Cyberman

The Quest for Pedler

CYBERMAN
THE QUEST FOR PEDLER

Michael Seely

publishing

First published in 2014 by Miwk Publishing Ltd.
This revised edition first published in hardback in 2022
by Fantom Publishing, an imprint of Fantom Films
www.fantompublishing.co.uk

Copyright © Michael Seely 2022

Michael Seely has asserted his moral right to be identified as the author of this work in accordance with the Copyright, Designs and Patents Act 1988.

All rights reserved.

A catalogue record for this book is available from the British Library.

Hardback edition ISBN: 978-1-78196-390-6

Typeset by Phil Reynolds Media Services, Leamington Spa
Printed and bound by CPI Group (UK) Ltd, Croydon, CR0 4YY
Jacket design by Connor Adkins

For Michelle,

with love

Contents

Introduction: A Man for Change		1
1	A Lot to Live Up To	6
2	The Two Doctors	14
3	The Reductionist of Judd Street	26
4	The Computer in Your Eye	36
5	The Genial Hokum of *Doctor Who*	50
6	Dehumanised Medicine and Modified Men	67
7	Of Cybermats, Angry Parents and Biomims	91
8	The Ivory Laboratory	113
9	Doom Writer	126
10	The Prophet of Clapham	146
11	Pedler's Meddlers	164
12	Luddite Desperadoes and Defrocked Scientists	197
13	Conditioned Brutality in the Lab	222
14	Diabolical Knowledge	240
15	The Road to Gaia	258
16	Educational Kit	274
17	The Pyramids of Rotherhithe	286
18	All in the Mind	301
19	He Could Be Watching the Sunrise	321
Appendix 1: Medical Papers		326
Appendix 2: Known Writing		334
Appendix 3: Known Radio Broadcasts		339
Appendix 4: Known Television and Film Appearances		350
Bibliography		358
Acknowledgements		374

CHAPTER 3

Introduction
A Man for Change

FOR MANY, THE NAME Kit Pedler will forever be associated with the Cybermen, a race he created for *Doctor Who* in 1966. The Cybermen were never the money spinners that the Daleks had been for their creator, Terry Nation, yet they undeniably had appeal in both concept and design to both adults and children. Some would argue that the menacing giant silver cyborgs with handles on their heads were more frightening than the exterminating dustbins armed with a sink plunger.

In 1982, the Cybermen were successfully brought back to the series after a long absence, impressively updated to thrill and excite a new decade of children and adults alike that watched and adored the programme. Sadly, Kit Pedler had died the previous May, halfway during a run of his seven-part series on ITV which combined ESP and subatomic physics. He had undergone a huge personal journey of change and experiment in the sixteen years since he wrote his first ideas for *Doctor Who* when he was a research scientist. He was now shaping plans to build an eco-city on the banks of the river Thames that would demonstrate how life would continue when the oil and gas runs out, as it will surely do one day.

Yet it is the Cybermen for which he will always be remembered. It's the way of these things, but without the Cybermen, the Kit Pedler who emerged as an environmentalist (although he did not consider himself one) would probably have remained unknown to the public except for the odd appearance on television or radio, hidden within the medical teaching institutions where he was discovered by Gerry Davis, *Doctor Who*'s story editor. Doctor C. M. H. Pedler PhD, MBBS, MC Path was reader and director of his own research department at one of the world's leading ophthalmological teaching establishments in the University of London where he was trying to decode the secret structures within the eye.

In the space of a few months, he had gone from being a would-be writer to having scripts made by BBC Television. He was brought into *Doctor Who* to put the science fiction into the series and take it away from fantasy and history. Unfortunately, the term 'scientific advisor' has been used over the years as a sort of catchy and totally misleading shorthand by those he worked with at the time and is sometimes used by unkind commentators when they spot an error in the 'science' of the programme.

Forming a productive partnership with Davis, he was quickly elevated into creating a successful series called *Doomwatch* which perfectly captured the feeling of the new decade that technological and scientific advances were not the panacea their advocates claimed. Because of some remarkable similarities between his stories and real life, he became celebrated as one who had the power to foresee the next man-made disaster and the media courted their charismatic 'Doctor Doom'.

Soon, Kit had turned his back on this scientific world that he had grown weary and suspicious of as he agreed with the current thinking – which had yet to become mainstream – that there was an environmental crisis looming and it was of our own creation.

Apocalyptic warnings sensationalised by the media were not enough. Something *positive* had to be done about it. Our whole way of life, and of looking at life, needed to change. Kit rejected left/right politics just as he had cast aside religion early on in his life. He believed in the reduction of waste by conserving energy and natural resources, but above all, in the Human Being itself against the industrial and urban juggernaut swamping our lives, dictating political allegiances, and taking us further and further away from our true relationship with the planet and the eco-systems we inhabit. He eventually found the perfect description for this relationship: Gaian, based on James Lovelock's theory of the Earth as a self-sustaining unit.

Kit was, perhaps above everything else, a teacher. He was not another tub-thumping documentary-producing prophet of doom (and there were a lot of them about in the seventies) giving furious polemical lectures on how mankind had another couple of decades before overpopulation, pollution and exhausting natural resources caused the collapse of society, which could only have a detrimental effect on their book sales. He certainly shared most of these views, but wanted to show how there was an alternative to industrial life, if only we could see it.

Kit set about to do just that. He knew where change should and could begin. So did Confucius, all those years ago: if you want to change the world, change yourself. Kit began to change. Unlike some of his contemporaries and friends, he did not retreat to a Welsh farmhouse to reject the twentieth century and start again from scratch; he started in London. In 1979 he wrote an account of his findings called *The Quest for Gaia* which detailed these changes in his lifestyle, of the modern artefacts he rejected. In a lot of cases, he replaced them with something just as ingenious and encouraged us to try and do the same.

The Quest for Gaia explains very lucidly the con trick of modern conveniences and how we are conditioned by those he called 'the ingenious toolmakers' into accepting whatever they wish to give us for what they say is our benefit. If this sounds more like a recipe for a conspiracy theorist then you would be mistaken: that's not Kit at all. His arguments were always far more insightful and cogent than that. If nothing else, the book made you think. I have heard from readers of my first edition who tracked down his book and benefited from it very much.

When I first picked up *The Quest for Gaia* from a second-hand bookshop, I had no idea that the Kit Pedler I knew from my favourite programmes *Doctor Who* and *Doomwatch* had gone this far. I won't go as far as to say that this book changed my life, but it opened my eyes at a time when Greenpeace was trying to prevent the Brent Spar platform from being dumped in the North Sea, and protesters were trying to prevent the course of the Newbury bypass destroying ancient woodland. The cause of the thinning of the ozone layer from CFCs in deodorant propellants was still in the news, and recycling newspapers and tin cans was beginning to catch on, as were unheeded warnings that simply exporting them to another country for processing did not guarantee they would not simply be burnt or dumped.

Things haven't much changed since then; they are just different. Debate over whether climate change is real has moved over to the cause which is still disputed either by reluctant governments, vested interests, or paranoid contrarians. Road protestors have, at the time of writing, been replaced by Extinction Rebellion who are making headline-grabbing protests blockading roads. We are also experiencing another panic in our gas supplies as they force up prices because we are still very much dependent on fossil fuels and suspicious of clean alternative energies. And suspicion towards scientists, which Kit understood, is typified by those who refuse to take vaccines to fight the spread of the Covid virus which practically shut down the planet in 2020, giving us a pause in air and car travel.

Things will change, they predicted, because of the virus. In fact things have returned pretty much to the way they were before, except that the more suspicious of our society have better means to express themselves and spread their ideas through constantly updating technology that Kit could only have dreamed of. Whatever would Kit think of us now that we have willingly allowed technology to strip away our privacy, which he so desperately wanted to protect from big business and government? At the same time, he would have been delighted by its abilities, while horrified by its addictiveness and vulnerabilities and misuse.

Kit was a man of changing ideas. Some of these ideas seem, on first inspection, quite peculiar. He never settled on just one idea declaring: 'This is the final word on the matter.' There was always a journey of examination and scrutiny. Change was the essence of Kit's thinking. This is the Kit who interests me and the man whose ideas I wanted to explore and preserve. I had no idea he had worked with the RSPCA to change the law on animal experiments, which he knew all too much about. I had no idea that he designed and practically built his own nuclear bomb in his workshop in Kent; nor that he was one of the witnesses against the expansion of the controversial Windscale reprocessing plant at a famous inquiry in the late seventies; to say nothing of his initial career as an anatomist. I only discovered these things when I was in the early stages of researching my book about *Doomwatch* called *Prophets of Doom*.[*]

I feel this is the Kit Pedler who is in danger of becoming forgotten, obscured, misinterpreted and just a catchy name associated with the Cybermen who still regularly appear in *Doctor Who*. They had meaning in 1966, but beyond the sixties they became another bogeyman. Yet it was lovely to see the original 'Mondasian' Cybermen return in the series in 2017, looking sleeker than their original counterparts, but emphasising the medical nightmares Kit originally envisaged.

The Cybermen became heavily merchandised when the series returned in 2005, as well as any other creation that the series put on the screen. The

---

[*] Now available from Telos Publishing as a revised and expanded edition.

Kit Pedler of 1966 who enjoyed his fast racing cars, good food and with a large family to support, would have been delighted. The next Kit Pedler would have been uneasy about them. He would have broken down and analysed the toy's production in the same forensic manner as he did with a photoreceptor cell of a pigeon. Where was this toy made? How far and by what method did it have to travel to reach the shop? What was the product made from? Can it be recycled? What process went into gathering the raw materials? How much energy went into refining that material and how much pollution was created as a result? Is the packaging just as wasteful and unnecessary? Are those little metal and plastic tags that fasten the product inside the transparent moulded window essential? Or is it all more expensive than the toy itself?

He wouldn't have blamed you for buying it for your children – or yourself. But he wanted you to know the true cost of the toy in your hands. So, the next time you buy a Cyberman toy, think of Kit and do what he would have done: remove the packaging at the shop counter before you leave. It's the toy you want, not the packaging, despite its potential in a couple of years to be worth a few quid to collectors, the ultimate conservationists. If enough people did that, or sent the packaging back to the company which now delivers it to your doorstep, the message might get through to the manufacturers. It's what Kit would have wanted.

Michael Seely
January 2014 and August 2022

1
A Lot to Live Up To

> Vox began the morning meeting. 'I know what you're up to,' he complained. 'You're going for a nice romantic voyage round your childhood. You know it's dangerous, don't you?'
> – From Kit Pedler's unpublished novel *A Mirror for Your Vanity*

SOMETIME IN THE 1830s, George Stanbury Pedler left the little village of Frithlestock on the north Devon coast and moved into the teeming hell that was London. George may have visited towns before, possibly been educated in one, but nothing could have prepared a country boy for the sights, smells and sounds of one of the greatest cities in the world.

London was expanding as rural populations migrated into cities looking for work. It was a time of protectionist governments, whose stifling religious philanthropy believed the poor should only be helped in return for their obedience in social and religious matters. It was not this life that mattered but the next. Extremes in poverty and wealth were represented by overcrowded slums sited next to spacious mansions and overflowing graveyards. This was a world where access to water depended on street pumps from which you could catch cholera, where sewage and waste was thrown onto the streets or into the Thames which stank in hot weather. It was a city of illness and disease. High mortality rates among infants were common, often resulting from seemingly simple ailments. If you couldn't afford a doctor, prayer was one way of dealing with illness. Otherwise, you could try a druggist.

That was George's profession, a wholesale chemist, and he traded from 199 Fleet Street in St Dunstan's parish. Anyone could set up as a chemist or druggist and was just as likely to kill a customer. The more honest of the profession petitioned Parliament to have their trade regulated in 1841. Failing that, a group of chemists formed their own independent association where members were required to have a recognised qualification. They would unite their profession, protect their interests, but also promote new discoveries in science. George Pedler was among the founding members of what would later become the Royal Pharmaceutical Society, based at 17 Bloomsbury Square, a respectable area of London, which would one day become home for the University of London.

One of the problems which the Society identified was how to prevent accidents involving powerful and lethal medicines. In 1868, a Miss Campbell died from taking an accidental overdose of a concentrated medicine from a single ounce bottle which had enough for ninety-six doses. A letter headlined 'Accidental Poisoning' was later published in *The Times* explaining the problem was that since it had first been adopted as a measure for liquid medicine a teaspoon was now twice the size of the old one, and nobody had noticed. The letter was written by George Stanbury Pedler.

By 1872, George was on the City Commission of Sewers shortly after cholera had struck London again. The Commission was charged with the promotion of public health, especially during epidemics. That same year, the second Public Health Act was passed; as a result, local sanitary authorities were created and required to appoint a Medical Officer of Health. George chaired the sanitary committee representing his parish, a role he took seriously, and in 1871 wrote again to *The Times* in frustration at the lack of energy and urgency in the face of another cholera outbreak. 'As chairman,' he wrote, 'I then gave up my holyday [sic] most willingly to attend to the pressing call for work, and I am sorry now to find the city charged with want of energy.' Energy was the one thing George did not lack, and he was invited to speak to a parliamentary committee.

George was popular in his parish, and upon his retirement after forty years, he was presented with a silver tea service in the vestry of the church. He was described by the trade journal *Chemist and Druggist* as 'a true philanthropist' and was praised for his 'energy and scientific knowledge'. He died in 1893 in Camberwell.*

---

* A round glass bottle with its glass stopper for Paregoric Elixir, a camphorated tincture of opium, from George Pedler can be found in a collection at the Science Museum in London.

Two of George's children followed his example. Kit's grandfather, George Henry Pedler, was born in 1847, but it was the youngest son who was arguably the most successful in the family. Alexander Pedler was educated at the City of London School and won a Bell scholarship. He worked and studied at the Royal Pharmaceutical Society where he achieved a Certificate of Honour in practical chemistry. After a spell at the Royal College of Chemistry, where he was a lecture demonstrator to Sir Edward Frankland, he was appointed Professor of Chemistry at the Presidency College of Calcutta.

During his twenty-two years in India, he became Vice Chancellor, Minister of Public Instruction of Bengal and was a member of the Legislative Council under the Viceroy. He also found time to send papers on the poison of the cobra to the Royal Society and contribute three papers to the *Journal of the Chemical Society*. He was also Honorary Secretary to the British Science Guild. It was in this capacity that he attended a deputation to a Mr Burns MP at the Local Government Board to promote legislation to tackle pollution of the rivers. Alexander was knighted in 1906. Twelve years later he died suddenly during a committee meeting at the Ministry of Munitions. The British Science Guild created the Alexander Pedler Lecture in his honour, but Kit would remember him as the 'one who raped India'.

George Henry studied at King's College in London where in 1869 he won the Todd Clinical Medicine prize. A member of the Royal College of Surgeons, George was also a Fellow of the Obstetrical Society and a Clinical Assistant to the West Riding Asylum. He practised medicine from No 6 Trevor Terrace in Knightsbridge, first in partnership with William Martyn and then on his own from the same address for the rest of the century. George married the daughter of a Norfolk rector, Maria Stratford Howard Gillett.

The next generation of medical Pedlers included Hubert Charles George Pedler who was born in 1885. At first, he chose a similar path to his father, attending Westminster School, followed by University College Hospital, and finally being admitted into the Royal College of Surgeons in 1911. Before war erupted in 1914, Hubert had been a volunteer in the West Surrey Regiment, and with the 1st Life Guards where he reached the rank of Surgeon-Lieutenant. Hubert also volunteered with the Royal Army Medical Corps, so for the duration of the war he was attached to the Coldstream Guards as a medical officer and reached the rank of Acting Major in 1918. Hubert continued to volunteer with the RAMC after the war until he reached retirement age in 1935, finally earning the rank of Major.

In the middle of the mechanised slaughter and gas warfare, Hubert married Mary Johnson who lived in Highgate. A Catholic, her family had both Irish and Shetland ancestry. Their first child was born in 1915, a daughter they christened Valerie. In 1924, a year after his father's death, Hubert was awarded a Diploma in Public Health by the Royal College of Surgeons.

For a while Hubert practised medicine in London before moving to Aldham, just outside Colchester, where he entered public service and worked as a Medical Officer and Public Vaccinator at the Colchester Infirmary before in 1929 becoming the Medical Officer of Health for a large part of the Eye district in Suffolk.

They were going to take to Suffolk their second child, a boy born in London at 7 Lancaster Road on Saturday 11 June 1927. His name reflected his ancestry: Christopher Howard Magnus Pedler. Howard came from Hubert's grandmother's family, and Magnus was his still living maternal grandfather. As for Christopher, he might have been named after his great-grandfather, but he would rarely be called that. He would always be known as Kit.

If he was going to follow in the footsteps of the Pedlers he would have a lot to live up to. However, initially it looked as if he was going to be the first Pedler who failed.

Suffolk life

The Pedlers lived outside Mendlesham, a village in Suffolk. One of Hubert's passions was for history, and he enjoyed writing potted histories of East Anglian kings and queens. This love was reflected in their home, an Elizabethan property called Park Farmhouse which they renamed Mendlesham Manor. Hubert stripped away the plaster from the exterior of the building and restored the look of a quintessential timber-framed house. Not all the interior features were original. Part of Hubert's job was to inspect houses and condemn them if he found they were unsuitable for habitation. That way he came across a lot of antiques, including Tudor wall panelling, which would end up back at the Manor. Hubert also collected clocks including an eight-silver-barrelled bracket clock, which sat on the mantelpiece and rang the Westminster chimes.

Mendlesham may have been rural; idyllic it was not. A childhood friend of Kit's, Hugh Cutting, remembered Hubert inspecting the children at Mendlesham school, part of his duties as an assistant tuberculosis officer. Children from Mendlesham Green and outlying farm cottages had to walk two miles to reach the village school, regardless of the weather, and they often arrived in wet and muddy clothes. Chesty coughs, sores and head lice were all too common. Here he saw life that contrasted greatly with his own. Those dependent on farms for employment experienced genuine hardship; wages were low as the price of wheat had fallen over the years.

The Pedlers got on very well with their neighbours, such as the Lockwoods who were farmers. The locals looked up to Dr Pedler, as they called him. He was described by those who remember him as a highly respected resident of the parish: a gentleman who had a very pleasant manner, and an aura of authority about him.

Hubert's grandson, Kerry Glasier, remembers his grandparents well:

> He was a large man, but very quiet, not given much to talking. He had the most impressive, deep voice. Just by sitting at the head of the table at breakfast time and saying something like 'Eat your porridge' he could instil fear into us kids. Granny was a birdlike person compared to him. She would call for him at mealtime by his nickname, which was Man. She would call to his study and say 'Man? Man? Lunch is ready.' And the voice would come back, 'Coming, Ladykin!'
>
> She was the most wonderful grandmother and I miss her to this day. She had a very lively mind. Come bedtime she would tell me a story, and that story would go on from night to night and then on the next visit, she would continue it again, all out of her head.

Kit benefited from her imagination, and on one occasion he wanted to impress his mother when, in bed at night, he mistook the shadow of a model aeroplane for that of a grotesque bird. His mother was a talented artist and very knowledgeable of art history, which Kit credited for his own artistic skills, though he never felt he could paint as well as she did.

From what he would later tell his family, Kit was a lonely child. His sister Val was seven years his senior. According to his future wife Una Freeston, he wasn't fond of 'grown ups' or 'proper people', for they all plotted against him. He was being raised as a Catholic by his mother which may explain this feeling.

Although now you could choose to belong to whichever religion you wished, a practising Catholic attracted prejudices, and the church was determined to retain and expand its numbers. In theory, a Catholic accepted their faith and the authority of the church without question. Kit did not enjoy his faith, nor Catholic school which may have been some distance away as they were few and far between. Catholic schools had a reputation for strictness far beyond the standard school and the nuns who taught him punished children with a rap on the knuckles with a metal ruler. Hubert was Protestant, but Kit had several maternal aunts who were very strong in their beliefs. This kind of mixed marriage was not uncommon, but it could create tensions.

Kit rarely explored his childhood in writing except for a short ghost story written for an anthology in 1972 called 'Terence and the Unholy Father'. A young boy, brought up in rural surroundings, wrestles with the rituals of the Catholic Mass, such as how can 'a silly bit of ice-cream wafer' turn into the blood and body of Christ which he would have to eat in the morning. 'His stomach heaved at the prospect.'

In Kit's unfinished semi-autobiographical novel, *A Mirror for Your Vanity*, the main character, Howard Riker, is also a Catholic, and remembers the priest as he delivered his sermon:

> A tall satanic man with a long Syrian nose, brilliant predatory eyes and close grey curls. His sermon in the grey coke fumes of the early morning church had struck terror into his childhood. He used to watch the great, angular bird figure working itself into a boiling rhetoric of sin and damnation. His images of hell struck with the ferocity of a baleful and terrible truth from which there was no possible escape. The only release was a string of badly made beads and avalanches of Hail Mary's and Our Fathers… At the end of his sermon the priest would writhe and gesticulate in a paroxysm of frustration and Riker used to watch fascinated, as his spittle sprayed out and glittered in the morning sun. An exploding man.

Terence feared hell, a place you were sent to if you were bad during your life, and you had to stay there *forever*. But, like Kit, Terence was a logical boy. He saw the loophole in the Catholic act of confession. You confess your sins on a Sunday and have them forgiven, which gives you the rest of the week to commit fresh sins ready for the cleansing on Sunday.

School in Ipswich

In 1935 Kit went from one institution into another: 'the grim austerity of a boarding school', as Terence described it, at Ipswich, coming home only for the holidays. Kit stayed at the school for ten years and was again not happy there. This may explain why in later life one of Kit's favourite films was the savage 1968 satire *If*, set within a boarding school.

Howard Riker was also sent to a boarding school, and on a return visit the memories washed over him:

> ...a bell clanging harshly, calling everyone to roll call... the impossibly perfect square of the playing field... the copper clad tower, which he once walked round in fear of his life, to scratch his initials through the soft verdigris covering the dome... black clad masters seemed to scurry away like rats into hiding from the rain, and there were crowds of boys running for shelter with exercise books over their heads as protection... Old corridors that smelt the same smell of damp towels and books... There was one dormitory where he didn't go... The wind always blew there. It used to rattle the windows, altering the reflection of the street lamps on the raindrops. There was always a wind. It used to furrow between the blankets. It blew straight out of hell, whining and clattering in a black stream of desolation. There was a woman, who used to walk between the dormitories. Her white starched uniform crackled as she walked. She kissed everyone goodnight, in a stark death's bed ceremony. There was no love anywhere to be found in the school, only shouted orders and obligatory codes of honour.

Kit enjoyed spending his holidays with his friend Hugh Cutting, boating on a pond at the Manor they called the moat and shooting sparrows with an air gun. He would play war games with his models, some of which he built himself from balsa wood.

But it would only be two weeks into his holiday before Kit became bored. Kerry Glasier remembers his grandmother 'telling me that Hubert had some very old watches, two hundred years old, some of them just works, sitting in a drawer, and Kit would take them to bits and try and put them together again'. This is an early example of Kit wanting to know how things worked, a fascination he would never lose.

The one thing at which Kit did excel at school was sport. He played for the School Rugby First XV and was in cricket and swimming teams. In 1942, he won all five of the under-fifteen events, including high and long jumps, and the hundred yards sprint. The following year, now a senior, he won the high jump, and in his final year the Slator cup for the hurdles. An early interest in science was represented by his membership of the School Scientific Society, in which he served on the committee. He also became School Prefect, and Captain of School House.

In a humorous résumé of his life written in 1969, Kit described his course through school as 'indifferent... and without any clear idea of purpose [I] ended up studying medicine'. Ipswich School did not offer biology as a subject, so when he was in the sixth form, the school arranged for Kit and hopeful veterinary surgeon Paul Ryde to attend classes at Ipswich High School for Girls.

This held certain risks. On their first visit they used the front door, and were summoned to see the formidable headmistress, Miss Neale. She told them in no uncertain terms never to use the front entrance again because the girls' parents would be shocked to see boys going in that way. She indicated a side door for their future use. Their new route to class took them through the locker room, where they would run the gauntlet of girls who could have come straight out of the St Trinian's films. Kit and Paul enjoyed the freedom of leaving school for their class at will; but one time they took their liberty too far and visited the Gaumont Cinema to see the 1943 film *Stormy Weather*. Inevitably, they were spotted by the chemistry master.

For half of Kit's schooling, the world was at war. Ipswich was a natural target for enemy bombers because of its docks and the town suffered from air raids. At one point, a British plane crashed close to the school, something Kit vividly remembered. During the summer holidays in 1941, Kit helped his mother raise funds for the National Air Raid Distress Fund by selling little flags; and Hubert Pedler did his 'bit' in Mendlesham, taking charge of the Local Defence Volunteers, a forerunner to the Home Guard.

Hubert and Mary moved to Ipswich during the war where they would be closer to Kit. Valerie had married Philip Glasier in 1939 and started a family, but the marriage was not successful and was dissolved by the end of the 1940s.

Kit's time at school ended along with the war in 1945. He did not perform well in his exams. However, becoming a doctor was not in dispute. The next stage of his medical training was going to be at the Chelsea Polytechnic[*] in war-damaged London, the chief centre for classes in the biological sciences and pharmacy. It also had links with the University of London of which it would later become a part in 1971. It was a good place to start, and it was here where Kit Pedler met his wife.

---

[*] Now Chelsea College of Science and Technology.

2
The Two Doctors

> Kit said to me how in one of his first lectures, this bright senior consultant came in, with a white starched coat and a stethoscope round his neck, and said, 'Ladies and gentlemen, I've only got one thing to tell you: a little bit of what you fancy does you good. That's all you need to know.' – Richard Mervyn

UNA DE HAVILLAND FREESTON was one of three daughters of Sir (Leslie) Brian Freeston, KCMG, OBE, one time Governor and Commander-in-Chief of Fiji and High Commissioner for the Western Pacific. In 1936 he was appointed Secretary to the East African Governor's Conference and High Commissioner for Transport for Kenya and Uganda, and in 1941 became chief secretary for the Tanganyika Territory which now forms part of Tanzania, before being appointed Governor of the Leeward Islands in 1944.

Una had wanted to become a psychiatrist from an early age and had her father's full support: 'My father was very advanced for his time. He was very much in favour of women's education. He insisted on my mother, Mabel, going on with her medical studies and not having any children until she had qualified.' Having begun her education in Africa, which involved a great deal of very difficult and challenging travelling to and from the school, Una became at sixteen the youngest student at McGill University in Montreal, Canada, before she went to Chelsea Polytechnic in 1945.

Una first noticed Kit while she was in the basement laboratory with her friends:

We were chatting about dirty jokes. I said I just blocked my ears, so I didn't hear them. They said, 'Let's try you out.' They brought over Kit because he was noted as being rather wicked. He told a story about an old lady who spoke to a sergeant and wanted to know what chevrons and spots were on a soldier's arm. She was told that the spots meant marriages and the chevrons meant children, and she slapped the sergeant's face. That was the dirty joke. I was a bit miffed because I didn't block it out, I could hear it!

He was in a mild sort of way the naughtiest in the class. He did the ordinary student sort of things. If anybody threw welds of toilet paper around, he threw more than other people. If people were pulling themselves up on the bars in the hall, Kit was the one doing the most pull-ups.

And Una noticed. Kit was enjoying the social life but was not putting much effort into his studies. He was not a lounge lizard, but his nickname was Snake Hips.

One of Kit's girlfriends had been the daughter of the stage magician Jasper Maskelyne, but it was Una who caught Kit's attention:

We were going to a party, and I went with somebody called Brian and Kit went with this other girl, and then they did a swap and I walked home with Kit. The only other thing I remember about that party was there was a game of postman's knock and, as you know, when you do something wrong you go outside and all the other boys, at my request, only pretended to kiss me. Kit, being the wickedest, kissed me. After Kit and I walked back from that party, we became regular friends and we used to go to Battersea Park to study and go out onto the boating lake. We studied a lot together, and after nineteen months I'd let him kiss me! Then I thought, well, I suppose we ought to get married, because that's how things were done in those days.

By 1947 Kit wasn't achieving the results he required. He failed his exams to get his MB (Bachelor of Medicine), which were necessary if he wanted to continue his path to becoming a doctor. It also meant he could not avoid being called up for National Service. Medical students were normally exempt from conscription, provided they had a hospital which would take them in. 'He had done so badly no one wanted to have him,' said Una. 'I went on to St George's Hospital, and he was conscripted into the army.'

National Service

The newly reintroduced National Service was unpopular, but for many young men it gave them a chance to meet people from all walks of life. Una recalled: 'He was in a dormitory with a lot of poor Scottish people. He had never mixed with that kind of person before, but Kit was very good at adapting himself to any company he was in.' National Service also offered training and education that many would never have had the opportunity to take before. Life could also be harsh, mind-numbingly dull, strict, and dangerous. If it moved, salute it: if it didn't, paint it. Everyone remembers their sergeant. Kit may have described him in *A Mirror for Your Vanity*:

> A compact sergeant quivering with authority striding into a freezing barrack room, glistening boots beating in time on the wooden floor. Swagger stick jammed under arm like a weapon; he stood absolutely still, looking round from one to another. He had a brick-red face, and eyes set close into the sides of a beaked nose. Close blond hair supported a sharply creased forage cap. After studying each watchful, nervous face, he drew himself up, took a deep breath and shouted in staccato phrases:
>
> 'My name's Walters, Sergeant Walters to you and "sir" as often as you can bloody remember. For the next six weeks I'm your bloody master and you'll do what I tell you, I'm giving the orders, you're going to obey them and if you don't that's mutiny! If you don't like what I tell you, you double march smartly down to the office and ask to see the Company Officer. And he's a reasonable man! He'll listen to you and then march you straight back up here again, register your horrible little complaint and then write in your call-up card: "barrack room bloody lawyer", that's what he'll do...'

The war was over, but there were flashpoints around the world involving the army. Kit had been conscripted into his father's regiment, the Royal Army Medical Corps (RAMC). Having gone to public school, Kit could have applied for a commission and become an officer, but this would have meant extending his service by a year. Una remembered Kit hating almost everything about his time from beginning to end. 'He went to various places like Egypt, Palestine, and Greece. I used to be shocked by the stories he told me. They used to sell antibiotics or army blankets, all that kind of stuff, but he was never caught. He just went along with what other people were doing.'

Private Pedler achieved the 'unimagined height of unpaid acting lance-corporal' for three weeks, he later recalled in his brief autobiography, and described himself as 'the most uncooperative and sullenly resentful soldier of his own particular intake'.

Howard Riker and his inner, critical voice, Vox, remembered the deserts:

Shooting, terrible deserts and a sergeant-major who had kept snapshots – taken with a Box Brownie – of all the corpses he had created. A fat lazy-eyed man; a frustrated rapist. He disappeared from a troopship, thrown overboard by his own men out of embarrassment.

'There was a company officer – in the desert – an even cross between Ronald Colman and David Niven.' 'The one who became a priest?' Vox remembered. 'That's right. He blew an Arab in half with a Besa gun just because he was running near the wire.'

However, Kit discovered his true calling when, during his training as a physiotherapist, he studied anatomy. Discovering how something worked inside the human body suited the boy who had enjoyed taking timepieces apart and seeing if he could put them back together again.

Kit needed to find a place to live after he left the army. Una was living in Canterbury Hall, a hall of residence:

> He had been talking for some time about his interest in psychical research and wanted to join the Society for Psychical Research. Canterbury Hall was about ten minutes' walk from where it was based at 31 Tavistock Square. We visited the place and met the secretary, Doctor Donald West, who was later to become Professor of Criminology at Cambridge and a close friend. He invited us upstairs to his flat and we had a cup of coffee with him. The society used the basement and the first three floors, and he lived in the top two floors. He said Kit could become his lodger when he came out of the army.
>
> So that's what he did. By now I was two years ahead of him. We weren't officially engaged but we had been a couple for quite a long time. When I finished my studies late at night I used to go over and visit him. The matron or director at Canterbury Hall used to ask me what we did at that time of night? I'd say, 'We talk…'

Kit resumed his studies, this time at King's College, and he didn't look back. 'Whether it was because of me or whether it was because he was so shocked that no hospital would take him, he really studied. His RAMC training helped him.'

Getting married

In 1948, Kit and Una officially got engaged:

> I was twenty when I wrote to Kit's mother about our engagement. She said that Kit was on a grant, and he could never afford to support a wife. I was

absolutely astounded! Who said anything about support? I was very lucky that no one ever said to me, 'Oh, you're only a girl, and when you get married, you won't have to do anything at all.' That's why it never occurred to me that I would be supported by Kit.

I was very upset by this, and my father arranged for Kit's parents and us all to have a lunch near Liverpool Street, which was a very grand place where the waiters wore evening dress. After lunch we the children were sent away, and after half an hour my father came and said we should go back. He asked everybody's permission if he could speak and said that they had agreed we could get married, but out of the kindness of their hearts, we could not get married until I was twenty-one. That was September, and I would be twenty-one in March. That was fine.

One of the reasons the Pedlers were wary was that their daughter's marriage had failed, leaving Valerie with three children to support on her own in Camberley. Una had differing opinions on her future in-laws:

> I didn't like his mother and she didn't like me. I thought she was vain and snobbish, and she thought I was boring and moralistic. I think we were both right about each other, but we never had a cross word. We just tolerated each other. I liked his father a great deal. He didn't talk much, but he was a very kind and upright sort of man.

The marriage took place on 4 March 1949 at the Unitarian Church in Kensington High Street, with the reception at Canterbury Hall. They decided to follow the example set by Una's mother and have no children for at least five years, after which they would have finished their training and qualified. Although Kit did not regard himself a Catholic, Una wondered if it would it last? 'I never was a Catholic and the thing I had against them was that they didn't allow contraception. Since I didn't want children yet, I was always worried Kit might go back to being a Catholic, but he never did.'

> Kit's rejection of his mother's faith did not go down well with his aunts. There was one aunt called Dorothy who was very poor and very nice, but the others were rabid Catholics. By the time we had three children, his relatives still thought we were living in sin. I had a Catholic friend during my studies who wrote to me twenty or more years later when I had all the children and she said that she hoped I wouldn't deprive them of their Catholic heritage.

Following the honeymoon, Una moved into Kit's flat where she experienced her first taste of daily life with her husband:

We were painting this upstairs attic and he showed me all my mistakes. I said, 'Oh yes,' then I went downstairs and saw that his mistakes were worse than mine! I thought, oh, I see! You want admiration? Oh all right. I'm good at admiration.

Wartime rationing was continuing. You had to make do with what you could buy to eat, and use your imagination, especially living in a city where you couldn't easily grow your own food. Una was completely undomesticated, having been brought up with 'lots and lots of servants':

> I could make coffee and boil an egg, but that's all. When I used to visit Kit before we got married, we used to put things from all the shelves into a big pressure cooker to flavour what little we were cooking. It could be yeast, marmalade, herbs, honey; and that's how I learned how to cook. My children say I'm a good cook, but all my food tasted the same.

Keeping warm was also a problem:

> We had little money and the only heating we had came from a little oil stove. The good ones had blue flames, but the one we had gave out yellow flames, and they weren't very warm. We used to study wrapped up in blankets with a hot-water bottle on our knees.

There was a new member to the family:

> As we thought we weren't going to have any children, we got a cat from the RSPCA. Kit was very fond of animals, and we got a little kitten called Caius. It didn't know how to lap milk, so we used to dab our fingers in the milk for him. He used to follow us when we went out to the cinema or anything like that. He was a lovely cat, but he was very put out when the baby came.

There were mixed reactions to the discovery that Una was pregnant: 'The baby was unplanned, but by me she was not unwanted.' Kit, on the other hand, was less than sure. They were still studying, and neither of them was bringing in much money to support a family, nor were they living in an ideal place in which to raise one. Kit's other reaction set a pattern which he would follow with his next two children. 'Kit got sick every time I was pregnant,' Una remembered. 'He had a pain in the chest and had to go into hospital. Nobody knew what it was. I can remember going to work with Kit lying in bed.' Kit was eventually diagnosed with Bornholm disease, which includes chest pains as one of its symptoms.

In December 1949, they went with Donald West to see a performance of *A Streetcar Named Desire*, starring Vivien Leigh. Una suddenly realised that their baby was about to make its own entrance. After a difficult labour, a healthy baby girl was delivered on Christmas Day, and they named her Carol.

Una's mother thought that this was going to be the end of her daughter's medical career, leaving Kit to become the breadwinner, but after six months she carried on regardless:

> It was extremely difficult to manage, but it never crossed my mind to stop my studies. I used to get up very early in the morning, study for a couple of hours, and then take a bus right across London to the day nursery where I left Carol and travel all the way back to St George's Hospital where I was studying. The difficult bit was that we didn't always finish at five o'clock and I became very agitated in case I got to the day nursery too late. Obviously, they wouldn't turn her out into the street, but they would be angry if I was late. They couldn't have her in the end. Although it was an extremely difficult time, I didn't fail any of my exams.

They accepted an offer from Kit's sister's Val to look after Carol, but making regular visits to Camberley was difficult. Una visited every week, and Kit would accompany her every fortnight, usually by hitch-hiking:

> We were quite badly off, and we weren't very experienced hitchers. One time, we were dropped off in some village, and we didn't know what to do. There was nobody to hitch a lift from. We were sitting there, having a cup of coffee, wondering what we should do, when a lorry driver overheard us. He said: 'Have you the money for the bus to get to Camberley?' and we said no. He gave us ten shillings – which was a lot of money in those days. He wouldn't give us his address, but I've given money to strangers ever since in memory of him because it was such a kind thing for him to do.

One person who was especially delighted to see his uncle was the young Kerry Glasier:

> Kit had a special place for me because whether he liked it or not, he became a surrogate father. He was very good with his hands. He could repair things and build things from scratch. He'd go down to a shop, buy a sheet of balsa wood and help me build a model plane. An hour later this thing was flying. It was fantastic, I loved it.

Westminster

After finishing his studies at King's College, Kit won an entrance scholarship in anatomy and physiology, and this secured him a place at Westminster Hospital Medical School.* All the new intake were addressed by a consultant, who was next only to God. He said that they should keep their fingernails clean, always wear a suit and that a consultant liked to be called 'sir'. He also said: 'A little bit of what you fancy does you good. That's all you need to know.' Future friend and collaborator Richard Mervyn remembered this resonated with Kit:

> He would often have two cigarettes in an evening. I said, 'Oh, you smoke,' and he said, 'No, I have two cigarettes. It's a bit like saying if you have a whisky in the evening, you are an alcoholic. But I find that after a really good meal I feel relaxed after two cigarettes. I am contented and it is doing me good.'

Kit was a habitual smoker until he reached twenty-eight. Cigars, on the other hand, he never stopped enjoying.

One of the things Kit would discover during his training was that patients needed more than surgery and pills. Kit wrote in his 1981 book *Mind Over Matter* about one doctor who could cure people by simply looking magnificent:

> He would sweep into the ward in a cloud of cologne, grey curls elegantly in place and leonine head inclined benignly... He dealt with ordinary mortals by attentive paternalism. I carried his case. He would stride into the ward leading a fawning retinue of mortal doctors and blushing nurses, like disciples from a Biblical film epic. He would sit on the bed of the first patient reaching forward to hold his wrist between manicured fingers then, for some seconds, he would stare meaningfully into their eyes remaining absolutely still. Finally, with a sense of timing he could have taught at drama school, he would intone with exquisitely measured mellifluence: 'You are much better.' Next day, the patient would be much better. The doctor was an intolerant pig to work for and is now a knight. I have no doubt at all that this particular doctor did cure people with the aid of practised melodrama, and the fact that he was a bit of a laughing stock among the common ruck of students does not diminish his healing ability. He did have it and he was also an intuitively

---

* It is now the Charing Cross and Westminster Medical School.

accurate diagnostician. We ended up by respecting his clinical abilities and disliking only his Rolls Royce.

Una remembered that Kit won 'practically all the top prizes at Westminster; he did very well indeed'. These prizes were in surgery, medicine, public health, and pathology. Kit also performed in a pantomime, and played with a jazz band, although his taste in music was usually more conservative and traditional. For one student review, he played bits of plumbing like wind instruments while dressed in Arabian headgear.

By now, the family wanted their own home. Una remembered how they 'used to walk around all sorts of places to see if they had any flats, and nobody had'. Undaunted, Una borrowed £2,600 from her father for a deposit on their first house, and they moved into 88 Park Hill in Clapham in 1952. In return for childcare, they allowed a Scottish couple with their daughter Margaret to move in rent-free.

The Pedlers became great friends with their next-door neighbours, the Zorn family. The artist and builder in Kit discovered that he had a lot in common with John Zorn. He was an industrial designer and had designed and cast the Dunlop tyre logo. He also freelanced in the film industry; he had recently sculpted the icebergs for the Pinewood film *Scott of the Antarctic*.

Diana Baur, Zorn's daughter, remembers her father's relationship with Kit:

> They just had a real meeting of minds. When he sat with my father, I was aware of these conversations which were climbing dizzy heights of ideas, and they would get very excited about things, which is a lovely memory. My father would spend hours with Kit discussing all manner of things. Kit was always interested in my father's life and what he had done and as soon as they met, they just talked about processes and ideas.
>
> I remember being struck by Kit's intense, staring, almost Picasso-like eyes and his softly spoken, drawling voice. He always spoke fast; his words were falling over themselves as he tried to get out all of his ideas.

The Zorns were also ex-Catholics, but the church was never far away. In this case, it was the parish church of St Mary's. One day in the early 1960s, Kit was astonished to receive a visit from the parish priest, enquiring if it was true that he was a lapsed Catholic. But one visitor from the church was always welcome. He was a local tramp, who was given food by the church, and would wander up Park Hill regularly, picking up dog ends as he went.

Kit befriended him and regularly invited him in to share a bottle of wine and discuss their shared interests. The tramp had gone to Cambridge but dropped out of society. Diana Baur remembers 'Kit becoming fascinated with him and talking to my father about how we were missing a trick with him. It was different then; a tramp was a tramp, a reject really... Kit had what many brought up in the Catholic faith had: an empathy with other people; maybe they've been brought up to think of others.'

Doctor Pedler

Kit qualified as a doctor in June 1953, and Una was currently working towards a Diploma in Child Health. The Medical Act of 1950 introduced the requirement for any newly qualified doctor to spend twelve months as a house officer in a hospital before they could enter general practice. 'Basically, you have to live in,' recalled Una. 'Six months in surgery and six months in medicine minimum. It did seem to me that we were always getting parted, one way or another.'

Kit began as house surgeon at Westminster Hospital where he worked with Sir Stanford Cade, a decorated surgeon whose primary interest lay in cancer. He was a pioneer in using radium for treating tumours, an early form of radiotherapy. Una remembers surgery could be grisly:

> They were doing the most terrible operations for cancer, not just removing the leg at the hip but also what were called hind quarter operations, the whole of the pelvis. The patients died just the same. Kit was doing very big operations and it was very hard work, but it was a prodigious job.

One of their patients was the celebrated opera singer Kathleen Ferrier who for several years had been suffering from breast cancer, and Sir Stanford was her surgeon. She died on 18 October 1953 at the University College Hospital. Since he loved opera, Kit was very fond of her, as indeed were all the staff who cared for her.

Had Kit's life not gone the way it did, he would have been happy to continue his training as a surgeon. He enjoyed the bonhomie and gallows humour of the surgeons and was proud of his cross-herring stitch which held together the subcutaneous wound after surgery.

Next, Kit spent six months as house physician at Kingston. As a junior doctor, Kit would have been on call at any time of day or night, a very arduous job. This meant another stay away from home. 'When you are a houseman,' explained Una, 'you have to pay for your accommodation. I remember one month he brought home just £16.'

This was a problem because in 1954, their second child was born, Mark Howard. Una recalled:

> By that time, there was Kit, me, two kids and a £50 per month mortgage, and here we had £16. That was the worst period. Every month we took out an overdraft which we paid off for a few days when he got paid. We also used to get thirty-six shillings a week maternity benefit. I once sent one of the children to the butchers with a shilling and they came back with two small chops and that was our dinner. The greengrocers were very kind, they gave us spoilt fruit, like a melon that was half bad.

Diana Baur was young enough not to appreciate the problems:

> Una once dished up roasted heart. It was on the plate, and you could see the arteries and things sticking out, and I had to eat it. With it was red cabbage and that seemed to have been cut into four sections only and shredded. I never forget that. I'd think, how do I get out of eating this meal?

Soon after Mark's birth, Una went into part-time work. 'I did public health, schools and day clinics which I liked because I did not have to be on call for emergencies.' Diana's mother, Helene, had been trained as a nanny and soon helped to look after the growing family next door. She was German and had been orphaned at the age of eight:

> In my mother's eyes then, a woman's role was to stay at home, raise the children and look after your man as he was the breadwinner. Mark had arrived while they lived next door to us. I remember once his carrycot being left on the ground in the front garden by the open gate and my mother absolutely horrified what with dogs being about. Una had been brought up on the idyllic island of Fiji, so presumably gates and fences meant nothing to her.

Finally, Kit entered general practice, probably as a locum, before quickly giving it up. This period has been reported as lasting anything from three days to six weeks before he realised it was not for him, and he would give different reasons why. For example, he told the *Guardian* in 1967 that 'helping humanity wasn't my metier. There was no scope to be original.' When the *New Scientist* interviewed him in 1971, Graham Chedd wrote that he didn't like 'having to make decisions on inadequate data'. Una had a different recollection. 'He didn't like patients! He said it. He didn't like patients.'

There may have been another reason – it wasn't interesting. He disliked the system, thinking it was little better than a medical supermarket. Kit's 1969 autobiography explained how he had spent a 'hilarious month' dispensing coloured placebos to patients who were lonely and not ill.

Richard Mervyn remembers:

> Kit felt that a lot of young doctors were worse (in the 1980s) than they had been at the turn of the century. The GP back then would say, 'Plenty of rest, plenty of fresh fruit and you'll get better.' Now it's pills. He thought that modern doctors had closed their minds further than they had pre-war because they know they've got a pill for it, and if they haven't got a pill, they'll cut out the ailment.

Kit was temperamentally not suited to being a GP. Looking back at this period, he would probably have described himself as a 'reductionist'. He preferred to discover what made something work by dissecting it down into small parts, and studying the detail, out of which a fundamental truth would emerge. From 1955, he would do just that.

3
The Reductionist of Judd Street

> One of my teachers said that 'there are two types of research, the effect of A on B, and good research.' – Kit Pedler in a book review for *The Guardian*, 1970

MANY PEOPLE OWE THEIR EYESIGHT to Professor Norman Ashton, working from a laboratory in a dirty, four-storey red-brick building in central London.

In 1941, there had been a sudden increase of blindness developing in prematurely born babies. Now known as retinopathy of prematurity (ROP), it was then called retrolental fibroplasia. The retina within the developing infant eye would detach itself, resulting in blindness. Ophthalmologists believed that the cause was an inflammation of tissue behind the lens that occurred before the child was born. This was true in some cases, but not all. There was a theory that there may be a connection with the level of oxygen given to premature babies who were kept in oxygen tents.

In the early 1950s, Dr Ashton designed what the *New Scientist* would later describe as a series of 'elegant' experiments to test this hypothesis. For his test subject, he chose the newly born kitten, whose eyes quickly develop as they mature in a manner similar to a baby. He subjected each kitten to a measured dose of oxygen, injected Indian ink into their retina, and traced its path through the tiny blood vessels of the eye using a light microscope. Ashton demonstrated that if the dose of oxygen was too high, the blood vessels shut down.

Ashton played a time-lapse film at the International Congress of Ophthalmology in September 1954, and you could watch the blood vessels contracting within a matter of hours. Despite the grumblings from a few researchers who couldn't replicate this work in rabbits, the hypothesis was accepted. In America, Arnall Platz of the Gallinger Municipal Hospital in Washington took the research one step further. Much to the alarm of the nursing staff, Platz reduced the oxygen levels in a couple of incubators to test Ashton's hypothesis. Other studies were performed in America during 1953 and 1954 which experimented with oxygen supply levels at the measure suggested by Ashton and others. Incidences of infant blindness were reduced to a negligible level. From then on, the level of oxygen given, and its subsequent withdrawal, was carefully measured. The epidemic was over.

This was a major success, not just for Ashton but for the newly created Institute of Ophthalmology, part of the Faculty of Brain Sciences within the University of London. A pathologist by training, he had been invited to join the Institute in 1946, a year before its formal opening by its first director of research, Sir Stewart Duke-Elder. In conjunction with the Moorfields Eye Hospital, where most of the original staff came from, the Institute would train a new generation of ophthalmologists from all over the world. The plan was to advance the study of ophthalmology by embracing disciplines such as biochemistry, virology, immunology, bacteriology and biophysics, alongside their other function which was to provide clinical laboratory and anatomic pathology services for Moorfields, and consultation services around the world.

The Institute was on the corner of Judd Street and Tavistock Place in Bloomsbury, in a building that had been the Central London Ophthalmic Hospital before it merged with Moorfields to become a teaching hospital. By 1959, the Institute had expanded into six departments. As well as Ashton's pathology unit, there was one for physiology which was headed by Duke-Elder himself, surgery, clinical ophthalmology, neuro-ophthalmology and glaucoma research. In the basement, there was a bar and canteen, and in what used to be the nurses' changing rooms there was now the animal house, where the test animal subjects were looked after. The rest of the building was taken up with offices, stores and a workshop.

Like Kit Pedler, Dr Ashton had no prior experience of the eye himself. In a speech he gave accepting the Proctor Medal in 1957, Ashton remembered that he wasn't terribly interested in what he felt to be a 'dull fibrous globe that had already been fully explored'. However, he later realised 'how rich… is the eye in opportunity, containing as it does so many types of cell, and so many specialised structures of its own, arranged with such nicety that pathologic changes may be seen, both in vivo and in vitro, with greater clarity than in almost any other tissue'. Consultants at the Moorfields Eye Hospital were surprised to discover a pathologist in their midst. Pathology was a new field and had yet to be accepted as a discipline.

Kit had studied pathology and demonstrated qualities that attracted Ashton, who invited Kit to join him as an experimental research pathologist and a junior lecturer, specialising in diseases of the eye. Kit seized the opportunity to spend the next five years of his life attached to the coat-tails of a rising star, and work towards a PhD.

Ashton's work was trying to discover the mechanism behind 'vaso-obliteration' and discover why oxygen poisoning only affected the eye in infancy. Kit also assisted Ashton's glaucoma research until Duke-Elder took over.

Kit needed to be trained in how to use animals for experiments, which required a Home Office licence. A contemporary of his was a visiting Japanese ophthalmologist called Saiichi Mishima, now considered to be the leader of Japanese ophthalmology. He wrote in 2003 that it was the duty of all workers to keep meticulous records: 'Such as individual timing of experiments, methods of anaesthesia, types of experiments and experimental details, etc… This was… a surprise for me, and it gave me the basic concept of handling experimental animals.' There was no room for sentimentality, but equally there was no place for inflicting needless suffering.

Kit did not immediately begin work on retrolental fibroplasia but on identifying sex nuclei in ocular tissue which involved taking samples from cat's eyes, proving that it was possible to identify the sex of an animal from eye cells alone. Kit learned how to correctly dissect the eye and stain the virtually invisible sample for the cellular detail to show itself under the microscope.

In March 1955, Kit and Ashton submitted a paper on the subject to the *British Journal of Ophthalmology*, which was edited in-house, but published by the British Medical Journal group. This was his first published scientific paper. Three months later, Ashton's third paper on retrolental fibroplasia, written with Norman Cook, saw one Christopher Pedler acknowledged for his assistance.

Watching the flow of Indian ink reveal the invisible pathways of the retinal vessels fascinated Kit. With his neighbour, John Zorn, they came up with an idea to see something similar but in three dimensions. They forced a liquid metal through the veins and arteries of a kidney, and once it had set, removed the flesh. What remained was a beautifully intricate silver network of veins which resembled a tree. Set into a block of Perspex, it remained within the Zorn family until quite recently. A photograph of 'Metal Cast of Vessels' was used as a frontispiece for the fifth edition of *Medical & Biological Illustration* in 1955. The Institute were impressed enough to include a reference in their seventh annual report in 1955.

Experimenting on cats

In 1956, Kit had his first independent paper published, which was included within the annually published *Transactions of the Ophthalmological Society of the United Kingdom* concerning the relationship of 'hyaluronidase to aqueous outflow resistance'. *Transactions* was available only to members of its society and ended up on a few library bookshelves, so papers like these naturally did not have a large readership.

By the end of the year Kit submitted two further papers to the *British Journal of Ophthalmology*, which would be published together in the following year. The first paper was called 'A Method for Direct Retinal Observation in the Experimental Animal'. Kit had been working on how to improve Ashton's own technique of observing the kitten's eye during experiments.

This is how he did it. The live kitten, probably only a few days old, was anaesthetised with Nimbutal. A dead one would be quite useless to study if you wished to observe blood flow. The eyelids and the cornea were removed by using a cutting diathermy knife. A 'limbal window' was then inserted into the eyeball itself. This was a small metal cylindrical chamber with a flat glass bottom, designed to prevent the retina from detaching itself. Once the limbal window was inserted, the animal was then placed into an airtight transparent container – which in this case was an ordinary lunch box with a hole cut into its sliding lid to coincide with the position of the rim of the eye chamber. The head was fixed into position with clamps. Carefully measured and controlled oxygen was fed into the sealed box, whilst another tube supplied anaesthetic from a syringe, clamped to the outside of the box, which would be regularly applied during the experiment. The results could be viewed through a standard Zeiss stereoscopic microscope which was lowered down into the limbal window.

The lighting source was kept inside a steel box which not only prevented stray ultraviolet radiation from affecting the experiment, but also in case the light source exploded. To prevent heat from affecting the test animal, the light was reflected off an angled mirror opposite the light box and above the test animal. All of this was set within a rigid framework of steel scaffold tubing. A newly developed GSAW Gun Camera could be fitted into the base of the microscope, capturing a frame of film every six seconds for half an hour. A time-lapse film called *Oxygen and Retinal Vessels* was produced in 1956 by Dr P. Hansell with Kit and Ashton and was available for hire for another ten years.[*]

The apparatus described above could be modified as was seen in Kit's second paper, which concerned the destructive effects of ionising radiation, such as we experience in X-rays, on developing blood vessels. 'Effects of Ionising Radiation' was the fourth paper in a series started by Dr Ashton on 'Studies on Developing Retinal Vessels', but this was the first one towards which Ashton himself did not contribute anything except advice. Cobalt, supplied by the Westminster Hospital's Physics Department, was kept in a container which was mounted on a swinging arm above the kitten so that it could be moved away and swiftly lowered into a protective lead surround within a very few seconds. The microscope used for these observations was also mounted on a rotating arm, so that when the cobalt was swung away into its 'safe' position, the microscope could be moved very rapidly into place over the animal to observe the retina. Three groups of kittens were used in the experiment, each exposed to a different dose of radiation, and briefly kept alive while Kit studied the vessels as irradiation occurred. The purpose was to see if the effects of radiation on the eye caused damage like oxygen. Was the mechanism a breakdown of certain enzymes? The answer was no. Negative answers were just as valuable as positive results.

Kit's next paper was submitted in May 1957, a preliminary report before more detailed could be carried out. This time Kit worked in collaboration with Ashton and Clive Graymore to see if the vessel closure phenomenon could be mimicked by injecting sodium fluoride into the eye, creating swelling in the tissue which might be a crucial factor as it constricts the vessels. Kit continued this line of enquiry with his next and largest paper yet, which was submitted in October 1958 and concerned the adult retina. The retina at the back of the eye is so small that any inflammation would not necessarily be noticeable even under a microscope, so the retina had to be

---

[*] A copy of this film exists at the British Film Institute.

weighed. To weigh the retina, it must be first extracted from the eyeball within a minute of the death of the subject. Kit designed a special plastic holder into which an eyeball could be placed and secured, ready for dissection. It would take no great stretch of the imagination to wonder if Kit discussed this problem over a bottle of wine with John Zorn.

'Dad was absolutely passionate about his work,' remembers his daughter Carol Topolski. 'I remember him coming home from work, having supper, and then going back to the lab to check up on how one of his experiments was going. He would be communicating that hyper-excitement about what was going to happen, explaining how he had mounted an experiment to prove a hypothesis.'

Mark Pedler remembered: 'He used to do the odd scientific thing with us when we were younger like get an onion, stain it with this dye, stick it under a microscope and let us look at it.'

Although Kit loved animals, he was not concerned about their use at work. Kittens were always needed, and in 1957 there was a shortage at the Institute, and Graymore had to use rats instead. Kit was willing to help to provide the Institute with a new source of kittens. An eccentric couple who lived in what Carol describes as a 'huge gothic Victorian house like something out of *The Addams Family*' kept what seemed like hundreds of cats and they were released when one of the couple died. One of these cats chose to give birth in Carol's bedroom. Kit's name for her was Ladypuss.

Unfortunately for Ladypuss, a couple of her kittens fell prey to a large tomcat which jumped in whenever the window was open: 'My mother was furious, and so Dad borrowed an airgun from someone and sat in the greenhouse at the back of the house. When the cat came back, he swears to whatever he swore to in those days that he hit the cat in the middle of the forehead and the pellet bounced off. The cat was deterred from coming back. The remaining kitten we had for about twenty years, but Ladypuss was taken to the lab, and she bred more kittens for vivisection. He was very sentimental about animals. Both he and his sister would ventriloquise animals, imagining what they were thinking; but at the same time, he was unsentimental enough to have this cat we were rather fond of, living in the lab as a breeding machine.'

During the school holidays, one of the treats for Kit's children was to visit the animal house. Carol remembers:

There was this menagerie of animals that were there for experiments. One of Dad's colleagues called Adam used to have a pet white rat that would run around his office. When I objected to the animals being killed, Dad would bring me up quickly and ask, 'Would you rather have a dead rat or a dead child?' And I probably would have preferred to have had a dead child, but I didn't think it was politic to say that, so I would say, 'A dead rat.'

Not all the animals were killed. John Baker, who worked in the animal house during the mid-sixties, remembers:

There was an iguana that Dr Patricia Silver used in her light observation tests. She found it was too stupid to respond and gave it to a family who kept it in their bathroom. Her other animals, including grey squirrels, recorded a very high score and were rewarded with a nutty treat. There was also a monkey called Olly and he could not stand up straight in his own cage. His cage faced the baboon cages, and they felt threatened by the other's presence.

119 Park Hill and fast cars

In the late 1950s, both of Kit's parents died within a year of each other. Hubert had retired in 1950, having seen enormous improvements in the lives of the people he inspected during that time. They eventually settled in Winchester, living next door to a derelict bakery. It was here where Kit's mother passed away in 1957. Hubert returned to Fonnereau Road in Ipswich where he died the following year.

Kit was left some money, and with that the family decided to move across the road to a larger house, number 119, and here they would stay until 1975. It was an eighteenth-century house with an acre of garden at the back which was good for the children and their friends to play in.

It might have been this extra money that allowed Kit to indulge in another pastime: fast cars. His father had driven a very large Morris car, but Kit wanted something different. Over the next decade, Kit owned a Lotus, a Maserati, kit cars, anything if they were fast. He would repair them, improve them, and then sell them. In the mid-sixties Kit drove a 1953 Ferrari. 'It does nine miles to the gallon and there are only nine of them in the world,' he told a syndicated newspaper interview in 1967. 'There is something Wagnerian about racing cars: lots of colour, noise, spectacle. Perfection!'

He claimed in another interview that he had raced in a Lotus at Brands Hatch, but only as an amateur. This may have been where he bought a car that had belonged to one of the greatest relay race drivers of his time. Carol Topolski takes up the story:

> He built an entire chassis for it, put in a V8 engine, and then took the car out for a drive. The engine blew the back of the car off! So, he didn't always get it right. He was obsessed with cars. He would change them like other people would change their underwear. I spent a lot of my early childhood terrified in the back of a car that he called the Osiris, which was a red sports car which he drove far too fast.

Diana Baur sometimes went for a quick spin in one of his cars:

> I must have been about thirteen at the time, and was treated to a ride down Park Hill at what seemed like an amazing speed, but it was probably only about 40 mph. The passenger seat was constructed in such a way that you saw more of the sky than the road in front. It was very difficult to get into and very difficult to get out of, but he loved that. He obviously got a kick from having made something like that, impressing people with it. I remember his laugh.

It was the end of austerity as far as the Pedlers were concerned. Rationing was a thing of the past. Consumerism was starting to emerge as an economic force, making labour-saving gadgets affordable, adding a 'feel-good factor' to life. With Una working, they could spend money – just – and enjoy life. At thirty, Kit was still a young man. He might have been losing his hair, but he wasn't losing his energy. 'Both Una and Kit were "larger than life" people,' remembers Diana Baur:

> Their lives were crammed with interest, work, research and activity and they managed to rear children as well. The house seemed always to be full of interesting objects, children, pets and visitors. It was pretty much like that, but my mother had strong views that Una was not looking after Kit. She'd get very frustrated. She'd go over there and do the ironing and see what it was like. She would do things like take a cake over that she made, and I remember her feeling quite motherly towards Kit and concerned.

In 1959, Una gave birth at home to their third child, Lucy. Once again, Kit fell ill, but there was a benefit for Mark as he explains: 'Dad had glandular fever and gave it to me. I was unconscious for three days. We were put in the same ward. He was in for two months, and I was in for a month. It sounds silly, but it was one of the more pleasant times of my life, because I got to spend a month with my Dad!' Carol remembered her father and Mark being isolated in a ward together, whilst the house was being fumigated 'which is what I suppose they did in those days'.

The PhD

Kit submitted another paper in January 1959, studying how little oxygen and fluoride poisoning affected the mature eye. By now, Ashton's team had developed a hypothesis that the closure of the blood vessels was due to a metabolically induced rise in tissues that surround the tiny blood vessels. When they swell, the vessels are constricted, or closed off completely, but only in the infant.

The work he had been engaged on was written up and explored as his thesis for the degree of Doctor of Philosophy (or PhD) called *The Mechanism of Oxygen-induced Vaso-obliteration in the Immature Retina*, which he submitted in March 1960. In the preface, he wrote: 'It is a pleasure to record the friendly help and continual encouragement I have received from Professor Norman Ashton during the performance of this work.' His PhD was awarded by the University of London. This secured him a permanent position at the Institute, and allowed him to hold a teaching post at London University. Although Ashton's career in the pathology of the eye was only thirteen years old by this point, his work was being recognised with more and more awards and prizes and he had been Professor Ashton since 1957.

Kit had five years' experience and was demonstrating enough talent in research and critical thinking to achieve his second doctorate. Where would he be in ten years?

It was while he was researching for his PhD that Kit decided the retina would make a marvellous fundamental study by itself. Ashton encouraged this thinking, and by 1960 Kit was listed in the *Scientific Register*, a directory for the scientific research world, as working on the 'normal and morbid anatomy of retinal glial tissue'. He submitted a paper on the inner limiting membrane of the retina that October, which Ashton described in the Institute's annual report for the academic year 1958-9 as having 'led to a new concept of the nature of the internal limiting membrane and of the neurological architecture of the stratum opticum'.

Kit's study would coincide with the arrival of a new piece of equipment, the electron microscope, and it was going to be the microscope that would define Kit for the rest of the sixties in the ophthalmologic community with his pioneering investigations into the previously unseen world inside the eye. The days of experiments on live kittens were over, which was something he was pleased about.

However, before he could turn his attention full time upon the retina, there was still some bread-and-butter work to do involving an unusual case of blockage in the optic nerve, which caused a child under the age of two to have his eye removed. This case was written up and published but, significantly, would be the final paper in which 'Christopher Pedler' was connected to the Department of Pathology.

The new decade opened with Kit on the verge of establishing himself as a force to be reckoned with, but there would be casualties along the way. Kit later reflected that he was 'becoming increasingly egocentric and quarrelled repeatedly with his professor [presumably Ashton] which inevitably led to a break'.

His wife would be another casualty. 'I was quite pleased for him to be a glittering star but what happens is that when someone is standing on your shoulders, they may look very tall, but you get squashed.'

4
The Computer in Your Eye

> He was given the opportunity to start and build up an electron microscopy and anatomy department which he still heads. He is a fairly incompetent head, since he dislikes both administration and being a father figure. Has gathered about him a small group of rather scruffy individualists, which he rather prides himself on since he is fairly scruffy himself. – Kit Pedler's short autobiography, 1969

In 1961, Dr Kit Pedler PhD, MBBS, now senior lecturer and teacher of pathology for the University of London, became the head of Anatomy, a new department at the Institute of Ophthalmology which gave him a seat on the Institute's academic board and research committee. This arose from an exciting new piece of equipment the Institute had recently acquired.

In October 1959 Sir Stewart Duke-Elder secured funding from the Wellcome Trust to hire and install an Associated Electrical Industries Ltd Electron Microscope model 6 (EM). A conventional binocular light microscope did not allow the microscopist to see structures any smaller than one thousandth of a millimetre. The EM could see something as small as a few millionths of a millimetre. An electron microscopy unit was created and from this arose Kit's Department of Anatomy. The machine was supposed to be housed in the basement of a stable building, away from vibrations of passing traffic. Yet, a later newspaper piece indicated that the microscope was next to Kit's office, and through his window he could observe the latest London landmark being built, the Post Office Tower, and daydream about silver beings converging around the base of it. They soon advertised in the

New Scientist seeking physicists or biologists to assume responsibility for the machine.

The earliest electron microscope was developed in 1931 by the German engineering firm Siemens. Scientific director Reinhold Rudenberg wanted to study a virus that was afflicting a family member, and assigned two engineers, Ernst Ruska and Max Knoll, the job of developing a microscope that fired a narrow beam of speeded-up electrons through lenses aimed at a target, which either absorbed or scattered them, forming an image on an electron-sensitive photographic plate. There were limitations to the machine because samples were scanned inside a vacuum which meant you could not study living tissue.

Despite this, Kit wrote in the 1961/2 annual report that the EM had 'the ability to provide a ready means of solving an almost infinite number of fundamental and applied research problems, and the main difficulty is clearly going to be how best to select work for the instrument'.

During its first year, they explored the capabilities of the instrument and developed and refined new techniques. Any specimen viewed under the EM needed to be coated in gold or immersed in chemicals such as osmium tetroxide; but methods of preparation, the thickness of a slice of tissue suitable for scanning and the interpretation of just what you were seeing were discovered through fascinating trial and error.

A number of research projects were initiated, and Kit's job was to educate and train people in electron microscopy. In this he was assisted by Mrs Rita Tilly. She became a valued 'technical assistant', whose expertise on the EM would become essential. She prepared for the job by attending courses in EM techniques at the Molecular Biology Laboratories in Cambridge. She would collaborate with Kit during the rest of her stay at the Institute and, like her colleague, would frequently suffer the indignation of having her name misspelt. Kit's first paper to mention the EM was also his first from the Department of Anatomy, another in the series of studies on developing retinal vessels co-written with Norman Ashton from Pathology.

Geoffrey Arden, a fellow PhD graduate at the Institute, remembers the routine type of work Kit was expected to carry out:

> He had about two people to manage, and two to three technicians. He would have made slides from electron microscopy of bits of patients' tissues for clinicians at the eye hospital. He would have lectured to our interns and residents and our students, but this was about a hundred hours a year. In those halcyon times, we were supposed to do 'blue sky' research.

Lucy Pedler, Kit's youngest daughter, went to see the machine:

> He was unbelievably enthusiastic about it. I remember going into the room where it had been installed. It was a very dark room with a huge machine, and as a small child I really didn't get why he was getting incredibly excited, but understanding that it was important because my Dad got so excited about it.

By April 1961, Kit was giving EM demonstrations at an open-day event at the Institute, marking the 150th anniversary celebrations of the founding of the medical school at the old Moorfields Eye Hospital. Kit became a Fellow of the Royal Microscopical Society in May 1960, which was soon celebrating the hundredth anniversary of being granted its Royal Charter, although as a society it had been functioning since its foundation by Joseph Lister and Edwin Quekett in 1839. Like so many other societies formed around this time, they wanted to elevate the microscope from being just a pleasurable pastime for enthusiastic naturalists and transform it into a useful field of science.

Kit threw himself into the workings of the society, and achieved membership of the council within eight months, described in their obituary for him as a 'meteoric rise'. In 1961, he served on the Library Committee, the Microscopical Journal Cover Revision Committee, and as convenor of the Biological Committee. In 1962 Kit became convenor of the Education Committee and co-founded a successful course on the 'Principles of Electron Microscopy'; the first week-long course was held in his Judd Street laboratory in February 1964. Twenty-six students attended, all of whom were young, qualified research workers from many different scientific disciplines.

As well as practical work on the electron microscope and ancillary equipment, the lecture theatre was modified so that each student was provided with a fully equipped research binocular light microscope which could be used immediately after a lecture so that theory might be put into practice. The Institute received many requests to repeat this course on a regular basis.

In 1964, having resigned all his other posts, Kit was elected Honorary Secretary to the Society, whose royal patron was the Duke of Edinburgh, a man who was also interested in the workings of the Institute.

As a teacher of pathology, Kit sat an exam in 1964 for the newly created College of Pathologists and earned the letters MC Path which would be placed after his name. The purpose of the college was to set a standard for their infant profession, and to have pathology taken seriously as a discipline. No doubt Professor Ashton encouraged Kit and his other students to join up following his early experience where pathology was dismissed by hospital consultants as something to do with swabs.

Overseas

One of the perks for Kit was attending international conferences, either as a delegate or a participant. You would normally have to pay for your own travel and hotel expenses, but not if you were officially representing the Institute. Conferences and symposia were good places to test your work and receive rigorous scrutiny and cross-examination, not all of it constructive. Many a scientist has returned from a conference with years of research swept away by inattention to detail, or by being too close to their subject and unable to see the flaws. It was also a chance to meet fellow researchers and form lifelong friendships, perhaps even explore new career opportunities.

One of Kit's first ventures abroad was in August 1960 when he attended the first European Conference on Microcirculation in Hamburg. He was one of just three British participants out of a gathering of fifty, which included P. A. G. Monro, a lecturer in anatomy at Cambridge University. The conference itself was conducted mainly in German but with an English translation provided. The social side of a conference was always a good counterbalance to a dry series of lectures, and delegates enjoyed a boat trip on the River Elbe, and a formal dinner and dance, which reportedly carried on late into the night 'principally due to the enthusiasm of the Scandinavian contingent', Monro wrote in a memoir.

In December 1962, Kit travelled to India to attend the 19th International Congress of Ophthalmology at Delhi. The Indians were proud to host the event for they felt their contribution to eye research was finally being recognised. Kit delivered a paper on the synapse of a visual cell, which would be published in an account of the congress called *XIX Concilium Ophthalmologicum*. Kit did not stay at a hotel but was a guest of the family of a student who was lodging with the Pedlers in Clapham. Kit brought back to Park Hill a love for curry and would learn how to make strong ones which complemented his hobby of brewing his own strong beer.

During one of these conferences Kit had what his wife Una would describe as 'a sort of opening. He was going to think about everything. Think about everything fresh from the beginning.' It would begin with himself, and then, everything else, and that included his wife. Una felt she was being excluded from his professional life, and there was a very good reason for Kit to do so. He had been conducting a long-term affair with a member of the non-academic staff.

Colleague Helga Kolb remembered Kit and the times well:

> He was something of a flamboyant personality. His black velvet jacket and bow ties mode of apparel characterised him. He drove a fancy low-slung sports car at great speed. He had a reputation for womanising. The Institute of Ophthalmology seemed at the time to be full of alcoholics and womanisers, and there were many parties, so he was not atypical.

One member of staff interviewed for this book was under the impression that Kit had already been divorced by this point.

'They used to have lots of parties,' Mark Pedler remembered. 'Some of the staff would drink lab alcohol and work out which one made you blind. There was a picture taken of Kit with lipstick marks all over his back from one of these parties.'

Naturally, the one person who did not suspect anything untoward was Una, but she had unconscious suspicions:

> It was when he was at the Institute that things started to go very wrong between him and me. I never had a thought which I wouldn't share with him. I didn't know for a long, long time; but for a long time I knew, but didn't know... I ought to have guessed, but anyway... It became progressively more difficult. It was really very, very bad.

Despite her own career, it was Una who arranged the schooling for her children who now numbered four when Justin was born in 1964, but the Zorns would always help out when she was busy with her work.

The hidden world of the retina

Kit was now being published more than ever before, either on his own or in collaboration, but no longer by the Institute's journal. In 1962, Kit was published in *Documenta Ophthalmologica* which was the official journal of the International Society for Clinical Electrophysiology of Vision; and in February that same year, Kit submitted a paper to a new journal called *Experimental Eye Research*. A lot of his papers around this time featured examples of visual cells from various animals such as alligators and geckos. Kit had spent a short spell in 1964 at Plymouth University researching the eyes of a genus of fish called the Callionymus. But his discoveries, combined with the work of other electron microscopists around the world, were generating a fundamental rethink in just how the retinal layers of the eye functioned. As Kit would have written in one of his papers, it would be useful now to consider precisely what the retina is, and its historiographical position in the early 1960s.

The retina is a thin membrane that is stretched across the inner surface of the back of the eye. Early microscopists, such as the Nobel prize-winning Spanish neuroscientist (and science-fiction writer) Santiago Ramón y Cajal, had studied the retina at the turn of the century and, from what they could observe, deduced that the retina was basically no more than just three layers of pillar-shaped cells with nothing in between.

Absorbing the light which comes through the eye were thousands of light-sensitive photoreceptor cells called rods and cones, which captured their own bit of an image the eye was seeing. This image is then sent up through two layers of bipolar cells, and then passes along the optic nerve into the brain, where the image is interpreted.

The problem with the accepted position on the retina was that the eye does not keep still when it is looking at an object. It makes tiny little darting movements, scanning if you will, and thus with each movement a rapid succession of images is impressed upon the mosaic of rods and cones with no ghost left over from a previous image. The image implanted upon the photoreceptors is having to constantly change, and no single receptor is seeing the same image for more than a fraction of a second. But there were simply not enough cells in the retina for the eye to be as acute and adaptable as it was known to be. To produce a sharp and stable image from such a mass of constantly changing information required a highly complex system of data processing, which might not necessarily be performed in the brain. Was there some more elaborate mechanism going on within the retina itself? Kit saw through the electron microscope that this was indeed the case.

It was decided to concentrate the greater part of the department's research on their 'further elucidation'. The EM revealed that the gaps between the two layers of retinal cells were teeming with cellular structures, perhaps a hundred thousand within a square millimetre. Kit concentrated his studies on the synaptic layer of the retina called the outer plexiform layer, where the nerve impulses from the rods and cones discharge into the receiving ends of the bipolar cells. Kit observed that there was an intricate system of cross-connections in the outer plexiform layer, and these connections were made by a tangled mass of branches from the bipolar cells called dendrites. Kit thought they acted like wires and are 'plugged' into the top of the photoreceptors, which are called pedicles. It had been thought that information from a photoreceptor was transferred (more or less) straight through the bipolar cells on its journey to the brain, without any cross-connections between the different columns of cells. This was not the case. But the way in which these cells were now seen to be interconnected suggested that the retina was, as Kit told Anthony Tucker in the *Guardian* in 1965, 'an appallingly complex version of the electronic machines which process and transmit information according to the laws of the new science of cybernetics'.

Cybernetics

Cybernetics is the science of communication and control in animals and machines. A relatively new science, it was becoming more and more important as a philosophy, directing research into machines that could 'learn' from their own experiences, and into understanding how a neural system, like the human eye, regulates itself. Kit wrote in the annual report for 1964/65:

> The cybernetic hypothesis can provide help: in man-made computing devices the 'logic module' is the basic functional block and this is simply a group of interconnected electronic components performing a certain logical function which might, for example, be equivalent to the meaning of the words 'and', 'or', and 'not'. The modules do not, of course, speak these words but instead provide electronically equivalent signals which can be used singly or in conjunction to carry out highly complicated logical patterns of activity… Looking at the retina with this idea in mind, the question can then be asked: are there any such equivalent units in the retina to do the work we know it can do? A search has to be made for other ordered systems composed of parts of many cells. Some evidence of these systems has been shown by Professor Vrabrec using special techniques revealing extraordinarily regular, geometric patterns which have more resemblance to the wiring diagrams of an electronic device than to living tissue.

Kit believed that the retina was performing data processing within the eye itself, improving the picture quality, adapting itself to light and dark, and distinguishing between different parts of the image. Was there a part of the brain in those two eye stalks? He believed so. 'Within something little bigger than ten thousandths of a millimetre,' he told the *Guardian*, this time in 1967, 'it has its own computing system... It does the brain's activity and processing on the spot, saving time and space.'

Kit put down his thoughts in a 1964 paper entitled 'Rods and Cones – A Fresh Approach...' which he delivered at two different symposia in London. The second was at the first International Symposium on the Biochemistry of the Retina in front of a gathering of forty-seven participants from England, America and Europe. Kit's work on the retina was introduced by fellow pathologist Clive Graymore as a 'relatively unexplored oil field'.

Some of his colleagues were sceptical. One of them was Helga Kolb:

> Kit was certainly an interesting man with, at the time, enthusiastic and glorious fantasies about the way the retina was wired up, so he inspired me to go into that line of research. Kit was very creative and very verbally persuasive of his ideas. Kit was probably already beginning to think in a more philosophical grandiose way than being dedicated to retinal research and neuroanatomy, at the time I joined his lab. So, he never made any discoveries of note in retinal anatomy, given that those were early days and electron microscopy and determination of even the synapse was very new then.

The slice of retina for study was typically about two hundred microns thick, and it needed to be embedded in plastic for it to be further sliced into strips *one tenth* of a micron thick. The pedicles which fascinated Kit were between five and ten microns in diameter. The slicing was performed by Rita Tilly on an ultramicrotome machine which used a piece of broken glass to perform the astonishing cross-sectioning required. A few years earlier in 1962, with money from the National Research Development Corporation, Kit and an engineer at the Institute developed a unique pneumatic driving mechanism for the machine made from brass and steel. This made the job easier, and more accurate to perform when more than a few slices of material are needed. They needed at least fifty to a hundred of these slices, although once Tilly achieved three hundred and fifty.

Once these slices are prepared for microscopy, each one being *a third of the wavelength of light* thick, an electron micrograph is taken of each cross-section in sequence, a very time-consuming business. In the early days of their study, the main features of each micrograph were traced onto a sheet of transparent plastic. With a hundred of these sheets, it was possible to assemble them and approximate what these cells looked like in three dimensions, and how they related to each other.

The procedure was difficult and laborious, 'hampered by a lack of rigorous criteria for the identification of transmissive connections between nerve cells, and by the difficulty of identifying isolated cells within a single section'. This method showed that there were more than two hundred dendrites contacting a single photoreceptor cell. But it was still very difficult to visualise just what one looked like from two-dimensional plastic sheets. 'It is as if we were trying to construct the connection details in a bowl of spaghetti,' Kit told the *Listener* in 1969.

The tyranny of reason

There was another research project within the department which excited Kit: a study of electrical signals originating in the retina, and how to localise them under the electron microscope. Here, he would be working with Dr R. Fatehchand, another PhD graduate. Initially they proposed to investigate the signals generated in fish, first discovered in 1953. These were easy to record, and it was presumed that they had important functions in all vertebrate retinae. For this job, a new laboratory had to be fitted and equipped. The study of fish retinae was interesting, considering the demands met by their bodies under enormous pressures deep beneath the surface of the sea.

Projects such as these were pushing the definition of anatomy to the point where Kit felt that it was becoming an anachronism, and he had to address the issue: what is the proper study of structure? Electron microscopy had brought morphology – the study of the form and structure of organisms and their specific structural features – to such a state of accuracy that molecular detail now demanded some attempt at explaining how they functioned, which is the realm of physiology and neurophysiology.

Kit believed that scientific research wasn't just a series of 'boring old facts'. Carol Topolski observes:

> His mother was a trained painter, and his father was a doctor, so he always had those twin cultures working inside him, a creative mind as well as a scientific one. I remember him saying that for him, and by association other scientists,

science was a creative act. It wasn't just rooted in pedantically following one fact after another; you had an inspiration which you then explored in an empirical way. He had an imagination. I remember him telling me about Friedrich Kekulé, who discovered organic molecules. He saw a puff of steam coming out of a kettle and imagining it as a snake biting its own tail. That visual image provoked him into exploring the look of the ring shape of the benzene molecule and how it worked. Dad always had that combination.

After a day or night studying cells on the screen of the electron microscope, he would relax at home, do some painting, or perhaps a little sculpting (which he once described as being done in a 'bad Barbara Hepworth style') of what he had been seeing: 'Even if they're scientifically valueless, they're aesthetically satisfying,' he told the *Guardian* in 1967.

Staring at the greenish images of an electronic scan of an animal skin cell had a profound effect on his imagination. At least, he assumed it was his imagination. He described the experience in *The Quest for Gaia*:

> At this degree of magnification, all species look very much alike, even animal and vegetable. I began to understand that in life there were atoms of the air, oxygen and nitrogen, stretching beyond the skin of the animal like an interwoven lacework of matter connecting the skins of all animals, all plants, and all humans… I also saw images which told me that they are all interconnected and so, in this microscope sense, are all one single whole.

In a waking dream, he saw a blizzard of 'small dark specks flurrying and colliding in a dynamic dance of interaction. Then people, animals and plants started to appear through the storm of specks as moving silhouettes.' They were softly drawn images, constantly changing and interacting, the blizzard passing through them, becoming them, and Kit felt that he too was a dynamic and interacting part of this:

> I realised that the static image in the microscope was only a frozen event… From this time on, it has been impossible for me to maintain the idea that my skin limits my individuality. My body only allows my thoughts to move about, my hands to make things, and my sense and experience to travel the planet I live on. But as I move, the matter of the universe moves through me as easily as the wind through the branches of trees.

This discovery left him feeling very ill at ease and with no language to describe what he felt. He certainly did not go around telling his colleagues about this experience. It would have been dismissed as over-tiredness, eidetic imagery, even delusion. It flew in the face of the confining dogma of reductionist science in which he had been trained, and in turn was training others. He had been happy in the belief that painstaking research would eventually reveal ultimate truths of a natural process which was tidy and explicable if you first took it to pieces. He saw his insight not as a rejection of reason, simply the tyranny of reason.

A need for recognition

Kit needed a better way to visualise the connections between the retinal cells. What if, instead of tracing them onto clear plastic, they were traced onto a sheet of expanded polystyrene foam, from which you could build up a model, slice by slice? The reductionist was becoming an expansionist. To do this, Kit adapted a standard pantograph, which designers use to make enlargements from plans or sketches, but replaced the pen with a heated wire so it would cut out from a thin foam tile (the thickness was also to scale) what he was tracing from the micrograph of a cross-section of cells. 'It worked first time,' Kit told the *Illustrated London News* in 1966, 'and we went off and had a drink.'

At last, they had a much better idea of what a dendrite looked like in three dimensions. Once you put thirty or forty cut slices on top of each other, a shape emerges. It was calculated that if Kit and Tilly reconstructed the whole retina this way, and to the same scale, they would have made a model four and a half miles wide. The first model of dendrites and pedicles revealed features that could never have been spotted from single sections. Kit and Tilly would refine the process, discover errors previously made in interpretation, and improve techniques in preparing specimens before they went under the EM.

The reconstruction of three-dimensional objects from two dimensions is called stereology, and they weren't the only biologists struggling with the problems of visualising cells. The International Society for Stereology was formed in 1962 and held irregular congresses around the world. Kit and Tilly would attend the second one in Chicago in 1967 to discuss their technique. Some of their earlier models were displayed at Westminster Halls during October 1965 as part of a two-day event celebrating the hundredth anniversary of the Quekett Microscopical Club. In April 1966, Kit's adapted pantograph was seen by the Institute, and by the National Research

Development Corporation, as something worth developing and a patent was taken out.*

Kit's work did encourage him to indulge in a little private daydream. Kit and Una had been invited to an Institute function, and Geoffrey Arden was joking about the Nobel prize. Una takes up the story: 'Now Kit every year thought he would get the Nobel prize, and when I said that to Geoffrey, he laughed.' Kit was not happy with this remark, which added to their growing estrangement, much to Una's distress. However, it was not outside the bounds of possibility that a Nobel prize could have found its way to him; in 1967, three retinal research scientists did indeed win the Nobel Prize in Physiology or Medicine.

This was symptomatic of a need for recognition in a very competitive environment. 'During my stay at the Institute,' Dr S. S. Hayreh remembers, 'I was awarded several national and international prestigious research awards. Kit complained that he was never informed that such awards were available, so that he could have applied for those, without realising that I found out about those myself while reading various ophthalmic journals, and not that anyone told me to apply.'

There were reasons why prizes and awards were valuable other than as a boost to one's ego. Research costs money, and Kit was engaged in time-consuming and costly work. The Institute of Ophthalmology was facing a financial crisis as short-term grants were coming to an end. There was to be no additional help from London University because, as with every other university in the country, government funding was being reduced or frozen.

The Institute calculated that there would be a shortfall of £30,000 in 1966, increasing to £90,000 by 1968. Projects such as Kit's would be frowned upon by those who saw research as 'the effect of A on B' rather than a speculative 'fantasy' on the wiring of the retina. Professor Ashton had recently identified that toxoplasma in cat mess could cause blindness in unborn children if handled by pregnant mothers. The Wellcome Trust was still giving Kit's small department financial support into 'serial reconstruction of neurones and examination of fresh, unfixed non-embedded tissue'. Surely Kit would be better employed on the electron microscope than creating a nasty smell of melting polystyrene?

---

* GB1153163 is its modern numbering and is listed as 'improvements in or relating to the contouring or profiling of articles'.

'One unfortunate side-effect of the cutback is that university professors are having to spend too much time in the search for funds to support research in their departments,' the 1966-68 Wellcome Trust report noted. On 13 April 1965, the Institute launched a campaign called the Fight for Sight. Its aim was to raise £1 million. Fundraising methods ranged from TV appeals to little ads in the newspapers such as: 'Did you SEE Lt General Sir Brian Horrocks on BBC1 last Sunday? Thousands cannot see. Help Sir Brian FIGHT FOR SIGHT.' One notable fundraising event was the royal première of Charlie Chaplin's new film *A Countess from Hong Kong* in December 1966. By April 1967, the campaign had raised £430,000 and a thanksgiving service was held in Westminster Abbey, although it is doubtful if Kit attended as his name was not in the commemorative booklet of department heads who attended.

However, Kit's need for recognition was going to be satisfied in a different way as his work attracted the attention of the media, and it began in 1965. On Friday 2 July, Kit was interviewed at his home by Paul Vaughan for a BBC World Service programme called *Research Project*. The subject was 'The Computer in Your Eye'. The thirteen-minute programme was broadcast on 19 September at 5:30 am GMT, for which Kit was paid twenty guineas. It merited a mention in *London Calling*, the listing magazine for the World Service, and featured a picture of Kit and his microscope. A month later, the *Guardian*'s scientific correspondent Anthony Tucker wrote an article about the new science of cybernetics and its application to biological studies, focusing on Kit's work.

Kit was beginning to review books on his specialised subject, first in the *British Medical Journal*, and then in 1966 for the *Guardian*, where he went slightly beyond his remit and touched upon a growing frustration. The book in question was one for the layman to read, and not for the specialist:

> There is a particular variety of scientist who will always be affronted by a book of this sort. He will say that it is a 'popular' work not to be taken seriously. He will also gleefully point out a minor mistake and use the mistake to reject the book as a whole. This type of comment usually comes from a closed community of specialists who have spent years erecting an ivory tower of jargon and obscurantism and woe betide anyone who dares to reinterpret their work within a broader context.

They were the enemies of communication, he concluded.

Kit was proving to be an excellent communicator and had an ability to make the most complicated subject accessible to the lay person. Science, he felt, was easy enough to understand if it was explained properly and did not descend into deliberate overcomplication to preserve a mystique.

In November, it was the turn of television to take notice of him. *Tomorrow's World*, the BBC's popular scientific showcase for 'the men, women and discoveries which are changing the way we live' as it was billed in the *Radio Times*, came to his laboratory for two days where they filmed an interview and demonstration. The edition was transmitted on 9 December. Excellent publicity for the Institute and for their appeal, but Kit could not have foreseen just what effect it would have directly upon him.

'I love my work here at the Institute', he told one newspaper in 1970, 'but the thought that I might be a scientist – and only a scientist – for the rest of my life began to bother me. I wanted to explore other facets of myself. There were so many subjects racing through my mind.'

The family story states that Kit asked presenter Raymond Baxter about writing for television which intrigued him. 'He doesn't like "not understanding",' he told the *Observer* in February 1967.* 'I had never written before except research papers,' Kit told *World Medicine* in 1967. 'As a medical student, I was as illiterate as the rest. I had to learn the craft somehow. Science fiction fascinates me.'

Their time with Kit was remembered by the film crew, and this eventually led him to a recommendation to the man who would help shape the next part of his life, and together, that of millions of children of all ages to this very day. His name was Gerry Davis.

---

* This article also began the much-repeated myth that Kit Pedler was visited by the *Horizon* documentary team. This did not take place until 1968.

5
The Genial Hokum of Doctor Who

> Come to Mondas and you will have no need for emotions. You will become like us... We have freedom from disease, protection against heat and cold – true mastery. Do you prefer to die in misery?
> – Krail, from the camera script of 'The Tenth Planet', Episode 2

Doctor Who was a regular fixture in the Pedler household, even if it met with a mixed reaction from his four children. For the past two years it had been on BBC1 virtually every Saturday night, and had become a part of the television furniture. It seemed to be a programme designed for children, but adults could get just as much enjoyment out of it as any child, and there was little else like it on 'the box'.

Doctor Who had moved away from its remit to be semi-educational following the success of the Daleks, which made their creator Terry Nation a wealthy man. In 1965, a new production team wanted to strengthen the storytelling with more imaginative and dangerous stories, taking it a few steps further from being a children's programme. But after just six months that team of John Wiles and Donald Tosh became disillusioned and tired with the resistance from their leading actor, William Hartnell, who saw the programme as primarily a children's fantasy, with himself playing a wizard, rather than a scientist.

A new team was put into place, and they soon formed very definite ideas as to what to do with this series. The first one to join was the new story editor,

Gerry Davis. Born in London in 1930, Gerry started his career working in repertory theatre, first as a student actor and assistant stage manager before eventually directing pantomime in Tunbridge Wells and Liverpool. Moving to Canada, he wanted to write for a living and submitted plays for Canadian radio when he was only twenty-two, before moving into television and later working under television legend Sydney Newman at the National Film Board.

Gerry returned to England in 1960 with his young wife, who was dying from leukaemia. He quickly found a job at Granada TV, helping to nurse the soap opera *Coronation Street* through its earliest days; but having been away from England for so long, he did not feel that he could contribute much to a series about everyday life amongst the terraces of Salford. Following his wife's death, Gerry left England and his writing career behind and took a scholarship in Italy to become an opera singer. On his return to England, he began writing as a freelance for the BBC, where Sydney Newman was now Head of the Drama Group.

In March 1965, Gerry wrote an episode of *Doctor Finlay's Casebook,* a successful series about a general practice in Scotland. Unfortunately Gerry's episode, 'Art or Science', was not accepted by the programme's producer, Gerard Glaister, who considered it 'an improbable melodrama.' Nevertheless, on the strength of creating a course on television scriptwriting for international correspondence schools, Gerry was offered a job as a script editor in the Serials department. His first task was winding up a twice-weekly serial called *199 Park Lane*, almost as soon as it had begun, before transferring to *United!* which was based on a fictional football team. Having remarried, and with a daughter on her way, he asked to be transferred onto a London series, and in particular *Doctor Who,* a programme that fascinated him.

Gerry would soon be joined in early 1966 by new producer Innes Lloyd, who had agreed to the programme only reluctantly as he did not like science fiction. Like so many other producers and directors who worked for the BBC at this time, Lloyd had previously been an actor, but then moved behind the camera and joined the Outside Broadcast Unit, and then started to direct for the Drama Group.

When Gerry Davis and Lloyd arrived, they were disappointed by the stories that the previous regime had left in place. There was a whimsical fantasy story called 'The Celestial Toymaker', and a comedy cowboy serial called 'The Gun Fighters', which no one seemed keen on. Meanwhile, a successful twelve-part epic called 'The Daleks' Master Plan' was on air. The story that followed lasted four weeks and was a serious historical drama called 'The Massacre of St Bartholomew's Eve'. Maybe it was the earlier start time, or maybe dramatised discussions about Huguenot persecution in medieval France disappointed the audience after the thrills, spills and general weirdness of the Daleks, but the programme lost three million viewers.

This slump (and the prospect of a comedy Western) sealed the fate for *Doctor Who*'s trips into the past, and Lloyd declared that he wanted less history and more guts for the programme. He might not know much about science fiction, but he knew what the kids wanted: monsters, and lots of them. Alien creatures were certainly popular, but none of them seemed to have the enduring fascination, story flexibility or commercial appeal of the Daleks. Previously, a new Dalek serial was on screen practically every six months, but not this year. Gerry remembered that when he started on *Doctor Who*, 'The Daleks' Master Plan' was to be their final outing for a while.

Like his producer, Gerry was no aficionado of science fiction, although one of his childhood idols was H. G. Wells who used science fiction for social commentary. Together, Gerry and Lloyd wanted to generate new science fiction-*based* story ideas with concepts that would fire the imagination of the audience. But they were aware writers might share their blind spot and were more comfortable writing for *United!* or the day-to-day suburban life of *The Newcomers*.

Interviewed in 1983 by Jeremy Bentham for the *Doctor Who Magazine Winter Special*, Lloyd remembered that he 'wanted to get someone in to write for the programme who had a good scientific background, who could provide us with real information, and who could show us where science was perhaps going wrong'. They needed someone who could bring plausibility into the science fiction and replace the fantasy. They were *not* looking for someone to vet the scripts for scientific accuracy, but to use the imagination of a scientist to bring ideas into the programme, fly with them, and see where it took them.

Gerry also knew what else he didn't want from an advisor. He had worked with footballer Jimmy Hill on *United!* and sometimes felt his contribution was less than helpful after he stopped a recording because he objected to a hat worn by one of the characters:

> I wanted people who would be adaptable so if I had a writer and he said, 'Look, I'm stuck over this,' I could say, 'Well, phone up the scientific advisor and he will help you.'

> I met with a number of scientists at that time. I met with Alex Comfort, Professor Laithwaite from the Imperial College, I even met with [astronomer and BBC broadcaster] Patrick Moore. I used to chat and try out a little fiction with them to see if they were flexible; if instead of just saying, 'No, it can't happen,' they say, 'Well, it doesn't happen this way, but there's another way it could happen...' They couldn't.

Lloyd continues:

> I contacted my old friends in Outside Broadcasting and asked someone in the science slot if they knew anybody that had that kind of creative mind. They recommended me to Kit Pedler whom they said was both a brilliant doctor and had a very wide view on science.

The first approach was made by Gerry Davis in early 1966. He went to see Kit at the Institute and was suitably impressed. He found that 'the research department he had created was rather like a sci-fi adventure itself, attempting to reproduce vision for the blind,' he wrote in David Banks' 1988 book *Cybermen*.

Gerry was delighted to have found a man who had a great love for mainstream science fiction, both in books and on film, and wasn't concerned when the demands of a story sometimes pushed aside orthodox accuracy. Gerry invited Kit round to the *Doctor Who* production office on Shepherd's Bush Green, and there they began to talk, and didn't stop talking for another ten years.

Writer of the future

Kit had a great love for science fiction, citing Ray Bradbury as his favourite author. It didn't have to be *serious* science fiction either. Another benefit in having children in the 1950s was that it gave you an excuse to read the *Eagle* magazine which Kit thoroughly enjoyed, especially the 'Dan Dare, Pilot of the Future' comic strips. This imagined a future with amazing technology and trips beyond the Earth in rockets, piloted by men who displayed the same heroic spirit as Royal Air Force pilots. Instead of the Nazis, they were fighting a sinister alien supervillain called the Mekon. Diana Baur, whose brother was also an avid reader of the *Eagle,* remembered 'feeling that Kit was a more human version [of the Mekon] with a large cranium and slightly bulging eyes – a brain on legs no less!'

Kit remembered how the Dan Dare strips seemed to interest his hospital colleagues in an introduction he wrote for a collection in 1979:

> I particularly remember the caustic dismissal of the strip by some of the staff in the hospital. 'The Biggles of the spaceways', 'cardboard characters'; you name it, it was said. And then I realised that everyone who was rude about it, knew and discussed every single detail of the storyline; they were not only reading it, but they were speculating about the next instalment; 'If I were the Mekon, I would...'

Gerry told *DWB* in 1988:

> Innes and I thought we'd start Kit off by giving him a story to do and we were sitting in the office one day and looked out and saw the Post Office Tower... and I said to Kit, 'What would happen if...' and somehow some magic happened and we suddenly found our minds moved together, and I said, 'Well, could something dominate the city from there because it's the tallest structure in London?' and he said, 'Well, it would have to be a computer,' and I said, 'Ah, that's interesting, but how would it get around?' 'Oh, it would have to have a control network of sorts, possibly using the telephones.' And eventually we thought about the telephones and pillar boxes, and we'd have all the kids so scared they wouldn't post a letter or pick up the telephone. Then we thought, because a computer is stationary, it would have to impose its power upon people to get them to make war machines which would then go out onto the streets and be capable of dominating the city, and that's how the computer would take over. All that came in one meeting...

'Every time we met, we'd talk for hours, and ideas would start bubbling out,' Davis told *Doctor Who Magazine* (*DWM*) in 1987. A nice bit of 'genial hokum', as Kit once described *Doctor Who*.

Computers couldn't be creative. They were logical and therefore had no artistic imagination. 'At the time,' Kit later wrote in 1979, 'I was obsessed as a scientist with the differences between the human brain and advanced computing machines, and I was thinking that although I could easily imagine a logical machine reasoning to itself and manipulating events outside it, by no stretch of the imagination could I visualise a machine producing a poem by Dylan Thomas.'

Kit was using an idea that was new for *Doctor Who*, the idea of a computer deciding to take over the world. Computers were still a relatively new concept in 1966 and were starting to become viewed with suspicion, especially in America where automation was a dream coming true, but with little thought as to the consequences. Although it was doubtful computers could hypnotise people into becoming their slaves, people's judgements were skewed because of the idea that a computer cannot be wrong.

Gerry told David Banks: 'Kit said, "If we use computers to do all our thinking, calculating, designing, feeding and healing – making all our decisions – one day the machine will decide we are a redundant species like the dinosaurs and replace us."' The story Kit came up with was not designed to be a parable, or a warning to the future, simply a bit of entertaining science fiction for a Saturday-night audience. But even in this early stage, the way Kit's mind worked out his suspicions was beginning to reveal itself.

Happy with these ideas, 'Doctor Who and the Computers' was handed over in March 1966 to writer Pat Dunlop, whom Gerry Davis had worked with before, but he had to pull out of the project and work on another series. The early work was then handed over to Ian Stuart Black, who had only recently finished his first serial for *Doctor Who*, 'The Savages'. In later interviews to various genre magazines, Black couldn't recall why Kit Pedler's name was associated with his script.

'The War Machines', as the story would now be called, was the first story that the new regime had originated by themselves, and they wanted it to have an impact. It would require location filming in London, a greater number of sets than before, and a much larger cast. Scheduled to be shown in June and July, it would be the last story before the series paused for a break over the summer. It would also be one of the first *Doctor Who* stories to be set entirely in modern times. The Post Office Tower was due to be officially opened that summer, and its appearance would make the programme feel relevant and topical. It would also usher in new contemporary companions called Ben and Polly, and see out, with very little fanfare or ceremony, the last of the old ones whose name, appropriately, was Dodo.

Kit was available during production for any advice that was needed by the production team making the story, headed by its director Michael Ferguson. 'I remember Kit very well, he did have a lot to do with it,' he told *DWM* in 1996. 'He was one of the early computer buffs and would sometimes say, "No, this couldn't happen like this," at script meetings.' The director was also encouraged to visit IBM's headquarters in Hammersmith to research computers, but there was only so far you could push authenticity in *Doctor Who*. One of the ideas for the War Machines themselves was that they would be a parody of a human shape with a 'head', 'eyes' and a squat 'body'. This didn't manifest itself in the final product, which in the end looked like a large Z-shaped tank which squirted corrosive gas as a weapon.

Filming for the story began in May around Bedford Square very close to the Institute, where Kit's correspondence and contracts from the BBC went to. His colleagues thought that his venture into children's television was amusing, if a little eccentric, especially since Kit was about to be conferred with the title of Reader of Anatomy for the University of London, which is a professorship in all but name. For his work on the story, Kit was paid £25 per episode in March, and a contract for ideas and advice was issued in May. Kit did not have an agent to take his slice from the fee – or fight any battles with the BBC bureaucracy that he may need one day to fight.

By the time Ian Stuart Black was writing 'The War Machines', Lloyd and Gerry Davis were looking ahead towards the next series of *Doctor Who*, which would begin filming in August. There was still one more story to make before then, a trip back in time to Cornwall to meet 'The Smugglers'. After that, the approach brought to 'The War Machines' by Kit was going to be tried again, but this time Kit asked if he could write his own story. They agreed.

It was astonishing for an untried writer to land a commission to write a four-part serial of anything. *Doctor Who* and the BBC generally employed experienced television writers, who could turn their hands from hospital dramas to thrillers, or 'apprentices' learning their trade on twice-weekly serials where the stories are worked out in advance. *Doctor Who* had a small budget, limited resources, and tight technical limitations; it was a huge gamble and a potential headache for the editor who needed to 'fix' the script, or find a replacement in a hurry, sometimes writing one himself.

Kit had the imagination and the ideas, but could he knuckle down to the nuts and bolts of television writing and approach structure, character, and dialogue to the required standard? Indeed, where would he find the time other than evenings or weekends? He was also paid a much smaller fee than any professional writer would have earned. Gerry Davis would act as a mentor, giving Kit a grounding in production technique, and he would have had the chance of watching episodes currently being recorded in the studio on a Friday night.

The pair would also discuss ideas at the Contented Sole, an expensive fish-and-chip shop in Knightsbridge where, as Kit later recalled to the *Guardian* in 1973, science and show business met in order to save *Doctor Who* from too few Daleks, and too much fantasy.

Monks and vampires

With time on their hands, Kit and Davis started to discuss ideas. One of their starting points was a speculative science-fiction theme based on the type of discussion Gerry had when he was sounding out people for the role of story advisor. An unknown planet emerges to join the solar system and comes into orbit alongside the Earth. It starts to drain the Earth's energy supply. Then astronomers notice that it is a reverse image of the Earth – what happens next? 'I loved working with Kit because we both got excited about working with images,' he told *DWM* in 1987. 'The image of that time was... space flight, which was still comparatively new, so we suddenly thought it would be fun if we had this space capsule going along and then finding its energy being drained by something.'

The capsule would be monitored during its orbit around the Earth by an international tracking station set at the South Pole. Gerry Davis remembered how 'we thought of a South Pole setting, because of the atmosphere it gave, with the tracking station and something – what? – affecting it. Also, the South Pole is so inhospitable that nobody would expect anything to come out of those howling blizzards.'

Another inspiration for the polar setting was Kit's love for the 1951 classic science-fiction film *The Thing from Another World*. Kit once told his daughter Carol that there was a sequence in the film that was one of the most frightening things he had ever seen. A group of scientists and military personnel arrive at a North Pole station to investigate what turns out to be a crashed spaceship, and there was something out there that was threatening them. 'The brilliant thing for him was that you hadn't seen what the thing was, you just knew it was out there because the Geiger counters went completely bonkers whenever it came close.' The conflict between the military and the scientists in the movie might have informed Kit and Gerry in their thinking too. Gerry found that the tracking station would serve as one big expensive set, with smaller, less expensive ones (cabins, storerooms etc.) surrounding it.

The next question was, who were going to be the main protagonists coming from this new planet? With the future of the Daleks uncertain, the production team ideally wanted a new regular monster that would be as popular. Kit's first thought was of a race of Star Monks, but something similar had already been done. With this new planet draining Earth's energy,

Kit may have thought of vampires, but he was told in no uncertain terms not to go down that route. What Kit and Gerry came up with would owe both to monks and vampires, but not in the manner you might expect.

'By that time,' says Gerry, 'we had a real rapport, and we could strike sparks off each other, and I said, "Look Kit, forget sci fi, forget everything you've read. What do you feel about medicine?" and I soon found that he was afraid that medicine would become a matter of machines; that you'd hook people up to computers and they would be the doctors and nurses.' There were some clinics in America planning to do just this. Kit imagined a computer controlling a hospital ward, and the power of life and death it could yield. What if it decided to act upon it, and let patients of no further value die? This idea was not pursued further – at least not for *Doctor Who*, but the idea of the victims of dehumanised medicine was kept in mind since there was something else in the air that touched upon it.

Cyborgs

There were concerns over where the biological sciences were going to take mankind by the end of the decade. It would soon be possible to transplant organs from one body to another, and fertilise eggs outside of a mother's womb, but there were those who thought we could replace a defective biological organ with an artificial replacement, or indeed replace a healthy one with a more efficient design.

The term 'cyborg' – or cybernetic organism – was coined in 1960 by Manfred Clynes and Nathan Kline, who fantasised about self-regulating human/machine systems designed to survive the hazards of deep space travel. Clynes argued in his introduction to the 1965 book *Cyborg: Evolution of the Superman* that a cyborg would be more flexible than a human being because 'it was not bound to a lifetime of hereditary'. He – or it – could pick and choose its own augmentations.

Dr Alex Comfort,* one of the men Gerry Davis had seen before he met Kit Pedler, had been writing about spare-part surgery since the early 1960s, most recently in an article called 'Modified Men' for *New Scientist*: 'Some of

---

* In the week 'The War Machines' Episode 1 was transmitted, Dr Comfort had contributed a story idea called 'The Devil's Eggs' for the Plays department, and this was written by David Weir. Eggs believed to have come from outer space are found at the scene of several disasters.

it may be used to enhance the performance of the whole rather than [allay] the deficiencies of the sick,' Comfort mused, before asking a fundamental question. What would it mean for the person receiving such a replacement? 'Who am I? Am I a true human being?' If you have an artificial organ, you may feel perfectly normal, but how would others regard you? 'One is regarded as being less human for having a wooden leg or for being blind; such handicaps are "judgements"...' A disability can be regarded by 'normal people' as horrific or abnormal, even just a small disfigurement on the face.

Scientists in America were certainly looking at ways of making human beings much stronger. In October 1965, Neil Mizen in the *New Scientist* wrote an article called 'Amplifying Man' discussing his own work on behalf of the US Air Force at the Cornell Aeronautical Laboratories. His 'Man Amplifier' project was studying the feasibility of a powered 'exo-skeleton' with hydraulic joints matching those of a man 'that provide the necessary torque and power under the control of servomechanisms. The servos respond to movements of the wearer and cause the powered structure to follow his natural movement.' The photos illustrating the article showed a man in a flimsy jump suit with bands across the joints in his arms and joints with tubes running along the length of his body.

Kit told *World Medicine* in 1967, 'If you're going to replace people with bits of nylon, plastic and stainless steel, you might as well go the whole hog and construct a completely survivable man. Humans are very weak with soft flesh and so on. If you replace them completely you produce something that is very strong physically, completely survivable, and also totally undesirable.'

the *Guardian*'s Anthony Tucker, also writing in 1965, was at pains to explain that the science of cybernetics was:

> ... comparatively new... it possesses a lunatic fringe and a cloud of popular misconceptions. Its purpose is not to create mechanical or electronic devices which imitate human behaviour... its purpose is to develop very precise theories of feedback control which have practical application and which, by analogy, may lead to an understanding of the extremely complex ways in which human beings work.

Supposing the space travellers from this new planet had undergone surgery, but had extended their 'improvements' to the brain? Kit had heard of alarming experiments being carried out on the brain to treat mental illness. Kit told the *Sheffield Evening Telegraph* in 1967 that experiments had been performed in planting electrodes permanently into certain areas of an animal's brain which could transform the subjects by remote control into either a state of rage or acquiescence. Imagine if they could just switch off their emotions.

Kit was mulling over these ideas in his back garden with his wife: 'We were discussing spare parts surgery and conceived the idea of someone with so many mechanical replacements that he didn't know whether he was a human or a machine,' Kit told the *Radio Times* in 1968. Una remembers that discussion: 'He was sitting beside me in the garden. He said it was his worst horror of what he was like, that is, all intellect and no love.'

Una also coined the title of the story Kit was thinking about: 'The Tenth Planet'. It would be Earth's long-lost twin planet, which looked like Earth, and had evolved its own human race. The *New Scientist* had recently asked 'Is There a Tenth Planet?', reporting the work currently being performed by Gleb Chebotarev of the Institute of Theoretical Astronomy at Leningrad.

Kit took these thoughts to Gerry Davis, who liked the thinking and imagined how their conversation would have gone in his foreword for *Cybermen* some twenty-two years later:

> You start with artificial arms and legs – very necessary and beneficial – but what if medical science eventually makes it possible to replace all of a human's organs – hearts, lungs, stomach – with metal and plastic replacements? At what stage would that person stop feeling human emotions and become robotic?
>
> 'That's it! Men with everything replaced by cybernetics, lacking the human feelings of love, pity, mercy, fear, compassion – and invulnerable to cold and heat. What terrible adversaries they would make! Cybernetic men. Cybermen!'
>
> 'They would be like computers motivated by pure logic,' said Kit. 'If it was logical to kill you they would – if you got in their way.' What could motivate these loveless, sexless beings? We decided on power. History, after all, was full of human monsters who sacrificed love and family for the thrill of power. 'And survival,' added Kit. 'These men have sacrificed their arms, legs, their entire bodies in order to survive and become immortal. When a part wears out, they replace it. They could survive indefinitely. Perhaps we shall all go that way in the future.'

Kit created a little back story for these creatures, as he related in *Dan Dare*:

They were an ancient race on a dying planet who had made themselves immortal by gradually replacing their worn-out organs and limbs with cybernetic spare parts. They had become strong in the process and always behaved logically, but had lost their feelings and humanity as they became more and more machine-driven – very much like the Treens and Mekons against whom Dan and Co waged their long battle.

They became very excited by the Cybermen. They had the potential for appearing in more than one story. In Gerry's office, they sketched out on a blackboard their idea of how a Cyberman would appear. Kit was keen to break up the human form and make these creatures as inhuman as possible. They wanted the heads and arms to appear lower down the body, for example, but realised that it would be too difficult for the designers to realise.

There was no doubt that silver was to be their colour, harking back to Kit's daydream of the Post Office Tower. They became excited over the image of indistinct silver shapes marching through a polar blizzard... Kit knew all about marching from his National Service days and was struck by how robotic a parade had seemed. They were still to have attractive *human* faces, but with computerised brains suggested by a metal skull cap like the bald plate of a monk.

The idea of a religious quest could still be found. The Cybermen have come to Earth to save us from destruction and convert us to their ways. Kit was beginning to see the world of medicine and science as quasi-religious, in that it generated a faith in those who used it and saw its practitioners as above the rest of us who did not question them. It has been speculated that the Cybermen might be a representation of communists, then the West's adversary, but they represent Kit's ultimate vision of himself and his ilk, as he relayed to his wife: cold, logical scientists, technocrats, who had surrendered their humanity to machines to survive, and had become monsters. The Cybermen were not a warning to the television viewers of 1966, just an expression of a personal nightmare.

The Cybermen would claim to be invulnerable to the elements and from bullets, but radiation was their weakness. Alan Barnes argued in *DWM* in 2005 that this could have been because transplant patients were irradiated to weaken the body's defences and prevent organ rejection. Unfortunately, the result was that the patient was so weak they died anyway from ordinary infections. Cybermen had transplants and may have been irradiated and could not tolerate no more. More likely, the use of radioactive isotopes was a suitably science-fiction manner of dispatching a superhuman.

Their greatest vulnerability turned out to be their dependence upon power from their own planet, Mondas. The Cybermen had returned to their original solar system, and to their twin planet, and tried to take away our energy. Precisely how this worked is never explained nor rationalised in the finished story; it may have been envisaged as a natural osmotic process since these Mondasian Cybermen were unable to control it. This resulted in the destruction of their own world as it absorbed too much energy, and the end of the story. The Cybermen seemed to be instantaneously powered by their own world, or at least from some generator on it; once that was destroyed, they instantly died and shrivelled up, like vampires exposed to sunlight.

Having worked out how the Cybermen would be defeated and knowing that they would be aware of this probability, Kit and Gerry came up with the Z-Bomb, the ultimate doomsday weapon, one of which was kept inside the tracking station. Part of the story would feature the humans arguing over whether to use it against this new planet, until the Cybermen plan to use it against the Earth itself.

Writing the script

Now all Kit had to do was *write* the story. He was issued a contract for 'Doctor Who and the Tenth Planet' on 17 May, with the scripts expected to be delivered to the BBC on 6 June. Kit's fee was £250. The contract does not specify whether this was a commission for just one episode or the whole story, although it does say that the length of each of the four scripts is to be twenty-five minutes. £250 is remarkably cheap for an entire story, suggesting they may not have expected Kit to fulfil his brief. The BBC normally paid a writer half a fee when a contract was agreed, and the other half on delivery if the scripts were acceptable.

The story originally took place in the fashionable science-fiction year 2000. This was later amended to 1982 in an early draft of Episode 4, and finally 1986, a neat twenty years into the future, when it was thought manned missions to the Moon would be commonplace. The polar base tracking station (later given the name Snowcap) was based on a smaller version of Cape Kennedy, and the Zeus IV capsule (which was probably nuclear-powered) on the current Gemini programme. Kit put in a reference to a tool used in ophthalmology to study the eye in a patient, the retinoscope, but here it is a camera on board the capsule sending images back to Earth. There would be scenes set within the Geneva headquarters of International Space Command, an organisation which seemed to be a mixture of NATO and NASA, with no communist bloc characters appearing. Apart from a female secretary in Geneva, the tracking station would be male-dominated. Kit wasn't *that* far forward in his thinking.

It is always tempting to suggest that writers cannot come up with names for their characters and try to imply some deep subtext that only a handful of people can decipher, but some of the names do imply scientific origins. Wigner, the secretary-general of International Space Command, may have been named after Eugene Wigner, the Hungarian-American physicist. The name of the tracking station's supervising engineer, Dyson, was perhaps taken from the well-known theoretical physicist Freeman J. Dyson.

An issue needed addressing, but not just yet for Kit. William Hartnell was being persuaded to leave *Doctor Who*. To this day, over half a century after the event, there is still great debate over how, why and when Hartnell left the programme. Those involved have displayed great tact in downplaying the events. The serious illness that would eventually cost him his life was still to come; but even so, Hartnell was becoming difficult to work with, finding himself out of sympathy with the different production teams which had replaced the one that gave him the job. He found making one episode a week for most of the year a strain and was tired. It also upset him that the co-stars who played the companions, some of whom had become good friends, were being changed regularly. Newcomers Michael Craze and Anneke Wills were from a generation he was not in sympathy with, and they had contrasting attitudes.

Innes Lloyd was a tough producer and had a new Head of Serials, Shaun Sutton, to back him up. The previous producer, John Wiles, had wanted to sack Hartnell, frustrated by the way he would go over his head and complain to Sutton's predecessor. Sutton agreed with Lloyd that it would be best if Hartnell could be persuaded to relinquish the role that he loved. This did not mean *Doctor Who* had to finish, despite the recent spell of low audience figures which were causing concern amongst the higher-ups at the BBC. But if another actor could be found to play the Doctor, it could give the show a new lease of life and possibly reverse the ratings slump, giving the programme one last chance – provided a good explanation was found to explain just why the Doctor looked completely different.

Actors, such as Hartnell's eventual successor Patrick Troughton, were being sounded out as possibly taking over from him when 'The Tenth Planet' was being written, and in the middle of June, Gerry Davis was being informed about William Hartnell's holiday arrangements for early 1967. It wasn't until recording on the current block was nearly concluded in the middle of July that Hartnell agreed it would be best to leave.

Any references to the impending changeover which would be a physical transformation could be worked in later. The script that Kit Pedler began to write would not feature any hint of such a major change.

A partnership

Gerry Davis told *DWB* in 1988 that Kit felt daunted at writing a whole *Doctor Who* story by himself and, after a few pages, suggested a writing partnership. 'I said, "It's a bit tricky because I'm employed by the BBC, but we'll see if we can do it."' Kit found that all he could really write was characters giving speeches, and he was getting bogged down in detail. He simply didn't know how to move a story along.

Story editors were not allowed to write for their own programmes except under special circumstances and needed permission from their head of department. Without this bar, editors would just commission each other for reliable stories and freelancers would be left unemployed. Writers' unions were informed to prevent serious disputes. Gerry had used up the number of television hours he was allowed to write each year, so his collaboration on 'The Tenth Planet' would have to be done secretly, above and beyond the type of work he would have been expected to perform on a finished script.

In the normal course of events, Gerry would brief the writers, talking them through plot, characters, situations and so on. He would not be expected to have a hand in writing the script even if he rewrote it, and could not claim a writing fee or receive any credit for it. He had his day job to keep him busy, but the last story in the current series had already been written and edited and production was winding down, leaving him with far more free time. He just needed to be available to approve changes made during rehearsals, for routine administration and to answer viewers' letters or correspondence with would-be writers. New stories were not needed until the early summer. He also had leave to take.

Exactly how the collaboration worked at this early stage is unclear. Gerry has often stated in interviews that it began with 'The Tenth Planet' in a manner that would last them throughout their time together as writing partners. Gerry would write a draft of the episode, putting in the structure and the characters that had been decided upon, and then Kit would 'put all of the science into it', which was either accurate, gobbledegook, or plausible, and then the two of them would get together and thrash out a third draft. But in the case of 'The Tenth Planet', what science? Gerry must mean science fiction and attitude. Kit would have written speeches, for example.

In later collaborations, science and attitude would be at the forefront of Kit's thinking, but that was for the future. However, Kit's contribution was much more than simply putting in a phrase or a word like 'electrode'. It is worth pointing out that in later interviews, Gerry sometimes muddled events and programmes together. This is not to denigrate him in any way, but while their successful collaborations would certainly take on the form described above in the future, it was not so yet.

Gerry summed up their later writing technique to *DWB* in 1988:

> Kit Pedler was flexible, and he could write, not dramatically but very movingly and very well about science, and that's where we were sort of able to come together; he didn't really interfere with my dramatic side, and I didn't interfere with his scientific side. We both respected each other's abilities whereas, if you get two writers together, they've both got different ideas on drama and characters, and you sometimes get a conflict going on (and the same thing happens when you get two scientists together)…

According to BBC records, Kit officially delivered all four scripts during May and early June, and had supplied rewritten Episodes One and Two by mid-June. In correspondence with the copyright department at the BBC in July, Kit is adamant that he wrote and delivered all four episodes when they suggested his fee should be for two episodes, and synopses for Episodes Three and Four. This was something that an agent would have looked out for.

The confusion arose because the assistant head of copyright, John Henderson, had been told by Innes Lloyd that Kit had only delivered the first two episodes. What he meant was the first two *rewritten* episodes. Kit wrote back stating his case and Henderson conceded that he had been misinformed. Kit's unofficial deal with Gerry was that any money he received would be split in half between them, and this may have been a way of making sure four episodes' worth were paid for. Gerry would not receive a credit other than being the script editor, but that would soon change.

Meanwhile, the fruits of Kit's first contribution to *Doctor Who*, 'The War Machines', moved into the studio in June 1966.* When it began transmission at the end of the month this new-look *Doctor Who* achieved very low ratings compared with the previous year when the Daleks were chasing the TARDIS through time and space. At the BBC's Programme Review Board where senior management discussed the previous week's output, Sydney Newman thought that the programme had taken a turn for the better, but the Controller of BBC1, Michael Peacock, asked if this had not come too late. The programme had seen depressing figures since March, and not many series in the past had recovered from falling from so low. The writing was on the wall.

There was some publicity: an amusing segment in *Blue Peter* featured a visit from the War Machine itself, ruthlessly slamming down cardboard boxes. Innes Lloyd tried to interest the BBC2 arts programme *Late Night Line-Up* in an appearance by their new advisor, but they declined the suggestion – for now. Kit would be credited as having come up with the story idea in both the *Radio Times* and in the end credits, with his surname misspelt Pedlar on all four episodes.

But Kit had far more important things to worry about. He was suddenly taken ill. The man who imagined the effects of dehumanising medicine was himself about to have a dehumanising experience, become a modified man, and never be quite the same again.

---

* The guest star in 'The War Machines' was William Mervyn, whose son Richard Mervyn would be one of Kit Pedler's future friends and collaborator. Richard had been to see one of the recordings. Gerry Davis later told him, '"Your father was one of those wonderful actors who, if he could, would write down his lines, which would save him learning it." There was a phone call scene [in Episode 3, added at the last minute to pad out an under-running episode]. He comes to doing it and then my father starts speaking and he suddenly realises that the flat or piece of scenery with his words on has been moved away. So, he makes it up! Up there in the gallery: "What the – what's he talking about?" He got the sense of the scene, but not according to the script.'

6
Dehumanised Medicine and Modified Men

'It was years after I had qualified as a medical doctor before I realised that I had been subjected to a six-year-long conditioning process. I had been turned out of medical school as an efficient medical and surgical technician but woefully bereft as a healer.'
– Kit Pedler, *Mind Over Matter*

K IT HAD LONG SUFFERED from what his family had christened 'Daddy's funny tummy'. There was nothing funny about it now. Mark Pedler, who was twelve at the time, remembered how 'Mum and Dad went to a dinner party, and they had to break down the door to the loo because he had collapsed in there. He always had trouble with his guts. Unfortunately, he passed it on to some of his children as well. We call it the Pedler bottom in our family!'

Kit was first taken to St George's Hospital in Tooting Bec where he was diagnosed with ulcerative colitis, a serious inflammatory bowel disease. No one knows what causes these ulcers, although Kit could have listed a ream of possibilities learned from medical school: psychosomatic, allergic, auto-immune, dietetic, infective... It could have been derived from his rather rich food and drink lifestyle. An operation was required, and the former house surgeon was under no illusion what that would mean for himself. The procedure usually saw the removal of the whole of the diseased gut, replaced with a colostomy bag. But not this time.

Kit went to the Gordon Hospital on Vauxhall Bridge Road, part of the Westminster Hospital Teaching Group, which specialised in diseases of the colon. Kit was put into the care of the surgeon Stanley Aylett. A tall man possessed with charisma and passion, Aylett did not believe that a total colectomy was always necessary, and felt that this was the case with Kit. Since the 1950s, Aylett had been performing operations where he kept the patient's rectum and connected it to the small bowel. This was a very controversial procedure, and he received a great deal of criticism. The word 'pilloried' was used in his 2003 obituary. His critics argued that this procedure would create intractable diarrhoea and allowed for the risk of cancer to develop in the retained bowel. Whilst waiting for his operation, Kit might have read Aylett's latest paper in the April edition of the *British Medical Journal*: 'Three hundred cases of diffuse ulcerative colitis treated by total colectomy and ileo-rectal anastomosis'.

However, Aylett did have a good success rate which his rivals could not compete with, leading some to believe that he simply convinced his patients to 'belittle' their problems after surgery. But Aylett and his outpatient nurse (and future wife) Kay Page believed in good post-operative care, with regular checks to allow for the cancer risk. This was the procedure he recommended for Kit.

On the day of the operation, Kit's eldest daughter Carol was in Cambridge visiting some friends, where she had a very strange experience. 'I'm not a great believer in ESP – although Dad was – but in the middle of one afternoon I had a very, very powerful feeling that I should phone home. I didn't, and I later discovered that when I had that powerful feeling, that was when he was at his most ill, and was briefly considered clinically dead.' Mark Pedler remembered that his father died twice on the operating table: 'He kept haemorrhaging and collapsing. He "died" on the operating table.' When Carol went to visit her father afterwards, she was shocked by the sight of him walking down the ward and corridor. 'I was very frightened by how thin and frail he was.'

To make matters worse, after the operation Kit developed a general peritonitis. Kit described the experience in *The Quest for Gaia*: 'I had no idea, even as a doctor, that such pain could exist.' It was the worst night of his life; the 'whole universe turned into pain. The walls and the ceiling were pain, the bed was pain, every smell was pain, every touch and sight and noise was pain.' He remembered a patient from his days as a hospital doctor who was in such agonising pain that he was subjected to a leucotomy, an operation which cut the connections between the front and middle part of the brain. 'I remember asking him how the pain felt after the operation, and he replied that it was exactly the same, but he smiled easily as he spoke. His reaction to the pain had changed. The pain was still there, but he did not suffer from it.'

That night, Kit could not make anyone understand the condition he was in, but eventually a nurse gave him some drugs. But it wasn't the drugs that made him feel better, it was the relief of having 'communicated across the harsh gulf of the darkened ward'. Pain, he realised, was partly suffered out of loneliness. 'I felt I was in the midst of a hard, chromium-shining, uncaring institution.' It may not have been that night as such, but he soon came to realise that 'I was successfully indoctrinated in the curative powers of technological medicine; and it was not until I had left the field of clinical medicine to pursue research into vision that I discovered a flaw in that confidence. It was that I was untrained in healing, or in the relationship between healer and patient.'

The patient was just a piece of material to be processed through the technological health service, serviced by white-coated savants who ticked off the symptoms on a checklist and computed which pill to prescribe. Furthermore, the patient accepted whatever the doctor told them because he was a highly trained man, someone not to be questioned, only looked up to. A few stubborn people might ask difficult questions, or not take the first answer given to their hypochondria. They were simply 'attention seekers'.

Later in life, Kit would talk about how he wanted to metaphorically take off the doctor's white coat and demystify them, so that they were not unassailable authorities apart from us. He didn't like the direction medicine was heading. He had noticed how recent advances in medicine and surgery were rapidly becoming viewed as the *only* important part of curing a patient. There was more to the art of healing than just that.

Richard Mervyn remembered how, towards the end of his life, Kit had become interested in the dubious area of 'alternative' medicine, and the placebo effect, although he was suspicious of any claims of a miracle cure for, say, an acute appendicitis. He understood the suspicion of powerful drugs with their horrific side effects, but he also knew that patients needed reassurance. At times, Kit was just plain cynical: 'If I've got an appendicitis,' he told Mervyn, 'I'll go to hospital and get it cut out. But for a lot of other things, I'd rather not go. I don't think they know anything.' But Kit appreciated that the operation he underwent had been performed with very high technology methods. The surgeons who performed the operation – Tom, James and Stanley – are thanked by Kit in *The Quest for Gaia*: 'I am alive and well writing this book.' He was also very appreciative of antibiotics, drugs that rendered once fatal infections impotent, but he was aware of their overuse.

Kit was working towards something in his mind, something symptomatic with the whole of technical society. That human element was starting to vanish; the machines were taking over.

Back to work

Una remembered how Kit adjusted to life with a reduced abdominal gut:

> He was very brave and after he had the operation, he didn't moan and groan about getting up and rushing off to the loo. Funnily enough, he was a great hypochondriac. He once thought he had a sarcoma – which is fatal – of one of his muscles, but it turned out to be varicose veins. It was a disappointment for him really.

Kit would in later life readily admit to this side of his character, but developing a sarcoma was a distinct possibility after the operation.

His illness had frightened his wife: 'After he was so ill, I asked him would he get some medical insurance so that I had something, just in case? But he wouldn't. If he had died, it would have been very difficult for me, bringing up four children with part-time work.'

Kit did not like being idle and hated having to take a holiday. After a short recuperation, it was back to work and there was a lot to catch up on. At the end of August, he was well enough to attend and deliver a very short paper to the Sixth International Congress for Electron Microscopy in Kyoto, Japan. He may well have visited the Twentieth International Congress of Ophthalmology in Munich, earlier that month. In September, Kit and Rita Tilly demonstrated their three-dimensional reconstruction of nervous tissue technique in a lecture at the Royal Microscopical Society. Kit was already trying to develop a technique for tracing the outline of cells from the screen of the electron microscope itself, saving time and money. Instead, they developed a roll film camera for the electron microscope, which provided better quality images than those reproduced on a photographic glass plate.*

---

* Tilly demonstrated this technique to the Institute of Biology in July 1967.

In the early autumn, the *Illustrated London News* came to visit Kit's lab and did a feature on Kit and Rita Tilly's work. It mentioned that he had recently been ill but was much better now. It also advised readers to watch out for 'Doctor Who and the Tenth Planet' later in the year…

'The Tenth Planet'

During Kit's stay in hospital, Gerry Davis visited him. It may have been the weak state that Kit was in that created their writing partnership, rather than Kit's lack of confidence in his own ability. At the end of June 1966, Gerry had, in the eyes of the BBC, officially taken over the job of rewriting the last two episodes of 'The Tenth Planet', and this would see to him not only getting paid but also receiving a credit. Those letters from the BBC's copyright department had been sent to Kit and replied to from St George's Hospital in Tooting Bec in early July.

The scripts were ready in early July. Each episode tells its own story in a sense, which means floating viewers who might not have watched each week would not find it too difficult to follow the action. This was essential in those days with no repeats, or any ability to record the programme other than with a sound recorder.

The story takes place in a space tracking station situated at the South Pole, monitoring a routine space capsule orbiting the Earth. After the Doctor, Ben and Polly arrive (much to the surprise of the base crew and its leader, a bombastic American general called Cutler), the capsule begins to experience a power drain and problems with its orbit, and eventually burns up in the atmosphere. The cause for this is a mysterious planet that is coming towards the Earth. Shortly afterwards, a flying saucer lands close to the base, and the Cybermen first make their appearance.

In the second episode, the Earth is now a dying world as its energy is being drained away by Mondas. The human scientists have been captured by the Cybermen, who offer them a chance to come back to Mondas and become like they are: improved cybernetic creatures with weaknesses such as emotions, and a heart, removed. They are overpowered and killed, but there are more on the way. The Earth is going to be invaded!

In the third episode, Cutler decides to launch the doomsday Z-Bomb, which the base is guarding, and destroy Mondas, much to the consternation of the crew, since no one knows the effect the explosion could have on the Earth itself. The Doctor knows that all they must do is wait because whatever process is draining the energy from Earth into Mondas cannot be stopped, and soon the Cybermen's home world will reach saturation point and burn up. Cutler is not thinking rationally because his own son had been sent up in another rocket to rescue the crew of the first capsule before it burnt up. The Doctor, with his companions and a few friendly scientists, prevents the Z-Bomb from being launched.

By sheer good luck, an original draft script of the fourth and final episode survives to this day with the Pedler family, giving a fascinating insight into how the episode originally played out before changes were made by the director, and from circumstances unforeseen when Kit and Gerry wrote it together. The story is the same as the final episode, yet so many lovely little touches were lost and scenes reduced in the process of getting it onto the screen.

The rocket launch has been thwarted, but another Cyberman ship has landed and takes control of the base, using gas to stun the guards. When they reach the Tracking Room, they kill the deranged General Cutler. The Cybermen have detected the missile aimed at them and want to know what it contains: 'You do not send an empty rocket to Mondas.' The Doctor explains that it was because of the late, misguided General Cutler that it was armed with a warhead. The Cybermen, led by Krang, insist that the missile is disarmed before they discuss their plans any further.

Meanwhile, there are Cyberman landings all over the globe, the fortieth being in Greenland. Secretary Wigner at International Space Command in Geneva wants to negotiate with the Cybermen at the South Pole, but his office is invaded by the Cyberman Gern who declares himself controller of the Earth. Only scattered pockets of resistance remain, and these are being 'dealt with'. Gern tells Krang via a radio link that there must be time to evacuate. 'There is much of value on Earth to be taken back to Mondas.' This includes humans, and selection processes are beginning. 'There would of course have to be certain changes,' Krang tells the humans at the South Pole. 'You could only survive on Mondas after conversion... This would be done on the space voyage.'

The Doctor soon realises that Gern intends to use the Z-Bomb to destroy the Earth, and warns Ben and the other scientists, who are disarming the warhead in the radiation room deep inside the base. There is a Cyberman on guard outside, but he will not enter the room. The scientists discover that the reason the Cybermen won't dismantle the bomb themselves is because they are afraid of the radioactivity. They trick the Cyber guard into coming into the radiation room, and watch it die. Angered, the Cybermen take the Doctor to join Polly in their spaceship where he is strapped into something like an electric chair:

> DOCTOR WHO: One moment. Why must we be left here?
> CYBERMAN: (MATTER OF FACT TONE) You are outside the surgery.
> POLLY: (FEARFULLY) Surgery?
> CYBERMAN: Of course, you are going to Mondas. You will both have to be operated on. To convert you to Cybermen.

The Cybermen use gas to immobilise the resistors in the radiation room, but Ben and the others use radioactive elements from the base's nuclear power facilities to kill them. They reach the tracking room in time to watch Mondas burn up. Ben rescues the Doctor and Polly, whose own captor is sitting down, quite dead. In a later version of the script, it was decided to show the effect upon the Cybermen when their world is destroyed. They collapse and shrivel up, like vampires exposed to sunlight. Vampires were never too far away from Kit's thinking process.

> DOCTOR WHO: Just as I suspected. All these creatures receive their life force from a central source of supply. When Mondas exploded they became lifeless as you see.

Cutler's son reports spotting Cyberman spaceships with no signs of life; they were like 'dead satellites'. The Doctor advises that Cutler should never learn how his father died. As for the Earth, the Doctor assures Polly that everything will go back to normal: 'The returning energy will produce some severe storms, high tides, but not for long.' Polly is relieved that the world did not end in 1982, and they head back to the TARDIS. Their departure is witnessed by some of the base crew:

> BARCLAY: If the Cybermen came from Mondas, just where did *they* come from?

The look of the Cybermen

The Cybermen were to have human features on display. The first time we were to glimpse the Cybermen, according to the first episode, was as 'a line of three lights moving in the murk,' accompanied by the sound of 'radiophonic bubbling'. The lights become 'three tall thin figures moving slowly, deliberately and in unison. We do not see any details…' When we do see them up close, they are described as 'tall, thin, clad in silver link one-piece suit,' and that when the sleeve of the suit slipped back, it would reveal that 'instead of flesh there is a transparent arm-shaped forearm containing shining rods and lights. There is a normal hand at the end of it. A close-up of their hand [actually 'head'] reveals a metal plate running between centre hair line front and occiput.' So, there you have it: the Cybermen originally wore clothes.*

In Episode 2, we would see their faces. The three Cybermen had disguised themselves in parka coats, headwear and goggles, taken from the bodies of base personnel that they had killed. The idea was that they would enter the base in disguise, unnoticed, until they reach the control room to the astonishment and horror of the crew:

> Their faces and heads are normal but under the hair on the head is a shining metal plate… Their faces are all rather alike, angular and normally good-looking. On the front of their trunks is a mechanical (computer like) unit consisting of switches, two rows of lights and a short moving proboscis. They carry (exotic) side arms. At elbow joints and shoulders there are small ram-like cylinders acting over the joints.

When they spoke, their voices were to be 'flat but not Dalekish, hard in tone'. These Cybermen had names as we have seen – Krail, Talon and Shav in Episode 2, and Jarl, Krang and Gern for Episode 4. They were presented as logical, pragmatic beings who killed without a moment's hesitation and without regret. Emotions were a weakness which they had removed from their brains.

As Kit recovered from his operation, he was available to talk to both director Derek Martinus, who wanted a swifter pace to the storytelling, and the costume designer Sandra Reid (now Alexandra Tynan) about how he envisaged the Cybermen to look, and any other technical detail he may be able to help with, or at least point them in the right direction.

---

* In a later *Doctor Who* story called 'Attack of the Cybermen' (1985) we meet partially converted humans one of whom takes off his glove and reveals a robotic hand. This story was one of the few to show how the Cybermen converted their victims.

Martinus, speaking to *DWB* in 1986, recalled that Kit didn't seem to show any signs of his recent ill health:

> Kit Pedler was a brilliant, brilliant man, always restless and on the move – quite the stereotype of a crazy doctor. He had his ideas, I had mine, and the costume designer had hers. He was a brilliant research doctor and was working on this sort of thing himself. That made it fascinating, the fact that this fantasy of cybernetic men was just an extension of what he was working on as a researcher in real life.

Kit explained the ideas behind the Cybermen to Reid. Pictures of the 'amplified man' from *New Scientist* helped to inform the basic 'clothing' of the Cybermen, with the black rings surrounding the arm or leg joints of an exoskeleton. Rather than show a human face, Reid gave each Cyberman a grey jersey mask with holes for the eyes and mouth. The eyes of the actor were clearly visible, leaving little doubt there was something human underneath. Some commentators felt that the masks resembled bandages covering the face of a burn victim, but it did lessen the impact that these were augmented humanoids, people like us.* The cranium was covered by a ridged skull cap to suggest that the brain had mechanical implants, with a lamp perched on top, held in place by three 'handles', two at the side and one at the back, which gave the Cybermen their silhouette, retained to this day.

The chest units were very large and heavy, being made from Perspex and metal and containing heavy batteries to operate lights. Add to that a thick polythene suit, and you had a very hot and heavy costume for the actors to wear. Cybermen had to fall over in the story, and once on their backs the actors had to be helped back up to their feet. Sometimes, parts of their costumes would break away and flap about, and this can be clearly seen in their only scene in the third episode, where they are ambushed on the polar surface.

A lot of thought was given to their voices, realised by Roy Skelton and Peter Hawkins, a veteran voice artist who voiced the original Daleks. The computerised tones were given a broken-up, sing-song quality. On a first viewing, it is quite surprising and unexpected. With the lines spoken off

---

* This first generation of Cybermen returned to *Doctor Who* in 2017, and writer Steven Moffat went to town on the image of people covered in bandages as part of the conversion process.

camera, the Cybermen would simply open their mouths, suggesting that there was a voice box inside. It's the sort of touch that children would enjoy replicating.

Kit visited the cast as they rehearsed the episodes at a church hall in St Helen's Gardens and took great interest in the proceedings as *Dan Dare* meets cybernetics. He volunteered suggestions as to how the action should be played out, telling the actors who were playing the astronauts how space suits would be worn. He got on well enough with William Hartnell to invite him to dinner at his home in Clapham. It would have been fascinating to have eavesdropped on their conversation since their views on how *Doctor Who* worked were at opposite ends of the spectrum. It must have been a bittersweet experience for Hartnell to sit and talk with the man who had written his final adventure.

Two days after Episode 2 had been recorded in September, Kit wrote to the production team to inform them that he was now recovered from his illness and was 'planning one or two nasty situations for the new and rejuvenated Doctor'. This referred to the last planned significant change made to the story, explaining how a younger actor would take over the role of *Doctor Who*. The Doctor begins to fall ill during the third episode (as did Hartnell who had to be written out of the proceedings) and drops hints at the beginning of the fourth that 'this old body of mine is wearing a bit thin'. The scene where Ben rescues the Doctor and Polly is changed into something more sinister, as the Doctor makes it clear that they must get back to the TARDIS as 'it is far from all over'. When Ben and Polly follow him into the TARDIS, all the machinery is working, a weird light is pulsing, and the Doctor has collapsed.

Kit collapsing from his ulcerative colitis and surviving 'death' on the operating table must have been the inspiration behind explaining the changeover from one Doctor to the next. There is no reason why the change had to be the result of a traumatic experience or injury as has been the case for every Doctor since. The term 'regeneration' was not coined until 1974, and the idea in 1966 seemed to be that the Doctor rejuvenates by a few hundred years, to explain why he looks quite different.

In the rewritten script, the physical change would not be seen as the Doctor's face would be conveniently covered up by his cloak, rather like a shroud – or a hospital sheet that no doubt Kit had seen pulled over many a patient – but late in the day it was decided that the face of William Hartnell would be seen to change into that of the new Doctor by simply mixing the faces from two different cameras, disguising the change by virtue of a faulty mixing desk which bleached out the picture at the critical moment.

Although no explanation would ever be offered in the following episode, as a biologist Kit would have had something to say on the way cells renew themselves. Gerry saw the changeover in literary terms, as something akin to *Dr Jekyll and Mr Hyde*. This is an example of how the two writers could complement each other with science and literature. But there can be no doubt that Kit Pedler had a hand in one of *Doctor Who*'s most famous abilities.

The success of 'The Tenth Planet'

'The Tenth Planet' Episode 1 was transmitted on Saturday 8 October, the same evening that the final episode was recorded. The new series had begun four weeks earlier with the historical story 'The Smugglers'. It achieved very low ratings which never reached five million viewers. It was hardly surprising that Episode 1 of 'The Tenth Planet' was watched by only 5.5 million viewers. One of them was the *Morning Star*'s TV critic Ann Lawrence: 'It is a little alarming to turn to the latest Dr Who episode and discover that in 1986 an international space station in Antarctica will be controlled by a bunch of moronic, trigger-happy Americans. Let us hope this serial gets better. It could hardly get worse.' Episode 2 was watched by 6.4 million, Episode 3 by 7.6, with Episode 4 dipping slightly to 7.5. The evidence was clear: more viewers tuned in if there was something original to be seen rather than a historical recreation, which the BBC could do on a Sunday night as a classic serial.

Children were fascinated by what they saw. One letter read out on *Junior Points of View* said: 'Please, please, please, can you tell me more about the robot men?' Even the Director General of the BBC, Sir Hugh Greene, relayed to the Programme Review Board his personal enjoyment of the Cybermen. A sequel was on the cards – assuming that the programme survived the change in its lead actor. When discussing the viewing figures, the Programme Review Board noted after Episode 3 that *Doctor Who* was now being given its last chance and would be dropped if no improvement occurred.

'The Cybermen hit the nail on the head in their very first adventure even though they were not as well costumed as they are now,' Innes Lloyd told *DWM* in 1983. 'Gerry Davis, Kit and myself all felt pleased at how that first one had gone so we decided to put them into some other situation, and spend a bit more money making them look more sophisticated.'

In November 1966, Patrick Troughton began his tenure as the new Doctor, a more eccentric and comedic figure than before, in an exciting battle against 'The Power of the Daleks', whose future in the programme was still in doubt. The final pure historical story, 'The Highlanders', came next. Set just after the battle of Culloden of 1745, it was mostly written by Gerry Davis after the original author Elwyn Jones went to work on a new police series, *Softly Softly*.

There was not much need for a 'scientific advisor', something Kit was not in the first place; but in the third story, there may have been a need for some insight. 'The Underwater Menace' was set in the ancient and submerged ruins of Atlantis, and featured a mad scientist called Professor Zaroff, who wanted to destroy the world by draining the ocean into the molten core of the planet. This was the stuff of 1930s children's cliffhanger serial, the sort that Kit and Gerry might have seen in the cinema as youngsters, and hardly a story to feature cutting-edge scientific research. Zaroff had somehow rapidly transformed an ancient superstitious people into scientists. They had a nuclear reactor, the ability to drill down into the Earth's crust, and could perform operations, but somehow Zaroff neglected to invent a fridge in which the Atlanteans could store their undersea food to prevent it from going off in a matter of hours.

Where Kit may have given some ideas were for the 'aliens' of the story, although they were once again modified men – sailors this time, rather than astronauts. They had been converted into Fish People who farmed undersea for the Atlanteans. In 1965, Dr Norman Dibelius from the General Electric Company gave a talk on the BBC's science documentary series *Horizon* about his research into fitting people with artificial gills made from a silicone rubber membrane, to allow them to work under water.

Kit was available to writers if they needed him. Gerry Davis hosted a writers' conference towards the end of 1966 where Kit was pointed out as the advisor, which is the memory of Roger Dixon who tried to write for the series in 1967. By this point, Kit and Gerry had delivered a script.

The Moonbase

Originally given the revealing title of 'The Return of the Cybermen', Kit Pedler was commissioned on Friday 18 November 1966 to write a four-part story. This time it would be a proper collaboration from start to finish, although only Kit's name would appear on screen, properly spelt this time.

There was another brief confusion over fees for Kit, who was going to need an agent if writing for *Doctor Who* was going to become a regular affair. He signed up with Gerry's agent Harvey Unna, who represented many television writers and would sometimes have to write to the story editor himself on behalf of an aggrieved writer.

Work began in late November and the scripts were finished by the end of the year. This time Innes Lloyd wanted a story set on the moon since Surveyor 1 had recently made the first landing on its surface to collect data to assist planned human flight later in the decade.

The new story was going to be set over a hundred years into the future, where mankind had established itself upon the moon. In story terms, it would be similar to 'The Tenth Planet' in that here is another base in a hostile environment which the Cybermen wanted to get inside. The humans required their ingenuity to keep them out. This time, the Doctor would play a much larger role in the proceedings, and he would be assisted by a new companion of Gerry Davis's devising, a survivor from the battle of Culloden, Jamie McCrimmon. His introduction to the series was a last-minute decision, and he was kept unconscious for the best part of two episodes, but there is no doubt that he was there from the beginning of the writing process, and not shoehorned in after the event as had once been surmised.

Like Snowcap in 'The Tenth Planet', the Moonbase would an outpost of International Space Command, controlling the Earth's weather by using a device called the Gravitron. 'It was [Kit's] idea to have a machine that alienated gravity so you could change the tides and the way the weather was going,' Gerry Davis wrote in *DWB* in 1990. 'It also featured as the Cybermen's objective. Their aim was to dominate the Earth by dominating the weather. We also created an international team along the lines of a United Nations organisation. This enabled us to get an interesting mixed cast of characters: Danes, French, lots of different nationalities.' Once again, there would be no representation from the communist bloc of countries and Kit and Gerry's blind spot could foresee no women personnel working in the base. Clearly the writers did not have an optimistic view of how the Cold War would play out a hundred years from now.[*]

---

[*] It was revealed in 1971 that around this time the American army were trying to extend the monsoon season in Vietnam by seeding clouds with lead and silver iodide. It was called Operation Popeye.

The political dimension of weather control was touched upon as the weather crosses the frontiers of nations, and the story demonstrated how vulnerable the Earth would be if such a machine malfunctioned or fell into the wrong silver hands.

Gerry Davis wanted one large set in which to play out most of the drama with several smaller chambers surrounding it. Two pages of the script went into detail as it described the Weather Control Room and its adjacent Gravitron set:

> The largest room in the Moonport and is quite extensive. In the foreground there are banks of controls consisting of the usual switches, meters and lights. To one side there are large computer assemblies showing magnetic tape memory heads and all the ancillary apparatus of computer machinery. The centre of the set is occupied by a large illuminated flat projection of the world. Over the top of this illuminated projection there are a number of ruled lines and figures. In addition, there are flat transparent plastic cursors which can be moved by remote control from the banks of equipment to one side of it. In part of the set there has to be room for several people, ten or twelve. In the background of this same set and separated from it by a transparent plastic or glass partition is the base of the gravitron. The gravitron is composed of a large torodal [sic] or doughnut shaped object, as large as budget will permit, standing alone in the middle of a large space. Coming from its external surface, there are a number of very thick and powerful looking cables. The doughnut shaped object is parallel to the Moon's surface. Through its centre runs the base of the gravitron probe. This is basically cylindrical and covered in extremely complicated and unfamiliar apparatus, again cables come from it and connect to the doughnut shaped object which lies about its base. Inside this room, people only move with special acoustic covering over their head because the machine, when in operation, emits a very low pitched and high energy rumble. We do not hear this rumble until the door to it from the remainder of the weather control centre is opened. Inside we can see operators moving around in their acoustic covering but cannot hear any noise. The scene opens with a number of operators engaged in their normal activity, that of controlling the weather on Earth. Each operator is dressed in similar clothing, which consists of a one piece tunic with no buttons or epaulettes or outward signs of rank. Each person has a number – from one to eighteen – which is clearly shown on left breast of tunic. This number is individual to the owner and applies to all his clothing including his space suit. All of which is similarly numbered.

In the story for the first episode, no one in the base seems terribly surprised when the Doctor and his three companions suddenly turn up out of nowhere, and happily explain the principle of the Moonbase, suggesting that either they have very lax security, or were simply not expecting any trouble to reach them. The episode gave Kit a chance to explore how a base would work and how humans would adapt to a world where a day lasted a fortnight. He also touched on how the personnel would eat and drink:

> On the racks are soft plastic bags containing shapeless lumps. The bags are labelled 'duck concentrate', 'algae block', 'general hydroponic concentrate', 'vegetable pellets'. One of the personnel, Ralph, number fourteen, is loading the bags into a small basket rather like a supermarket basket. He is ticking items off a list. He picks one bag up. It is broken. The powdered contents stream out. He throws it with disgust into a flap opening labelled 'dry waste disposal'.

Another idea Kit fed into the first couple of episodes was the Medical Unit. Here he could finally imagine how medicine would be conducted in a hundred years' time:

> A bare metal enclosure containing five or six 'beds'. The beds are light, cantilever, triangulated constructions sticking out from the wall. The 'bedclothes' are a single light quilted square. Each 'bed' has beside it an electronic unit to which each patient is attached by a thin leash of cables. The cables terminate in a small circular unit strapped to the centre of the chest.

The Doctor is impressed and takes delight in explaining it to Ben and Polly, both of whom are from 1966, but it is Polly who hits upon the one big flaw in this set-up, something that Kit experienced in the Gordon Hospital ward when his peritonitis was at its worst: it cannot feel or be 'nice' to the patient like a nurse could. Polly tries to make up for it by helping the unconscious patients already strapped into their machines.

That Kit turned the medical ward into a place of horror is unsurprising. In the story, the patients have been struck down by some mystery virus. Once infected, black lines follow the path of the nerves under the skin. The Cybermen have infected the base's sugar supply, and since not everyone takes sugar in their coffee, not everyone succumbs to the virus. Those who do collapse; as they lie unconscious on their medical beds, they are vulnerable to the Cybermen, who take away their bodies one by one for conversion.

The writers wanted the medical unit to be the place where the Cyberman presence is finally discovered at the end of Episode 2. This is an often-criticised sequence, as one of the Cybermen has taken the place of a patient in his bed, covered up by a sheet, but his booted feet are sticking out, bolt upright. It is a nice, creepy image, especially when the Cyberman whips off the sheet and stands up. Unfortunately, in the recording, the table wobbles alarmingly after the Cyberman climbs off the bed and strikes a strange pose with a gun.

In the script for Episode 2, Kit addressed the Doctor's own medical training, which he claims was acquired in Edinburgh by studying under Joseph Lister, one of the founders of the Royal Microscopical Society, of which Kit was now Honorary Secretary. Considering the Doctor spends the best part of the episode peering down a microscope, the 'in-joke' is simple enough. The script called for a 'binocular microscope' as opposed to an electron one, since the Doctor would be looking for living organisms as part of the plot. Kit also christened Hurricane Lucy, which the base was tracking, after his second daughter. This might have been intended ironically as Lucy herself remembers being a very shy child.

The scientific detail was to give 'The Moonbase' an air of plausibility, rather than the science-fiction fantasy of 'The Underwater Menace', where one jab of a needle turned you into a fish person; but Kit and Gerry did not forget that they were making a drama/adventure series 'strictly for children' as Kit once remarked, and not a documentary. They still wanted the sinister, the spooky, and the exciting. So, the Cybermen had tunnelled their way into the Moonbase? Sure, why not? There is no suggestion in the script that they had not tunnelled in from their own sealed spaceship, or from an airtight 'tent' to ensure that there was no serious escape of oxygen. They needed the humans alive, after all. They used large bags of sugar and stores to cover up their route into the base, not to block off the air. Every time the Cybermen entered and left the base, drops in air pressure would be recorded in the main control room.

In Episode 3, the Cybermen take over the base, and use converted humans to control the Gravitron and begin to use it as a weapon. Polly has an idea to mix up all manner of chemicals and solvents and throw them onto the Cybermen's chest units, in the hope that this will knock them out. One hopes this was not replicated at home… Jamie McCrimmon, coming from 1745, likens it to sprinkling holy water upon a witch. This is successful, and now all they must do is stop the Cybermen from entering the base again until help arrives.

One of the images Kit and Gerry must have had in their mind when conceiving the story was a low-gravity chase across the lunar landscape featuring the Cybermen. In Episode 3, one of the base personnel goes outside to find out what has happened to two missing crew members. Inevitably, he is spotted by a Cyberman and is chased back to the base. The only weapon he has is a concoction of chemicals that had been used to kill the Cybermen earlier:

> As Benoit bounds it looks like the dream situation of a chase where one can only run at a certain rate… (the solvent bottle) travels like a bullet (LOW GRAVITY) and bursts on CYBERMAN'S chest. As it bursts, a tremendous cloud of steam-like vapour shoots out from the chest unit (LOW VAPOUR PRESSURE). The CYBERMAN staggers, claws at its sagging chest unit, its mouth jerking in (COMPLETELY SOUNDLESS) screams.

Sometimes, plausibility was stretched to provide for a dramatic and visual sequence, such as when the Cybermen puncture the Moonbase dome in Episode 4, and the air escapes. We see liquid coffee evaporating in the low pressure, but some commentators have wondered whether the depressurisation would have been just a bit quicker, and fatal. The small hole was first blocked by a jacket, and then when that is sucked through, a transparent tray is used. The answer to this mystery is simple: there must have been a force field, in much the same way there is Earth-like gravity within the Moonbase. It's science fiction. Hopefully, future designers of a moonbase would think of some way to prevent a violent and fatal depressurisation.

The attitude within the criticism is that a scientist should know it all, especially if he comes with two doctorates. The scorn this scene receives is disproportionate and deeply unfair. Kit was a biologist telling an exciting story to be watched once, not writing a documentary.

The new Cybermen

The Cybermen were rethought, as well as redesigned, to make them sinister and creepy. Kit Pedler was clearly still inspired by vampires. They cast shadows around the base with their distinctive silhouette, silently kidnapping diseased and dying scientists. There is a possible reference to the pseudo-religious Star Monks, when the Cybermen describe their human slaves as having been 'converted'.

To get around the fact that their home planet Mondas had been destroyed at the end of 'The Tenth Planet', the writers decided that these Cybermen were early space travellers (another nod towards the 'lunatic fringe' of early cybernetic enthusiasts) and had come from a settled planet called Telos. Only one of the Cybermen had a name this time, their leader Tarn, and they had developed a fine line in self-congratulation and insults. They might have felt themselves removed from emotion, but this shows that they were suffering from a self-delusion.

The Cybermen had evolved from their 'Tenth Planet' models, and this would set the template for all future Cyberman serials. Episode 1 was designed not to reveal the Cybermen until the very end, and we don't hear them speak until the third, although they did originally have a few lines in the first episode, out of vision, as they monitored the humans talking to Earth control:

TARN: That is all. Is it all recorded on tape?
CYBERMAN: It is.
TARN: Turn off the receiver.

In 'The Tenth Planet' they rendered people unconscious by gripping their heads. They now can shoot sparks from the ends of their fingers to knock out their prey, which we witness a couple of times in the story. The ending of Episode 3 describes the Cybermen's march towards the helpless moonbase, preparing for their final assault:

> We now begin to hear the sinister 'CYBERMAN' theme. Accompanying it, the glinting row of reflections resolve into a row (several if budget will allow) of CYBERMAN [sic] marching in unison... The music is louder, the CYBERMEN are nearer, they are marching more or less in unison, but not in step. We see rows of expressionless heads, the eye holes staring out into the vacuum [sic]. Shots of the massive arms with excrams [?] over their external surface drawing a new weapon like an oxyacetylene torch and pointing it... The group of CYBERMEN is looming massively, the music is now very loud. Montage of swinging arms, lurching heads. There is a feeling of complete power. Finally, the creatures loom above and with crashing music ride over it.

The Cybermen are finally defeated by the very thing they had hoped to use to destroy the Earth – the Gravitron. The probe is lowered down to the surface of the moon, towards the marching Cybermen. The writers were certainly asking a lot for their images to be visualised:

> ...the CYBERMEN stop in their tracks. CUT The lowered probe blasting out the power. The movements of the CYBERMEN start to become jerky, their feet leave the ground. Then, one by one, they rise into the air frantically gesticulating, weapons and other items of their equipment swirling around them. They accelerate rapidly into the black of space and dwindle as gleaming spots of light, diminishing into the stars. CUT The lowered probe and the massive rumble of the machine. Finally CUT to three models of CYBERMAN space ships, shifting slightly on the crater floor, then rising slowly and massively into the air and then accelerating more and more rapidly again up into space as their gravity is neutralised. It too finally vanishes as a speck in the space backdrop one after the other, like giant Catherine wheels.

The first three episodes were delivered just before Christmas and the final one officially delivered on 4 January, although a version had been used by the production assistant a few days before. Revised editions of the script were delivered a few days after that. Producer Innes Lloyd was very happy with the scripts, and so were the production team assigned to make it.

The designer, Colin Shaw, told a colleague of his at the BBC design department how 'at the start of the production we all went round to the writer Kit Pedler's house to discuss the story. There were quite a few of us, the director, costume designer and the rest; and when we arrived, we discovered that Kit Pedler had no furniture in his house, and we all had to sit on the floor. Because Kit was a scientist, he had very definite views on what a base on the moon would look like and was very keen that it should be scientifically accurate.' The reference to the lack of furniture is a mystery to the family, suggesting this was not Kit's house Shaw visited. 'Kit wanted to make sure that the base didn't look like a bunch of flashing lights,' Gerry Davis remembered. He believed that 'the use of the money and Kit's help really gave things that added dimension'.

The director this time was a veteran BBC man called Morris Barry who also visited Kit's home. '[Kit was a] delightful man and very outgoing,' he told *Doctor Who Magazine* in 1991. 'He was fascinating; in his garage he kept vintage racing cars which he used to do up. He took an active interest as a writer and always came to recordings.'

Kit went to the filming at Ealing Studios, where they had previously built the polar surface for 'The Tenth Planet', and this time had constructed the lunar surface for the new serial. He was impressed enough by what he saw to promise a journalist from the *Observer* a few weeks later 'some splendid chases in low gravity'.

It was at Ealing that the new Cyberman costume was seen for the first time. Sandra Reid had not been happy with her original versions. This time she streamlined their bodies using a silver vinyl jumpsuit with distinctive rubber piping used in vacuum cleaners, and joints which were practice golf balls, which children from the 1970s might remember from their PE lessons at school. Their chest units were much reduced in size and weight, and their heads looked more streamlined and metallic, but they retained their handle motifs. The mouth had a flap which the actor could open and close with his own to indicate which one was speaking. Their voices were also modified from the slightly comic sing-song approach to a low, harsh 'buzz', generated by a dental plate attached to a loudspeaker. Peter Hawkins would mouth the dialogue, and the buzzing sound became speech.

Kit decided to take the costume out onto the streets of London to see just how the public would react to something unusual in their presence. Gerry Davis joined him on this expedition and took some photographs which today exist in private hands. It was either in the busy shopping area of St Pancras, or closer to home in Clapham, that they escorted one of Kit's taller medical students around the streets. This was an echo of what happened when the very first Daleks were taken out onto the streets of Shepherd Bush back in 1963, or when the Cybermen took to the streets of Ealing for a photo shoot for this very story. 'It takes a lot to catch the attention of busy London shoppers,' Gerry later recalled, 'but we noticed how they drew away from the tall, silver figure a little apprehensively. One woman thought it must be an advert for a cleanser!' One of the pictures shows the Cyberman walking down an alleyway, watched by a policeman, who wasn't too pleased that their experiment appeared to be blocking the pavement. Kit didn't mind. He wanted to be a nuisance. 'This motive alone, he agrees, is on a schoolboy level,' noted the *Radio Times* in 1968, 'but underneath it is a cry against dull and stifling conformity.'

Kit began to get to know the cast of *Doctor Who* and they were impressed at having 'a real scientist' on board. He became great friends with Patrick Troughton in particular. During rehearsals for the story, the cast had great fun with some of the lines written for Jamie McCrimmon: 'Well, dinna fash yourself, Doctor,' and in his delirium after sustaining concussion, crying out when he sees a Cyberman at the foot of his bed in the Medical Unit: 'It's you! The phantom piper!'

'The Moonbase', like most television from this period, has dated considerably when viewed against a modern production. There are some clumsy moments which are inevitable in a programme that is recorded as if it were a live transmission. However, the feel of the serial, with its 'plausible' approach and sinister nastiness, won approval as the new *Doctor Who* was finding its feet. Patrick Troughton's approach to the role was bedding in, removing the more zany and comedic excesses of his earlier performances. Kit and Gerry's approach to *Doctor Who*, which started with 'The War Machines' and which they had developed in 'The Tenth Planet', was cemented with 'The Moonbase'.

It was noticed by Ann Lawrence, the television critic for the *Morning Star*. She had no time for the previous serial 'The Underwater Menace' because she could not accept the idea of artificial gills. After criticising the new Doctor behaving like a clown, she wrote:

> I am quite prepared to accept that science-fiction writers are entitled to give free rein to their imaginations regarding things about which we generally know nothing, but when they appear not only to ignore, but to be completely ignorant of the most basic and observable laws of science then it's no longer entertaining… I feel that the futuristic stories of Dr Who are an awful let down. They are just not good enough for the children, and my own youngsters' interest has declined markedly.

However, on Monday 22 February, after Episode 2 of 'The Moonbase' had gone out, Lawrence was better pleased: 'The present futuristic episode of Dr Who is of a much higher quality than we have been used to for some time.' She knew whom to thank. 'Written by Kit Pedler, himself a scientist and research worker, the present adventure of the Tardis has a much better-balanced mixture of science and fiction.' She closed by wondering if Polly had to scream as much as she did in that episode. Anneke Wills would probably have agreed. Episode 2 earned the series its highest rating in almost a year with 8.2 million viewers. A later audience research report commended the serial for its approach. This might have made up for the fact that it was an expensive production.

The production team found that having Kit on board was noticed. Their publicity for the serial gave a short biography for Kit, which was featured within the *Radio Times* where it described him as a 'remarkable man... He is a doctor and leader of a scientific research team; he is also a painter and sculptor, and a builder of racing cars.' The *Observer* interviewed him at the Institute and thought it was surprising that the author of a children's television programme was also Head of Anatomy (although Kit may have preferred the term Director). On the night Episode 1 was broadcast, and the same day Episode 2 was recorded, Kit Pedler was a guest on the BBC2 arts review programme *Late Night Line-Up*, where he discussed his children's role as viewers 'who are as watchful and critical as a bunch of vigilantes', reported the *Nantwich Chronicle* a few days later.

He was also interviewed for a syndicated article which appeared in Sheffield's *Morning Telegraph*:

> The man who dreamed up the Cybermen... is an internationally known medical scientist by the improbably swash-buckling name of Kit Pedler, and he believes we are in danger of becoming too much like his disturbing creations. That fact is moving too close to the fantasy; and the worst of it is that we are letting it happen without protest.

Kit speaks of scientists living within their ivory towers, a phrase he had recently used for a book review he wrote for the *Guardian.* He is appalled by unnecessary experiments on animals such as strapping bombs onto dolphins, which he calls a 'prostitution of the world we live in', and criticises the dehumanisation of the human being in the world around them:

> A scientist must never not produce a piece of research because he thinks it may do harm. But there has got to be examination at the time, not in retrospect of each piece of research. The solution, as he sees it, is self-examination all the way, adequate communication with adequate knowledge. If scientists prove that man is the result of an ancient biological accident... we may all have to re-evaluate ourselves less arrogantly. We have lived for too long with the idea that we are a mystical race apart... If we encountered other forms of life elsewhere in the universe, we might not even recognise it as life.

Unless, of course, it took the form of Cybermen, the article concluded.

Donald Gomery, writing for an unknown newspaper at the same time, focused on Kit's views on what he felt was the dehumanisation process going on in society which he had also touched upon in *Late Night Line-Up*:

> The other day I saw a man knocked down by a car – it was a terrible thing. He lay by the pavement just as a rush hour crowd was streaming into King's Cross Underground. The people in the crowd merely gave a cursory glance at the man, then swept by in a mass down the steps... The blonde girl pushing a pram through the supermarket – she is a cardboard character careful never to get herself involved in anything outside the set way of her life, living to a programmed procedure in the pattern of the image maker.

We also get glimpses of Kit the man, 'pleasantly plump of face, with vanishing hair,' smoking a cigar (which he claims he has cut down to just four a day), who writes angry poetry, loves shapes, 'the flow of an aeroplane, a porpoise cutting through the water...' and sighs happily at his other 'madness', fast, petrol-guzzling cars.

> On Saturday, Dr Pedler and his family will be watching the next episode of Dr Who and his children will poke a little fun at dad and his story. But Kit Pedler will smile. He (like Dr Who) will be seeing the serious side of the Cybers – and will be worrying whether we, down here, are becoming too much like Cybermen too.

This was all very agreeable to Kit, a chance for him to express what his writing was trying to say, but he couldn't win them all. Anneke Wills invited him to a dinner party along with her friend, another artistic medical man, Jonathan Miller, to see what would happen when she got these two minds together. Unfortunately, Kit was out of his depth as he couldn't compete with Miller's versatile mind.

Kit's short autobiography, written in 1969, thought it knew where his thinking was coming from. 'After a serious and near lethal illness two years ago, he has now changed completely. Having half read Jung, he now talks about having "individuated" as if he really understood the word, making it sound profound.' He also described his success on *Doctor Who* as considerable and 'facile'. Yet, he had started to hit upon something with his developing views on the dehumanising society, and the responsibility of a scientist to ethically evaluate his own work and its consequences. He still had some way to go before he acted upon them.

Kit Pedler and Gerry Davis, supported by Innes Lloyd, had changed *Doctor Who* forever. They may not have realised it, but they had started to turn the programme from being a frightening (for some) teatime science-fiction adventure series into a horror serial, and this would continue to set the pattern for another year's worth of stories and long after when Gerry had left the programme. They had created a template *Doctor Who* fans describe as the 'base under siege' story, where a group of people, usually scientists, are trapped within the claustrophobic confines of a base containing a technological marvel that can work against them as well as for, threatened on one hand by hostile natural menaces and on the other by an alien menace.

Innes Lloyd asked for another Cyberman story which would launch the next series in September. It would also plunge *Doctor Who* into controversy: a small storm in a teacup over what was acceptable horror for a teatime audience.

7
Of Cybermats, Angry Parents and Biomims

'He has one particular paranoid delusion; that mankind will become redundant on a planet of duplicating intelligent machinery.'
– Kit Pedler's self-penned biography, 1969

INNES LLOYD WANTED THE BEST Cyberman story yet and commissioned Kit on 3 March 1967; but this time Gerry Davis received a credit on screen because he was going to write the story in between BBC contracts. He was moving on to another series to edit, and for a different department.

Allegedly, Gerry's relationship with Lloyd had not always been smooth since his producer had been a frustrated writer and never impressed Gerry with his efforts. Lloyd also wanted to move on to another programme having revived *Doctor Who*'s fortunes, but this would not occur before the end of the year. Gerry declined the offer of becoming the new producer. He told *DWB* in 1988:

> It's hard to explain, but at that time producing was not something a lot of people like directors or even production assistants wanted to do. Some of the editors did but I was making a bit more money by script editing and writing scripts as well. Also writing was what I was trained for, and I didn't particularly want to have all the cares and worries of the programme on my shoulders. I had freedom to commission and do whatever I wanted with the scripts and so why bother producing?

He suggested Peter Bryant, who had been his assistant for a couple of months. Bryant was made associate producer but was given the new Cyberman story to produce as a kind of audition piece at the end of the current production block, and then trail Lloyd before taking over in the new year. That meant they needed a new script editor. This was former actor and radio writer Victor Pemberton, who joined *Doctor Who* to replace Bryant, and became script editor on this story. He had appeared in 'The Moonbase' as one of the base members under the spell of the Cybermen and disliked the long make-up job that the role entailed.

Kit and Gerry now had two new people to please after they finished their script. Any concerns were quickly dispelled as Pemberton proved to be very supportive. Speaking in 2010, he remembered: 'They were two opposing characters, and yet their work gelled. One was a scientist and the other one was a dramatist. I thought this was never going to work, but the meetings we had together were absolutely spot on. They crossed swords occasionally, but not very often.'

The story would go through several titles such as 'Doctor Who and the Cybermen Planet', and 'The Ice Tombs of Telos' before 'The Tomb of the Cybermen' was chosen. Kit jovially tried his hand at getting a pay raise for his contribution since he had now written 'three series for Dr McNoo and in each case the viewing figures have gone markedly up. Do you think that the BBC might suggest slightly more?' They didn't.

This time the writers wanted to explore Telos, the world of the Cybermen. For once, this was not going to be a base-under-siege story since the object was for the humans to get *inside* the base. Whether they would emerge from it depended upon the whims of the writers.

They took as their starting point the 1932 classic horror movie *The Mummy* (recently remade in 1959), where a group of archaeologists wake up an ancient evil. In the case of the Cybermen, it was going to be a trap which only the cleverest humans could trigger. It was a chance for the writers to imagine elaborate set-ups, and for Gerry to explore his favourite phobia of claustrophobic tunnels, based on a childhood experience down in a coal mine. Above all, it gave them a chance to write another spooky horror serial, with a healthy dose of melodrama added into the mix.

Egyptology is a very attractive image for children, so the deserts of Egypt would form the basis for the sandy wastes of Telos. There would be a sarcophagus of sorts in the Cybermen's recharging room, and bas relief illustrations of Cybermen were plastered all over their base. Since mummies are the embalmed dead with some of their internal organs removed and kept in jars, it does not stretch the imagination too far to imagine how this relates to the Cybermen. They were to be found frozen in suspended animation within tombs deep below the surface of their city. Inevitably, they would be awoken, and emerge from their tombs in a set-piece scene. 'There was something very evocative about the image of the Cybermen being all frozen up and breaking through the honeycomb-like membranes,' Gerry explained in 1988.

The Cybermen were to have a new leader called the Controller. It would be a more sophisticated, taller and less cumbersome creature. The Egyptians revered scarab beetles, and so the Cybermen would have an equivalent: Cybermats. According to Pemberton, the Cybermats were entirely Kit's idea.

Enter the Cybermats

Kit had once visited a scientist who was working on artificial intelligence. The man had built a small box on three wheels, which he described as a blind man inside a room. The room in question was black tape forming the shape of a polygon stuck onto a flat silver board. As the box moved about within the polygon, it would never cross the black lines. The inventor challenged Kit to work out how the machine stayed within the black lines. Kit assumed it was a light sensor underneath the robot. 'Inside the robot,' Kit wrote in *The Quest for Gaia*, 'was a small model of the room and a sensor which "felt" the walls of the model room. In other words, the robot had a *memory* of the outlines of the room and so needed no senses to find its way about.'

This was an advanced version of 'the tortoise', a cybernetic 'toy' designed and built in the 1950s by the British physiologist William Gray Walter, a designer of electroencephalography machines which measured brainwaves. The tortoise was about the size and shape of one and was designed to explore the behaviour of biological organisms, such as goal seeking and learning from experience. With a scanning photoreceptor cell, it would seek out and approach a light source (as a Cybermat would home in on brainwaves), and Walter had constructed a very simple nervous system.

One of these was called ELSIE, which was demonstrated at the Festival of Britain in 1951. It could explore its environment, seek light and guide its wheels towards the light source. ELSIE also had a preference between strong and moderate light sources and would not get too close. It had a movable shell with pressure sensors which closed an electrical circuit if touched, causing it to react if it hit a wall. A later tortoise had its own light source attached and could attract another one; when they met, they performed a kind of strange dance. In 1950, Gray wrote that his work on tortoises could be adapted for use on a 'better self-directing missile'.

Naturally, Kit built his own versions. Mark Pedler remembered: 'Dad used to build electric cats, mice, little Heath Robinson devices, very sophisticated for those days, that would react to light. They were on wheels and their heads would move. He used to bring them home.'

As Gerry Davis recollected to *DWB*, they thought of insects rather than tortoises:

> We thought that the Cybermen would have some sort of ancillary animal thing and we basically wanted something rather horrific that would crawl along and then leap on you and clamp to the side of your face and home in on your brain waves. We envisaged them like silver fish with that sort of segmented body and much bigger of course. They didn't end up like silver fish, of course, but that was the original concept and we thought it would be interesting to have the scene where they were all sitting down unaware and then suddenly this thing starts coming... We also thought they might be marketed as a children's toy, but they didn't quite catch on.

The story featured the villainous Brotherhood of Logicians whose plan was to infiltrate the archaeological expedition going to the planet Telos, and plan to revive the dormant Cybermen and use their power to take over the illogical world that the Earth has become. Interestingly, William Gray Walter was a member of the Ratio Club, a small and select dining group who met to discuss new ideas in cybernetics. Included within the twenty or so members were former Bletchley Park veterans, the geniuses who had cracked the German Enigma code during the last war. Although intrigued by Gray's machines, the club members regarded the publicity that surrounded them, not to mention his large media profile, as vulgar. The Ratio Club dissolved in 1955. It was not a sinister group, but you can't help thinking of the Brotherhood of Logicians.

Its two members, the wealthy Kaftan and Klieg, appear to come from the Middle East, which does not go down terribly well with viewers in the early twenty-first century. Arabic nations were still regarded as exotic and sinister since Britain's relationship with the region was troubled to say the least, and television dramas of a certain genre frequently featured them in such villainous roles. The Cypriot actor George Pastell, who had played an Egyptian in the 1959 remake of *The Mummy* and was frequently seen as Middle Eastern villains, was cast as Klieg. For Kaftan, Shirley Cooklin was the wife of the producer Peter Bryant, and the character was written especially for her.

Toberman, a person of colour, is the strong arm of Kaftan and Klieg, tall, silent, and very muscular: another common stereotype. Toberman is a victim and not a villain, manipulated by all sides, but breaks free from his conditioning when Kaftan is murdered by the Controller. He helps the Doctor and Jamie as they try to freeze the Cyberman back inside their tombs, and finally gives his life, closing the electrified outer doors of the city. It has often been misinterpreted that Toberman's lack of dialogue was because he was originally written as deaf, and was wearing a hearing aid, prefiguring what the Cybermen would do to him later in the story, that is to say, replace some of his limbs with cybernetic parts. Martin Wiggins, who wrote the production commentary for the second DVD release of this story, explained that after his partial conversion, the original idea was for Toberman to be seen wearing a Cyber-control device in his ear, which *resembled* a hearing aid, and this can be seen in the costume notes for Episode 4.

Toberman's eventual self-sacrifice at the end of the story was originally dwelt upon in the draft script, of which only the last two pages survive amongst Kit's papers:

PARRY:	(SADLY) How terrible – another life gone.
DOCTOR:	A brave man.
PARRY:	(QUIETLY AND WITH GREAT SINCERITY) I shall see that his name is remembered in my official records.
JAMIE:	(BITTERLY) I'm sure he'll be grateful for that.
VICTORIA:	(REPROVINGLY) Jamie!
JAMIE:	(HOTLY) I'm just grieved that he's dead.
PARRY:	That's what I was trying to say.
DOCTOR:	(GENTLY) Of course.
HOPPER:	Come on Professor – blast off in nine minutes. Anyone else coming for the ride?

It is established in this story that the Cybermen have batteries to keep their mechanical components working and need frequent recharging. 'Our power devices had stopped,' one tells the Doctor. The original Mondasian astronauts seen in 'The Tenth Planet' took their power from their home world, but the space travellers seen in 'The Moonbase' made no reference to their power needs.

Logical though they were, the Cybermen were not very good at anticipating resistance, convinced that they would always triumph. Their recharging room was above the tombs, which was awkward when the humans escaped from the Cybermen and kept them away from it.

The dialogue featured a lot of mathematical and 'logical' talk, with references to symbolic logic, 'OR' gates and logic gates. Mathematicians Alfred Whitehead and Joseph Fourier and Boolean logic are also mentioned. It may have been this dialogue which Kit remembered later in his 1979 *Dan Dare* introduction: 'One of the teleplays I wrote had a robot speaking a real machine language called COBOL and a fourteen-year-old wrote me a disdainful letter pointing out an error in the COBOL which invalidated half the plot!'

The scripts were delivered in April and Victor Pemberton certainly liked them: '"The Tomb of the Cybermen" was an extraordinary piece of work – a very tight and well-constructed serial. I suppose my contribution to it was that I wanted more atmosphere.' This included a character scene written between the Doctor and his new companion Victoria, appropriately from the Victorian age, and serves as a pause before a couple of rip-roaring adventure scenes. In 2010 Victor said, 'Kit and Gerry really built up the tension. Gerry constructed this very, very well. You come into it very gently and slowly in the gravel pits and then suddenly you're into this and everybody wants to see the Cybermen and he builds up to this and you don't see them until Episode 2.'

With the writing finished, Gerry Davis moved over to the Series Department to become script editor of a Sunday-night drama, *The First Lady*, which was about the local politics of a northern town. If there were to be any more Cyberman stories, Kit would either go it alone, or see if Gerry was willing to collaborate and receive no credit.

'The Tomb of the Cybermen' went into production over the summer and would be transmitted on Saturdays in September 1967, launching the fifth series. It would receive a distinctive *Radio Times* cover, something of a rarity for anything other than the Daleks, and always seen as an honour for any programme. Kit kept a copy in his growing collection of newspaper clippings.

Starting from a low viewing figure of six million, the ratings once again climbed over successive weeks to reach 7.4 million. Generally, the story received a good reaction with a nice review in *The Times* by Julian Critchley, and from the BBC hierarchy. Peter Bryant remembered:

> I had a marvellous telephone call – I've never forgotten it – the following morning after one of the episodes had gone out. It was from Sydney Newman who just rang me to say how great he thought it was. It was the sort of thing Sydney Newman did, but for me, as my first job in television production, it was absolutely marvellous and very nice of him.

Huw Wheldon, the BBC's Controller of Programmes and a big supporter of the series, told the corporation's Programme Review Board that the Cybermen were in the 'true tradition' of the series.

As with many stories from this period, they were wiped by the BBC, and film copies that were sent abroad were destroyed when they were no longer of any commercial value. Some fans recorded *Doctor Who* each week onto reel-to-reel audio tapes so that the sound was preserved, and every episode of black-and-white *Doctor Who* survives in this form. Of Kit and Gerry's three *Doctor Who* stories, the first three episodes from 'The Tenth Planet', and Episodes 2 and 4 of 'The Moonbase' survived the purges.

For most fans, memories were all that survived, and their memory said that 'The Tomb of the Cybermen' was one of the true classics of the time. In 1992, all four episodes of the story were found to have survived in Hong Kong, and they were rush-released onto BBC videocassette later that year. The majority were pleased with what they saw from a vintage programme, but others were disappointed that the reputation did not match the visuals, or that there were holes in the plot. These stories were not written – or made – to withstand the incredible critical scrutiny and analysis that some *Doctor Who* fans subject the stories to over and over again, and television techniques had changed considerably since the sixties. Yes, you can see the wires that are lifting up Toberman as he is thrown by a Cyberman. Yes, that is obviously a polystyrene door the Controller is smashing down, and yes, that is a dummy in a suit being thrown across a room. But it is still a hugely entertaining story, well directed, and a rollicking yarn, like all their *Doctor Who* episodes.

Fear of the Cybermen

Children were terrified by the Cybermen. The visual effects designer on this story, Michaeljohn Harris, had been taking a Cyberman costume from his workshop to the studio and, as he emerged from a lift, a child, who was with his mother, came face to face with a Cyberman and started screaming. Ann Lawrence, writing in the *Daily Worker*, thought she had discovered the secret of the Cybermen's 'success' as she asked her daughter why they gave her nightmares, but the Daleks didn't: 'She replied that the Cybermen looked like terrible human beings, whereas the Daleks were just Daleks… these were robots in human form with distorted faces…'

Frights and suspense were one thing, but violence was quite another. A new BBC1 discussion programme called *Talkback* wanted to debate the violent content of *Doctor Who* in its first episode, which was due to be transmitted on Tuesday 26 September, apparently live. A pre-recorded pilot episode had already featured this very subject. Neither Innes Lloyd nor Gerry Davis wanted to appear on the programme, and Lloyd did not want to put up the relatively inexperienced Peter Bryant in front of a group of critics. They turned to Kit, a man used to the rough and tumble of academic debates with colleagues and students. He agreed and made his appearance on the programme from 6.30pm. The question was, how would he cope with emotional parents, and the presenter David Coleman?

This feature may have been in *Talkback*'s mind for some time, but the final episode of 'The Tomb of the Cybermen' had only been broadcast the previous Saturday. It featured a fight between Toberman, who had been partially converted and brainwashed, and a Cyberman. He got the upper hand, pinned it to the ground and then delivered a powerful blow to its chest unit. White foam oozed out of the cavity as the Cyberman clawed at the mess. Although it looks particularly tame today, it is still quite effective. The rest of the story featured electrocutions and shootings.

This edition featured a studio audience of over a hundred 'average viewers', each of whom were given a 'votemeter' which allowed them to express their displeasure at the press of a button. The popular chat-show host Simon Dee was there in person to defend himself against the view that 'our declining standards of morality are due to the filth we see on television', according to one critic, whilst another audience member was angry because of a perceived slight towards the Prime Minister on a recent edition of *Panorama*. Kit was up against it.

Introducing the segment, David Coleman described Saturday-night *Doctor Who* as the 'centrepiece of family viewing'. This was followed by a couple of interviews with concerned parents, one of whom had a six-year-old child who was often left 'gibbering' by the programme. Another child was convinced that there were Daleks behind an electric door rather than his elderly grandmother. Finally, one Mrs Dollar was appalled by the violence inflicted onto the Cyberman by 'the coloured man, Toberman'. She accused the camera of lingering far too long on its frothing body. 'I can't think of anything more disgusting and revolting and unsuitable for children, and this programme is put on when even small ones might be running around…'

Once they cut back to the studio, Coleman introduced 'Mr Kit Pedler', which he kept calling him throughout the segment. It is to Kit's credit that he did not correct anyone on this point. He was asked to react to Mrs Dollar's complaint:

> My reaction is, this is horror, admitted, of a sort; but it's horror perpetrated by unhuman beings. They're not relatable to Dad, at least I hope they're not, and it's entirely harmless in this context. If you produced a man who did this, or was responsible for doing this, or the man was identified with your dad or someone else in your home, then of course you wouldn't do it. What I think you have failed to realise is that the BBC have a very strong policy about this sort of thing. For example, I once wrote a story about vampires in *Doctor Who* and they said, 'Out! No graveyard humour.' They've got a very strong… They keep a pulse on what goes out, and wouldn't allow certain things. But I question whether you worry about this violence when you should perhaps be more worried about other things. I paid a visit last night to a public library; I went into the children's library to a shelf labelled 'fairy stories'. It just so happens that in my pocket I have some quotations from them –

David Coleman interrupted Kit to restrict him to television programmes and noticed some head shakes from the panel of guests. One woman asked if this was really entertaining for children? The Cyberman behaved like a human, which the children could identify with: 'All that gunge must put a picture in their minds of a real human.' Another woman remembered an episode where a man was stabbed 'horribly… the last gasp from his mouth, with blood coming out of him, was the last thing we saw. He was an ordinary man.' If she was thinking of the 1966 story *The Smugglers*, a churchwarden was certainly stabbed in the back, but there was no blood on screen, and the knife was not seen to enter him.

The star of the panel was a quavery-voiced gentleman who accused Kit of sidetracking the conversation by bringing in fairy stories: 'How can you sit there… I just don't know… There is no excuse for it to be on. It does no good.'

KIT: Have you evidence it does harm?
MAN: Yes, I have. My own child.
KIT: I see.
WOMAN: Then you should turn off the set if there's a programme you don't want your child to watch.
MAN: Should (I) have to watch every programme in case something violent comes on?
KIT: I think you should certainly do that. If you're worried about your children being upset – and incidentally, since the Cybermen began, we had one letter from a mother who had a problem with her child, one letter* – if you're worried about this, of course you should switch off. Are you powerless in your own home?
MAN: Certainly not.
KIT: I've got four children, they have varying opinions about the show, one of them thinks it's a rotten show anyway, and none of them are frightened by it.
(The man is still not placated and is annoyed that the BBC expects him to watch every programme they put out in case it frightens his child.)
WOMAN: Children vary enormously in their reactions.
MAN: I agree they might vary –

Academic Dr Hilda Himmelweit, the author of *Television and the Child*, was brought on to summarise the debate at the end of the segment. A wide range of children's ages were being discussed, from three to twelve, and she agreed that some incidents would frighten or disturb a child such as 'stabbing, grabbing and touching the inside'. These were disturbing not only to young children, but also to some adults. She disagreed with Kit's assertion that having actors dressed up in masks and costumes would diminish the adverse effect of violence or horror. She concluded by saying that 'children like to be frightened – but not too much'. A small majority of the voters in the audience agreed with the idea put to them by Coleman that children's programmes should be classified as suitable for certain age groups.

---

* Peter Bryant in *Doctor Who Magazine Winter Special*: '… in all my time there we only had one really harsh letter from a parent who said her child had been badly scared by the Cybermen. I wrote back and invited her to bring the child along to the studios the next time we did a Cyberman story, and when they came, I arranged for one of the Cybermen actors to take his mask off. After that he was quite happy.'

Thankfully, this segment ended with a vox pop of children who said that they had never been frightened by *Doctor Who*.

Carol Topolski, Kit's eldest daughter, wasn't impressed by what she saw:

> I was a film censor for the BBFC for twelve years and so I had twelve years of thinking about those things, by which point special effects had graduated from being just fairy liquid. I remember Dad being confronted by this furious father who also objected to *Tom and Jerry* cartoons! Well, yes, *Tom and Jerry* are fairly violent too.

When her father returned home after the broadcast, he was still fuming at the man who put *Doctor Who* and *Tom and Jerry* together like that.

Some of the children who watched *Talkback* were not very happy with the grown-ups' attitude towards their favourite programme and made their feelings quite clear on *Junior Points of View*. Still, the appearance was an extra twenty-five guineas in Kit's pocket. But he had been out of his depth. He won applause from the television critic of *The Times*, Julian Critchley, and the review found its way into Kit's collection of clippings.

Watching *Talkback* from home was Patrick Troughton with his son and biographer Michael, who wrote in *Doctor Who Magazine* in 2001:

> I recall my father asking me: 'Do you think we've gone too far?' Dad had always been concerned with the amount of violence that should be shown on *Doctor Who* and I know from what he told me that on a number of occasions he was instrumental in toning down certain violent and frightening scenes at rehearsals... At the time I never did understand why there was such a fuss from all those parents who had phoned the BBC to complain. I thought it was great to see a Cyberman collapse with its 'blood' squirting out all over the place. After all, they wouldn't have thought twice about killing the Doctor!

Indeed, during their next production, 'The Abominable Snowmen', the cast objected to a horrific special effect that would have seen a man's face melting during the climax of the story.

Perhaps Kit discussed the issue with Troughton on Bonfire night a month later. Their youngest son, Justin, celebrated his birthday on 5 November, and the Pedlers used to hold a joint party, and the cast of *Doctor Who* came along one year. Diana Baur remembers that 'the firework parties were always good there because it had to be bigger and better than anywhere else'.

In later years, Kit admitted to the *Guardian* in 1973 that they did go a bit over the top with the Cybermen 'spewing Fairy Liquid out of their joints and generally writhing about.' 'A great seethe,' Gerry agreed.

Kit was not against censoring what his children could or could not read. In her early teens, Carol used to enjoy a particularly lurid and controversial series of horror comics:

> Dad found one comic of mine where there was this story about this boy who whenever he was naughty, as children do, blamed it on his imaginary friend. His father became very frustrated with this and says to the boy: 'Right, I'm going to kill your imaginary friend!' In one frame, he has his hands in the air, pretending to strangle somebody, and this thought bubble comes out and he thinks: 'It feels like I've got a neck in my hands.' The final frame is of this boy's face but now completely demonic, saying, 'Heh heh heh, you've killed the wrong one!' Dad was completely beside himself with that. I think those comics were generally felt to be completely over the top. That was probably horror that was one step too far.

Australian broadcaster ABC occasionally found *Doctor Who* too violent and censored episodes. They proposed not showing 'The Tomb of the Cybermen' at all. In February 1968, BBC Enterprises promotion manager Guy Carr telephoned Kit on this matter and he sent in a letter which repeated his *Talkback* arguments. This formed the basis of an appeal against ABC's decision, which claimed that the BBC had a report prepared by Dr Himmelweit and Dr Pedler, 'two world authorities on child psychology' who had found the serial to be harmless to children, and ABC relented.

'The Wheel In Space' and 'The Invasion'

In early September 1967, Kit came to an amicable agreement with the BBC over merchandising, film and publication rights for the Cybermen in which the head of copyright agreed to a fifty-fifty split. This was a quiet period in *Doctor Who*'s history for merchandising in comparison with Dalekmania a few years earlier. The Cybermen would appear as regular villains in a two-page comic-strip *Doctor Who* adventure in the children's weekly *TV Comic*. The *Eagle* it wasn't, but children didn't mind. They probably wondered why the Cybermen were always the ones that had appeared in William Hartnell's day.

It wasn't long before the BBC wanted another Cyberman story, this time to close the fifth series. Kit would provide the ideas, but another writer would turn them into a six-part story. Victor Pemberton had not stayed with *Doctor Who* for long, and his replacement was Derrick Sherwin, another actor turned writer. Peter Bryant was now the full-time producer on the series. In December, the production team had hoped to do a story combining the might of the Cybermen and the Daleks, but this was vetoed by Terry Nation. The Cybermen were on their own, once again aided by the Cybermats. Kit's agent, Harvey Unna, also ensured that his client was properly credited in a manner similar to Terry Nation in any production featuring the Daleks which he did not write. 'From a story by Kit Pedler' would be part of the opening titles on 'The Wheel In Space'.

Kit returned to the 'base under siege' format which had been replicated so many times since, and decided upon a space station setting. Whatever notes he wrote for Sherwin and Bryant have long since been lost, but apparently he came up with the name for the station: the Wheel. This was a sort of space traffic control in a time where rocket flights between Earth and the other planets and stations within the solar system were commonplace. Kit envisaged how such a place would operate, how the stresses and strains of life on board affected the crew, and the seemingly scientific touches such as 'X-ray lasers' (always a sci-fi favourite but actually based on cutting-edge science of the time) and neutron field barriers.

This was a story where you were simply unable to move for the science fiction. Whether Kit thought it was plausible for seeds floating in space to have originated from Venus is debatable, but until the mid-1960s it was believed that underneath those thick, impenetrable clouds of Venus, there could well have been Earth-like conditions on what we now know to be an inhospitable nightmare of a planet. He probably devised the incredibly complicated plan the Cybermen concocted to gain access to the Wheel and take it over to use as a homing beacon for their invasion fleet.

Two Cybermen, dormant inside giant 'eggs', were placed on board a hijacked space rocket called the Silver Carrier. Controlled by a servo robot, which may or may not be of Cyber origin, the rocket was directed towards the Wheel. The crew, it was predicted, would be intrigued by the drifting derelict, but would probably want to destroy it in case it accidentally rammed them. Cybermats would be sent over to the Wheel in egg-type containers, that could somehow pass through the Wheel's hull, to sabotage the X-ray laser by consuming its fuel store. Meanwhile, the rest of the Cyberman fleet would ionise a star, which would send a storm of meteors to cross the path of the

Wheel, which only the laser could deflect. This meant that the crew would have to go over to the drifting rocket ship in the hope of finding fresh supplies of the fuel on board. And they would, inside large crates – large enough to conceal the two very awake Cybermen. The crates are taken inside the Wheel, in a manner of which Dracula would have approved.

Doctor Who's first story editor, David Whitaker, was given the job of turning Kit's ideas into a script. His own approach to science fiction was informed by the Jules Verne romantic vision of engineering, with more than a healthy dose of the *Eagle*, and this is very clear in the finished story. Whitaker died in 1980, and only gave a couple of interviews back in the early days of *Doctor Who* research, but his memory of the story was that the amount of plot Kit gave him did not add up to six episodes, so he decided to make it more of a character story, which certainly slowed down the speed of the Cybermen's scheme. Whitaker was supremely good at making even the smallest character stand out as an individual, and the story does have many colourful and distinctive characters.

The budget for the story only allowed for two new Cyberman costumes to be made, so Kit devised a new figure in the Cyberman hierarchy, the Planner. He saw it as having a massive brain on top of a thin, frail body, which reminded Whitaker of the Mekon. In the event, the designer made the Planner look more like a complicated machine than a Cyberman.

The story had one other task, which Kit may have had a hand in: the creation of the character Zoe, who was going to be the new companion. The idea of a child trained by logicians, and used as a walking data bank and calculator and suppressing emotion when expressing a fact, does smack of the Brotherhood of Logicians. The fantasy then being expressed by futurologists was that computers may one day become the teacher in the classroom.

'The Wheel in Space' went into production in April 1968, by which time Kit was producing more ideas for the Cybermen. The director was Tristan de Vere Cole, who certainly remembers Kit, but not, oddly enough, David Whitaker. Again, we do not know how the writing process worked this time, and whether Kit went through the script and offered advice. Yet Cole remembers Kit being at script meetings, agreeable to suggestions such as introducing a mixture of different nationalities in the crew. Derrick Sherwin also remembered Kit as being a nice man to work with, but the close relationship that Kit had with Gerry Davis and Innes Lloyd was not going to be replicated.

Another new addition to the production team was assistant script editor Terrance Dicks. Speaking in a DVD documentary on 'The Invasion', he recalled how 'Kit Pedler was very keen to be seen as a creative input as well as a scientific one... I remember he wrote Derrick Sherwin a very stroppy letter once saying, "I want to take part in the creative process. I'm not just a think tank to be plugged into!" And I thought, yes you are!'

'The Wheel in Space' did not go down very well with Patrick Troughton, who felt that the scripts were becoming tired and predictable. His character was going to be absent for an episode (giving Troughton a week's holiday), and would remain bedridden for the next two. What didn't help matters was that he was getting extremely tired with the production demands and had been required to work on his 'day off', doing location filming in advance for the next serial; but Troughton had done so many episodes by now that it was going to be hard to impress him. It is certainly true that the programme was becoming repetitive, based upon the formulae Kit and Gerry had inadvertently put into place.

This feeling that the scripts were getting stale was shared by Derrick Sherwin and Peter Bryant, and they wanted to try a new template for the series. Take *Doctor Who* away from outer space and put him down amongst the Earthmen of the 1970s. They devised a militaristic set-up called UNIT – the United Nations Intelligence Taskforce – headed by a character from an earlier story called Colonel Lethbridge-Stewart. The idea was that they were a type of world police force, defending the Earth against alien aggression, and the first aggressor they would fight would be the Cybermen.

Kit came up with 'The Return of the Cybermen', a title he had previously used for 'The Moonbase'. He was paid a fee of £280 for his storyline plus a copyright payment of £120 for use of the Cybermen and the Cybermats. Aware of Kit's sensitivities, Peter Bryant felt that although Kit Pedler's synopsis as submitted would only make a four-part serial, they proposed 'using little of his actual stuff; the whole thing is really to make him feel integrated with the project as far as possible'. The story would later be simply known as 'The Invasion'.

This time, Kit had to imagine how the Cybermen would successfully invade the Earth in 1975. Silicon chips and transistors were very new and promised to revolutionise technology. The first handheld calculator had been built in 1967. Kit created a huge, multinational company called International Electromatix (or IE, possibly derived from the manufacturer of his electron microscope, or even from the Institute of Electrical Engineers) which dominated the world's electronics market. Kit's fascination with the world of the miniature circuit was something he was investigating, as we shall see. Edinburgh was home to the Department of Machine Intelligence and Perception, and one of its founders was Richard Gregory, whose 1966 book Kit had reviewed for the *Guardian*. Whether the character of Gregory in the story was named in his honour is doubtful, since he is rather weak-willed, and meets with a sticky end.

The director of the company is called Tobias Vaughn, a name apparently derived from a book of Christian names. Vaughn was in league with the Cybermen, and was partially converted himself, as was most of his workforce. IE would manufacture a micro-monolithic circuit and place it inside every electrical machine that they manufactured. Its purpose was to receive and amplify a hypnotic signal beamed from an orbiting Cyberman spacecraft, which would place the entire world under Cyber control. This developed the Cybermen's mesmeric abilities first seen in 'The Tomb of the Cybermen', and again in 'The Wheel in Space'. The signal could be blocked by a metal plate and a transistor, taped to the back of the neck. The Cybermen had been secretly building up their forces on Earth and would use the sewer system to spread across London before they emerged to take control of the world.

Kit believed that a good 'monster' should have an Achilles' heel worth exploiting. He had thought of one for the Cybermen in 1967, and now had a chance to get it done. That same year Kit had given an interview to *World Medicine*, the author of which wrote: 'In real life the trend of politicians and planners to discount the emotions of those they control alarms Dr Pedler. Perhaps with this in mind he has something nasty in store for the Cybermen. He is considering confronting them with feelings – long repressed, upsetting feelings from way back in their mental evolution.'

In the story, Kit had International Electromatix develop a teaching machine called the Cerebration Mentor, a device that triggered emotional responses in its subject to award achievement. The Cybermen would be given a dose of the emotion fear, and their response was to go berserk, or die.*

---

* Teaching machines would appear in the next Doctor Who story, 'The Krotons', used to condition a subjugated race of humanoids, and attempt to boost their mental energies in order to power a spacecraft, hosted by a dormant alien race.

The careful continuity established during his first three scripts for the Cybermen, where each event took place a hundred years or more after their last appearance, had been abandoned. 'The Invasion' was set ten years before 'The Tenth Planet', while 'The Wheel In Space' was set at some unspecified point in the future, and none of the humans had heard of the Cybermen.

Originally David Whitaker was going to write this story, but in the event it was Derrick Sherwin himself who bit the bullet and expanded it further into an eight-part adventure, which would become one of the most popular and successful stories of its time. Whether Kit even saw a script or attended a studio session is unknown; when he spoke to the *Radio Times* shortly before its transmission in November 1968, he sounded quite relaxed, but did not discuss the story. He looked back at the appeal of the Cybermen and what they meant to him as a writer and scientist. They were 'strong and immortal but the antithesis of everything I conceive to be human'. This was the last time Kit would write for *Doctor Who*, but it didn't matter as much. Although he enjoyed his experience and was grateful for what it did for him, Kit now had a reputation within the BBC's drama department as a man of ideas.

In late 1969, *Doctor Who* underwent yet another period of change, as wide-reaching as the one Kit saw in 1966. The Doctor was now exiled to Earth in the flamboyant form of Jon Pertwee and advised UNIT. In the 1970 series, the Doctor went from one scientific establishment to another, some of which were trying to find the answer to what would later become known as the energy crisis. Scientists in their bases were still under siege. It sounds like a perfect setting for a genuine scientific advisor; but Terrance Dicks, now promoted as script editor, felt that it would be a pointless and time-consuming exercise to put scripts through any form of vetting. He was more than capable of coming up with good ideas himself and did not require a think tank.

Gerry Davis was invited to write a Cyberman story in 1974, but his script (called once again 'Return of the Cybermen') was remarkably out of date and written as if *Doctor Who* was being made as it had been ten years before. The production team who inherited the script were not impressed and gave it a top-to-bottom rewrite by script editor Robert Holmes, who did not have much sympathy with other people's creations, and therefore missed the point of the Cybermen. This would be their one and only major appearance in the 1970s, and it was an entertaining effort, featuring a race of albino gold-miners who echoed the recent conflict that had raged between the firebrand coal-miners' union and the patrician government of the day.

Kit might not have been involved, but the new Doctor, Tom Baker, was a guest at one of the Pedlers' firework parties in 1974. Kit cut out and kept a picture of Tom with a Cyberman from when his appointment was made public. Gerry did try to write a Cyberman 'origins' story for *Doctor Who* in the 1980s but his storyline (where he names a companion after one of his daughters, Felicity) was turned down, which left Gerry deeply hurt.

On call at the BBC

At the end of 1966, Kit was asked to help advise a BBC2 drama serial by Arden Winch called *The Paradise Makers* which was about an ex-spy and physicist who is asked to infiltrate a corrupt laboratory. Kit thoroughly enjoyed the scripts and the themes of the serial. He only had a few minor suggestions such as 'P.16: There is too much "sir" from Henderson. This doesn't occur between scientists,' or 'P.74: Money out of Russia – you try it!' and 'P.34: 'Integrated circuit. Suggest computer of average transient together with logic module system.'

Shortly before his *Talkback* experience, Kit was invited to the office of the Head of Series, Andrew Osborn, to watch a playback of a pilot episode for a new science-fiction series called *Counterstrike* to see if he could help improve it. This was the story of an alien disguised as a human called Simon Kane, whose job was to prevent the infiltration of Earth by alien refugees, who could equally pass off as human. They wanted to wipe out humanity and repopulate the planet. Kit was not impressed with what he saw, and in a letter dated 28 September 1967 he summarised:

> From the scientific point of view, it was convincing. The factory 'atmosphere' was well generated and realistic, except for some rather obvious technical clangers from the laboratory workers. I could also believe in the two principal factory directors – logical beings who were single minded. One, in particular – I forget his name – gave off an appropriately sinister aura.
>
> The principal 'goodie' – Simon Kane was it – was entirely unconvincing; the character was wet and chatty, no power there at all. The lady doctor would have made my wife spit into her stethoscope for the reasons I have already told you.
>
> The story did not succeed in exciting or involving me in any way, because the theme is over-familiar, and the pace was flat, downbeat and non-escalating.
>
> I think the basic feature about aliens is that they are 'alien', they are one point removed from our experience. Our senses do not succeed in generating their real image, there is a basic failure of fit.

> I am sorry to be so critical, but there is no point in buttering the 'pilot' up at all. It achieves nothing new and can never in its present form do anything except be the mixture as before.

Kit was developing a taste for speculative science fiction, and in 1968 he was known to be writing a book looking at the past fifty years from the viewpoint of 2016. The writing bug had bitten Kit deep, as had the success and public exposure it had generated. He wrote of himself in 1969:

> Since his name has appeared on television and articles have been written about him, there seems little doubt that he is gaining an increased idea of his own importance. He now talks of himself as a 'writer' to scientists and a 'scientist' to writers, a ruse clearly to avoid definition or pigeon-holing. At the present time he has no clear idea of his own future. If pressed he will emit pompous phrases such as 'creative people are permanently involved in an identity crisis' and so on.

Meanwhile *World Medicine* wrote:

> If he could find a theme in which he could become all absorbed, he might even consider abandoning research… 'I wouldn't give up research altogether. I enjoy it too much.' At present he is working on a film for which he is trying to express ideas which have been in his mind since student days. 'It will be a science fiction film. I think Ray Bradbury's stories are among the best. What I want to do is to explore some very private themes in very ordinary London or English settings. I am concerned with exposing the dehumanising effect of image-makers and pragmatists on ordinary people.' He cites the American policy in Vietnam as an example of the way in which the emotions of thousands of people are being coolly disregarded by politicians concerned with practicalities.

He had taken up writing poetry. 'I really must get up courage to publish it,' he said in 1967 to an unknown paper. 'People who have seen it have said "You must be terribly unhappy – how did you get into that state?" There's a lot of hate in it, you see.' This 'hate' raged against the patterned way of life that causes the callousness of society. He was also reported to be writing a cycle of six plays 'bits of each at the same time'. In all of them he is attacking the 'Cyber-like' attitudes of real men and women.

The biomims

In 1969, the *Listener* magazine commissioned Kit to write a short piece for their June issue to coincide with a Radio 3 talk he had recorded six months earlier called *Of Ombudsmen and Cybermats*. It gave him a chance to indulge in what he described at the time as 'one particular paranoid delusion: that mankind will become redundant on a planet of duplicating intelligent machinery'. Titled 'Deus ex Machina?', the article sees Kit looking at the robot; not the current traditional model of robot which he dismissed as mere sophisticated dolls, but towards the second generation, which he christened biological mimics, or biomims. He wanted to explore how such a construct would come into being and why they would eventually 'render man redundant as a consequence'. This wasn't Kit having fun; there was a point to be made. 'It is now becoming feasible to build into the original robot strategy many of the remaining properties necessary to bring it to the state of potential danger... They are: goal-seeking, intelligence, adaptability of behaviour, learning capability, and... the urge to survive.'

The biomims could not have portable Asimov-inspired 'positronic' brains since they would be far too big to carry around. Instead they would be modelled on arthropods, who have a 'ganglionic nervous system, a series of nerve cell aggregations connected together by a network of fibres linked to the sensory and motor periphery of the creature. They have no brain and no equivalent of the cerebral cortex – our pride and sometimes joy.' They display no compassion or creativity, yet they have societies – like anthills and beehives – with the individual totally absorbed by its activities. The biomims would behave in such a way. They would make themselves in factories, and would take memory, pattern recognition, comparison and avoidance of dangerous situations from a central brain by telemetry; and from all the data that flows into the centre, they would learn.

They would learn how to mine raw materials and 'develop circuits, fabricate sensory systems and alter their design strategy to further the cause of their own survival... One thing they would discover is how mankind was a threat to themselves, and logically this would lead them to including a defence strategy.' The biomims could easily bypass Asimov's laws of robotics, Kit theorised. They would evolve far more quickly than mankind could, possibly in a matter of hours, with each generation inheriting the acquired characteristics of the last.

Biomims would come about, Kit wrote, because we were:

> ... abrogating more and more human qualities to our machines due mainly to a thirst for leisure and a demand that the more repellent tasks of society be carried out for us.
>
> I would feel happier about the outcome if I thought that man had any serious objective for himself in sight. Progressively our gods are letting us down. God, Jesus, Karl Marx, Mr Wilson [Prime Minister] and the Beatles have all been rejected. Apart from the brainwashed millions of China, there seems to be little evidence of serious purpose in either western or eastern civilisation. The art of our age accurately depicts its formlessness and yet we progress technologically at an accelerating rate.

As the biomims take over, what would happen to man's 'dynamism, originality, decision and creativity?' Man would become a redundant tool, to be discarded by the biomims, destroyed by the product of his own 'technological greed... An automated structure to society will give battery man the illusion of freedom.' Kit wondered whether the first step towards this situation was already happening:

> The individual is losing his voice and is becoming irretrievably immersed in the complex systems of increasingly intelligent artefacts around him... What is happening now is that most aspects of our activities are considered in statistical blocks, programmed for efficiency. Are the diurnal inhabitants of multi storey office blocks really considered as individuals? Their lives and personalities are computerised, their output is compared to a 'norm', even the time they spend in the lavatory is measured and allowed for... Battery buildings for battery people.

'I see the modern city,' he told *Radio Times* in 1968, 'as a great technical mechanism. To get people to serve in it we give them the illusion of freedom. But the things being done to them to work are quite horrific. In multi-storied beehives their entire lives are ordered by systems analysts. It's loathsome and degrading to the individual to be considered in these terms.'

Kit wanted to explore how science could negatively impact on our ordinary lives if it was left unchecked. In his self-penned biography he wrote: 'He genuinely appears to believe in this... and rants about it at the drop of a hat. Unfortunately anger often bedevils his logic, rendering many of his comments ridiculous.'

However, he and Gerry Davis were about to create a series based on this theme, and together they were going to do for adults what the Cybermen had done for children. But this time it was a definite warning.

8
The Ivory Laboratory

> The days when you and I marvelled at the 'miracles' of science... are over. We've grown up now – and we're frightened. The findings of science are still marvellous, but now is the time to stop dreaming up science fiction about them and write what we call 'sci-fact'. The honeymoon of science is over. – Gerry Davis interviewed in *Radio Times*, 1970

1968 WAS A BUSY YEAR for Dr Kit Pedler in his job as reader and director of the Department of Anatomy. At the end of February, he had given the inaugural London Lecture for the British Optical Association on 'The Retina as a Biological Computer' at the Great Western Hotel in Paddington; an 'outstandingly fine lecture', the *Ophthalmic Optician* reported. In April, Kit chaired the Peter Le Neve Foster lecture at the Royal Society of Arts as he handed over to the new Honorary Secretary of the Royal Microscopical Society. In early May, Kit delivered a paper on 'Neurone Interconnections in the Vertebrate Retina' at City University's Department of Ophthalmic Optics research symposium on visual psychophysics and neurology.

Together with his colleague Rita Tilly, he had by now reconstructed eleven retinal cells, revealing all of their complicated interconnections as large polystyrene models. However, building polystyrene models of cells would soon be a thing of the past. The Institute now had a computer section and employed a full-time programmer and a couple of part-time assistants, one of whom was a physicist. In that year's annual report, Kit revealed that he had been developing a 'computer-driven method for the reconstruction of electron micrographs'. The pantograph used to trace the outline of a cell was now 'connected to a servo-operated XY gantry, and analogue data from the gantry is recorded by the use of shaft encoders so that profiles from electron micrographs can now be stored on Westrex tape'. This would result in a three-dimensional model revealed on a screen – or as Kit described it, 'the read-out tube-face of a drafting computer'.

Kit believed that the retina was the first stage of a biological pattern recognition system. 'If these cells are inter-relating in a logical fashion, it should be possible to build a machine which functions in the same logical manner,' he theorised. 'This should show what are the logical operations performed on visual signals in the retina before the impulses are fed to the central processor of the computer in the visual cortex of the brain.' If they could develop a machine which acted like a retina, this could become an aid for the blind, helping them to navigate, identify objects and recognising potential hazards.

This extraordinary idea took a step closer into becoming reality when he teamed up with Professor Douglas Young of the computing centre at the University of Manitoba in Canada. Kit had attended a conference on pattern recognition, subtitled 'The Retina and the Machine', in Manitoba in May 1968. Young had also investigated the feasibility of a simulated retina. He concluded that it was possible, and a design study was in progress. Kit would collaborate with Young – not an easy task considering the distance between them. It would be built in Canada since there was insufficient funding for such a project in Britain; Kit would make a lengthy visit there in 1969 as a visiting professor.

Kit was filmed discussing this work at the Institute over a couple of days in July by a crew from BBC2's *Horizon* programme, and in November he visited the Lime Grove studios of *Tomorrow's World* to give another demonstration, while his final *Doctor Who* contribution was enthralling children on Saturday nights.

It was as a *Doctor Who* writer that he had been on Radio 3's *My Life In Science* in January 1969 (transmitted as *Of Ombudsmen and Cybermats* in July) where he had discussed Cybermen, the retina, and his feelings on the responsibility of the scientist, and then introduced listeners to his current BBC project which had just been commissioned: *Doomwatch*.

Scientist: right or wrong

Without a doubt, Kit Pedler loved science, the method that allowed you to understand how something worked through observation, theory and test. But he was becoming disillusioned and frustrated with the academic environment in which scientific discovery was practised. The system had become institutionalised, possibly because of societies set up to instil discipline into their expertise. A hierarchy had become established within science. The seats of learning in colleges and universities had become reliant on government or commercial funding. Kit felt science had gone away from serving people, and was instead being used to advance individual careers, while technology was serving company profits.

However, to suggest such a thing was career suicide. This is what he wrote in *The Quest for Gaia*:

> During my fifteen years as a university scientist, I made many friends who were deeply driven towards the aims of the natural philosophers, people who loved nature and sought to understand a little about it: men and women of poetic and imaginative enthusiasm who exulted in the priceless beauties of the life form. But sadly, over the years I watched many of them first of all starved of research money, and then subjected to all the vindictive and bullying pressures for which the academic bureaucratic community is so notorious, until they gave in and directed their talents towards the prestige goals set by the state scientific committees holding the purse strings. The committees were always managed by older men with honours and titles, who 'rage against the dying of the light', and turn, at bay, finally to visit their frustration upon the young. The reward and punishment conditioning systems of the institutions are heavily entrenched and show little sign yet of change.

The pressure was on you to show results and beat the competition, which may include your own colleagues. Good results will reap rewards and advancement, but also, crucially, funding. Not everybody was being entirely ethical in how they achieved their results, from a little massaging of the figures in their favour, to downright fraud.

Unlike doctors, research scientists did not have the idea of the Hippocratic oath. Within the laboratory you needed to be cool-headed, and practise emotional detachment. An experimental animal was just material, not something to become sentimental over; but could this extend towards people? In 1967, Dr Maurice Pappworth, a teacher of postgraduate medical students, published a book called *Human Guinea Pigs*. 'During the last twenty years,' he wrote, 'clinical medicine, especially in the teaching hospitals, has become dominated by research workers whose primary interest is the extension of medical knowledge. Their concern with patients as such... tended to suffer as a result.' He had become concerned by articles from research teams who were performing 'extremely unpleasant and often dangerous experiments on unsuspecting patients'. Doctors felt powerless to intervene, and the public were unaware of what was happening to them.

Kit may have recalled the controversy over tests conducted on infants to evaluate the oxygen poisoning hypothesis of infant blindness. There had been no informed consent from the parents, and the care nurses were alarmed that the babies were being used as test subjects. This was a blatant breach of the Nuremberg Code, drawn up in 1947 to prevent the recurrence ever again of the extreme atrocities perpetuated by Nazi scientists on Jewish prisoners, given licence by their government.

Democratic governments did it too. Many years elapsed before western governments owned up to experiments that had been conducted on their own unwitting troops, when they were testing new atomic explosives in faraway places. Perhaps the best example was that of the brilliant minds recruited to the Manhattan Project, who built the first nuclear bomb during a period of total war. Nazi Germany had to be fought, and the consequences of what would happen if they got the bomb first were just too horrible to think about. They could justify their work by thinking that the weapons they devised would never be used, or that they would eventually save more lives than they took. The responsibility would lie with the people who decided to deploy them, not devise them.*

Political engagement was something a scientist was advised to avoid at all costs. Argue against such weapons existing, and you ran the risk of being accused of being unpatriotic or even a traitor. One man who worked on the Manhattan Project who did leave on moral grounds was smeared as a Communist spy. He was Joseph Rotblat, a Polish-born physicist who was appalled to hear one of his colleagues claim that the true purpose for the bomb was to subdue the Russians.

---

* For a fictional account of the moral conflict faced by scientists in Britain trying to create the first nuclear bomb during the Second World War, see C. P. Snow's 1954 book *The New Men*.

Wartime is one thing, but where was the justification during peacetime for developing greater weapons of destruction? Was this being done purely for defence, for prestige, or simply because it was lucrative for the bomb makers? Rotblat went on to campaign against further nuclear research and investigated the effects of long-term radioactive fallout. His work made a difference and led to the Partial Test Ban Treaty of 1963. He was also one of the organisers of the international Pugwash conferences which brought together scientists from the east and west, with the aim of ending weapons of mass destruction.

By the late 1960s there was growing alarm over chemical and biological weapons, which led to the formation of the British Society for Social Responsibility in Science (BSSRS). Several research workers, who had previously accepted without question that science was impartial, felt that they were being exploited by the military, and wanted their concerns heard. International protocols had been established restricting the use of certain weapons on civilian populations, but they could be easily 'reinterpreted' to suit the current political agenda. America did not agree to these protocols and used Agent Orange in the jungles of Vietnam.

Kit told *Hospital Times* in 1970:

> Scientists are basically opportunists; they're neither malefactors nor benefactors. They just get obsessed; they are men with a private obsession. This can often lead people into very dangerous areas. This is what has happened to those wretched doctors involved in research into chemical and biological warfare; they've become obsessed by a problem, and in so doing, they've turned themselves into intellectual prostitutes.

But Kit understood why they did it. He once went with his daughter Carol to see a film about Oppenheimer, who, when he saw the first nuclear bomb explosion, recognised the consequences of what he had been pursuing and declared: 'I have become death.' 'Dad said that, had he been offered that scientific conundrum – to build a nuclear bomb – he'd have been fascinated. He would have pursued it *because* it was fascinating, and had he not had any thoughts about the consequences he would just have gone straight ahead.'

The BSSRS believed that social responsibility had to extend into *every* aspect of scientific research. Recent advances in genetics and biology had profound implications for the future of humanity. A group of British scientists were about to achieve the first artificial insemination of an egg outside of a mother's womb. The motive was pure: to beat infertility, but this was a world approaching three billion people, a number some felt was unsustainable given the finite number of resources that the world contained. This was the theme of several books written in the late 1960s making doomsday predictions. The most popular of these was Paul Ehrlich's *The Population Bomb*. He foresaw by the end of the 1970s a world stricken by famine and wars as the fight for space and resources forced those who had little to take from those who had more.

A cooler collection of scientists, academics and industrialists got together in Rome in 1968 to study the results of overpopulation. The Club of Rome wanted to raise awareness of how finite economic growth was in a modern industrial and technological society. Computer models were used to predict future rates of consumption against current known reserves of natural resources.

Their ideas would feed into burgeoning environmental movements that were springing up around the world. America was already at the forefront of this, having received a rude awakening in 1962 from a hugely influential book. Rachel Carson's *Silent Spring* demonstrated how the overuse of pesticides was polluting the environment as far away as the Arctic. DDT would be banned within the next few years, yet new pesticides were still overused. In Britain there very few pesticide safeguards in place, most of them voluntary.

Pollution was often seen as a necessary, if unfortunate, side effect of economic growth. In Britain, one way of dealing with acidic smoke from industry was to build higher chimney stacks in the expectation that the pollution would be blown away by a predominantly westerly wind. Unfortunately, this smoke would come down on Scandinavian countries as acid rain. Britain was called the worst polluter in Europe by Friends of the Earth, and the Swedish chemist Svante Odén, the man who first hypothesised acid rain, called it 'an insidious chemical war' on Sweden's forest and lakes.

Governments were still confident that science and technology through industry would always find an answer to social problems. This was the original meaning behind the term 'technological fix', coined in 1966 by nuclear physicist Alvin Weinberg. He believed that nuclear bombs acted as a deterrent for war between the east and the west, that nuclear-powered desalination projects would bring a halt to the Arab-Israeli conflict by providing more water, that free air-conditioning would help reduce riots in the hot inner cities, and cheap computers would compensate for a lack of teachers in the classroom. Perhaps there wouldn't be a need for classrooms for all children if racial geneticists could 'prove' that the African-American was intellectually inferior to his white counterpart and that educating them was a waste of public money. Evil wrapped up in the respectability of a white coat.

Western governments were firm believers in the technological fix; jobs and a sense of prosperity mattered. Objections to industrialised food production, the sonic boom of a passing jet liner, and the computerised data banks cataloguing our lives were the province of cranks.

Kit argued that the scientist should think about the consequence of his research. He practised what he preached. His department was invited to study the effects of lasers upon the retina. Lasers could be used to treat detached retinas, but as a weapon they blinded and burned. Kit turned it down as he did not want to sign the Official Secrets Act required to cover the work taking place at Porton Down. Kit believed that scientific knowledge should be shared. The study was eventually carried out by two of his research assistants in collaboration with the Royal Air Force Institute of Aviation Medicine.

Interviewed on Radio 3 in 1969, Kit said, 'I think the scientist is a citizen and as such he has a complete responsibility as a citizen for the work he does. I don't think he can ever say, "Of course, it's up to the politician," or [that] it's up to the people, or something. He *is* the people, he *is* concerned with politics.'

Kit told the *Hospital Times* that there ought to be a Hippocratic ethic observed by scientists. Rotblat received a lukewarm reception when he called for one in 1995 as he accepted the Nobel Peace Prize for his efforts towards nuclear disarmament. But Kit was thinking of doctors working on biological weapons:

> Obviously no doctor actually swears the Hippocratic oath on a book, but he's brought up in the idea of it. In general, this implies that you shouldn't do harm to people as the result of your training, and in my view studying how to kill people more efficiently is a very strange way of using medical training... I think the time has long since passed when a scientist could abrogate any social responsibility for what he does. If he's got the imagination to do the work in the first place, he's got the imagination to foresee the potentially harmful effects.

He proposed one in the *Listener* by adapting one of science-fiction writer Isaac Asimov's laws of robotics: 'No scientist shall by his professional ability harm a human or by inaction in this sphere allow a human being to come to harm.'

'Obviously this is idealistic and impracticable,' Kit admitted, 'but I do feel that the time has come to attempt some sort of humanisation of the scientific endeavour.'

The creation of Doomwatch

Since they last worked together, Kit and Gerry had kept in touch, meeting regularly at their favourite fish-and-chip bar in Kensington to talk things over and put the world to rights. 'We were discussing what we would like to write next and gradually we came to realise that we both had similar views about what was happening around us,' Kit told an unknown newspaper in 1970. Gerry knew that the phobias he had tapped in Kit for *Doctor Who* would make for an excellent adult science-fiction drama series, and one with a relevant and contemporary message. He told *Doctor Who Magazine* in 1987: 'Kit would come back from conferences and say, "Do you realise what's happening?" and tell me about some dreadful ecological disaster that had been hushed up.'

'The man who impressed me most at the BBC,' Gerry Davis told the *Listener* in 1988, 'was Huw Wheldon. He used to give us pep talks and ran home the message that the way to get information across was by telling a story.' Kit agreed. Good science fiction should have social content; and, having found an audience for his 'sermons', he wanted to go on writing more of them for television and write about the conflict that had been building up in his professional life.

'To Pedler,' wrote the *Guardian* in 1973, 'the temptation of being able to reach out directly to a vast audience and express his own doubts and fears about the direction of science and technology through fictionalised drama proved irresistible.' 'I am sick of seeing learned sermons on TV about the dangers of science,' Kit told the *People* in 1970. 'People switch off, or just say "So what?" But put the message into exciting stories and it strikes home. We are going to shock people into realising the diabolical dangers that threaten health and peace of mind.' The audience would then (hopefully) question, and demand change, in order that fiction did not become reality. Kit was aware of the power of television, and how the image makers used the medium to submerge the public with a series of instructions by which to live, and the look that is best to have, or the things you need to buy.

They came up with an idea of a group of scientists working in an unloved government department, tasked with investigating new and dangerous threats to mankind from today's scientific research. Each week they would come up against the vested interests within government, industry, and scientific institutions who would resent the intrusion and the exposure of accidents and deliberate cover-ups.

With the blessing of Series head of department Andrew Osborn, Gerry and Kit produced an eleven-page document which detailed the premise and characters behind their new series. They needed to come up with a memorable and appropriate title for the series and selected a number of words such as 'doom', 'monitor', 'project' and 'watch'. In a cut section to his introduction to the *Dan Dare* anthology in 1979, Kit remembered the thinking behind the process:

> We spent nearly a day in front of a well-sized blackboard connecting up words, syllables and the appearance of words. We based part of our thinking on the psychology behind the OMO detergent logo. 'Doom' looked good, it had the two eyes and an apocryphal ring, but its sound was two [sic] soft and soothing so we added on '-Watch' which had a clipped, whip-like sound. The two syllables matched well together, fell easily off the tongue and above all looked right. And now we have just discovered, with some amazement, that we have put a new word into the Oxford Dictionary.

The series was to be set in present-day Britain. Kit and Gerry's format document explains:

> A newly formed government have been elected on a main platform of concern for the individual against the encroachment of the State and technological advance. When the series opens, several months after the inauguration of the Department, it has become obvious to Dr Quist, the Head of Doomwatch, that the government have had cold feet about the amount of freedom and initiative to be allowed him and his team. The pressures of both private industry and governmental research installations, alarmed at the reports circulating regarding the powers of Doomwatch, have resulted in the Minister, who is responsible for the Department, clamping down on the project and trying to clip their wings. But in Quist they have chosen the last man ever to submit to threats, pressure or bribes. A man of fanatical dedication to his job, and a deep-seated personal reason for wanting to make a success of it.

Named after an Australian tennis player, Spencer Quist was a mathematician who had worked on the Manhattan Project during the war. It was his maths that helped create the bomb, something he had never come to terms with. After the war, in the same year he won his Nobel Prize, his wife died from radiation poisoning. He returned to England to work at Ipswich University where he met Dr John Ridge, an organic chemist, and a former agent for MI6, which saw him working on both sides of the Iron Curtain, before unexpectedly quitting and returning to academia. Ridge was to be the cold, logical member of the team, a womaniser and action man. The third and youngest member of the team was Tobias Wren, a recently graduated scientist, designed to be the 'identification' figure for the audience with the stories played out through his young eyes. The rest of the team comprised Yorkshire-born computer specialist Colin Bradley, and the 'love interest' secretary Pat Hunnisett.

The group were to be based in a disused church that had been equipped with laboratory facilities, aided by a modern 'Rand' style computer which would not only be their database, but could come up with strategies for their investigations which they may or may not act upon. The guide ends with a few hints of what the series might be like:

> The men of Doomwatch are by no means omnipotent supermen. There are many failures on their files. On two occasions the computer 'Doomwatch' has broken down or its messages jammed with disastrous results.
>
> Sometimes their on-the-spot evaluation of a situation causes them to disregard the computer's advice. WREN habitually follows his own line of enquiry with varying results.
>
> All too often they work against the direct instructions, or prohibitions, of their official brief. This puts not only their jobs in jeopardy but, confronted with police, troops etc. they could face a possible prison sentence or bullet.

Osborn was keen on the idea and wanted to see a script as soon as possible. He took advice to see how Gerry's rights would be affected by his still being a BBC staff member. Gerry did not want to hide behind an anonymous script editor credit when he was both co-creator and writer of the series. When the script was commissioned in June, 'Gerard Davis' was therefore given permission to collaborate with Kit on the grounds that they had worked well together before.

'The Plastic Eaters'

Working at weekends, they developed their pilot episode, 'The Plastic Eaters'. They imagined what would happen if a technological fix went wrong. A man-made virus, designed to break down that modern problem of plastic waste into a disposable slime, accidentally escapes from a government laboratory and infects a passenger aircraft. A melting aircraft was an irresistible image. They added into the mix the Minister, who is hostile to what Quist's team stand for. He also wants the glory of being the one politician who had the foresight to tackle the problem of plastic waste and is forcing the pace of research too quickly.

The story begins with a British passenger plane crashing in South America. Having seen pictures of wiring inexplicably stripped of its plastic insulation, Quist suspects that it might be the result of some new solvent. Acting on a hunch, Quist wonders if it has been developed in government laboratories that Doomwatch have never been allowed to inspect. Quist allows Ridge to break into the Minister's office where he discovers that the government germ warfare laboratories at Beeston have indeed been developing a plastic-eating virus called Variant 14. Convinced that there is a link with the plane crash, Ridge is ordered to break into the laboratories and steal a sample of the virus. In its current stage of development, it has the potential to spread like a bush fire if it gets out into a city.

Toby Wren is sent to study the aircraft wreckage. He unwittingly brings on board his flight home a piece of the contaminated wiring, which he examines during the flight. Wren touches a plastic cup, before a stewardess takes it away on a plastic tray which she then rests upon a plastic surface. The virus is out and begins to feast on the plastics on board. It is a race against time for the plane to perform an emergency landing before disaster strikes again.

Faced with the sack for his department's unorthodox investigative techniques, Quist discovers that the link between the first disaster and the Beeston laboratories is the Minister's secretary, Miss Wills. She and the Minister had visited the laboratories a few days earlier. The Minister had secretly recorded the demonstration on a small Dictaphone, and the virus managed to contaminate the cassette. This was handled by Miss Wills, who later wrote out a cheque with a plastic pen for her cousin, an air stewardess on the doomed flight.

It was an ambitious script, which efficiently set up the premise and the characters of the series. It is part disaster movie, part scientific detective serial, and at the heart of the story is what happens when science is rushed. It is also left open-ended. The Beeston laboratories were preparing for a field test of the new virus variant, and this is simply delayed as stricter safety precautions are put into place. The implication is that the virus is going to be used, even if the consequences of another leak could be catastrophic. The Minister comes out of the story unharmed, if a little shaken. He is presented in the story as someone who wants Doomwatch kept under a tight political leash and wants to replace Quist with someone more politically attuned.

Kit was excited by the potential of *Doomwatch*, and he began discussing his ideas in a guarded way with scientists at the Fourth European Regional Conference on Electron Microscopy in Rome. He was delighted by the response. When Kit came back from the conference in mid-September, he immediately wrote to Osborn:

> During the various meetings I brought up the question of *Doomwatch* to groups of scientists... The response was really quite remarkable. Everyone would immediately flood the conversation with ideas. It was as if the collective guilt of the scientific community was suddenly unleashed and the most ingenious and, in some cases, appalling ideas were put forward. For example, an immunologist suggested a specific antigen which would attack the germ-plasma of a particular race: result – sterility. Given a racist immunologist in say Alabama and the colour problem would cease to exist in one and a half generations – and so on.

Osborn replied that although he had reservations over the script, there were no insurmountable problems. As autumn turned into winter, it was agreed that should the series be picked up, with Gerry acting as its script editor, Kit and Gerry would be recognised by the BBC as a science-fiction writing partnership and would always be credited together as creators and writers. Their producer was someone with whom Gerry was currently working on *The First Lady*: Terence Dudley.

Known to his friends as Terry, he was a very experienced and talented writer, director and producer. He had begun his career by running his own repertory theatre before he joined the BBC in 1958. He worked on a wide range of genres including science fiction and thrillers. He could be a charming and erudite man but was very determined to have his way.

Dudley had liked what he had read in the *Doomwatch* format, and was very much taken with Kit, who took him around his laboratory at the Institute to give him an idea of how a real scientist operates. Dudley knew that for the programme to succeed it had to be as authentic as possible in its representation, not just of science which Kit would ensure, but of scientists themselves. Kit and Gerry agreed: they did not want any *Doctor Who* style mad scientists threatening to destroy the world. They had to be real people.

It was going to be a fruitful, if stormy, relationship.

9
Doom Writer

> 'I know I'll probably get a lot of stick from scientists, but I don't care a damn. I don't want to moralise but it's time we examined the whole ethos of scientific research.' – Kit Pedler, unknown newspaper

Kit Pedler and Gerry Davis were not going to be able to write all thirteen episodes of *Doomwatch* by themselves. The programme needed writers who could tell a rattling good yarn while keeping the subject matter plausible, and away from the more fantastic realms of science fiction. Gerry explained to one writer that: '*Doomwatch* is a special type of scientific thriller and is extremely hard to write for. The action must be highly inventive and charged with edgy confrontation, and at the same time be entirely viable.' The theme of the series was stated on the contract issued to each writer: 'Adventures in the responsibilities implicit in scientific advancement when it ignores the human condition: A kind of science fact-fiction.' 'The idea was to write a type of science fiction which could actually take place next week, next year, or a few years on,' Kit told the *Evening Standard* in March 1970.

Dudley agreed to allow Kit and Gerry to prepare storylines as a starting point for the writers. For ideas and research, they scoured newspapers and journals, especially *New Scientist*, and kept scrapbooks and folders full of clippings. There were plenty of ideas: enough, Kit estimated, for a hundred episodes. Together, they would discuss an idea or a theme, come up with the setting and characters, and explore how the idea would work within the story. How would the team become involved and operate in each situation?

What opposition would they face? How would the incident be portrayed, and how would the team overcome it? They thought up striking images, set pieces and dramatic hooks. The storylines were then sent on to potential writers. Gerry would help them on the story construction, while Kit was available to advise on the background to the story and provide any research. Kit didn't want any extra payment on top of his writing fees, only a credit as scientific advisor under his professional name – Dr C. M. H. Pedler.

'It's... a fifty-fifty collaboration,' Kit explained. 'I had a head full of knowledge and Gerry has an intuitive dramatic instinct.' Their working relationship was summed up a few years later in the CV sent out by their agent: 'The combination can be best described as a small "think-tank" into which is poured an almost continuous stream of ideas for debate. The discussion which follows is always highly critical and sometimes heated, but eventually an original and viable idea emerges which neither one can put down.'

They began providing the storylines by the end of 1968, but it would be Terence Dudley who would choose which ones to take forward, and whether the final script got made. These first storylines were called 'Check and Mate', 'The Logicians', 'The Devil's Sweets' and 'The Battery People'.

'Check and Mate' dealt with government computers which not only stored an individual's personal details but were allowed to make a value judgement on whether they should work in sensitive areas of government. Kit hoped that the story would help 'destroy the complacency over the use of computers to store personal details about the way we as individuals work and live. This is a terrible invasion of privacy. People are already being hired and fired because of what some tycoon's computer says about them.'

Kit saw himself as essentially a private individual, and the thought of his life pattern being analysed by a machine appalled him. In 1975, he would campaign against continuing membership of the European Common Market because he saw it as a greater bureaucratic encroachment on our lives. He wrote in the *Sunday Times*:

> We meekly allow public officials to enter our homes on the production of a form. We accept the need to computerise our personal characteristics without asking the reason why, and we allow central planners to change our local surroundings permanently without ever being offered a part in the decision process... Nineteen Eighty-Four began in the real year of 1960, when the technology of data control really got under way... Until the era of high technology draws to a close, as inevitably it must, the steady erosion of

the gentle freedoms of the individual will continue under the heel of technological collectivism.

In the story, government security suspends Toby Wren on account of his drinking problem, and visiting scientist Stella Robson because of her family connections with Palestine. They were investigating a new and highly secret defoliant called Project Sahara. Quist discovers that the secret department behind the suspensions is being advised by a computer vetting personal records. He is outraged, but spots a flaw in its assessment which does not save Robson's job: she was indeed a security risk, but for reasons not spotted by the computer, because it needed a human being to spot her lies. This story would eventually be made under the title 'Project Sahara', but only after it passed through the hands of several writers, including Gerry Davis.

Kit was familiar with computers in his professional life, but a friend of his actively campaigned against them. He was a colourful American emigrant called Harvey Matusow, who had come over to London in 1966. He had become notorious back home during the 1950s when Senator McCarthy was conducting his anti-communist witch hunt. Matusow gave damning testimony but later declared that he had been lying and was an FBI agent. Convicted for perjury, he became the most hated man in America.

After a spell in New York, he reinvented himself as a wildly eccentric musician; but he also aimed for the destruction of the computer, which he thought was encroaching into our lives. He founded the International Society for the Abolition of Data Processing Machines and compiled a book in 1968 called *The Beast of Business* which listed examples sent to him by the public. His theme was how the word of the computer was accepted uncritically because it cannot be wrong. 'A computer should know its place,' Matusow argued; 'the computer is just an over-rated adding machine.'

Mark Pedler remembered Matusow very well: 'He was a bit avant-garde, although I thought it was rather put on. He had a bit of glamour and chutzpah behind him. I think it was him who introduced Dad to dope. He was a very pleasant man, nothing wrong with him, a bit full of himself.'

Computers also featured in the next storyline, one that would not get made for the first series. 'The Logicians' was about the use of teaching machines in schools. What would happen if children who were taught by computers on the basis of logic decided that the need to distinguish between a right or a wrong action was redundant if it was the logical thing to do? In the story, teenagers at an independent private school, educated by a logic-based teaching system, decide to stage a robbery of commercially sensitive pharmaceutical material, and blackmail the firm for its return. The children needed the money simply to keep the school running. As far as they were concerned, this was a logical policy to follow, and no one was harmed.

'The Devil's Sweets' was concerned with behavioural drugs being developed by a cash-strapped university department and misused by a former student, a failing advertising man. He puts the drug in free giveaway chocolates (given out by an unsuspecting confectioner client) which encourage the taker to smoke. But this desire is only triggered when they see a checkerboard pattern – the pattern of a brand of cigarettes, produced by another client. The drug is still experimental and causes an adverse reaction when taken in conjunction with slimming tablets. Soon the hospitals are filling up with reaction cases, including the Doomwatch secretary.

This story was given to teacher turned writer Don Shaw to script: 'I had read *Silent Spring* by Rachel Carson, and that book worried me and gave me motivation to write for *Doomwatch*. I was never happier than when writing about threats to our existence on Earth!' 'The Devil's Sweets' is a perfect example of the sort of story Kit and Gerry wanted to tell on *Doomwatch*, a scientific detective mystery. Here is the effect, what is the cause? In this case, why was there a sudden increase in smoking of one brand of cigarette in a small area?

It was one of the first scripts to be finished and Kit was so pleased with it that he telephoned Shaw to tell him as much. 'It was a pleasure to work with Kit. He was such a nice man. He told me he was working on an idea to connect the optic nerve from eye to brain via an invention that he thought was possible in the future – obviously to help the blind to see.'

The last of the four original storylines was 'The Battery People', given to writer Moris Farhi. The story matter is unknown, but the title featured in Kit's 'Deus ex Machina' article for the *Listener* in which he described how the population of London was controlled by systems analysts. The script was rejected by Gerry, but the title was too good to waste and was transferred to another story.

Rats, rockets and riots

More storylines were accepted by Terence Dudley in February 1969. These were 'The Pacifiers', 'The Flames of Hell', 'Rattus Sapiens?', and 'The Patrick Experiment'. 'The Pacifiers' featured a group of students who discover that the result of their research was a nerve gas that was going to be used for riot control. Kit was sympathetic towards the students who were becoming politically and socially active on issues such as the Vietnam war or the environment:

> I think the technologically profuse society we're growing up in is becoming so oppressive in its side effects that the individual's emotions have very little say. If a group of people want to protest about something then they're often forced into extreme measures, so that if they make a democratic, quiet protest about their misgivings about a particular subject, then I think no notice will be taken of it.

This was another storyline that would never make it to the screen, even after two writers, Jan Read and David Fisher, had a go at it. Within a few months of the storyline being written, the British Society for Social Responsibility in Science had been formed and took up the issue of chemical weapons. Its first president was Nobel prize-winner Professor Maurice Wilkins. His work on the Manhattan Project, and his subsequent rejection of working on further development of the bomb, bears some uncanny resemblances to Quist's fictional biography and may have had some influence on the writers.

Kit and Gerry had been writing their second script, which was called 'Operation Neptune', since the beginning of the year. Their original idea concerned a sunken nuclear submarine and how radioactive leakage had mutated swarms of fish into developing an appetite for human flesh, having acquired a taste for the dead sailors they found. Either it was too expensive to produce, or simply implausible, but by March the writers turned to one of their storylines, 'The Flames of Hell'. This was about the effect of supersonic noise pollution and how, under unique circumstances, it can kill.

The first supersonic aircraft, Concorde, was being built as a collaboration between Britain and France. There were concerns over the effects of the sonic boom, especially in a densely populated area like Manhattan where Concorde was going to make regular flights. No one knew what was going to happen. 'The Red Sky', as the new story was now called, imagined how a rocket-propelled jet plane, developed by a mighty air corporation, travelling at much faster than Concorde at Mach 4, creates intense shock waves. They resonate within certain enclosed structures on the ground, such as a lighthouse. The noise this generates is so fierce that it forces the retina in the human eye to react, creating hallucinations and eventual collapse. In the story it is a lighthouse keeper who is driven mad by the noise and falls over the edge of a cliff.

The script dealt with the tensions between Quist and Ridge, an antagonism based on their differing approaches to their job. Kit and Gerry wanted to show Quist as a totally dedicated man, pushing himself towards a nervous breakdown, while Ridge is concerned that Quist's behaviour during their investigation is detrimental to their essential work. Toby Wren would be in the middle of the conflict, and it was he who came up with the answer to the deaths in the lighthouse. These conflicts would only ever manifest themselves in the scripts Kit and Gerry wrote.

It was always likely that Kit would want a story on genetic engineering to feature in *Doomwatch*. In 1968, a book was published called *The Biological Time Bomb* by former *Horizon* editor Gordon Rattray-Taylor in which he surveyed the work on genetics carried out to date and tried to imagine its implications for the future of mankind. The announcement in February of a breakthrough in the field of in vitro fertilisation inspired the writers' imaginations to go into overdrive, and they rapidly wrote 'The Patrick Experiment', later 'Friday's Child'. It was now theoretically possible to conceive a human baby outside of the mother's womb, and then replace the fertilised embryo back inside the mother, a breakthrough for infertile couples, and there were many who were willing to become test subjects.

Added into the plot was another ethical minefield, organ transplants, and one which Kit felt was symptomatic of a general mindset in medical science: a demonstration of a 'ritualised and theatrical ceremony' of 'medico-technological power' in return for six months' extra life. The first heart transplant had been recently achieved in America, but it would take another ten years before it was performed successfully in Britain. For the purposes of the story, organ transplants were a regular occurrence. It was the *scale* of the procedure which offended Kit the most:

> It has been estimated that a heart transplant can cost up to £15,000. In social terms this must be regarded as gross irresponsibility. Surely such money would be better spent on research into those technology-induced diseases of our time, or into more effective methods of contraception – research that can help the masses, not the few.

This work, he would tell the Royal Society of Medicine in 1972, was a fool's game.

Kit did not doubt the motives of Dr Steptoe, who wanted to allow infertile women to have children. Kit felt that the medical arguments put up for this were:

> ... nothing less than a sentimental smokescreen for what was essentially a scientific experiment. They made great play with the childless mother, which is a very sad situation. But there are children who are crying out to be adopted. I think the medical arguments for this, as I said, are sentimental rubbish... I think this is going to extreme lengths to satisfy a need on the part of the mother. I'm not denying this need; obviously it's a very basic one; but I have a feeling that it's thoroughly selfish.

He also wondered about the effect on the child during its life, knowing it was conceived in a bottle.

The story begins with a grieving mother convinced that the surgeon, Mr Patrick,* who had operated on her dying child, had stolen his heart to put it into his own son. Doomwatch discover that the surgeon is innocent of this, but find that the number of heart transplants and the number of donors does not tally, so where did the heart used for Patrick's son come from? They discover that a monkey's heart had been used, but Patrick has made no announcement of such a major scientific breakthrough. Furthermore, he has created a test tube baby from a donor's egg, and his own sperm. The embryo is growing inside an artificial womb, and the resultant baby will be 'born' with no brain function. It is a homunculus, designed simply to give his son a new heart in ten years' time when the monkey heart begins to fail.

It is an ethical swamp. Quist wants Patrick to stop his experiment. Patrick gives him, and his estranged wife, the option to switch off the artificial womb he has constructed. No one can do it. No one can kill the artefact. Kit asked what would happen to embryos in research at the end of the day. Flush them away, or give them a Christian burial? Kit denied one journalist's suggestion that his views were informed by his Catholic upbringing.

The debate as to what constitutes life and how early it begins after conception is still fiercely debated, especially in America. 'This type of experiment... has a tendency to dehumanise the experimenters,' Kit told the *Hospital Times*, 'because they have a lessened regard for human life. I think

---

* Surgeons in Great Britain are called Mr rather than Dr, and Dr Steptoe's first name was Patrick.

this is very much a problem for our age. We are now bludgeoned with the effects of a thoroughly dehumanised society.' This story was given to Harry Green, and he produced a script that the *Doomwatch* team considered was one of the best yet.

Genetic engineering would be at the heart of 'Rattus Sapiens?' Terence Dudley wanted to write a script for the series, and it would transmit as 'Tomorrow the Rat'. Ministry pest-control worker Mary Bryant conducts biological experiments on rats at her own home-made laboratory with unofficial approval from her boss. The object is pest control, but she has been increasing the rat's intelligence, and switching their food preferences towards flesh. A new generation of super-intelligent rats escape undetected and attack the vulnerable, including children. They are also multiplying at an alarming rate. These experiments in pest control were only necessary because the more effective poisons had been banned due to their effects on wildlife and domestic pets. In the end, the only way to prevent a population explosion of the 'cannibal' rats is to flood the sewers with poisons 'and to hell with the Cruel Poisons act!' Dudley himself felt that the Great British public preferred animals over children.

Except for 'Friday's Child', Terence Dudley had not been impressed with the scripts as they were coming in. He was particularly scathing of Kit and Gerry's work, as he explained to Andrew Osborn in a memo:

> Entre nous, Pedler is brilliant in his field but doesn't understand (or chooses not to understand) the nature of the civil servant animal and consequently underestimates the *Doomwatch* opposition. The characterisation in his two direct contributions needs to be much tougher-minded and a good deal more sophisticated. To date I consider this Green script to be the series yardstick and the others don't yet measure to it. They will!!!!!!

Writing to Anthony Howe in 1987 Dudley elaborated:

> We quarrelled about over-simplification that Kit particularly wanted in the characterisation of Doomwatch's opposition. I felt that it was too tendentious – and too like propaganda… to be dramatically viable… Dr Pedler was, in my view, a great man with a gut mission in life, which I admired and respected. Unfortunately, he was so obsessive with the message of the series that he was convinced that all the villains should be depicted as fools or rogues, and I felt that to fall in with this view would depreciate the format. Aunt Sallies don't make for much opposition.

There was an element of truth in this. Kit told *World Medicine*: 'Parsons, planners, politicians, and pundits of all types make me hot under the collar with rage. I really loathe them and want to be able to write about them thoroughly maliciously.' That he wanted his message to be heard loud and clear is also true. 'I'm absolutely hooked on *Doomwatch*,' Kit admitted to the *Daily Mirror* in 1970:

> Writing it gave me a sort of God complex – for about five minutes. But I hope the serious message gets across through the entertainment. *Doctor Who* was strictly for children, but this is aimed at adults who are apathetic in their private nirvana of the telly, supermarkets, bingo, and all the superficial stimuli. One of my hobby horses is the loss of individualism – the abnegation of the human quality. We are becoming units instead of people. I am horrified by our impotence to stop it. I hope *Doomwatch* will show us the real danger of hyper-civilisation.

It was through Dudley's influence that *Doomwatch*'s sense of authenticity and plausibility extended itself from the scientific content to the world of government beyond and arguably strengthened the series. An experienced writer himself, Dudley had certain views in how characterisation should be handled. Although he had written thrillers himself, he was not inclined towards adventure. He preferred exciting, meaningful debate, without superfluous adventurous elements demeaning the drama. Dudley was supportive of *Doomwatch*, but he was aware of how message plays like *Cathy Comes Home* made the BBC nervous of criticism by the right-wing press.

Like Kit, Gerry Davis preferred the direct approach in his writing, and he was not afraid to spell out the message of the story in a speech by Quist. He did not feel it necessary to examine every angle of debate. Show, not tell, was his mantra. Gerry was certainly the quietest of the three who ran *Doomwatch* as Judy Bedford, secretary to both Dudley and Gerry, recalls:

> Gerry Davis wasn't very prominent in the team dynamic... Gerry doesn't feature very much in my memories of the group surrounding *Doomwatch*. He was either not in the office (probably working with writers elsewhere), or if he was in his office he tended to stay there. Terry could be very funny and witty and entertaining when he was in the mood, and we'd all sit around and enjoy the joke and his 'performances', but I don't recall Gerry joining in a lot of the time.
>
> Kit was very involved in the science of the series and maintained a sense of reality when 'creative' types came up with silly ideas. While I think he

enjoyed the fun of being involved in drama production, his conversation was very much around his work at the Institute, or science in general, and the notion of ecology and environmental issues which were quite novel at the time. He was also very much still a medical doctor in the sense that he was always immediately concerned if you had symptoms of illness and wanted to know more, ask questions, suggest remedies and so on. Kit had a self-deprecating sense of humour. I remember he had a sports car and made jokes about himself as a bald geriatric who bought the car while he could still manage to struggle to get in and out of it.

More adventures in science fact

Work carried on into the summer on more storylines. These were 'Hear No Evil', 'The Synthetic Candidate', 'Burial at Sea', and 'Re-Entry Forbidden'.

The theme of 'Hear No Evil' was like 'Project Sahara': technology being used as a means of intruding into someone's privacy with devastating effect. In this case, it was the bugging of an entire workforce by their employers to monitor trade union activity. Not even the bedroom was safe. Doomwatch discovers the bugging by accident and turns the surveillance upon the employers to expose their criminality. Harry Green, basking in the success of his first script, was given the story to write, but soon found that there was confusion between the script editor and the producer as to the extent of the bugging the story required. The story went through several rewrites, and the writer left the project demoralised. Gerry Davis rewrote most of the script.

At this point, Green had been working on a third script. 'The Iron Doctor' was to feature Kit's favourite theme of dehumanised medicine. Set within an experimental hospital ward, a third-generation computer with the ability to reason was giving health care to patients, such as dialysis treatment. Supposing the logical and compassionless computer was programmed to weigh up a patient's survival chances and evaluate whether it was cost-effective to proceed with treatment in order to prioritise cases? And suppose the computer had not been told *not* to act upon its recommendations and withdrew treatment resulting in death?

'The Synthetic Candidate' was originally about a group of extreme right-wing thinkers desperate to get their racist and bigoted candidates elected to Parliament. Realising that they generally repelled voters, a consortium created a candidate for election based on the latest scientific techniques, exhaustive research into voter preference, plastic surgery, and use of a computer to create his speeches, which are sent direct into the candidate's brain. Although this idea was given to Elwyn Jones, a writer Gerry Davis admired, it was abandoned, and in its place was a new story which concerned the misuse of hormones in food production, and how it affected the workers on an industrialised battery farm.

In the version as written, now given the title 'The Battery People', the manager of the farm was a former army colonel who used an abandoned secret weapons research project which had developed an agent to destroy the bone structure from within. The colonel secretly uses it in his battery farm to produce boneless fish, a revolution in food technology. It was harmless enough to those who ate it after cooking, but in its raw liquid state, the hormones used to destroy the bones in animals would in time affect the personality of the handler. The colonel knew of these potential side effects and did not vigorously enforce safety standards. He deliberately employed Welsh ex-coal miners who were desperate for jobs. Because of their age, any change in personality would be dismissed as a natural part of growing old. However, it is noticed by their wives. The colonel's employees lose their sex drive, indulge in cockfighting and switch from beer to gin, totally out of character. By the end of the story the workforce discover what has happened to them and the colonel is 'accidentally' pulled into one of his fish tanks, swallowing some of the liquid designed to destroy bone.

Kit and Gerry had thought this was a wildly speculative idea, based on how antibiotics were being put into the food chain to make an animal plumper and 'healthier' within its battery cages. A self-confessed hedonist like Kit was horrified by modern methods of food production. 'They're dreadful,' he declared in an interview for an unknown magazine in the early 1970s:

> Supposing you take that pathetic travesty of an animal that passes for a chicken in cellophane in a supermarket. You know how it's produced, by what seem to me abominably cruel methods. That's not the point – let's not be sentimental about cruelty to animals. But the fact is you should have printed on the wrapping covering that bleached piece of blotting paper on bone that this animal contains both sex hormone and oestrogen and is injurious to health. Because the people who euphemistically call themselves industrial farmers – the bastards who produce this kind of animal – add sex hormones, oestrogen, and antibiotics because it gives them a better figure – it's called 'flesh to carcass yield'. We shouldn't eat it.

Not so speculative was the idea behind 'Burial at Sea' which featured another topical issue, and one that saw Kit write a couple of letters in protest to the *New Scientist* during 1969. During their research, Kit and Gerry were astonished to discover in a report prepared by the European Nuclear Energy agency that some of the canisters containing waste to be dumped in the sea were designed to corrode rapidly. The writers fictionalised a genuine dumping ground for nuclear waste near Plymouth and it started leaking nerve gas. The story was given to Dennis Spooner and while he was writing it, mysterious drums were being washed up upon the Lincolnshire coast. The original storyline declared:

> The conversion of our oceans into lethal rubbish tips is often under the control of high-ranking military or naval personnel who are commonly so devoted to the successful prosecution of the task in hand that they fail to see the obvious dangers to people and to wildlife. Moreover, if a title and honourable retirement are at hand, they are not easily going to admit responsibility for a disaster which they may have initiated by a decision made many years ago.

'Re-Entry Forbidden' featured nuclear-powered rockets and a paranoid astronaut from Britain who is trying to cover up a simple mistake he made during the preparations for re-entry. Had the space capsule burnt up, half of Britain could have been contaminated with radioactive material. When Don Shaw wrote the script, Neil Armstrong had just walked upon the Moon's surface. Shaw found that Kit's advice was less helpful on this occasion, although he still appreciated what help he received. For example, Kit was out of date with the 'firing sequence' (the Mission Control countdown before launch) that would see Sunfire 1 launch at the top of the programme. Instead, Shaw wrote down a commentary from a tape recording of a more recent Apollo launch. 'He must be fallible sometime!' Shaw commented when he delivered the script.

Kit liked writing about rockets. Sometime in 1969, he wrote the first of what would be four short stories for a series of horror anthologies edited by Rosemary Timperley. His first story was published in *The Sixth Ghost Book* and was called 'Image in Capsule'. This too featured a paranoid astronaut, alone in orbit in a capsule called Dynasaur 9 – except the on-board computer starts to address the pilot by his first name, Saul. At first, he thinks it is a tape recording planted by an estranged friend who had committed suicide after discovering that Saul had been conducting an affair with his wife. Has his ghost entered the computer, or has the pilot been driven insane by the absorption of an unknown toxin?

Kit was under no illusion as to the true significance of the Apollo programme. It was simply a political demonstration of technological one-upmanship over the Soviet adversary. In *The Quest for Gaia*, Kit wrote:

> Apollo was a superb tool to put a man on the moon, but no new scientific knowledge was necessary to make it work. It was the result of a decision by an affluent military-industrial state to assemble large numbers of talented toolmakers. Following that decision, a landing on the moon was a near certainty. The necessary knowledge of metallurgy, ballistics, rocketry, and space physiology was either already in existence or to be had for the hiring. It was not 'one great step for man', it was just the apotheosis of a race of talented toolmakers.

The day job

Kit's involvement in *Doomwatch* was either writing alone in the evenings, or at weekends with Gerry, visiting the production office when he could, and speaking with the writers by phone or over lunch. He squeezed in some thinking time in the morning before he left for work. He also dealt with his correspondence at work and kept a folder of clippings in his desk. Sometimes he felt that he was working a ten-day week. He was not left with much time for his hobbies, nor for his family. He felt a tension develop between his two jobs: 'I have felt driven more and more lately and I must admit I'm very confused. I suppose sooner or later I shall have to come to a decision, or I shall blow a fuse.' This workload increased when Gerry Davis suggested they should write a science-fiction stage play together based on *Doomwatch* themes; in June 1969, they began working on the first draft which was reportedly ready early in the new year and had been given the thumbs up by a producer.

During the summer of 1969, Kit travelled to the University of Manitoba in Winnipeg, Canada, to see the artificial retina being developed by Professor Douglas Young. It was one of his longest stays away from home that his children can remember. He stopped off in New York on the outward journey to visit Carol who was going to be working at the Woodstock Festival in August: 'He kept saying, "Oh, I'm going to stay in your pad!" in the very groovy language of the time and we had a lovely couple of days at the time.' Kit enjoyed some good weather in Winnipeg; but during one of his winter visits, he discovered that it could get so cold they had to plug in their car batteries overnight, otherwise all the fluids would freeze.

Work on the artificial retina was progressing to the point where Kit and Young were ready to announce it at a lecture to the physics section of the university, and this was reported in British newspapers in early September. 'The man who invented the Cybermen robots in the Dr Who BBC TV series is working on building an artificial "eye" which will enable computers to see,' announced the *Daily Mirror*.

In the Institute's 1968/69 Annual Report, Kit wrote:

> The design of the machine is based on a newly developed multi-valued logical system which allows some plasticity of operational design. The object of the study is twofold: first, to give parallel processing capabilities to a digital computer assembly, and second, to construct a machine sufficiently similar to the biological organ to enable different inter-neuron connectivities to be rested against some of the known physiological properties of the organ.

The machine's 'eye' consisted of 2,500 light-sensitive detectors forming a disc about three centimetres in diameter. The individual outputs of the detectors were interconnected and processed in a complicated series of logic stages whose design was based on the known structure of the retina. The *Guardian* reported that:

> ... of all the elegant and complex seeing-machines that have so far been made, this one promises to be not only the most revealing in the scientific sense but also the most effective. Its practical advantage is that, unlike other machines which are based on scanning and can therefore see only very slowly, the Manitoba machine should be able to recognise a shape immediately...

The machine was being programmed to recognise thirty shapes.

Kit admitted to the *Daily Mirror* that 'there is no way of knowing where this sort of research could lead. But its obvious application is to give computers the ability to read print, or even handwriting.'

Young certainly agreed, and had his own ideas where the technology would be best served: 'With the increasing number and use of computerised data banks and information systems,' he told the delegates of the Society of Photo-optical Instrumentation Engineers at a conference in Japan in June 1970, '[there is] the threat to individual privacy, and the misuse of identity and credit cards… there is an urgent need for an efficient and secure personnel identification system."*

Kit and Young continued their collaboration at the Department of Machine Intelligence at the University of Edinburgh with Professor Longuet-Higgins, a theoretical chemist from King's College, London, who was deeply fascinated with artificial intelligence and perception. Together, Drs Pedler and Young wrote a joint paper for the *British Medical Bulletin* called 'Retinal Ultrastructure and Pattern Recognition Logic' which would be published in 1970. This would be one of Kit's last major papers on vision. He elegantly summed up his work to date in an article written for the *Science Journal*, a rival publication to *New Scientist*.

Although he offered papers with Rita Tilly to other journals on the retinas of the fruit bat and the pigeon, Kit's scientific output was appearing less and less in print. He was still refining electron microscopy techniques, but Tilly left the Institute to take up a post at the Mill Hill laboratories of the Imperial Cancer Research Fund. She would later head its own electron microscopy unit before retiring in the 1990s. Her loss was felt at the Institute, and some of Kit's colleagues felt that he never quite recovered his work rate after her departure.

Kit still gave lectures around the country and his department was at its busiest during this period, with many research projects in action. Kit would become president of the university's Optical Society in 1970, and his presidential address attracted one of the largest audiences that year. Kit and a couple of departmental colleagues demonstrated how closed-circuit television could transmit lectures and demonstrations across the country at a meeting entitled 'The Biologist's Eye' at City University. Dr Kit Pedler PhD, MBBS, MC Path, reader and director of the Department of Anatomy was at his zenith.

'Survival Code'

After his spell in Canada, Kit began to research his third and final script for *Doomwatch*, 'Survival Code'. He and Gerry wanted to try once more to write a story featuring nuclear hardware lost at sea, this time something caught up in the nets of a fishing trawler. They had an all-expenses paid trip to a naval base at Gair Loch in Scotland, where they were suitably impressed by what they saw to think that the story wasn't worth pursuing.

---

* Professor Young later applied for a patent for what he called a computerised face identity verification system, but nothing more seems to have come of this.

Instead, they devised a story about a nuclear bomb that had become accidentally 'armed' and was ticking down to oblivion. Called 'The Bomb', the surviving storyline is set in 1973, and features a new design of bomb nicknamed 'Calling Card'. It was designed to be armed in flight via a coded electronic system activated by two people simultaneously. It is then dropped by parachute and is finally primed when it touches the ground. It would explode eight hours later, presumably to give the enemy a chance to surrender. During a test flight, a fault opens the bomb bay doors, and both men and the bomb fall out… The bomb ends up in a dance hall, with eight hours until explosion, and no code to stop the countdown. The dead men's lives, and those of their families, are frantically trawled through in an attempt to discover the code that they used.

Kit told the *Hospital Times*:

> People said, 'It's quite a nice idea, but we just can't believe it – that a nuclear weapon can be armed by accident.' Then the Americans were extremely obliging; they dropped a nuclear weapon in Texas. This weapon had six interlock safety devices which had to go off one after the other from safe to unsafe. When it was examined, five of the six had gone to unsafe. When we told this story back to the BBC they said: 'All right, we'll look at your [story] again.'

For Kit, the story was not so much an attack on nuclear weapons, but something far more fundamental:

> I think the principal danger is putting more and more of what you might call human judgements into machine systems. And machine systems break down in a way that doesn't enable them to recover their breakdown. Now a human being may say: 'I've made a mistake – quick, let's do something.' The machine just permanently winks a red light and goes to sleep. I think this is very dangerous.

The explosives inside the Texas bomb did not detonate, but the coastal town of Palomares in Spain had not been so lucky in 1966. Following a mid-air collision between two planes, nuclear bombs fell to earth, and exploded on impact. The explosion was a 'conventional' one, but the radioactive material inside the bombs contaminated much of the surrounding area – and still does to this day.

Starting from scratch, a new script was written in two days and two nights. Thinking in images, they envisaged a Palomares style accident occurring just off the south coast, and imagined a bomb floating towards a seaside pier, where the owners of an amusement arcade fish it out of the water and, thinking it to be a weather satellite, open it up for spare parts. In the process, they accidentally start the countdown. They soon begin to suspect that what they have found is not such a harmless machine after all, although none of them recognises the international radiation hazard symbol on its casing. They don't want to tell the police since one of them has a criminal record. The bomb is damaged, the countdown cannot be stopped, and the nuclear core is leaking out radioactive material. Could the imminent explosion be the full nuclear holocaust or, like Palomares, a dirty bomb? Whichever way, it spells disaster.

The Doomwatch team discover the bomb thanks to a phone call from the frightened wife of one of the arcade owners, and have to disarm the bomb themselves with only a short time to go. Worse, the bomb is now wedged within the timbers of the pier after the owners tried to push it back into the sea. The script allowed Quist to come face to face with his own guilt over the Manhattan Project, clash with his colleagues, and deal with complacent military departments who, in a manner similar to the civil servants seen in earlier stories, refuse to allow for the possibility that their fail-safes could fail. Kit said in the *Strait Times* a year later: 'There's an attitude in the industrial military complex which says: "Do it until you're rumbled. Put in enough fail-safes for ten years. By that time, you'll be retired and no longer amenable to responsibility."'

The cast

Doomwatch entered production at the beginning of November 1969. Judy Bedford:

> I recall that during the making of the first series there was a sense that this was something new and exciting and the messaging was about important issues. Although I'd have to say my experience of TV production people in general is that there can be a tendency to dramatise oneself! Having said that I think it probably was quite different to anything that had been produced before. It all seemed quite new to me at the time, and it certainly wasn't anything I'd heard at school or read about previously.

This enthusiasm was shared by the cast and crew who would bring *Doomwatch* to life. Heading the cast was John Paul who would put in an electrifying performance as Dr Spencer Quist. Dr John Ridge was played by Simon Oates, a versatile performer who had been a heavyweight boxing champion in the Intelligence Corps during his National Service days.

The BBC was initially nervous over not casting a household name, but they needn't have worried; they were about to create one. *Doomwatch* would launch the career of an emerging young actor called Robert Powell. Both Gerry Davis and Terence Dudley had seen him in a recent Nigel Kneale play called *Bam! Pow! Zap!*, and both knew that they had found their sensitive and enigmatic Toby Wren. Kit's eldest daughter Carol knew Powell socially when she had wanted to become an actress, and he visited the Pedler household to discuss the role.

Kit made a great impression on the cast and crew, and he would form a close friendship with Joby Blanshard, cast to play the gruff Yorkshire computer engineer, Colin Bradley, a friendship that lasted long after the series had finished. Wendy Hall was cast as the secretary, Pat Hunnisett, and although she only met Kit a couple of times, it was enough to make a lasting impression.

One of those occasions was when the cast went to see his laboratory at the Institute for a photo shoot, which included a tour of a new electron microscope that had been installed that year, again provided by funding from the Wellcome Institute. Wendy told Anthony Brown in 1991:

> I thought he was a remarkable human being, and one of the most modest people I've ever met. He seemed to have very little regard for himself, and thought he was very insignificant. To him the significant thing was what was happening to the world, the pollution and how he could start doing something to remedy the situation he saw looming up. In that respect he was very far-sighted, because we're only just beginning to be aware of it now. I only met him a few times but of all the things I think of about *Doomwatch*, he was the outstanding person I remember… He was a very, very caring person, very genuine, and seemed enormously excited about *Doomwatch* in a way which spilled over. I couldn't wait to get started, though at the time, of course, I hadn't even seen a script! It seemed the most exciting thing I'd been involved with and something really worth doing because it offered the chance to contribute and do something of substance.

Unfortunately, Wendy's role would prove to be less than satisfying and she declined to appear in a second series, and so did Robert Powell. Unlike the rest of his colleagues, he did not have an 'option' on his contract for his services beyond the first year and he did not want to be tied down to an ongoing series this early in his career.

Even as the programme was being made, the production team still did not have all the scripts ready, and two new storylines were needed. The first of these was called 'Train and Detrain'. Once more, Gerry and Terence Dudley turned to the reliable Don Shaw. The story was about an unscrupulous pesticide company, which was about to launch a new product that could either make or break them. They also treated their staff in a very dehumanised manner. Detraining was a demoralising method American companies used to remove an employee whom they considered redundant, without angering the unions. The victim of the process was a chemist called Ellis, Toby Wren's former tutor at Cambridge. He had objected to the lax safety parameters of a recent field test for their new pesticide product, the side effects of which Doomwatch were investigating. The process begins with him first losing his parking space, then his telephone, and finally his office furniture, before he is told the truth and commits suicide.

Dudley wrote the final story required, called 'Pollution Inc' (though it would transmit as 'Spectre at the Feast'). It revolved around a conference organised by Quist to investigate the level of pollution being emitted by a chemicals factory into a river. The delegates staying at an exclusive hotel are struck by hallucinations caused by food poisoning from lobsters farmed at an estuary and which have absorbed the combined effluent from many different sources of pollution discharged into this river. The moral of the story is, we are poisoning our own food, but who pays to clean up the mess of industry? The public, Kit felt, had to decide whether it was going to pay twice as much for the plastic angel on top of the Christmas tree to fund industry as they find alternatives to voiding their waste into rivers.

The series was announced to the press in January 1970. The BBC saw Kit Pedler as one of *Doomwatch*'s greatest assets. He was commissioned to write an introduction for the series, which he recorded during the last studio day of the first episode. Exactly what this entailed is not known, but some episodes were given their own special trailer. For example, 'Friday's Child' asked the question 'whose baby?' over a shot of the young boy whose heart is not his own.

The *Radio Times* gave the new series a front cover, a piece of superb artwork which showed a melted plane inside a briefcase. Inside, there was a one-page introduction to the series, focusing more on the producer and the script editor as they explained the premise of the series. Unfortunately the article, written by Elizabeth Cowley, starts off with several 'facts', the very first of which (concerning deaths caused by the radar station at Fylingdales) was false; a correction had to be issued a few weeks later. The article featured a brief paragraph about Kit. Within a year, that situation would be reversed.

Doomwatch began broadcasting on BBC1 on Monday 9 February. By Tuesday morning, there was a new word in the English language ready for the new environmental and ecological awareness that the series would help to bring to the public's attention.

10
The Prophet of Clapham

'Either science completely and rapidly rethinks its motivation in relation to people or it will be left penniless and without honour.'
– Kit Pedler, *New Scientist* 1970

FEW IN THE PRESS could discern what type of drama *Doomwatch* was going to be when it was announced. Some homed in on the authors' *Doctor Who* connection, while others were expecting the BBC's answer to *Department S*, a stylish ITC series currently transmitting on ITV, which investigated mysterious events no one else could solve, and also had a computer to help.

After 'The Plastic Eaters' went out, *The Stage and Television Today* was disappointed: 'I was favourably disposed towards *Doomwatch*... and was looking forward to watching a well written, exciting science-fiction based series. In the event, it turned out to have more in common with the *Boy's Own* paper of the fifties than with even the immediate future.' The critic for the *Daily Express* suspected that she was being 'preached at', but it was Nancy Banks-Smith in the *Guardian* who realised that the series might be making an interesting point, noticing just how much plastic there was around. More tellingly, a report in the *Sunday Telegraph* revealed how a group of scientists complained to the BBC about the subject matter because they were 'dabbling with just such a bug as the saviour of our (plastic) refuse problem'.

Doomwatch had arrived. The first episode was watched by seven million viewers, but it was with the broadcast of 'Friday's Child' that the press took notice of Kit Pedler. Initially, they were more interested in guest star Mary Holland's former role in a long-running Oxo commercial. But shortly after transmission on 16 February, *Horizon* featured Dr Patrick Steptoe's work with test-tube babies, and Kit was interviewed on Radio 4 and then recorded an interview for BBC1's early-evening magazine programme *Nationwide* 'on the ethical and social implications of test-tube babies'. Kit was attending an ophthalmological conference in Mexico when it was transmitted, but his comments on mass-produced soldiers were widely reported in newspapers for both home and worldwide syndication.

As the series continued, each week's theme rang bells of recognition in the viewer or appeared to foreshadow an event which subsequently reminded them of an episode. This was picked up by a BBC executive who sat on the Programme Review Board and had watched 'Burial at Sea'. The minutes of the meeting noted that he 'thought one great value of the series was that it was not just pure entertainment but dealt with issues which were now often in the news. It was noted that a very similar story to this adventure, arising from the dumping of cyanide drums in the ocean, had just been covered in *Nationwide*.'

Ten and a half million viewers watched 'Tomorrow, the Rat'. Terence Dudley had not only written the episode but directed it too, taking full advantage of the post-watershed slot. He did not shy away from visually shocking moments (and a few unintentionally embarrassing ones) such as lingering shots of a rat-eaten horse, a grieving mother slashing with a carving knife the woman scientist responsible for the carnivorous rats which killed her child, and finally the scientist herself, a chewed-up corpse left lying on the floor in her own rat laboratory. The complaints which poured into the BBC made the newspapers both home and abroad. Privately, the BBC agreed that the episode had gone too far, and Dudley was advised to tone it down.

Kit didn't mind the controversy one little bit. 'You have to shock people,' he told *Saturday Titbits* in 1972:

> They aren't interested in documentaries. You have to create characters and situations which the public can identify with, then bring the danger down the chimney into their living rooms. That's what'll make them sit up and shiver and think 'Could that really happen to us?' Civilisation is balanced on a razor's edge. It doesn't take much to knock it off. Really, it's terrifying how soon a sophisticated society can crumble.

'I am helping to create the series,' he told the *People* at the beginning of March, 'because I feel that the technocrats and scientists are leading us on a doom-bound course. The way things are going today little distinguishes man from apes. What is left which dignifies man is so damned precious it has got to be bloody well kept.'

His opinions were wanted. Towards the end of February, Kit was a guest on the late-night BBC2 programme *Line-Up*, where he discussed *The End of the Twentieth Century?* by Desmond King-Hele, another book that wondered where science was going to take us by the end of the millennium.

As the series continued, the press referenced the series to highlight current issues. There was a huge public outcry when the American government planned to dump chemical weapons 280 miles off the Florida coastline. Highly intelligent rats were discovered in Australia, and poison-resistant ones were found in Wales. A few weeks after 'Re-Entry Forbidden', the crippled Apollo 13 captivated 31 million viewers on both BBC and ITV as they averted disaster and managed a successful splashdown. 'Project Sahara' with its tale of computer data storage caused the *New Scientist* to speculate that 'future governments may depend for their survival on computerised dossiers on private and political lives'. An MP quoted a line of dialogue from 'The Red Sky' while debating the effects of noise pollution.

Hormones affecting workers in 'The Battery People' also had real-life echoes. Male workers at a contraceptive pill factory were replaced by middle-aged women because of the effects of the hormones on their bodies. 'This [episode] seemed a little over-speculative at the time we thought it up two and a half years ago,' Kit told the *Radio Times*, 'but just a few months before it was screened a similar incident actually occurred on a farm in Leicestershire.'

When *Doomwatch* returned in December for its second series, the *Radio Times* ran a two-page feature highlighting the 'success' rate of the first series with its prescient subject matter, focusing on Kit Pedler. This infuriated a BBC further education producer, Dr Robin Brightwell, who criticised the alarmist nature of the piece and the series itself, pointing out that the technology seen in some of the episodes was still very far from reality and claiming that other issues like test-tube babies or sonic booms had been blown out of proportion:

> Articles of this type undoubtedly lead to fear, as well as condemnation, of science and technology, so they must present information in a responsible and unambiguous way… I agree *Doomwatch* could inform viewers of real

dangers, but it must not be used as an excuse to magnify and distort those dangers. Nor, and this is worse, must those same distorted dangers be used as an excuse to blow *Doomwatch*'s own trumpet.

Kit Pedler defended the programme's stance and the research that went into each episode:

Does Dr Brightwell really think it is irresponsible of us to transmit a story about leaking toxins in the sea off Plymouth when, even as I write this, a cargo ship full of herbicide has foundered off the coast of Italy and wiped out a local fishing industry? Does he think it wrong to put out a story about a nuclear weapon armed by accidental release and impact when a precisely similar event occurred in Texas some years ago? I would remind Dr Brightwell that we are producing a fictional programme and not a series of documentaries. In each episode we take what seems to be a reasonable jump forward from a real contemporary event and create an exciting story around it. In my view, the most dangerous *Doomwatch* theme at present is the extent to which ordinary people have become conditioned to accept an intolerable environment. Is Dr Brightwell quite free from this process, I wonder?

'*Doomwatch* had a reputation for being prescient,' recognises Carol Topolski, 'but my father had a very fiendish imagination. He understood what the verges were like in scientific research. He imagined what it would be like to step over that verge.'

The success of the series was also due to the cast. John Paul and Simon Oates had their fans, but it was Robert Powell, playing the sensitive and enigmatic Toby Wren, who became the series' sex symbol, attracting a legion of admiring fans. He was also the unluckiest of the *Doomwatch* team and faced peril far more than his counterparts ever did in that first series. Our final sight of Toby Wren was when he was perched underneath a dark seaside pier, trying to cut the wires to the explosives inside a damaged and armed nuclear bomb. It was leaking radioactive material and was quietly ticking down to zero. This was the nail-biting climax to the final episode of the series, 'Survival Code'.

Eleven and a half million viewers watched Toby Wren's failure. Ten years after the event, Kit Pedler was still being asked by viewers why he had killed off such a popular character. The *Radio Times* received more letters of complaint for this than on any other previous subject, and the BBC received its fair share of grief-stricken letters, some genuinely tear-stained. Each letter was replied to by *Doomwatch* secretary Judy Bedford, and signed by Robert Powell.

It was the presentation of the three lead characters, and in particular the flirtatious Ridge, that drew criticism from scientists. Graham Chedd of the *New Scientist* wrote a leading article on the subject:

> They inhabit a two-dimensional world (the other dimension, more often than not, being sex) in which it is impossible to imagine personal relationships that are not consistently charged with high emotional voltage or a domesticity that has no insistent melodramatic overtones. If we ever caught Quist boiling an egg, it would probably blow up in his face…

The criticism was put to Kit in person in 1971. 'Pedler is immediately willing to concede almost every one of these criticisms,' Chedd smugly wrote:

> He has the grace to look uncomfortable as one spells out specific examples of grossness, but counters with the argument that he isn't the programme's producer, and that often he disagrees with the production committee's decisions. He agrees that the characters don't behave like real scientists – the John Ridge character, for instance, 'is a sub-James Bond type who wouldn't last five minutes in a laboratory' – but contends that the programme doesn't set out to convince scientists, who make up only a tiny proportion of the audience. In any case, the constraints of producing a popular TV series mean that the fictional Doomwatch 'can't really bear a strict, rigorous relationship with what is needed in real life'.

Kit was also getting stick from his own colleagues: 'They call me Dr Doom in the laboratory where I work,' he told the *Evening Standard*. 'I get a terrible clobbering if one of the TV sets is not quite accurate.' He elaborated in June to *Hospital Times*: 'I allowed an eighteenth-century retort to appear in a twenty-first-century laboratory, which they got cross about – quite rightly; I just missed it.' He was also criticised by his colleagues and employers for commenting on subjects outside of his field, such as test-tube babies.

However, one criticism he would not accept: that he was simplifying science for the masses. 'The trouble with so many scientists is that they live like a monastic order,' he remarked. 'With all that said,' Chedd added, 'the fact remains that *Doomwatch* has undoubtedly got more about science and its concomitant dangers across to more people (some twelve million watch each programme) than a host of earnest, learned documentaries.'

The people loved the programme and its message, and took the heroic characters to their hearts. 'At last, the scientist is shown in a better light – as an intelligent, hardworking, understanding, broad-minded, sociable, and, above all, honest humane person. Diametrically opposite to the administrator,' wrote Mrs Marshall in the *Radio Times*. One senior BBC Review Board member 'looked forward one day to an adventure which would star a dim scientist and an efficient civil servant and an obviously able Minister of the Crown.'

Kit told the *Evening Standard*:

> People tell me they like the programme because it sets them thinking, even though they may not agree with it. This is what we are trying to do. Its message is that any scientific discovery can produce two opposite faces: one that can help man and the other which can harm him. I want people to know where science may lead us unless we control it.

A real Doomwatch

'I remember a conversation between Dad, Gerry Davis and somebody else in the front room at 119 Parkhill,' Mark Pedler remembered. 'This was during *Doomwatch*, and Dad and this other bloke were talking. Dad said, "I think it was about time a real Doomwatch agency was formed." Gerry Davis turned round and said, "I agree. I can't wait to be a part of it." Dad's face went green! Gerry Davis wasn't a scientist, he was a scriptwriter; what could he bring in?' As Kit was to discover, for such a creation to exist, it would need the very real support and clamour from the lay public, and there was always the need for an artist to bring across an idea.

Interviewed for the *Evening Standard* on 6 March, Kit explained that 'I am basically on optimist, but I think time may be running out quickly for all of us... The members of a real-life Doomwatch would be chosen by the public and there would probably be a scientific chief. But the group would answer to no one, not even the Prime Minister, except the public.' One of the first things the outfit would explore, Kit said, was 'the worrying new development of stored and computerised information kept on many of us today, much of it by industrial and commercial organisations.'

Kit first spoke in public about the need for a real Doomwatch during the Easter weekend in the less than luxurious environment of the Royal Hotel in London. He had been invited to address Sci-Con 70 (aka Eastercon), an annual gathering of science-fiction fans. This was normally a weekend of hard science-fiction coverage, but this year was going to be different. Arthur C. Clarke was attending but had not been invited to participate. Instead, the attendees listened to a lecture on the banned 'religion' Scientology; the artist Keith Albarn discussed Spaceship Earth; Dr John Clarke from the Department of Psychology of Manchester University gave a talk on the scientific theory of mysticism; and finally Kit's friend Dr Christopher Evans spoke about computers.

Kit was there to debate 'the need for a genuine scientific ombudsman'. Government intervention could enforce such a safeguard, but it needed the political will to create such an agency. But Kit told the *Evening Standard* that he would distrust any committee appointed by the government: 'It will at some time start to compromise itself about what is to be done.' One of the guests at Eastercon was Labour MP Raymond Fletcher, a sympathetic voice; within a month, the *Daily Mirror* reported that, together with a group of colleagues at Westminster, he was keen to form a Doomwatch committee within Parliament itself, independent of government. 'The idea is to discuss regularly with scientists, technologists, architects and planners what sort of dangers future holds and to get Ministers to act out on their warnings,' the report, probably from a briefing given by Fletcher himself, said. Who was said to be 'extremely interested' to participate? 'Dr Kit Pedler, who helped devise the television series.'

Unfortunately, Fletcher would have been unlikely to be listened to by any government. An ardent critic of the nuclear arms race, he had been under surveillance by MI5 since he was in contact with the Czechoslovakian secret services, despite his assurances that the Home Office knew about it.

There was an election due. In late 1969, the *New Scientist* predicted that the quality of air and water in our towns and cities would become a major election issue, just as in the premise of the series. The Labour Minister in charge of overhauling governmental bureaucracy dealing with pollution was Anthony Crosland, the Secretary of State for Local Government and Regional Planning. Public unease, the *New Scientist* commented, had grown too rapidly for the department to keep up with. A Ministry of Pollution was not a practical idea since it would find itself dealing with anything from Concorde to DDT, exhaust fumes, oil slicks, and waste disposal problems, issues which touched virtually every other government department, who would resent any intrusion into their sphere of influence. Prime Minister

Harold Wilson decided to create a Royal Commission on Environmental Pollution, which would issue its first report in 1971. *New Scientist* favoured an ombudsman who could draw attention to the ecological problems that had been mishandled or overlooked by government departments, initiate long-term research and coordinate responses to events such as the *Torrey Canyon* oil slick which polluted the coastline of Cornwall in 1968.

The general election was called for 8 June 1970. To everyone's surprise, the Conservatives took control under Edward Heath. How would the 'party of business' feel towards the environment, or the need for scientific checks and balances? They might have taken their cue from America.

US Senator Gaylord Nelson had witnessed at first hand the results of a massive oil spill in Santa Barbara, California in 1969. He was inspired to create Earth Day, which was first celebrated on 22 April 1970. Some consider this to be the birth of popular environmental activism which 'capitalised on the emerging consciousness, channelling the anger of the anti-war protesters and putting environmental concerns front and centre', as its own website puts it. Twenty million Americans from all walks of life and political persuasions took to the streets to campaign for a healthy, sustainable environment in a land where pollution was all too visible. Even President Nixon, who was prolonging the Vietnam conflict and using napalm and defoliants, was speaking publicly about the public's right to clean air and water.

The previous Labour government had at least wanted to investigate the issues that could no longer be ignored, and the Conservative government agreed. The Department of the Environment was created in September, and the Royal Commission continued to study the issues. But the danger was that they would be just sticking plasters, little concessions to middle-class cranks. It would be a brave government that would dare to scale back industry, redirect technological growth and temper free-market capitalism to protect and safeguard the environment. Industry was, after all, the backbone of our economy, an entrenched view.

Kit and Gerry were invited by the first Secretary of State to the Department of the Environment, Peter Walker, to discuss how a real Doomwatch would operate. They also met his opposite number amongst the Labour opposition, John Silkin. Nothing came from it. A similar thing would happen to Teddy Goldsmith, whom we shall meet later, when he was invited to see the Minister following the publication of a landmark issue of the new *Ecologist* magazine, 'A Blueprint for Survival' in early 1972. Goldsmith realised that 'Walker was only interested in being able to tell MPs that he had seen me.'

Goldsmith was right. Later in 1972, Walker told *The Times* that he did not think that a national Doomwatch committee as recommended by Goldsmith should be set up to prevent mankind from destroying itself.

Getting wrong with the BBC

Readers of the *Radio Times* were the first to receive the news that the BBC wanted a second series of *Doomwatch* to begin before Christmas – and they wanted it fast. Scripts were commissioned from April, before the first series had even finished on television, and the first filming was planned for the end of June. It was a tall order, but not uncommon for a drama to be this quickly recommissioned. Theoretically, this time new writers had a chance to watch the show they would be writing for.

To save time, Kit and Gerry resurrected some previously unused ideas like 'The Pacifiers', 'The Iron Doctor' and 'The Logicians', which still left them needing to very quickly dream up ten new storylines.

They also had to devise a replacement for Toby Wren. The new character was first called Jeep, before eventually being christened Geoff Hardcastle. He was basically similar in age and experience to his predecessor. To address the issue of sexism that had been identified in the series over its presentation of two irresponsible female scientists, it was decided to create a second regular and make her female, Dr Fay Chantry. She would be a former medical research scientist who had abandoned her career and briefly returned to the NHS wards.

Terence Dudley wanted to improve the standard of the writing, stung by *New Scientist*'s criticism of 'cardboard characterisation', and he also wanted to tone down the character of Quist to make him less of a proclaiming demigod, delivering potentially controversial political messages. Success sometimes makes the BBC nervous, and the larger a programme's profile the more vulnerable to attack it becomes.

The problems began almost immediately. The new storylines had some evocative titles: 'Lonely the House', 'Darwin's Killers', 'A Condition of the Mind', 'Massacre of the Innocents', 'Inventor's Moon', 'Death of a Sagittarian' and 'A Will to Die'. But Dudley felt that the writers were veering too close towards *Doctor Who* territory. He rejected 'Death of a Sagittarian' and 'A Will To Die' outright; but feeling vindicated by their success, Gerry

Davis went ahead and briefed writers. Dudley reluctantly agreed, providing substantial changes were made. Gerry agreed.

Some writers were only given as little as a fortnight to script their episodes; when they were delivered, Dudley did not like them either, and started to reject a number of them. Not every script was needed as early as June, as production would stretch into 1971, but the delivery dates on writers' contracts implied that early delivery was necessary. The BBC drama department seemed to be putting an impossible workload on their shoulders. All this should act as context for what happened next.

Relations between writers and producer had not been smooth. Although there had never been any stand-up confrontations or rows, a deep feeling of unhappiness festered between the camps. They both had very strongly held views on how *Doomwatch* worked. Gerry and Dudley would fire angry memos at each other, written down and delivered by Judy Bedford. They no longer exist. Andrew Osborn was called in to arbitrate over the quality of the scripts, and he came down firmly on Terence Dudley's side.

Martin Worth, an experienced writer for television, had been brought in to script the episode 'Lonely the House' (transmitted as 'Invasion'), and considered himself a spy for his friend Osborn:

> Gerry Davis's office was next door to the producer's office, and they couldn't stand each other. I had to go up in the lift, and I had to walk past Terry's office to get to Gerry's, and he always had his door open. As soon as he saw me, he would say 'Oh, just a minute Martin,' and I would have to go in and talk to him first. Gerry knew this was happening because he could hear us talking next door.

When Worth finally saw Gerry about his script, he would be greeted with 'What has that bastard been saying now?'

Since there appeared to be no way to break the impasse, a radical solution was proposed. Since 'Invasion' was the only script that everyone agreed was excellent (although both 'The Iron Doctor' and 'The Logicians' did become scripts and were first in production), Osborn invited Worth to act as an unofficial script editor for a couple of months, and get six scripts written and edited in time for production. At the same time, Terence Dudley's wife fell ill, and he needed a break before the juggernaut of production began all over again. Osborn would act as associate producer (which as Head of Series was actually a good way of describing his job) during Dudley's absence, signing the contracts with the writers.

Suddenly, Kit and Gerry found that they had lost creative control of a series they had created and shaped to become a success. What happened to Gerry during May and June 1970 is not known, although he may well have gone on leave, which might account for the need to get so many scripts in so short a space of time. He did not commission any scripts during that period. He was also writing his own episode, 'The Web of Fear', about an outbreak of a disease on one of the Isles of Scilly being misdiagnosed as yellow fever, but which was in fact, a man-made virus, created by a sloppy, reputation-driven scientist investigating pest control.

John Gould, a young writer who had great success with thrillers, was going to script 'The Will to Die' which would eventually be made at the very end of the production cycle as 'In the Dark'. This was a story of a scientist who refuses to allow an incurable disease to destroy him and becomes simply a head sticking out of a life-support system. He has fantasies of being just brain and intellect; even when his illness robs him of the power of speech and sight, he will still be living inside his mind. His scientists are devising ways for him to communicate via his brain waves. But would they hear him scream? Doctor Quist is invited up to their Scottish mansion by his daughter to persuade him to simply let go and die. It certainly has Pedlerian overtones as an idea.

Gould was a supporter of Dudley's views on how *Doomwatch* should be played and felt that Kit and Gerry had compromised too much with the 'cowboy/adventure' school of drama: 'The inevitable levity is a total error,' he wrote in a letter to Dudley. He also implied that when he had worked on the script, Gerry Davis was alarmed by some of his writing. Quite what he meant by this is unknown.

With only a few changes to their storyline, 'Massacre of the Innocents' became 'No Room for Error', based on a recent tragedy. Dozens of babies did not respond to antibiotic treatment during a gastroenteritis outbreak in Hull. Their deaths became the subject of an upsetting and deep-searching government inquiry. In the story, there is a typhoid outbreak, and again the sick children do not respond to antibiotics and are given a brand-new and powerful drug. Some of the children react as if they already had some in their system, which they had. The farm on which the drug was tested had accidentally infected the milk supply, which these children then drank at school. This was a very down-to-earth story, so it is not a surprise that it passed Dudley's test.

Of the known rejected stories, 'Condition of the Mind' was about mentally disordered people who were being used as human guinea pigs for psychiatric tests. They were shut up in rooms for days, treated like virtual prisoners. 'It is research gone sick,' Kit told the *People* in March 1970. For this idea, Kit was helped by his psychiatrist wife, Una. The idea was offered to Harry Green in July, but he was too disillusioned by his own experiences on the programme to commit to it. 'Darwin's Killer' was Kit and Gerry's final attempt to deal with the threat from a sunk Russian nuclear submarine and both attempts by Dennis Spooner failed.

The situation with the seven storylines devised by Kit and Gerry became further complicated as Terence Dudley, on his return from leave, decided that they should only be paid for the five stories he had originally accepted, and not for the two he had rejected – even though he had agreed for them to be turned into scripts. Osborn agreed to pay them off since 'I do not... feel that it is worthwhile fostering any form of enmity in a situation which I am sure we are all anxious to cool by the saving of a few pounds.' On one BBC memo regarding this payment, someone had highlighted Gerry Davis's name in red ink: 'I spoke to them – they're off their heads.'

The Daily Mirror

Despite the series slipping out of their hands, its success meant that there was no shortage of offers for either Kit or Gerry, and one came from the *Daily Mirror*. It was hardly surprising that the press should get in on the act and see if they could develop a Doomwatch reporting style of their own. Newspapers tended to receive short shrift from scientists in the television series itself, and Kit himself had reported the *Daily Express* to the Press Council for their coverage of the creation of a virus as life in 1968 which he considered to be dangerously inaccurate reporting. The left-wing *Daily Mirror* had been a supporter of *Doomwatch* during its run, and in the next few years it would take up a campaigning stance on environmental issues, achieving a notable victory in 1972 exposing the illegal practice of dumping industrial waste in the countryside. The right-wing press would later play 'catch up' as they discovered that their readers also shared the same concerns, and could no longer dismiss them as naïve.

Agreeing to be their 'chief scientific advisor', Kit teamed up with the *Mirror*'s science editor Ronald Bedford and writer Michael Hellicar to form the paper's own self-styled Doomwatch team. It would be an interesting exercise to let the people come to them with their concerns, the type of thing a real democratic Doomwatch would need.

The infrequent series of articles was launched on Monday 22 June 1970:

> CALL IN DOOMWATCH! THEY ARE READY FOR ACTION!
> TODAY we launch an important venture: the Mirror Doomwatch Team. Its object: to probe and crusade against the dangers that threaten the world around you.
> Many people in Britain fear the effects of scientific progress. Technology is all very well – but what are the scientists doing to YOUR lives?
> … Now they are waiting to hear from YOU about the things that worry you – from aircraft noise to insecticides, from the state of your breakfast kipper to the state of your local river. In fact, anything, however trivial or baffling, that disturbs you about the conditions of your daily life.

Their first case might not have been what Kit had expected, although it was a gift for the tabloids: The Case of the Tattered Tights…

Geoffrey Arden remembered how Kit appeared to have been out of his depth:

> *Doomwatch,* which had great success, turned his head completely, and he ceased to do much at the Institute at all. He courted the press, and they responded. One tabloid paid him to do a real-life Doomwatch – they would find the problem and he would solve it. I came in to see him one morning, and he was entirely surrounded by nylon tights. The newspaper had picked up a story that amorous young ladies on Clapham Common were frequently embarrassed by finding holes in their stockings after their horizontal trysts. The obvious explanation was that some unknown pollutant was dissolving nylon – one of the Doomwatch scripts was close to this, if I remember rightly. I found Kit forlornly dabbing tights with pH indicators – he had no idea whatsoever what to do.

The story featured women from Erith in Kent, and at Barrow-in-Furness, who had noticed holes appear in their tights after either spending their lunch break on their firm's sports ground, or playing a round of golf. Assisting with the case were two researchers from the Greater London Council's Environmental Research Group. They discovered microscopic samples of acidic particles or 'smuts,' within the affected nylons. According to the article, Kit tried to reproduce the damage by dropping four types of strong acid – sulphuric, nitric, hydrochloric and formic – onto the stockings, in various stages of dilution, but could not reproduce the same effect. He also tried alcohol, cigarette ash, and ether. The conclusion was that the particles came either from a factory boiler burning oil which contained too much sulphur, a chemical process discharging acid fumes, or a factory boiler with an unsuitable chimney.

The main problem for the articles was that rather than opening a floodgate of horror stories regarding pollution, killer noises, dangerous laboratory experiments and hazardous industrial processes, the issues were rather small and trivial. Kit would be called to talk about why one side of a man's garden didn't do so well as the other (it was probably someone using a weedkiller that had drifted into his garden, they concluded). Each infrequent article would begin with a dramatic warning, an overdramatised alarm call, but by the time you'd read down to the end of the article, it didn't appear to be as bad as all that after all. Kit would then be quoted in summing up the piece with a few sage words of wisdom, no doubt edited and sub-edited down to a couple of sentences.

To confuse matters further for the readers, the word Doomwatch was used as a tag for any similar type of story. In August, the *Mirror* trailed an article with the headline: 'Threat to Newborn Babies'. The story here was that there was a risk to a baby's health from water supplied to Lincolnshire homes by the North Lindsey water board because it contained too much nitrate. The nitrates were either coming from fertiliser spread upon agricultural land or derived naturally from bacteria which live around the roots of plants. The Farmers' Union pointed out that the water board had been over-abstracting water from the ground. A board official downplayed the problem, claiming that the nitrate increase had been levelling off for some time. Kit was nowhere to be seen in this, but interestingly, just as this article went to press, the television *Doomwatch* was making 'Invasion', an episode which started with the team concerned about high nitrate levels found in the water supply of a Yorkshire village.

One notable article published at the end of July regarded the menace from an increasing number of rats and 'super-mice' in major cities, echoing neatly 'Tomorrow, the Rat'. The figures Kit used to describe the menace in the newspaper might have come from his research into the original storyline.

For the August bank holiday weekend, they looked at the sewage disposal problem following a new report issued by the government called 'Taken for Granted'. The newspaper listed the seaside towns that were pumping their waste into the sea: some of it piped out half a mile offshore, and some directly into rivers and harbours. Every day, five hundred million gallons of sewage was being pumped into the Thames Estuary, while the Humber carried a thousand tonnes of sulphuric acid waste daily.

When it was asked of the British Resorts Association why their own members appeared to be discharging crude sewage into the sea, they referred the paper back to a report prepared in 1959 which felt that bacteriological contamination from raw sewage was too trivial a risk to act upon. Its author, Dr Brendan Moore, chairman of the Medical Research Council's committee of the time, was reported as having said: 'I stand by the findings. There is no evidence that points to disease being caused by sea bathing in sewage.' He had rejected in 1959 rigid bacteriological standards that were beginning to appear in America, in favour of informal, visual assessments of pollution. The new report suggested that waste should be pumped out further into the sea than at present, but that disinfection should be carried out only in extreme situations. A recent World Health Organisation report begged to differ, and Kit seized upon it as he wrote: 'Water which has been contaminated by sewage can carry many diseases – such as typhoid, polio, hepatitis and dysentery. It is time for an up-to-date examination of dangers in the sea.'

A wounded series

With Andrew Osborn's blessing, Terence Dudley decided that Kit and Gerry should no longer originate the *Doomwatch* stories. Kit's official role in the second series was not agreed upon until September, but by then half of it had been recorded. He would simply be allowed to comment on the scientific aspects of each script, acting as, in Dudley's own words, a 'sounding board' for ideas, and discuss possible themes for episodes. This was backdated to 1 July until the end of January 1971, for which he would be paid £100 per month. However, writers were encouraged to seek their scientific advice elsewhere. Martin Worth particularly enjoyed doing his own research with a BBC staff member called Anna Kaliski.

At the beginning of July, Gerry Davis returned to the programme, but he found that while getting his own stories commissioned was a simple enough process, getting them accepted by his producer was another matter. One writer who failed to get his script made into an episode was Keith Dewhurst. His contribution was provisionally titled 'The Home-Made Bomb Story':

Gerry Davis and I knew each other for a good while. We liked each other and were on more or less the same side in what I call 'the theatre wars'. I was commissioned to write this script from a basic idea by Kit Pedler who had realised it was possible for someone, who knew how, to make a small nuclear bomb in a suburban garage. I had lunch with Kit and Gerry to discuss ideas and met them again when I delivered. I have a very strong recollection of Kit's intensity. I think that it was after I delivered a final script that Terence Dudley took over. What Dudley proposed was to reject the script, not pay its acceptance fee and start again with new people. He would have his own chums, so to speak, whom he had used on other shows. Writers worked in all good faith to a brief but when they delivered were told that the brief had changed, and that they would not be paid for acceptance. They and their agents objected strongly.

The changing brief was because of the characterisation of Quist, whose guilt over his part in the Manhattan Project was to be addressed and put to rest in the opening episode of the series, 'You Killed Toby Wren', written by Dudley himself, reformatting the series the way he wanted it to go.

Writer after writer was briefed, paid their first half of an agreed fee, and then found that Terence Dudley either did not like their script, or some other problem arose. In some cases, it was the characterisation that annoyed the producer; in others, the style of the story. There were very angry writers and agents who needed soothing and paying off. There was also bad luck involved: one script was turned down because its subject matter clashed with an episode of *Doctor Finlay's Casebook*, while other writers simply did not deliver their script for various reasons. By the autumn, Terence Dudley had brought in his preferred writers, such as Martin Worth, to write other stories.

The final blow came for Gerry with a script called 'The Inquest' by series writer Robert Holmes. The inquest was into how a young girl came to die from rabies in a Suffolk village. The prime suspect was a nearby laboratory experimenting with changing the DNA of the tsetse fly to render the lethal pest harmless. Could a bite from an escaped fly have given the girl a deadly infection similar in symptoms to rabies? The answer was no. The girl really had died from rabies, after being licked by a rabid dog. The idea in this part of the plot was the reverse of what Gerry had written in 'The Web of Fear', where symptoms of a man-made virus were misdiagnosed as yellow fever. Holmes claimed in an interview that his script was the reason Gerry walked out. It simply wasn't a *Doomwatch* script, and the regulars played far too minor roles in what little action there actually was.

Gerry asked to be moved onto a different programme since he was still under contract with the BBC. Even without him the scripting problems continued, and Dudley effectively script-edited the programme on his own, something he was more than capable of doing. But soon Andrew Osborn put his foot down and told the producer that there were to be no more commissions. Something like thirty-two scripts had already been commissioned.

There were two contrasting styles of *Doomwatch* episode. The earlier recorded episodes were more in the tradition of the first series: an intriguing, exciting scientific mystery for the team to solve. The second style, which Dudley preferred, were more character-driven, philosophical, and calmer in action, but intense with emotion. Gone were thrilling sequences such as Ridge breaking into laboratories or impersonating civil servants, and the science-fiction elements were toned down or eliminated entirely. In other words, everything that made the series popular and special in the first place had been eroded. Despite still being very good writing, *Doomwatch* was in danger of becoming just another series, rather than the unique format Kit and Gerry had created. This was something that the more conservative BBC types were comfortable with.

The absence of Kit and Gerry was felt in the rehearsal room early on. Simon Oates felt that the character of John Ridge, which he enjoyed playing, was being watered down and the conflict with Quist removed. He also felt that the stories were not as effective as before. Ironically, he thought that the series was veering towards *Doctor Who* in places. Kit Pedler certainly attended early rehearsals for the new series, and met Jean Trend, the actress selected by Terence Dudley to play Dr Fay Chantry. She remembers the way he was thinking by the summer of 1970:

> I was a very big fan of the man. He cared so desperately about the planet. Such a modest man too, but once you got him on the environment he buzzed with energy and enthusiasm. My sons were little when I did *Doomwatch* but some things Kit told me I passed on to them and in turn (I believe) they have passed on to their own children to follow. Water was the main thing: when cleaning your teeth only put on the tap to rinse your mouth and brush, don't let it run. He also was horrified at our use of clean water for flushing the toilet; why couldn't sea water be used?

Kit's visits to the rehearsal room were rare as he lost whatever influence he had. He was basically going to be used as a source of useful publicity material, a stamp of authority on the premise of the series. In private he was angry and dismissive of other people's scripts. One was based not on some scientific or technological idea, but a piece of literature, which Kit should have approved of: Ibsen's 1882 play *An Enemy of the People*. The episode was called 'Public Enemy', and it was certainly commissioned around the same time Kit was investigating factory pollution for the *Daily Mirror*. Dudley and Osborn thought that this was the best script of the entire series. 'It is what *Doomwatch* is all about,' Osborn enthused. There was nothing that could be construed as science fiction, or as an imaginative piece of speculation.

The story features an industrial factory that is developing a new secret alloy to replace carbon fibres. It proves cheaper to close the plant down rather than address its pollution which has inadvertently caused two fatal accidents. The town's politicians, once supportive of Doomwatch and critical of the company, now switch sides once they see their future without a major employer. Doomwatch face pressure from all sides to change their mind.

Although it contained sentiments Kit agreed with, it was a health and safety versus economics story; he pronounced it as 'both jejune and scientifically unsound', which astonished Dudley. Kit asked for his name to be removed as scientific advisor from the episode. He also demanded that in the event of there being a third series, Dudley should be removed as producer. The BBC was inclined not to agree.

The series began a few weeks before Christmas 1970. Despite a strong start with 'You Killed Toby Wren' with its animal-man hybrids in a university lab, and 'Invasion', where a village is evacuated following a leak from an abandoned germ warfare laboratory, it became obvious to some viewers that the programme was changing. The clash of styles soon began to show, and some within the BBC noticed. The inevitable backlash to a success showed itself in the media with criticism of the series appearing, some of it rather petty.

Doomwatch was still popular with its audience, and still achieving good viewing figures on average; but there was a distinct feeling that it was not as good as before. However, a third series was commissioned, but this time the BBC gave Terence Dudley total control, and a whole year to get his stories together before production would begin.

11
Pedler's Meddlers

> Some people would be happy to see the last of him... I sometimes think that what they really dislike is the idea that every Tom, Dick and Harry in the mass television audience should have these topics dished out to him in dramatised form. There is always the danger that the public might really get interested. – Colin Ward, from a speech printed in *Perspectives in Public Health*, June 1972

It wasn't just the media who became interested in Kit Pedler and *Doomwatch*: it was a new generation of scientists, more politically active than those who had trained them. One influential group was called LASITOC, created in 1967 by Jan Fjellander. LASITOC was an international theosophical summer camp based in Sweden, taking its initials from Look At, Search In, Try Out Camp.* From this camp emerged a committee who wanted to explore and grasp 'important global social, environmental and scientific topics'.

The core group came from Europe, meeting every three months to discuss and plan an expanding agenda. By 1969, the United Nations was planning an international conference on the human environment to be held in Stockholm in 1972. They wanted to debate and plan action with as many countries that would attend to protect the environment worldwide. The youthful LASITOC wanted to arrange alternative activities and influence the conference. They started to contact well-known intellectuals and scientists

---
* Later the C stood for Committee.

who in turn wanted to understand this new generation after the student unrest of 1968 and the growing radicalisation of the student movement around the world.

LASITOC was invited in September 1969 by the Nobel Foundation to a symposium called 'The Place of Value in a World of Facts'. They wanted to discuss the generation gap, but as one commentator observed, the true meaning of the meeting soon became: 'How can mankind cope with the rather frightening world that science and technology has thrust upon it?' Quickly, the meeting dismissed the generation gap as irrelevant. One delegate from America, Harrison Brown, remarked: 'Perhaps the greatest tragedy of the human experience is that our understanding of man and his behaviour has not kept pace with our knowledge of how to control nature. We have now reached the point where from a technological point of view starvation and misery in the world are inexcusable.'

Robert Cowen wrote in *Technology Review*:

> The elders listened, as they have many times before, and shared Dr Brown's sense of tragedy. But the students wondered why, if scientists know such things, more of them aren't trying to do something about it personally? Why, one of them asked publicly, don't they put aside such frivolities as space research and heart transplants and work to banish hunger and misery? Again, symposium members outlined the potential horrors of nuclear or biological warfare. And again, other members joined in the familiar ritual of decrying war's dangers. To which the students responded by asking why did some of them work on military projects if they know all that? One student wondered whether these people came to symposiums like these to help the world, or whether they 'have a comfortable position and salary and they like to go to meetings to eat the good food and talk with their friends, saying the same things over and over again?'

Fjellander and the man in charge of the British side of LASITOC, Peter Harper, decided to host their own conference in London in 1970. Harper was twenty-five years old, a postgraduate who was working towards his PhD in experimental biochemistry at the Laboratory of Experimental Psychology at Sussex University. He had begun to doubt the value of the work he was doing there which involved experiments on rats. They wanted to see if they could transfer memory by removing one part of a brain and grafting it onto another.

Titled 'The Threats and Promises of Science', the object of the week-long meeting was to investigate the role of science in the resolution of problems of human welfare and to examine the relationships between science and society. It was to be held at Imperial College in July 1970. Harper had an ally in the shape of the President of the Student Union, Piers Corbyn, who is today a notorious and controversial figure for his free thinking on global warming and vaccination. Although Harper did not have a television, he had heard of *Doomwatch* and invited Kit Pedler: 'I wrote asking him to come to our conference… It was novel then even to mention "threats", but he was doing it on the telly! He replied by return saying, "The only way you will prevent me from attending your conference is by physical force."'

Eighty young academics from fifteen different countries attended. The intention wasn't to solve the world's problems in one week, but to bring together ideas from as many disciplines, nationalities and generations as possible. Among the subjects to be discussed was the deterioration of the environment, population distribution, the development of new weapons, depersonalisation of the individual, and the exhaustion of world resources. Although billed as a conference, it was really a workshop, concerned with studies of alternative futures. By exchanging and documenting ideas, Fjellander believed that the pool of informed opinion would swell. The *Daily Mirror* quoted him as saying:

> We want informed change. We are adding something like 50,000 new chemicals a year to the environment. Many do not occur naturally. We are not against science as such, but we are alarmed at some of the ways in which it is used. We think this effort is more important than getting men to the moon or building new atom smashing machines.

As Harper later reflected, the conference spoke a lot about the threats, but never got round to the promises. He wrote a few years later in *Undercurrents*:

> That doughty old Stalinist Eric Burhop valiantly defended the gods of science, but it all fell on deaf ears. Ted Roszak was the hero of the hour, and we sat there chilled and enthralled as he quietly anathematised the whole technical culture. We were all set for a pathetically joyous return to the Stone Age.

The conference received some good publicity in the papers. *The Times* covered the conference twice during the week, including an interview with Harper, who explained why he had resigned from Sussex University. 'I think there are certain things it is just as well not to know, and I wrote out my resignation. The professor told me "I think you are mad but the best of luck." I finish at the end of term, but my views have not changed. Most science is a waste of time and sometimes it is positively harmful.' He believed that some people felt that the only way to change things was by the application of more science. An attractive theory, Harper agreed, but it was only a guess, and nobody knew what the effect would be for the future.

Harper was not alone. Back in January, Dr James Shapiro at the Harvard Institute had stopped his work after having successfully isolated a single gene. Fundamental research such as this, designed to understand and cure inherited diseases, could easily be abused. The eugenics research being carried out into 'proving' the racial superiority of whites was evidence of that. Eleven other young scientists, including Harper, had given up their work to help LASITOC, and set up what Fjellander described as an international college of change, an informal world university. The *Daily Mirror* inevitably nicknamed them 'Junior Doomwatch'.

A conference like this must have been an interesting experience for Kit. Here, at last, he could discuss themes with like-minded people. A real Doomwatch had to come from within the scientific community, requiring a huge shift in attitude, and here it was emerging from the next generation. But even that might not be enough. Later in the year, Kit wrote in *New Scientist*:

> If a new ethos did develop within the scientific community, how would it have its effect? Even if the majority of laboratory workers decided that… all their work would be directed towards furthering the cause of man's happiness and to prevent the continual exploitation of Earth's dwindling reserves, who will listen? Who, among the industrialists and politicians, will say: 'Yes, the scientists are right – we must abandon our industrial complexes, and run down our systems of mindless ingenuity'? Clearly, no one.

The New Science Group

A voice was slowly emerging in Britain with the British Society for the Social Responsibility in Science. Barely a year old, it was beginning to challenge the government's uncompromising attitude towards chemical and biological weapons. Its General Secretary, David Dickson, was a young mathematician and had recently been a journalist writing for *Medical News-Tribune* before he took up his new post in the summer. He worked from a small basement office opposite the British Museum and next door to the Bernal Peace Library who had sponsored the meeting which gave birth to the society in 1969. Along with Harper, Dickson organised a small, informal weekend meeting of people to discuss the issues of the day, but to go further than that, and think of what to do next. It was very easy diagnosing the problem, but where do you go from there?

Dickson prepared a flyer which he sent out as an invitation to a limited number of people, one of whom was Kit Pedler. He gave it a title which he thought was rather pleasing – 'A Blueprint for Survival':

> Are we fiddling while the world burns? Has man created an environment incompatible with his own survival? Have we outstretched our own intelligence? Is there an intrinsic contradiction between man's technological ability, and his ability to survive on limited resources? Can we identify the weak links in the survival chain and ensure that these are adequately protected? Is there a future for science in a world that has already sown the seeds of its own destruction? What must we do NOW to maximise the chances of survival into the next century?

Dickson elaborated on what he hoped would come from this meeting for Michael Allaby's book *The Eco-Activists*:

> I feel that the reductionist, problem-solving approach must be replaced by an imaginative, creative approach in which convergence must give way to divergence. This comes into ecology, because ecology seems to be very much a divergent activity in which you must use your own imagination. Conflict between human and scientific values must be resolved. We must create an aesthetic appreciation of the scientific process and scientific problems themselves must take on a new nature.

What was needed was a new approach to science, one truly beneficial to mankind, and not for a few vested interests.

Dickson and Harper invited Piers Corbyn, Robin Clarke, the editor of the *Science Journal*, in which Kit had recently been published, and Jerry Ravetz, Senior Lecturer in History and Philosophy of Science at Leeds, and currently working on a massive tome called *Scientific Knowledge and Its Social Problems*. Ravetz only met Kit a few times at the meetings of the group: 'I was enormously impressed by him and worked quite hard to get over my prejudices about the way that radical thinkers should look and behave. With my puritanical streak, I could not find racing cars an attractive pursuit. Certainly, with *Doomwatch* he was far ahead of the official consensus about science.'

The final member of the group was the impressive Gustav Metzger, a computer expert and artist. Born in Nuremberg in 1926, Metzger came to Britain in 1939 as a Polish citizen but had become stateless since the 1940s. He became active with the anti-nuclear campaign, and developed an artistic style called Auto-Destructive Art in the 1960s. Revolutionary artists from Britain and America had already formed an informal organisation called the International Coalition for the Liquidation of Art, and a call was issued inviting artists to demonstrate their opposition to the monopolisation of art in the hands of museums, banks, auction houses, and other evils in society. 'All artists who refuse to join in attacking the present system – are shit,' declared its manifesto. 'All artists who continue to work with the system will be required to produce nothing but miniatures in order to limit the growing art pollution. Those who desire may also be permitted to make artistic painting on bombs before they are dropped on people.' The BSSRS had formed an Art and Technology group with Metzger at the forefront. Its aim was to provide graphic demonstrations of environmental problems to bring these issues before the public.

One such piece Metzger created was called *Mobbile*. It was a Perspex box, mounted on top of David Dickson's own car. Inside the box were meat, vegetables and flowers. A tube fed from the car's exhaust pipe into the box. The message was clear. It was first demonstrated outside the Arts Council-sponsored Kinetics exhibition at the Hayward Gallery on the evening of 24 September. Dickson remembered that Metzger was angry that he had been excluded from the exhibition:

> He was a slightly gnomic character; he was very determined and cut quite a reputation as a non-conformist artist. Quite an intriguing character, he was a bit of an iconoclast, and didn't make himself popular in the art world because he was difficult to frame. He generated quite a reputation for himself.

The group christened themselves the New Science Group, and they first met together one weekend in September 1970 at Kit's house. 'It was quite a curious group we had,' remembered David Dickson. 'We were all pursuing our own slightly offbeat ideas, and we got together as a group of people with offbeat ideas who might enjoy spending a couple of days together, which is how we did it.' 'Luddite desperadoes' was how Peter Harper described themselves. 'The group met only a few times,' remembers Jerry Ravetz, 'but it was very exciting. I was detailed to do a draft of a manifesto.'

The manifesto of the New Science Group

The manifesto set out to identify the problem inherent in 'old science', and develop their aims as they saw it, not so much of the group, but as a mission statement for the development of a 'new science'. It begins with a piece by Ravetz called 'Harmony' examining the basic philosophy of their thinking, and then Gustav Metzger: 'We are situated at a point of a renaissance of science and technology. The past development has brought us to a dead end in the most literal sense. The new approach does offer a way out of the dilemma – how can man manage to support existence?' Their struggle to oust the existing science was a revolution from within. They needed to attract the young to their side. 'Infiltration and expansion of our ideas within the existing academic institutions. Takeover of departments and of entire institutions within a ten-year period from now.'

Robin Clarke offered 'Thoughts for a Non-Rapine Scientist': 'a social utopia defined by a science and technology which neither manipulates man nor rapes nature is going to raise severe semantic problems. Is it manipulation, for instance, to extort or to order scientists to work only within these loosely defined confines? And does stepping on a cockroach constitute the rape of nature?' He discusses how the burning of fossil fuels was a one-way process, an unnatural loop introduced into the natural cycle. Governments were realising this, he said, but their solution was fission energy which was 'a historical accident derived from a military blunder of the 1940s. As the only renewable and constant source of energy is the sun, that is where our future supplies must come from.'

David Dickson contributed 'Towards a New Science'. What conditions would a new science have to meet in resolving, to take an example, the conflict between the values of the scientific man and human, yet retain the integrity of traditional science, and lead towards a deeper 'understanding' of the world in which we live? 'Our present science gives us mathematics as a tool that can "explain" physics, physics as a tool that can "explain" chemistry, chemistry as a tool that can explain biology, biology, etc., thus constructing a highly ordered picture of the world that conveniently fits into our cultural traditions of structural development and progress.'

Piers Corbyn took a realistic look at the current industrial-capitalistic system, which is:

> ... geared to ever increasing consumption and production since essentially this is necessary to maintain the rate of profit on wealth invested into costly production machines... if the whole of the production and consumption of industry and society were democratically and socially controlled with proper regard for the present and future social and environmental wealth, rather than forming profit, then decisions of science and industrial policy concerning growth and application could be correctly taken.

Kit's contribution was called 'The Scientific Method or Antisocial Dogma':

> Science students are conditioned to believe that the scientific method is a uniquely powerful means of acquiring some special aspect of truth. They are also asked to accept that to use it successfully demands an almost religious submission to a highly structured dogma.
>
> The method when considered alone, within the confines of a laboratory, is obviously powerful. The testing of a hypothesis by experiment and prediction from experimental results can produce information which has already led to an unprecedented control over the physical universe. Thus the method stands upon its own operational strength, but only within clearly defined limits. To use it the scientist knows he must operate within its canons, otherwise he will probably be unsuccessful in his laboratory and certainly be subject to excommunication by those of his colleagues who still retain a classical belief in its purity.
>
> The reasoning processes peculiar to the method may often lead an individual scientist to a form of self-examination, whereby he is able critically to examine his own intellectual integrity. In relation to an experiment, for example, he may discover just how far he can maintain a separation between his own personal wishes and ambitions and the necessary process of the experiment.
>
> Within the now crumbling dynasty of the old science, this process is perfectly satisfactory. He can go on for the whole of his life, seeking internal and external evidence of his probity as a laboratory worker and satisfy himself that he has never allowed his personal hopes to interfere with the purity and elegance of the method itself. By definition, the method demands the complete removal of all human qualities during its practice, and thus, again by definition, its validity as a social instrument is never considered by the classical purist.
>
> But if a scientist looks beyond his laboratory walls and is made aware of external socio-political problems he may be subject to serious anxiety and

doubt. Because although he knows the effectiveness and problem-solving capacity of the method in the laboratory, he now sees it to suffer from two crucial defects. First, it is totally unsuited to study the problems in this area, and second, it has conditioned him to reject any problem which is not soluble by its particular closed system.

It can only work perfectly in a perfect situation. And a perfect situation is a laboratory situation which has been especially contrived for perfect solution.

To have one's basic training revealed as a process which has systematically reduced one's status as a human being is obviously of profound importance and there are two remedial courses of action available. Either to go permanently back into the laboratory and re-accept the power of the method within a strictly limited framework or to remain exposed to the problems raised by an overpopulated globe and a sagging ecosphere.

To remain determinedly exposed to the global problem is probably to start a frontal assault on the multitude of incipient disasters which require the most urgent attention. This is self-defeating simply because of the size of the task.

But there is a third constructive alternative: for each individual scientist to attempt a total reassessment of his status as a specially skilled citizen and to see where his expertise can best be applied to help man to live in a more symbiotic relationship with the environment. To design 'risk-free' experiments which will not pillage the earth's resources, to agree never to work in secret and to take active, prior steps to ascertain whether any research undertaken could conceivably be of any harm to man.

A detailed examination of the consequences of this simple affirmation can provide relief from the otherwise intolerable knowledge that the classical scientific method has little future relevance for society unless it rediscovers a primary, social drive. It now stands revealed as a moribund and monastic leviathan, in the throes of a last attempt to rediscover a sense of motivation without affecting its sense of purity.

It is relatively simple to agree to a general statement about the future ethos of science, but more difficult to plan a practical course of action.

How can a new principle lead to political action? By teaching students to carry through a fully scientific investigation in a politically sensitive area.

To take an example. Many seaside towns discharge untreated sewage into the sea. The Medical Research Council in 1959 pronounced that there was no significant health hazard in bathing in raw sewage, but were prepared to admit that it might be anaesthetic.

A recent WHO (World Health Organisation) publication (September 1970) tells of the discovery by three American virologists of recoverable and virulent viruses both in raw sewage and in treated sewage.

A field investigation by the student group would involve: oceanography, bacteriology, virology, biochemistry and mathematics. It would inevitably lead directly to a number of political confrontations. First, with the local town council and health authority, secondly with the Medical Research Council and finally with the Department of Health. The confrontation would succeed if, and only if, an adequate and safe replacement scheme was presented in detail. This would present to the students the effectiveness of a new science; that by using their ingenuity and training as scientists within the classical scope of the method referred to above, they were able to take effective political action through a factually based investigation within the scope of the new science.

Kit tentatively made public some of their ideas in November when he wrote a review for *New Scientist* on Professor Rene Dubos' 'important' book *Reason Awake: Science for Man* which shared the views that had been expressed by the New Science Group. The book argued, in Kit's own words:

> ... that ecological constraints on population and technological constraints on population and technological growth will inevitably lead to new social and economic systems. And that to survive, Mankind will have to develop a 'steady state' formula entirely different from the philosophy of endless quantitative growth which has been the mainstream of industrial civilisations during the past century... He states that, far from leading to intellectual stagnation and decadence, it will provide an exciting stimulus for scientists to develop new ideas and concepts within the structure of a closed system. To examine new technologies specifically designed to minimise pollution and to recycle natural resources; to redesign the general distribution of energy and to work out in more detail a global spaceship ecology.

Kit threw in his own sixpence:

> There was a time after the end of the Second World War, when almost any laboratory discovery was automatically given obeisance by a wide-eyed enthusiastic public. But now the lay eye is beady and suspicious. Does the glittering array of science spectaculars help us to live in true symbiosis with the environment, does it even help someone to get coal to their fourth floor flat? Basically, it does not, so the public are trying to find a stronghold where they can successfully resist the conditioning process which has taught them that every new product – however useless, however depleting to the environment – is good for them.

Kit sensed that Dubos felt overwhelmed by the scale of the problem. 'It is as though he has really seen the complex scientific and technological future rolling onwards almost of its own volition: without purpose, compassion or serious utility,' and that he can offer no clear solution. Here, Kit offers his own ideas – politically aware students had to be mobilised, and once again offers the example of sewage and the sea.

Dubos was right: the scale of the problem *was* overwhelming. Just how were they going to get their message across? Kit Pedler had the natural advantage.

Taking the message to the masses

Out of the group, Kit was certainly the best known to the public and with a growing media profile on radio, television and in print. A few days after the July LASITOC conference, Kit was filmed at home for an edition of an educational programme called *New Horizons* dealing with 'People and Computers', a subject close to Metzger's heart, and in August he contributed to a debate on Radio 4's *The World Tonight* on pollution: 'Are we making too much fuss?' He made an appearance on *The World at One* to talk about the Americans dumping nerve gas close to the coast of America. He also recorded an interview for a strand of educational radio programming on Radio 3 called *Prospect*.

The second series of *Doomwatch* was launched in the middle of December with another *Radio Times* cover, and this time the article focused on Kit and his prescient ideas from the first series. The article ended with the claim that one of the thirteen 'frightening new predictions' had already come true. This was 'The Islanders' which followed the fortunes of a group of evacuated Pacific islanders who discovered that their fish had been contaminated with organic mercury from a First World War wreck, killing off the vulnerable.

Whether Kit had any actual involvement in the writing of this episode is forgotten, but it certainly did him no harm. In mid-December Kit was again on Radio 4's *The World at One*, talking about the mercury contamination of fish which had recently been discovered in America and was generating controversy, confusion and alarmist headlines. By the time the episode was screened a few weeks later, the Prophet of Clapham had struck again. This led Jean Trend and others in the cast to wonder whether Kit was a witch!

Kit was on hand for a publicity whirl by the time the second series ended in March 1971, with interviews appearing in the press, on radio and television.

He made no reference to the fact that his involvement with the programme was effectively over, but pushed his case for a real Doomwatch. Kit was accompanied by a film crew from BBC1's *Nationwide* to London's busy Oxford Street on an average working day. London had been notorious in the 1950s for its thick smog which was the result of smoke from domestic and industrial fires, and the Clean Air Act came into force in 1956. In 1968 the bill was strengthened to ensure industrial chimneys were built higher, but as we have seen, the pollution became Scandinavia's acid rain.

Exhaust fumes from cars were not covered by the Act, because they weren't generating the smog seen in Tokyo or Los Angeles. In the finished piece, Kit surveyed Oxford Street. The noise and the carbon monoxide fumes 'have made this whole area of London absolutely intolerable for human habitation. I think the cities have long ago become intolerable for people.'

Kit discussed a test which he had performed for his final contribution to the *Daily Mirror* the previous year:

> I did a small test on myself involving measuring my own carbon monoxide content in my blood. I went to the country, took some readings there, came into the town, and spent all day wandering around London and Oxford Street, and so on, taking repeated measurements of my own blood carbon monoxide level, and towards the end of the day my blood level had reached a point which was only one per cent below the level at which some performance tasks are badly affected.

In 1971, the dangers over lead in petrol became a very big topic, with Professor Derek Bryce Smith from Reading University presenting his research on the harmful effects of the metal on our own biochemistry to a hugely sceptical scientific community. Other countries had banned the substance from their petrol, but not yet in Britain, and his stance was dismissed. People were, as Kit said, conditioned to accept exhaust fumes. This was where a real Doomwatch group, attached to a university, would come into play.[*] Their very first task would be to assemble all the available pollution data from around the world and centralise it in a rapid access computer system. Based on this data, it could be possible to make a prediction of current trends and put in place preventative measures. These students would be encouraged not

---

[*] A college in Plymouth had already launched a 'Doomwatch diploma' in 1970, based on environmental health issues.

to regard themselves as isolated from the political and social world around them, and to allow emotion and ordinary human feelings to enter the scientific arena as Kit had argued in his New Science Group paper.

'The use of students to do most of the scientific data gathering in the seaside example also points up the real Doomwatch's other key role: in education,' wrote Chedd in *New Scientist* when he interviewed Kit in March:

> Hopefully, it would engage in, perhaps, the design of simple biological testing equipment for schools, and the making of films. The leading of field trips for university students would give them valuable experience in applied ecology. But perhaps even more important than any of these specifics is the prodding of people into an awareness of the fact that technology is a two-edged sword: that there is a price to pay for every 'advance'. People must be given an idea of this price – they should be aware of what goes on behind the scenes in the production of a battery chicken, for instance – and be allowed to consider if they are prepared to pay it.

Kit continued this theme on *Nationwide*:

> I think the public now is inaccurately and incompletely informed. One of the things I would like any Doomwatch group to do is to produce data for public consumption. Quite a lot of this work gets tucked away in obscure journals which the public never read. There is nothing wrong, it seems to me, with the proper presentation of data, in an attractive way, to the public, repeatedly, providing the data is accurate. The best way of doing it is to go on showing the public that we are using up our planet… [This is a] leasehold planet, and we don't ever pay the ground rent… If they are properly informed about the data which might come out of any such organisation, I believe in the end they will take action. They will demand changes. In the end, the only pressure can come from the public.

People were conditioned to accept the unnatural:

> I worked out the other day, for example, in London, I hadn't walked on earth for three days. I've walked on concrete or tarmacadam or something like that. It's almost as if we're producing a new species, a sort of man of the city who is an adapted creature and, in my view, already slightly dehumanised.

An unknown magazine asked if he was getting the response he had hoped for from *Doomwatch* viewers:

I take the view that everybody has discussed the dangers of air, ground and water pollution, but what hasn't been discussed is the degree of acceptance that people are showing to the problem. If you like you can call this a pollution of the mind. People have become so used to the horror stories they are continually hearing that they almost accept them as a way of life. Soon they'll be looking with benign smiles at the patterns the foam makes on the rivers.

Then there was another issue: who would foot the bill? Always a good excuse to prevent action at any level from being taken, especially if you were already paying water rates or council levies or purchasing a heavily packaged but legal product. Kit did not know in detail how much it would cost to resolve these issues, as he told *Nationwide* in a London high street, watching the fumes belching out of the back end of motionless cars:

One has to start from the assumption that money is spent for people, not just to fill this whole street up for no reason. If you think of all those cars down there... they're all burning petrol, but they're not moving. We've taken oil out of the ground, we've refined it into petrol, put it into cars, and the cars are remaining stationary. This is not only irrational, it is quite mad. What you have to do is take cars out of this... This is going to cost money and upset shop owners, but it simply has to be done. We have to find a method, a democratic method whereby this can be done.*

Initially, the real Doomwatch would get its funding from a university, or from a few large private donations. Kit felt that once it had a success or two under its belt, the organisation could appeal for funds directly from the public: it would be science for the people, paid for by the people. In this way, it could avoid political pressure or vested interests. Kit hinted to the *Guardian* that he had very rich friends whose consciences might be prised open.

One of these friends may have been Teddy Goldsmith, who had launched the *Ecologist* magazine the previous summer. Goldsmith was a fascinating man, once described as 'the uncle to the radical wing of the international green movement as well as one of its most potent intellectual forces'. The son of Frank Goldsmith, a former Conservative MP and owner of a chain of luxury hotels, Teddy studied Philosophy, Politics and Economics at Oxford,

---

* There was a precedent Kit may not have been aware of. The first pedestrianised city street in the United Kingdom was in Norwich in 1967 called, ironically, London Street, the first of many.

all of which disillusioned him enormously. The world was going to the dogs, and history was designed to justify the process. Having failed in business, he travelled the world looking for rare species before concluding that it was industrialisation and the spread of western-sponsored economic development that was the root cause of social and environmental destruction. He supported the Primitive People's Fund (which became Survival International in 1969) who wanted to protect the right of isolated tribes and indigenous peoples to choose their own path, rather than being forced to become assimilated into modern-day technological societies. Having turned away from conventional academic thought, he moved into the realms of cybernetics, ecology, anthropology and general systems theory to better understand how societies functioned. With the PPF, Goldsmith launched the *Ecologist* magazine calling for a unified theory in science rather than the current reductionist view that Kit too deplored.

The opposition

Laudable though the scheme was, there were those who resented the implication that at the heart of the problem lay the scientist himself. This was the central point of an inaugural lecture at the University of Cape Town by Professor of Electrical Engineering, N. C. de V. Enslin, called 'Should Scientists and Engineers Call a Halt to Research?' He had been alarmed by a series of articles in a South African newspaper which laid the blame for society's ills solely at the doorstep of the scientist. He quoted Kit Pedler's view of the need for a Hippocratic oath for scientists and accepted that the environment needed protecting. However, for Enslin, the villain of the piece was commerce:

> Commerce has availed itself of mass media and conditioned the consumer and worker to fit in with the optimisation of its production system and profit. Industry likes large quantities of the same article, bulk handling and the reduction of the range of different articles that have to be manufactured. It is therefore not surprising that supermarkets have been so successful.

Kit's example of how sewage was expelled into the sea brought in a very angry response to the *New Scientist* after his March 1971 interview. Henry Brinton and Donald Payne had recently been part of the Parliamentary Working Party on Sewage Disposal, who had produced the August 1970 report that angered Kit. They vigorously defended the original 1959 report which had been compiled by 'scientists better qualified than Dr Pedler in this branch of medicine'. They criticised Kit for not mentioning inland towns and their contribution to pollution at sea, and then got to the nub of the issue:

> If the supply of money were illimitable for public purposes, any fool could improve safety standards. What is needed is a cost/benefit analysis. To equip every seaside town with full treatment works would cost many, many millions of pounds. There is not a scintilla of evidence that such expenditure, as against properly sited outfalls of crude sewage, would save a single human life. The same money spent on hospitals or roads would save many hundreds, or probably thousands. Heaven preserve us from self-appointed guardians who cash in on a wave of popular emotion to misdirect the use of scarce public resources.

Meanwhile, out in the Mediterranean the pollution flushed into it from two continents was more acute, and forecasts were being made that it would become a dead ecosystem by the end of the decade.

In the same letters column where he was attacked for his views on sewage disposal, he received support. H. C. Burford from Warwickshire wrote:

> I believe Pedler has put his finger on one of the main causes of the current distaste for science when he talks of its misapplication. Even if his Doomwatch proposal never succeeds in overcoming prejudice and apathy in establishing itself, Pedler will do a great service to science and technology, and to mankind, if he only manages to break open the barriers to allow, as Chedd says, 'emotion and ordinary human feelings of aesthetics to enter the scientific arena'. Pedler certainly won't lack volunteers.

Kit told Chedd that he 'thrives on opposition, and hopes that this article will provoke people into pointing out the weaknesses of his scheme: he wants to get it watertight before he actually launches it out into the world...'

Throughout 1971, Kit continued to push and lobby and lecture the case for a real Doomwatch, trying to make it become a reality. He hosted a seminar at Linacre College in Oxford on 7 June, addressed the Conservation Society in Bayswater, and was invited to return to Imperial College to speak to their branch of the BSSRS.

By the late autumn of 1971, Kit's project was to consist of a nucleus of forty scientists, economists and artists, and would produce a magazine like the consumer protection guide *Which?* A year later, Kit was a guest of Commitment, the Young Liberals environmental group, at a fringe meeting at that year's Liberal Party conference. The meeting was well attended, and he was reported in *New Scientist* as saying that his group would feature a team of fifteen scientists, lawyers and media men. Kit was hoping to extend his work by forming groups all over the country.

By this time, events had somewhat overtaken him. The American pressure groups Friends of the Earth and Greenpeace were becoming established, and a call had been made to set up a British branch. But groups like these operated in a manner different to the one Kit envisaged, and he would not approve of some of their publicity stunts, although he deeply sympathised that it was an effective way to get their message across.

The official guardians

If Kit and his 'ilk' were the self-appointed guardians (or a lone ranger in a lab coat, as Graham Chedd offered), who were the appointed ones? The architect and anarchist Colin Ward, Education Officer for the Town and Country Planning Association, delivered a lecture in 1972 in place of Kit, who was abroad at the time. It had the pleasing title of 'A Doomwatch for Environmental Pollution (a) Pollution of Land – an Enemy of the People':

> The battle for environmental health is fought by thousands of real public health inspectors, medical officers, pollution officers, and officials of local and central government high and low, all of them subject to the constraints that a rigid hierarchical and paternalistic public service tradition involves, together with that minority of the general public which feels a concern for one or other of the issues involved. All of them fallible, few of them powerful, and all operating in a densely populated country which, economically and socially has higher priorities than the health of our environment.

Councils were being deliberately kept in the dark by the polluters themselves, and official reports used the term 'satisfactorily low' to describe pollution levels but would not define what that meant in real terms. Furthermore, getting accurate information as to what was being pumped into your river was virtually impossible. Only the polluter and those in their immediate vicinity were entitled to know, and no one else, not even those living downstream of a discharging plant. Permission was needed from the river authorities to discharge waste into the river, but any monitoring controls were always in the favour of the job-creating polluter.

Ward praised Kit's stance that a real Doomwatch had to be *for* the people:

> Now investigating on behalf of the people is exactly what the professionals of the pollution-monitoring services are supposed to be doing. As their lips were sealed, the growth of independent environment watchdogs in university departments is not only what might be expected but is very much to be welcomed, and the story of the involvement of the University of Bristol's Sabrina project in the Rio Tinto Zinc smelter at Avonmouth indicates how very much in the public interest this independent involvement can be.

There had been lead and zinc smelting plants at Avonmouth since 1917, owned since 1962 by the Rio Tinto Zinc corporation who expanded the site in 1968. There were concerns expressed about the health of the workers on the site, and contamination of the environment beyond the plant; but the company was only interested in meeting minimum standards of pollution control as they increased the productivity of the plant.

Management ignored concerns until the discovery of an employee who had been passed as fit for employment by the company but was found by the local hospital to be suffering from lead poisoning. Another man died from an unrelated illness but had also been contaminated. The company refused to cooperate, and the official Factory Inspectorate were concerned enough to apply for a court order. There had been many cases of lead poisoning in the workforce since 1968, with twenty-five in 1969, and forty in 1971.

Meanwhile, the environment beyond the plant was being monitored by the Alkali Inspectorate, working under weak sixty-year-old legislation. Everything was fine, they said, and Peter Walker made a statement to this effect in Parliament on 3 February 1972. It was fine because the outside monitoring results were based on findings performed by RTZ itself, who reported to a committee on which the Alkali Inspectorate sat along with officials from the city of Bristol and RTZ themselves. On this committee, and under the strict provision that they were not to publicise what they heard, were two scientists from Bristol University's Sabrina Project, who were studying the overall pollution patterns of the Severn estuary. They started to publish results which proved that the pollution from Bristol industry was much higher than the official accounts suggested, and they were promptly forced off the committee.

Ten days after Walker had made his statement, two Sabrina scientists decided to make public their own work into environmental lead pollution.

They were hurriedly invited back onto the committee but were once again barred from disclosing any facts. In a written question to the Minister, Walker was asked whether he would make a further statement on pollution in the neighbourhood of Avonmouth considering reports from scientists at Bristol University. Walker confirmed that the scientists had been asked to prepare a statement of their findings and make it available to Bristol Corporation. An inevitable inquiry investigated the cover-up.

Shortly after this came to light, the Royal Commission on Environmental Pollution issued its second report, 'Three Issues in Industrial Pollution'. It called for an early warning system against the introduction of new products which could cause pollution. The issue 'was not being given adequate priority by the government,' it said. 'While it would not be reasonable to regard substances as guilty until proved innocent, it is reasonable to regard them as under suspicion…' Firms were legally permitted to keep the composition of pollutants a secret on grounds of 'commercial sensitivity'. It urged the government to act sooner since the current plan was to wait until 1975 when a new system of local government would begin to operate 'new comprehensive control of waste disposal'.

Leaving the Institute

In 1971, television and radio wanted Kit's punditry more than ever. He was invited onto the *Today* programme to talk about President Nixon's state of the union address, and for a discussion on 'air versus space' in June. He gave a twenty-minute talk called 'Doomsday or Doomwatch' in the middle of February and spoke on population issues on *Woman's Hour* in July.

Over the summer months, Kit could be seen on television in the first programme of a Sunday teatime discussion programme called *The Eighties*, hosted by Bernard Levin. As the title suggests, it looked towards the next decade, and the first subject was health. *The Times* reviewed it the next day:

> The real need, expressed by both Kit Pedler and Brian Inglis, was for medical education to aim at producing doctors more aware of the whole ethos of modern life, and less disposed towards pill pushing. Fine – but the very fact that Nye Bevan had said it all first emphasised the lack of novelty in the concept; and it is an unfortunate fact that a discussion programme in which – for once – all the participants agree tends very rapidly to become boring.

Punch was less kind:

The introductory film was a dreary aperitif and almost the only useful point to emerge from the discussion – that doctors might be paid for keeping people well rather than for treating their ailments – was one made donkey's years ago by Bernard Shaw, Cyril Joad and Aneurin Bevan.

But, as Kit would argue, repetition was essential.

Controversy on BBC2 might have been more to the critics' taste. Each week, a scientist would put forward his viewpoint (and it was always a he), which was considered controversial in the scientific world, and would be vigorously challenged by a panel of critics. The first programme featured Professor Sir Ernest Chain whose thesis was that scientists working for the defence of their country 'merit our highest respect and esteem. We are surrounded by enemies... capitalism should be maintained at all costs.' Chain had been a refugee from Hitler's Germany, and believed that scientists who commit themselves to work on weapons of mass destruction should not be allowed to opt out – even if they disapprove of the governments they are working for. This was, of course, the antithesis of how Kit believed a scientist should behave. 'When Professor Chain was defending the use of science for what could be called patriotic purposes, he quickly found himself involved in a verbal dust-up with more than one member of the panel,' the *New Scientist* gleefully reported.

Another programme featured Professor Hans Eysenck defending the thesis that some races were incapable of intellectual attainment; a demonstration of 'twenty young, black, beautiful and militant negroes' halted the recording until they were allowed a five-minute say at the end of the programme. One of the other programmes in the series featured Derek Bryce-Smith whose 'controversial' stance was on banning lead from petrol. At this point, Bryce-Smith was advising *Doomwatch* on an episode Terence Dudley was writing about this very issue.* In fact, Bryce-Smith had approached Gerry Davis with an account of a vicar whose erratic behaviour had been caused by lead poisoning. Dudley seized upon the story and, during his research, interviewed the Under Secretary of State at the Department of the Environment, who assured him that, as matters stood, lead was perfectly safe in petrol.

Kit's hardening stance was now too public for it to be ignored at work. Writing children's science fiction was one thing, but what could be seen as

---

* The episode was called 'Waiting for a Knighthood' and is among the few which survive from the third series.

attacks on research scientists were too close to home. One event occurred before *Doomwatch* was transmitted. To the astonishment of his peers at the Institute, he handed in his Home Office licence to experiment on animals on the grounds that it was 'emotionally distasteful'. According to 'canon law', wrote Graham Chedd, 'emotion is not meant to enter into science, so his action to many of his fellows is totally inexplicable, particularly as it is likely to hamstring the progress of his research'. Geoffrey Arden suspected that the real reason for this was that Kit was fed up with the form-filling experiments required. The mistake Kit made was mentioning it in public: 'At one point I was nearly kicked out,' he told the *Guardian* in 1973. 'I wrote about animal experiments which were being conducted for careerist rather than scientific purposes. I knew perfectly well that it was true but I made the mistake of saying so in a daily paper and so they tried to grind my testicles in public.' His growing sideline in *Doomwatch* was alienating his colleagues. 'I got a tremendous amount of crap flung at me. I was a popularist, I was a fiction writer. I had to take this and my skin was no thicker than anyone else's and it upset me a great deal.'

Carol Topolski: 'I know he was terribly hurt from the attacks that he experienced from the Institute, from his friendly, cooperative colleagues, and I can only speculate what lay behind that. I certainly think they wanted him out.'

Some have suggested that there was an element of jealousy and resentment by rival colleagues towards Kit and his profile. Others felt he was becoming vain and egotistical, and there's no denying that. He did have a large ego and enjoyed the attention. Dr S. S. Hayrah, who was now working in Edinburgh, was surprised to find Kit on the television 'as the BBC's expert to give opinions totally unrelated to his work at the Institute of Ophthalmology and I suppose his professional training'. He certainly wasn't afraid to raise his unpopular views at the University of London's Senate House meetings.

On Thursday 10 June 1971, Kit gave the prestigious Edridge Green lecture at the Institute for the Royal College of Surgeons. The annual lecture was devoted, although not exclusively, to subjects relating to colour vision, and a bronze medal was awarded to the lecturer. His chosen subject was 'Retina Ultra-Structure and the Signal Pathway'. It was to be his apotheosis as a university academic.

Una remembered that he wanted to work part-time towards the end of his career but this was not allowed. He had been in ophthalmology since

1955; perhaps a change of direction was needed. There may be no more television writing to do at present, but he and Gerry Davis had a three-book deal and a movie lined up. Even the stage play was still an open possibility.

Carol certainly felt the attitude developing within the Institute helped him make his final decision to leave behind his academic career. 'It was push and pull. The pull of really enjoying the writing and getting onto a different stage but also push from his colleagues who were falling out with what he was saying and believing.'

Kit resigned and was gone by October 1971. In the annual report for 1970/71, the Department of Anatomy is listed as having no director, simply the lecturers and research assistants, and in the following year there was no longer such a department. Kit's departure was not mentioned in either of these two reports. People came and went all the time, but for such a senior man not to have his departure noted may have been indicative of how they felt towards his leaving behind academic life.

Freed from an environment that was increasingly feeling alien and sterile to him, Kit could now speak his mind without fear of ridicule or censure. In the years to come, he would launch fierce broadsides against the conditioned mindset in the scientific community, giving voice to those who dare not put their heads above the laboratory table, fearing harm to their careers, or reputations. No wonder Kit would begin to describe himself as a 'defrocked scientist'. He had a new way to describe scientists who helped industrialists: 'ingenious toymakers'. Kit was never elected an FRS, a Fellow of the Royal Society, yet he had another meaning for the acronym in mind whenever he heard it: Failed Responsible Scientist.

A plethora of radio series called on his scientific knowledge; in December alone he appeared on *Speak Easy, New Worlds* and *Dial-A-Scientist*. On more than one occasion he could be heard, on different radio stations, twice on the same day. His appearances did not go without some teasing from his family. 'Whenever there was a crisis, it was "Send for Pedler!"' Mark Pedler remembered.

It gave him a platform, and would prove very useful indeed, but Carol Topolski did have a serious concern with his ubiquitous appearances:

> He was a terrific communicator, but I felt that he was diminishing his currency by being so available for comment on absolutely everything. But it goes to people's heads, doesn't it? He loved all that. I remember thinking, for

God's sake, you don't need to be commenting on floral arrangements in some hall! I'm satirising, but he was very willing to talk about anything.

There had also been a broadcast in November reminding listeners, in case anyone had forgotten, that he was still in a science-fiction writer partnership. *Ideas in Science Fiction* was hosted by his friend Dr Christopher Evans, and had been recorded a year before in November 1970. Evans and his guest for that week would talk about 'the philosophical ideas underlying science fiction and try to discover what relation it bears to man's present condition'. Kit's subject was alternative life forms.

From time to time Kit was also called upon to provide an article for the newspapers, such as the *Daily Mail* in 1972 about natural pest control, or an interview with a physicist for the *Radio Times*. As in the latter case, they weren't always accepted. A joint venture between Kit and Gerry was proposed in August 1971: a series of articles on topics like pollution but from the viewpoint of 1978, called *The Doomwatch Files*.

Mutant 59

They may have lost control of *Doomwatch*, but beyond television, Kit and Gerry were free to continue writing their prophetic tales, freed from the restrictions of a cautious and traditional broadcaster. Through their agent, Harvey Unna, they secured a publishing deal with Ernest Hecht, creator and owner of Souvenir Books Ltd.

They wanted to tell an exciting scientific thriller with brand-new characters and situations, unrestrained by budget. They could wipe out half of London if they so wished, and very much did. They decided to go back to their very first idea about a man-made plastic-eating virus and see what would happen if it was unleashed into the modern world. It seemed to have caught the imagination of those who watched the episode earlier in the year, more so than any other concept of the first series.

Since their original script had been written in 1968, there had been some more developments in solving the problem of plastic waste. One research group under Professor Gerald Scott of Aston University in Birmingham looked into how to make a plastic bottle crumble into an easily disposable powder when it became exposed to sunlight. Scott was not thinking of developing a virus, and was actually against the idea when such a thing was proposed for clearing up oil slicks in 1971. Scott's work was mentioned in a comment piece in the *Daily Mirror* in July, where they mentioned that their own Doomwatch team were looking into the problems of plastic waste. 'Hurry up with that secret weapon, Professor!' urged the anonymous author. This was enough to give Kit and Gerry their first push. If plastic, sealed between two sun-proof sheets of another biodegradable material, does break down into a powder when exposed to sunlight, the remains will probably be washed away down the sink. Supposing the process is perfected, and that this material (which they christened Degron) becomes used under licence for the making of disposable plastic bottles? That means there will be a lot of powder residue down in the sewers. Now if a plastic-eating virus was being secretly developed by a scientist at his home, and the virus was accidentally released, say washed down the sink, it would have access to a huge supply of food. As a virus, it could rapidly multiply, learn, evolve and gorge on any type of plastic, perhaps excreting a toxic and flammable gas as part of the process. Trapped gas could build up under certain points until it is ignited by a chance event, say a lit cigarette chucked into a drain. Once the virus had built up in strength, changing and evolving, nothing could stop its spread across the world, or even onto other worlds.

Kit and Gerry imagined how dormant spores of the virus could find their way inside a factory that was building a particular microcircuit component. All the spores had to do was wait for warmth and moisture to wake them up, and then they would start to feed on the plastic insulation around it. In the story they imagined the failure of Logic Gate 13 to be the prelude for a series of disasters. There is a plane crash near Heathrow; a Polaris submarine vanishes without trace; an Apollo launch explodes; a computer system designed to regulate traffic flow breaks down; and a giant toy robot in a department store runs amok. At first, the cause of the malfunctions is put down to component failure, and then the explosions that rock central London bring forth the discovery of a foul slurry underneath the streets of the city, obviously sourced from the residue of Degron.

Kit and Gerry produced a strong and exciting plot, describing how London is brought to its knees in what would be described by one American reviewer as 'the most riveting novel of speculative fiction since *The Andromeda Strain*'. As the story unfolds, we are privy to events which the major protagonists are not. We learn how the virus came into being, and what lay behind the catastrophes which the book vividly describes. It was an excellent mixture of Gerry's narrative skills, and Kit's experience of putting across a plausible scientific point of view, perfectly complementing each other. Gerry enjoyed writing situations within claustrophobic settings and set a large section of the book in the underground railway system.

Kit's 'attitude' is on every page, but there are passages in the book that are clearly written by Kit alone, demonstrating that he did more than just offer ideas which Gerry then turned into prose. He explores his view that London was ground, rather than land. In one section he described the complicated network of tunnels that are beneath your feet at King's Cross where the first major disaster occurs, some sixteen years before a genuine tragedy struck the station. He describes the passenger entering the underground system, escaping the polluting stench of car exhaust pipes 'from an area which has long since become intolerable for any real man-machine coexistence'. The licence to produce the Degron bottles is purchased by a soft-drink manufacturer who 'wanted a new gimmick to sell the mixture of tartaric acid, citric acid, saccharin and colouring which he shamelessly called Tropic Delight'.

There are several sections that take us inside the mind of a scientist who has a 'good and original idea'; how they are developed, and the problems faced with getting them accepted and turned into practical expression. One such development is the Degron bottle itself; another is proposed by one Lionel Slayter, whose PhD in communications theory led him to study traffic patterns in Brooklyn whilst flying overhead in a helicopter. He likens the cars moving along congested lanes to blood cells in a vessel, and develops an idea to take a localised system of roads and turn it into something resembling a biological unit, echoing his previous work as a biologist. This gives him the idea of how to develop a traffic control system for London that will keep traffic moving, controlled by a computer system that learns from the pattern of traffic behaviour.

Kit's most obvious solo effort is the story of the man who nearly wipes out London, Dr Ainslie. He is a bacteriologist leading a dull, academic life in a teaching hospital, where medical students scare him with their 'sense of youth and attack', and sets up whimsical experiments in the hope of gathering enough material to be published in a journal. One day, while removing a piece of plastic which is blocking the drain outside his house, Ainslie hits upon a novel idea. What if bacteria could be induced to attack plastic debris? Kit describes how Ainslie becomes very excited by the idea as he works out the practicalities. He has indulgent fantasies about being awarded an FRS, or even a Nobel Prize. Kit also notes how Ainslie begins to slowly imagine results, nudging a figure here and there, something he himself had witnessed in other researchers over the years.

After a few months, Ainslie produces the fifty-ninth strain of a bacterium which consumes plastic. In his excitement, he suffers a cerebral haemorrhage; in his death spasm, the variant ends up in the sink and passes down into the drains. His obituary opens the book. Kit would reuse some of Ainslie's background for his last published short story called 'White Caucasian Male', in which a similar scientist called Anderson experiments with a section of cells taken from a dead donor. He invents a new, original and exciting technique, replicates them, and sends samples to other laboratories around the world. Unfortunately, the cells exert a malignant influence over him which drives him to his death, but not before he imagines the effect on those who received the samples.

The most familiar attitude on display was deployed with the major characters in the book. Arnold Kramer is a scientist who creates a consultancy in London designed to put science to good use for the benefit of mankind. Unfortunately, the money brought in by their breakthrough product – the new plastic aminostyrene, and later the self-destructing plastic bottle – changes Kramer's attitude and he becomes the businessman. All that matters is whether The Idea makes money. Another scientist, Gerrard, had been invited to join the consultancy during its early idealistic days, but he had only been able to join it two months before the events of the book unfold. His belief in the original purpose remains, and he is saddened to discover the change in Kramer. The consultancy is part of the investigation into the alleged component failure, and the possible failure of aminostyrene, and eventually into finding a solution for the rampaging virus. In the only scene that was lifted from the original *Doomwatch* episode, Kramer takes a sample of the virus over to America by plane, and it escapes on board. The major difference this time is that the flight does not reach its destination.

Gerrard is the one to connect the virus with the Degron in the sewers, and is aware that the consultancy bears part of the responsibility for the disaster by having created Degron in the first place. As he says, 'None of us set out to do anything more than be technically ingenious. We succeeded and London nearly died.'

The book was finished by March 1971 and was called *The Death of Plastic*, before settling for the more lurid *Mutant 59: The Plastic Eater*. Kit had hoped that its royalties might go towards funding a real Doomwatch. It was published in February 1972 in hardback in Britain, Canada and the USA, and Pan produced its own paperback edition in Britain, reusing Julian Cottrell's *Radio Times* cover which promoted 'The Plastic Eaters'. It would later be published in Germany, Italy, Japan, France (as *La Mort du Plastique*) and Holland.

The *Guardian* promoted the paperback edition in 1973 with a rare joint interview with Kit and Gerry, where their previous work on *Doctor Who* and *Doomwatch* was discussed, as well as the origins and purpose of their book:

> It may seem unlikely that, as the first biodegradable milk bottle goes on sale in their novel, another scientist working in the same area of self-destruct plastic should release a plastic-eating virus into the sewers of London. But then no one ever thought the Americans would accidentally drop a nuclear warhead in Texas. The fact that we can read such a book and then toddle off to bed for a peaceful night's sleep is a small example of our conditioning which scientists like Kit Pedler would like to change.

The big screen

In 1971, *Mutant 59: The Plastic Eater* was optioned by Tigon British Films Ltd, which was just as well, for they were about to make the *Doomwatch* movie, with a chance for it to be released in America. So far, the only other country to have seen *Doomwatch* was Canada in 1971, but they only saw the second series and a few selected episodes from the first beginning with 'Tomorrow, the Rat'. Tigon Films was based in London, and since 1966 had been making and distributing films including those for which they are best remembered – lurid horror movies. Kit and Gerry worked on the storyline and script, which was developed into a final screenplay by Clive Exton, who was a business partner with Dalek creator Terry Nation.

The producer was Tony Tenser, Tigon's creator. At first, he did not want any of the television characters to appear in the film, but Kit and Gerry insisted. It wouldn't matter if they were 'unknowns' in America; their roles in the film would be explained, as would any other character. Tenser insisted on a new *Doomwatch* character who could be played by a name, and this was Ian Bannen. He would get the plum starring role in the film, playing Dr Del Shaw, whose role was similar to the one Simon Oates had played on the television. This sidelining of the regular cast did not go down too well with Oates, who readily admitted that he took the part simply for the money.

Kit and Gerry took ideas from their deep-sea dumping episode 'Burial at Sea', and combined them with hormones getting into an isolated community's diet and dramatically affecting them, which came from 'The Battery People' and 'The Islanders'. The story sees Dr Shaw being sent to an island community called Balfe that has recently recovered from an oil slick. He discovers a paranoid and hostile community, trying to keep secret a hideous deformity that is spreading across their population, for which they blame themselves following centuries of inbreeding. This was based on a genuine condition called acromegaly. Shaw discovers that they have been ingesting a hormone that has been illegally dumped in an area of sea reserved for radioactive waste. Shaw and the Doomwatch team fight to uncover the truth, in the face of the hostile community and official cover-ups. Despite their best efforts, the islanders must admit defeat, and leave their island home forever.

The oil slick Shaw was investigating had occurred in real life back in 1967. The BP-chartered supertanker *Torrey Canyon* hit a reef between Land's End and the Scilly Isles. 119,328 tonnes of oil leaked out into the sea, heading for the coasts of Cornwall, France and Guernsey. The smell got there first. BP and the Dutch tanker owners sent in experts to help, but eventually the British government sent in the RAF to bomb the vessel and set fire to the oil. This did not work, even when they used napalm. A week after the shipwreck, the oil reached the west coast of Cornwall, which got off lightly compared to Guernsey. A rapid clean-up operation transferred the oil to a nearby quarry where it still sat in 2010. The detergents used in the clean-up turned out to have worse effects on the ecosystem than the oil.

The film was made during the autumn of 1971, directed by Peter Sasdy. He was new to film directing, and took the message of the film quite seriously, favouring a documentary style: '*News at Ten* plus entertainment,' as he put it. Kit was on set, helping to set up any scientific equipment, and showed Bannen how to dissect a fish for analysis. He brought his family down to the studios to watch some of the filming. Mark Pedler recalled:

> Dear old Dad, he was vainglorious, and he was showing off because he wanted to look his best in front of us kids. He had the script in his hand. They were rehearsing a scene and we were up on some kind of a gantry, overlooking the studio. Dad shouted down to the director, 'Oh, can we change that word from such-a-beam to such-a-beam?' He wanted to demonstrate he was part of the ongoing thing, but I thought, you silly old fool!

'Scientist Doctor Kit Pedler… has done it again!' shrieked the *Daily Mirror* in January 1972. Kit began to wonder if he did indeed have powers of prophecy when, a month after filming had finished, an environmental catastrophe threatened one of their filming locations. 'When we read of the incident we were absolutely shattered,' he told *Saturday Titbits* in 1972. 'For one moment we began to believe there must be a little devil sitting on our shoulders.'

They had filmed at a Cornish coastal village called Polkerris. It had avoided the worst of the *Torrey Canyon* disaster, but it didn't escape this time. In December 1971, a Spanish freighter called the *Germania* was shipwrecked near the Channel Islands. A couple of weeks later, its cargo of 'Drums of Death' (as the *Daily Mirror* put it) started to wash up upon the Cornish shore. The navy and government scientists from Porton Down ('Nothing sinister in that,' stressed a government spokesman) began a search along a hundred miles of coastline to recover them. However, the number of drums estimated to be at sea had risen to three thousand. These orange canisters each contained forty-five gallons of toluene diisocyanate. It gave off a highly irritating vapour and was potentially explosive. The ethyl acetate drums were white, and contact with the liquid was harmful to the skin.

If this wasn't enough, a few days after the alert it emerged that a *second* cargo of toxic chemicals was heading towards the same coast. This cargo had been washed from the deck of a Somali-registered ship during a gale somewhere off Land's End on 19 December, two days before the *Germania* sank. The new menace was termed by the insurers Lloyds of London 'flashpoint zero'. In other words, potentially lethal. That two cargoes were mingling together was not known about until a Cornish fire chief had a talk over a cup of tea with a ministry chemist. The film makers seized upon this piece of enormous serendipity, or coincidence. 'A chilling story from today's headlines!' boasted their publicity material. Kit told the *Daily Mirror*: 'I wish we could put [the film] on general release tomorrow.'

It was released in June and, like the *Germania*, sank without trace. Plans to make a follow-up movie based on *Mutant 59: The Plastic Eater* were abandoned, despite a script being written.

In light of the canister spill, and perhaps with memories of the sheer breathtaking amateurism in dealing with the 1967 oil slick, Kit called for the creation of a National Disaster Force, which would deal with environmental disasters such as the two that had afflicted Cornwall:

Recent events in Cornwall have emphasised the potential dangers involved and have shown very clearly that there is no organisation equipped and trained to deal with these materials in time. Days elapsed before any effective action was taken, and then once a recovery operation was seen by the media to be in operation, one of the ministers involved visited the area and was reported to have said 'I came looking for a disaster and couldn't find it.' This type of continued complacency does nothing to help a situation which is rapidly growing more dangerous. It was purely by chance that the Cornish people were protected from exposure to lethal material, and the fact that no one died reflects credit on no one at all.

He spoke on this theme at a seminar organised in June 1972 by the London Co-op Summer School at Longborough called 'The Alternative Society', where he was the principal speaker.*

At the end of March 1972, Kit and Gerry set about distancing themselves from the new series of *Doomwatch*, no longer confident it still represented their message and needing to protect themselves. They wrote a joint letter to Terence Dudley to protest at having been excluded from the scripting process. Dudley suspected that the 'originators' were looking for a quote to give to the press. The BBC wrote back to Kit and Gerry, suggesting that any statement they wished to make regarding their lack of involvement in the new series of *Doomwatch* was down to them, and not the BBC. Dudley had noticed Kit's ubiquitous appearances on the subject and wrote to John Gould, hoping that Kit's conversion to the cause of ecology hadn't made him a bore.

The third series went on air in its traditional Monday-night slot but in early June. 'Fire and Brimstone' was written and directed by Terence Dudley himself. Because Simon Oates would only agree to do four episodes, John Ridge was to be written out as a permanent cast member in this episode; the way Dudley chose to do it was for his character to crack under the pressure of his job, and demand that governments make wholesale changes to the way they respond to environmental issues, and to completely overhaul our industrial and technological way of life. His demand is backed up by six stolen phials of anthrax, which he sends to major cities around the world.

---

* Gerry Davis subsequently drafted a proposal for a series called *Worldforce 5* which featured an international Doomwatch, headed by a man once again called Kramer. In memory of his daughter who had died after swimming in mercury effluent discharged offshore, he and his team ruthlessly investigate and solve ecological disasters.

The rest of the story dealt with Special Branch trying to trick Ridge into revealing where he had sent them. The Doomwatch team sit back and watch the events unfold. By the end of the story, Ridge attempts suicide, and the episode ends ambiguously as it appears that he might die in his prison hospital bed, muttering his farewells to Quist.

Perhaps Terence Dudley hoped that the episode would generate a reaction as great as that which greeted Toby Wren's death and put *Doomwatch* firmly back on the TV map. It drew a reaction, but not the one he was hoping for. The reviews were uniformly bad. Seeing a popular character like Ridge acting completely out of character, and in a plot *Doomwatch* previously took care not to do, was too much to be credible. It played right into Kit and Gerry's hands. In the *Daily Express*, Kit was reported to have said: 'This was a travesty of the programme's intention to reflect the dangers of science based on realistic scientific ideas. Instead the BBC reverted to a 1930s style mad scientist epic. It is no more than horizontal toothpaste.' Kit and Gerry had their names removed from the *Radio Times* as 'originators' of the programme. Mary Holland, writing for the *Observer*, decided in light of Kit Pedler's denunciation of the series not to bother writing her own review lamenting the trivialising of a series 'which was originally so exciting and intelligent. In the event, Dr Pedler said it all: "Just a spy thriller." Absolutely awful, a mad scientist going amok yet again.'

It was later explained that Ridge had been suffering from lead poisoning, but by then it was too late. The criticism of credibility, mingled with complaints that the stories were boring, set the tone for the rest of the series. There were a couple of positive responses to the new series in the *Radio Times*, but in general the reactions to this and other episodes were similar in tone: without Kit Pedler's imagination, *Doomwatch* had lost its way, and was now just an ordinary drama programme. The BBC themselves privately admitted that the programme had run its course, and that they had used up most of the available ideas. *Doomwatch* limped off the air in August, watched by barely five million viewers.

Privately, Terence Dudley was deeply hurt and angered by Kit's statement. He received support from his colleagues, in particular John Gould, who shared the same taste in drama presentation. 'Kit, to say the least,' Dudley wrote, 'is being highly unprofessional, but who's to know that? Internecine squabbles make good copy. I can't hit back – hence a letter such as yours is doubly welcome. One's peers are all that matter in the long run.' When all is said and done, Terence Dudley was firmly committed to the programme, and was very proud of its achievements. Interviewed many years later, Dudley regretted the falling out that he had had with Kit Pedler, and still considered Gerry Davis a friend.

Although Kit had burnt his bridges with the BBC's drama department, another BBC producer called John Percival wanted to use him. Percival was a groundbreaking anthropologist and film maker. He was putting together the first documentary series devoted to environmental themes, intended to advise the public on how to take action for themselves in the manner of any other consumer affairs programme. 'I want to show how the environment affects all of us – in our jobs, in our homes, our food and our leisure time,' Percival told the press when the series was announced. 'Some of the problems will arouse gloom, but we believe they need not spell doom.' One edition of the programme revealed how a road in the Snowdonia National Park was created simply to film a commercial for Milk Tray, while the trade in pickled songbirds prompted six hundred viewers to write in to the RSPCB.

Kit scripted a series of parodies of commercials, 'the best of which,' wrote Mary Holland in the *Observer*, 'was a seductively photographed send-up of Coca-Cola's peace and love commercial, done to a background of a clattering rubble of empty Coke cans'.

Kit and Gerry still hoped to make another series and developed a new idea called *1999: The Year of the Rat*. We were to see what the world was going to be like by the end of the millennium, should no action be taken. Envisaged as a kind of *Dr Kildare* of the future, the prognosis was not pretty. Thanks to antibiotic resistance, a plague breaks out in 1978, spread by poison-resistant rats. By 1999, the city state just manages to function, but it remains on a knife edge. Even as a set of notes, it was prophetic in one respect: 'It became clear that the environmentalists had hysterically overstated their case, and thus their credibility dropped almost to zero and the process of unlimited technological growth gathered weight once again, straining the control system of government and order to breaking point.'

Curiously, April 1975 saw the launch of a new post-apocalyptic series called *Survivors*, dealing with those who had survived a devastating flu-like epidemic which had wiped out most of the world's population. It was produced by Terence Dudley. The series followed the efforts of a group of survivors making do in a world with no electricity, running water, antibiotics, supermarkets, law and order, or those other modern conveniences we take for granted. The press latched onto Dudley's *Doomwatch* credentials, and some thought that this was another creation by Kit Pedler and Gerry Davis. In fact, it was the brainchild of Dalek creator Terry Nation, a writer very much attuned with the prophets of doom the early seventies and late sixties had produced. He envisaged that any survivors would try to live without anything that they couldn't replace and would obviously have to turn to self-sufficiency once scavenging had run its course. Self-sufficiency was a popular theme for the time and, as we will see, there was no one better qualified in 1975 to advise on a programme like *Survivors* than one Kit Pedler. Except, of course, he didn't. And Terence Dudley fell out with Terry Nation over the quality of his storytelling too.

12
Luddite Desperadoes and Defrocked Scientists

> The road back to our green and pleasant land won't be easy. Please don't make it at all sound simple, because it's not. But at least everybody can become involved. It will mean changing our style of living, doing without some of the conveniences we've grown to expect... If we don't do something about our environment soon, there won't be a planet for us to look and smell beautiful on.
> – Kit Pedler in *Saturday Titbits*, 1972

THE DRUMS ALONG THE Cornish coast began what was to become an amazing year for environmental awareness. Had Kit Pedler and Gerry Davis not already created the word 'doomwatch', it would surely have been invented for 1972 as the battle lines for the environment were firmly laid down. It boiled down to one simple issue: economic growth generated by expanding industry, increasing consumption, and rampant pollution, versus sustainability and minimal waste.

A special edition of the *Ecologist* magazine called 'A Blueprint for Survival' (later to become a book) was published in January 1972, borrowing David Dickson's phrase from 1970. Endorsed by scientists (and criticised by others such as *Nature* magazine), it looked for answers to the pollution and population debates. It identified unchecked economic growth as the problem and recommended that society needed to be broken down into smaller, localised units of living. This flew in the face of conventional economic wisdom. When questioned by *The Times* on 15 January, Peter Walker, who headed the Department for the Environment, commended the authors for their concern but disagreed with the suggestion that economic growth should be stopped, returning to what Walker described as 'primitive living'. Without economic growth, he argued, he would be unable to find the resources to clear slums, improve public transport, restore derelict land, and clean the air and the rivers.

This debate was touched upon in the pages of *New Scientist* later that March. An editorial spoke of the need for five per cent growth in the British economy, and a letter quickly arrived to criticise this 'deplorable naivety'. Restraining growth was anathema to politicians and industrialists. Growth was limitless, and supply would always meet demand, creating more jobs, therefore generating greater taxes, which creates a better standard of living.

In March, the Club of Rome published their report into *The Limits to Growth*. It asked the question: could mankind continue consuming the world's resources of fossil fuels and minerals and supply food at the current rate of population increase? To find the answer, three systems scientists used a computer at the Massachusetts Institute of Technology, and developed a systems theory later called the Meadows-Meadows model named after two of the authors, husband and wife Dennis and Donella Meadows. The report demonstrated the contradiction between unlimited consumption and finite resources. The Earth is a finite system, and can only provide so much material, and can only absorb so much waste. More capital and energy must be used to provide more energy and resources. If current trends continued, the limits to growth would be reached within a century, followed by a sudden and uncontrollable decline – the post-industrial age. This could be avoided if proper alterations were made immediately. The world would then establish a condition of ecological and economic stability, sustainable far into the future even with a larger population.

The report was a work in progress, and the reaction it generated was polarised along familiar lines, but it was difficult to ignore since the Club of Rome were not a fringe group of radical students or counter-culture hippies. They were not making alarmist predictions, nor prophesying doomsday, nor is there anywhere in the book a prediction that oil would run out by the end of the millennium, as is often believed to be the case.

Kit felt it was the most significant study of the subject at that moment and was not surprised by the negative reactions to either 'Blueprint' or *Limits*.

The basic point had a huge impact on his thinking, reinforcing his belief that a new direction for science was desperately needed. Sounding something like an Old Testament prophet, Kit declared in *Saturday Titbits* in 1972: 'For years, for the sake of a quick profit and boosting the economy, we've taken the riches out of the earth. We've snatched at all her materials without putting anything back. Now she's demanding payment.'

He knew that the message would be ignored because the goal of twentieth-century western society was to demonstrate your wealth through status symbols, escaping the shameful poverty and starvation. Kit told Patrick Rivers for his 1975 book *The Survivalists*:

> Technical man is totally conditioned to accept the artefacts from a great industrial complex, without any regard for the consequences to all – globally or environmentally. He still thinks that as long as there are Concordes, deep-freezes and ten different varieties of frozen peas, with the enormous and totally mendacious commercialisation that goes with them to induce him to buy them all, all is well. He is totally conditioned to accept it all. Technical man, particularly in the cities, has never been shown the effect of all those things on the earth around him. He sees a new factory going up and he thinks 'Great – that means more employment for more people'. He omits to realise, to quote just one side-effect, that the area covered by the factory is an area of potential agricultural land gone forever. He doesn't see the full circle because he has never been educated to think this way. Everything around him in the commercial world, where he lives, teaches him that all this growth is good and produces civility for him.
>
> In fact it is a short term thing which is already collapsing from the inside, but he is not allowed to hear this. The forces of large, industrial and political organisations teach him that all is well when it manifestly isn't. In a cash-based society we only recognise changes in costs, so that economists talk about 'inflation'. But what is really happening is that the earth is becoming like a wrinkled apple and drying up...
>
> It's a terrible conditioning system. There's no board of evil managing directors doing it, no one man at the top saying 'right, we've got to keep these people quiet'. It just happens. The profit motive is at the root of it. Your top industrialists bent on profit – they are the victims as well, pathetic creatures who have to work to keep the system going. They would like the alternative but they don't know how to do it, because they're as conditioned as anyone else – they're just richer.
>
> At the end of the day, it was us, propping it up. We need to take a look at ourselves and see the changes we had to make. If we could. If we *would*. We

have got ourselves conditioned like trained rats in a cage to accept the rewards in the form of a continuous stream of shining artefacts and conveniences. Much like primitive tradesmen who accepted glass beads in exchange for their birthright, we accept a gleaming car or brilliantly enamelled washing machine – but in exchange for what?

In another interview for an unknown magazine, Kit was asked what people could do to cut down on their own pollution:

Well, apart from the classic middle-class outlet, which is to buy a nice little place in Wales which you then proceed to pollute in the same way that you do in NW1, you could for example examine the refuse that goes out from your house, and see just how much of it won't rot down… The people with a big case to answer for are the packagers. You buy an object and it's wrapped in polythene, polystyrene foam, brown paper – I always refuse it in shops. I say 'Listen, I bought the article; you can keep the bloody wrappings, you can throw them away.' The packaging is just done to condition the public, because the wrappings look nice; they simply serve to tart up the product.

Occasionally, Kit would be stopped by store detectives, convinced he had been shoplifting. This could be acutely embarrassing if anyone accompanied him on such an expedition, as Gerry Davis once did. Packaging was not just unnecessary in most cases but could also be more expensive to produce than the product it contained.

In a 1974 conference in Amsterdam called 'The Truth About Garbage', he spoke about a 'certain well known soft drink' whose can is made from steel and aluminium: 'Ninety-two per cent of the cost of this product is in packaging. The rest is teeth-rotting rubbish. Anything more insane would be hard to imagine.' He examined the cost of an aerosol deodorant and discovered that eighty-two per cent of the contents was propellant. The remaining eighteen per cent was deodorant, two per cent of which was a chemical which Kit could buy in bulk for fifteen pence, and that was enough to charm five hundred pairs of armpits for three years.

He admired the recycling methods practised in America where you would find giant bins for broken bottles outside their supermarkets. 'You just bring along your old bottles, sling them in and they're taken back to the factory to be ground up and reused.' He wanted to see milk bottles delivered to your doorstep (which was the style of the time) done away with and replaced by a tanker which would arrive in your road to top up your supplies. Supermarkets had yet to drive the milkman practically out of existence.

He could find examples of needless waste in his beloved cars. The bumper was merely for decoration and could not save the bodywork of a car in a collision. Why not have wooden ones instead? 'We could leave the copper, nickel and chromium where it is and plant more forests... Properly polished or painted, a wooden bumper could be just as decorative and more effective. And what's more important, wood can be recycled,' he told *Saturday Titbits*.

To drive home the point that we were all culpable, he used water as an example. 'Britain's water table is sinking. People tend to blame industry, but householders waste a tremendous amount. I was watching one of my sons clean his teeth the other day. He was letting the water run. Next time I put the plug in and measured how much he would have wasted – nearly a gallon. If half of London's population clean their teeth once a day and leave the water running, they waste four million gallons.'

These were simple examples that anyone could relate to and understand, but Kit did not want to go around simply ticking people off. They needed to be shown the alternative.

Soft technology

A significant idea which emerged from the New Science Group was written up by journalist Robin Clarke and titled 'The Third Alternative'. It recognised that we needed a new 'softer' technology, reflecting our real dependency upon the natural world from which industry and technology had taken us away. Soft technology would use renewable energy sources and easily accessible materials which would generate recyclable waste where possible, and without any dangerous artificial by-products. It would impact not just on how we lived within our world, but with each other. Technology could be adjusted to suit the local environment since one size would not fit all. It would allow for a greater personal freedom, one no longer totally dependent on the state or large organisations. At least, that was the theory.

Clarke had been influenced by the work being carried out by the New Alchemy Institute in America who had been exploring these issues since the late sixties. Created by a Canadian biologist called John Todd, it had been studying the impact of man upon the natural world. Based at an old dairy farm at Woods Hole in Massachusetts, Todd and his wife Nancy wanted to create 'human support systems' derived from 'renewable energy, agriculture, aquaculture, housing and landscapes', to achieve 'a minimal reliance on fossil fuels and operate on a scale accessible to individuals, families and small groups'. The idea was not to create profit but to create rich and stable lives 'independent of world fashion and the vagaries of international economics'. Nancy wanted the Institute to show scientists had a human face.

Clarke wanted to import the Institute's ideas to Britain. Peter Harper was impressed enough by what he saw to 'wrangle' some money out of UNESCO to fund a report on soft technology and present a case for paid research. With Andy McKillop, he organised a conference to discuss the new approach to technology at University College London in February 1972. The name Harper gave the meeting, and the new science, was Alternative Technology (AT).

Clarke announced his plans in a paper called 'The Soft Technology Research Community'. He proposed setting up BRAD – the Biotechnical Research and Development centre. This would be a working commune containing a handful of families, living in an abandoned farmhouse in a depopulated part of Wales, where they could experiment with wind and solar power, farming and housing practices. Biotechnics was a new word coined by MacKillop to emphasise the ecological aspect of their work. 'Perhaps the most valuable part of the paper,' Harper wrote in *Undercurrents* a few years later, 'was a table contrasting 35 features of "hard technology society" with ideal features of "soft technology society". It was outrageously partial but unrivalled as a kicking off for discussion.' A lot of hard work lay ahead.

Ultimately, Harper felt that the conference was a shambles as it revealed a serious fault line: politics. Most of the people who were interested in AT were scientists, engineers and architects, but a lot of them were younger and political students. The left saw alternative technologies not just as a way of lessening the environmental impact on the Earth, but as a complete liberation from the state and the end of destructive capitalism. 'I particularly remember the plaintive cry, "What's all this about revolution? I came here to talk about windmills."'

Kit was not going to withdraw with his family to join Clarke in Wales, nor explore self-sufficiency in Somerset as BBC producer John Percival had done. This simply wasn't an option for most urban dwellers with one low-paying job and who did not own their own home. Teddy Goldsmith was producing the *Ecologist* magazine from a farm in Cornwall, Clarke had writing to fall back on, Percival was still a documentary film maker, and his wife was a writer. Although the appeal was understandable, the idea of quitting your job, selling up your home and moving into six acres of land soon became seen as, and was sent up as, a middle-class eccentricity. Kit was certain that the primary place for experimenting in alternative living should be urban, simply because that is where most people lived. Like Harper, Kit recognised that AT had to be employed in the west, the biggest consumers of resources in the world, and that its use should be encouraged in developing third world countries, steering them away from our industrialised trap.

Kit told the *Daily Express* in 1974:

> You would have to be damned incompetent to fail to be self-supporting with a farmhouse and several acres of useful land. There is a technology for that. We call it agriculture. You've got to approach it on an urban basis. But no one has yet solved the problem of producing an urban house, with extremely low energy requirements, virtually self-sufficient for water and providing conditions for a humane existence that are as good as if not better than anything now available to ordinary people.

Kit also disliked the commune idea because it smacked of parasitic 'dropping out' of society and solved nothing. There were young radical architects calling themselves the Street Farmers who had set up inner-city communes by squatting inside unoccupied buildings. 'Peace and love' communes were popular in America, such as Drop City, where a group of 'dropouts' had set up an artistic community. Drop City had been inspired by the work of architects Buckminster Fuller and Steve Baer, and they built award-winning geodesic domes, using available materials such as car roofs. Kit got his hands on a prototype dome and assembled it in the back garden of 119 Park Hill. It didn't stay up for long.

After two years of preparation, Harper and members of LASITOC finally went to Stockholm in June to lobby the United Nations Conference on the Human Environment. They set up an exhibition called 'People's Technology' and attended a round-table meeting where the issue of decentralisation was widely explored. Nothing came of it, except the discovery of how much effort something like this took to organise.

Designers and architects

Habits are hard to break. It would be down to the designer of the product to make the change, and for the manufacturer to see that there was a commercial incentive to become what we now term 'green'. This was an issue discussed at a Lisbon conference in October 1972 organised by the Design and Industries Association; Kit was a member and was invited to speak. The DIA had been created in 1915 with the slogan 'Nothing Need be Ugly'. The theme as advertised in the journal *Design* was 'Wants, Needs and Sustainability': 'Ploughshares or electric toothbrushes? Artificially created wants or real human needs? Can designers and industrialists meet the challenge and still show a profit? Where does the designer stand in the fight against pollution?'

Kit proposed that the scientist should now work closely alongside the designer, and that no responsible person should put any idea to paper without first considering the ecological and environmental results of his artefacts. The *Guardian* reported how he 'proposed four principles, his own Hippocratic oath for the scientist and designer:

1. No designer shall create an artefact from raw materials which he knows to be in short supply.
2. No designer shall create an artefact from a man-made material which carries a high environmental price.
3. No designer shall create an artefact which assists in the manipulation of the human mind.
4. The artefact which a designer creates should meet an overt social need.

Kit's contribution, noted *Design*, added 'a new word to the language – "pedlerism" – used in gentle reproof by the planners who really believe that they have everything under control. Like Geoffrey Shuttleworth whose control of everything he touches – words, ideas, ideals – is most consoling.' Shuttleworth was a systems analyst, a job Kit loathed, working for Environmental Planning Assistance, a section of the Canadian Department of Public Works. The *Guardian* liked Shuttleworth 'for sheer lucidity':

[His] contribution on office planning, with its reasoned statistical approach – and the fact that there will be increasing numbers of office bound workers and decreasing numbers on the factory floor – sobered everyone. It was the first time he and Kit Pedler had met. One result of the three days is that Kit Pedler disagrees violently with Shuttleworth, and they plan to meet and thrash things out. Out of which friction good things may come.

Kit wanted architects to take seriously the challenges of the coming post-industrial age, which they could do if only they stopped being so frivolous with their designs. Like scientists, Kit wanted them to become socially responsible, and stop producing outlandish designs that were more attention-grabbing than anything else:

> Architects often seem to me to be one of the most arrogant species at liberty. Having absorbed a sprinkling of philosophy and a crude knowledge of technological concepts, they develop the ability to translate what is largely impudent dogma into concrete and metal reality, and then have the sheer nerve to justify the initial ideas by post hoc rationalisation. What probably started as an absolutely 'sooper' idea in the intellectual wastelands of NW1 turns into a fraudulent justification for a real building where people are rather regrettably inserted.

This was taken from a review of *Experimental Architecture*, a book of 'technological nightmares' published in 1970 by architect Peter Cook. His bold and radical designs did allow for 'the gentle human frame' which otherwise 'appears to be a rather tiresome protoplasmic appendage, to be fitted in somewhere at the end of a designer's monument to his own frivolity'. His views on ugly architecture would be echoed by Prince Charles in years to come. On the other end of the scale were architects who designed the cheapest box in which to contain a human being. 'Buildings are not really buildings any more; they are concrete realisations of a cost-benefit analysis.'

Kit wanted to create housing self-sufficient in energy production and cut down on heat waste. In the 1970s, at least thirty per cent of heat generated to warm a house escaped through the roof and the walls. Insulation was not then considered integral to a house's design. The idea of cavity wall insulation was not new, but tales of clumsy installation encouraging rising damp put off many who could have benefited from having it installed.

What Kit had in mind was to transform a house into a self-contained 'urban spaceship', based along the lines of the Apollo command module. This idea had been floating around since the mid-sixties. In 1967, a magazine called *Progressive Architecture* headlined its October issue 'Needed – Life Support Systems for a Dying Planet'. The issue suggested that architects and designers needed to learn from NASA's self-regulating capsule for its astronauts and apply the same 'salvation mechanisms' for our own closed system of a world. An ordinary house could replicate the closed system ecology of a space capsule, recycling all waste products, just as within the natural cycles of Earth there is little waste.

No one was suggesting living in resource-gobbling high technological space capsules in the post-industrial age, and AT enthusiasts did not want a corporation like General Motors to monopolise and standardise the field. They envisaged localised light industry, serving the needs of their urban communities. Kit wanted technology to be reproduced in a simple manner, so it could be replicated by practically anyone rather than a specialist. Kit was going to spend the next couple of years looking at how he could achieve this within his own home.

Engines

The first issue to be addressed was energy. Electricity was here to stay, but the manner of its production had to change. Ninety-five per cent of America's energy consumption in 1971 was generated from fossil fuels, and only two per cent from nuclear plants. Hydroelectricity made up for the remaining three per cent. Once oil or coal is burned, it is gone, and it pollutes, not just as fumes and smoke, but as heat. Kit wrote in *The Quest for Gaia*:

> If the electricity company running the power station generates and delivers electricity into a national grid system, only twenty-eight per cent of the energy in the fuel turns into electricity. The remaining seventy-two per cent is released as waste heat… The process has therefore contributed massively to the net disorder of the planet, and the electricity generating company should more properly be *a waste heat generating company*, since its prime product is entropy not electricity… We have to get away from the idea that bigger factories and power stations are necessarily more efficient or economic.

Heat waste is not often seen as a form of pollution, but for Kit efficiency became the key issue. Heat could be used elsewhere.

Imports of fossil fuel were also vulnerable to political, economic, and international pressures, especially if you relied on imports from Middle Eastern countries at this time. In 1973, Egypt and Syria launched a surprise attack on Israel, starting the Yom Kippur War. A confederation of oil-producing states, including some Arab countries, stopped selling oil to America and other pro-Israeli countries. Although the embargo did not affect Britain, soaring oil and petrol prices did. The government issued petrol rationing coupons which in the event were not needed, but they did advise that people should heat only one room in a house.

The price of coal soared, and British miners worked to rule as part of fresh industrial action about pay. From January 1974, the government was panicked into rationing electricity, implemented a series of power cuts, and introduced the three-day working week to preserve their coal stocks. In February 1972, the miners picketed power stations, exposing the fragility of the power supply system. This forced schools that depended on coal heating systems to shut down.

If the power went out in a city, the results were appalling. No number of systems analysts could have helped parts of America and Canada when they experienced a thirteen-hour-long power outage in 1965. This was down to simple human error when a power relay was incorrectly set at too low a level and tripped. Something similar struck New York city in the hot summer of 1977, and this time riots and looting broke out within hours.

You can see why being independent from the main power networks was an attractive proposition, but was it possible in the late twentieth century to generate your own energy to supply your needs? Indeed, who would want to invest in natural power sources when in 1971 two giant oil fields had been discovered in the North Sea.

The most natural source of energy is the sun. The energy from the sun is absorbed by the land and sea. This energy is behind the movement of the wind and water, the waves and ocean currents (but not the tides), all of which could be harnessed to generate electricity. Even in a country like Britain with its low amounts of sunshine, solar power could still produce results which were believed to be far from negligible. Wind power is certainly the most difficult to harness, and in our contemporary age, still the most controversial. Kit knew in 1974 that based on 'presently available technology, even the most enthusiastic of autonomous house designers will have to accept that, in Britain's urban area, sunlight and wind power will not together provide all the energy needed'.

Kit had an answer for that. He built a gas-powered engine, adapted from a 750 cc Austin 7 engine and a radiator which he picked up from a scrapyard. The gas engine would heat water and power a dynamo and generate enough current to power the lights. Lucy Pedler remembered: 'When we had the power cuts and the three-day week, he hooked it up to a couple of fluorescent lights. He was so proud that we were the only ones with lights when the power cuts went on. He was just bursting with pride that he generated light.'

Kit's engine used gas created from a digester, fed with food or garden waste, producing methane gas. Methane is highly explosive, so great care was needed. If there wasn't enough methane, propane could be utilised, but he appreciated that this type of generator could not be used on a large scale because present levels of propane could not meet the demand. The engine could also be plugged into the mains electricity supply when all else failed. The digester only produced one to two cubic feet of gas per day, compared to the thirty-six cubic feet needed for an average domestic cooker. Kit also experimented with peanut butter oil, which later attracted media interest.

The best source of methane would be ourselves via the sewage system. This idea made his neighbours chuckle, as Diana Baur recalls:

> I remember Kit talking to my father about his plans for turning his house into it all being run on the methane produced, and we used to laugh about that because they lived hard and strong, and there was probably a lot of methane going on in that house. I remember my father saying, 'They'll be able to run everything over there!'

The gas-powered engine was central to what Kit called his Total Energy System. He presented his finished prototype in a 1976 book called *Radical Technology*, edited by Peter Harper and *Undercurrent*'s editor Godfrey Boyle. He calculated it was eighty per cent efficient, and even the hot exhaust gases could be condensed and removed as a liquid.

Another method for heating water came from the sun. Kit built two solar thermal collecting walls, one for summer sunlight and another for winter, each constructed using non-flammable foam materials with a black over-glazed external space through which water would trickle when the sun was shining. Some of this water would be rainwater run-off, cleansed through a sedimentation tank (a small version of that used by waterworks): 'This way you get a large volume of water being heated to quite high temperatures which can then be stored.' The water was pumped into a very well insulated water tank for storage, either by a small wind turbine or by the gas engine. After use, it would flow back into the system via a heat exchanger in the large heat store after passing through further sedimentation and filter systems. Providing no detergents are used, the water could be safely reused.

Kit argued that in the post-industrial age, the definition of efficiency had to extend towards how and from what the engine was built:

When the conventional engineer talks about efficiency, he refers to the number of calories of heat which can be extracted from the fuel by the engine to do useful work and says that efficiency is the amount of work done by the engine while it did the work. I believe that this idea of efficiency is incomplete and that any definition relevant to the future must include factors which represent machine lifetime, design simplicity and the amount of energy used in fabrication, as well as the amount of energy used to refine the raw materials used in construction.

Engines did not have to be noisy. Kit was particularly impressed by Stirling engines, one of which powered a ten-ton boat belonging to his nephew Kerry Glasier. The engine had been invented by a Scottish parson in 1816 as a rival to stream engines. They had recently fallen out of use, despite being more efficient than steam. They were quieter, safer, and could use almost any heat source including solar. Kerry remembered Kit was impressed by the silence and simplicity of Stirling engines. Kit was also impressed by modern attempts to create a liquid piston engine by Dr Colin West at the Atomic Energy Research Establishment at Harwell. He visited for his edition of the BBC documentary strand *Choices for Tomorrow* in 1975. The heat source used was an infra-red light, playing on a closed volume of air inside a glass tube: 'Now the beauty of this is when the air is heated it expands and then cools and displaces water pistons and the water piston has displaced mercury from one end of the see-saw to the other so that the whole thing rocks; when it begins to rock it can do work.' A sophisticated prototype was being developed where it could be used to pump water:

> This makes it useful because it means you can take it and put it in some remote area and leave it working away pumping water to irrigate land; and best of all it wouldn't need any attention at all, it would work month in and month out. But there's another feature to these new machines which I hold to be very important for the future. They are beautiful, they are quiet, and they are elegant to look at and they don't pollute the world we live in.

It was a good use of resources, Kit decided.

Wind power

Kit was fascinated by the problems of wind power. In the past, windmills had been used to grind corn and pump water from the ground, but they could also be used to generate an electrical current. He built his blades from fibreglass. 'He loved his fibreglass,' remembers Lucy. 'That smell always brings me back to Dad's workshop.' Now, fibreglass contains plastic, but this was an admissible use, Kit said. He found aluminium beer cans bonded with resin between fibreglass sheets to be one of the best structural materials he had come across.

Kit believed in the small scale where practical. It should be possible that each part of any windmill design should be capable of being copied by somebody else. He built one small windmill which added interest to the Park Hill skyline. It could spin at a top speed of ninety-four miles an hour even in a modest breeze, and this was enough to keep one bar of an electric fire going all day. He demonstrated one of his windmills at an Architectural Association conference in Bedford Square in 1975. Kit's example was mounted 'conveniently near the bar on the roof of the AA, and was toasted in light ale', according to *Undercurrents*.

They could be also quite dangerous if the blades broke off during high winds. Mark Pedler recalled: 'At Clapham he built at least one windmill, if not two. The last one woke him up in the middle of the night as it was shaken to pieces.' Kit admitted that he was Europe's number one windmill breaker. 'He was building a wind turbine when I got my O level results in the post,' says Lucy. 'My mum was at work and my Dad was in the garden building a wind turbine, and I ran out to him as they were okay results, and said, "Dad, Dad, I've got my O level results!" He said, "That's lovely, darling. Now, this wind turbine…"'

Kit did not dismiss the need for conventional power stations, only how they generated the electrical current, which was another difference between himself and the more radical alternative technologists. During the mid-1970s, Kit's growing expertise with windmills was utilised to help design what was hoped to be Britain's first ever wind farm in Wales at what is now the famous Centre for Alternative Technology in Machynlleth,* a place Kit said you needed a cleft palate to pronounce. It wasn't a happy experience, and the project was cancelled. Kit quarrelled with the company who were going to build the blades. This may have been alluded to in a 1974 lecture called 'Science Fiction and Science Futures' given to the South Place Ethical Society at Conway Hall in London. In *Ethical Record*, Peter Cadogan reported: 'Recently, he spoke to Welsh steel workers and nearly got lynched.

---

* The Centre opened in 1973 and runs to this day.

The oxide or nitrogen that they produce for their steelworks could… be used to make nitric acid. We can make pollution work for us if we wanted to.'

Kit visited CAT many times, but during one trip he had a car crash, and suffered from whiplash as a result. Una came to Wales to take him home, unaware that he had gone to Wales accompanied by a new girlfriend, whom he had met through the AT movement.

Lifestyle choices

Kit knew that in the post-industrial age, living a lifestyle with a low impact upon the environment would result in changes that could be very hard to sell to the public who did not want to return to the house slavery that modern technology and convenience was liberating them from. Who would want to return to the mangle? From 1972, not only was he lecturing upon the subject, but also putting it into practice himself.

Baths would be replaced by showers, not just because of the amount of water used but for how they were made. Washing machines would go, at least in their current form. 'The housewife,' Kit declared to G. Franks in the *Strait Times* in February, 'will have to get used to doing her own washing by hand, largely because washing machines of the conventional type will no longer be produced economically, and will use too much heat… The housewife, incidentally, will be doing this sort of work in a cotton overall – cotton needs a fifth as much energy for its production as nylon.' It was also less dangerous in its manufacture. In June 1974, there was a massive explosion at a nylon precursor plant near the Lincolnshire village of Flixborough, killing several workers. The entire plant was wrecked, and homes in five surrounding villages were damaged.

Kit told *Value* in 1974:

> I can foresee a time when our taxation system will be based on the amount of energy used by the consumer. On that basis, a nylon shirt might be taxed at, say, 100 pence, while a cotton shirt that needs about a fifth as much energy for its production would be taxed at only 20p. Even life assurance policies and other financial transactions might be based on energy values, because energy is the life blood of our civilisation – of the whole world.

Kit stopped wearing any clothes made from artificial materials, or which needed ironing. 'It is the individual consumer who is responsible for disasters like the one at Flixborough,' he declared to Bob Klass in 1974.

Cooking would be different in the future. 'I've no intention of living entirely off nuts and raisins,' Kit told *Value*. 'I like my food, and I want to be able to make a curry or stew when I want.' Kit designed his own slow cooker. 'If you insulate the sides and lids of your pans properly, you can cook a stew on one candle. All it needs is redesigned cooking utensils.' He also developed a heavily insulated polystyrene box, which would allow a preheated dish to continue cooking without a continuous source of heat. It was very, very low tech, but by his account, the stews he produced were delicious. Kit told *Woman's Day* that it is possible to eat 'quite acceptably' on three to four pounds, which is an eye-watering £38 at today's prices. 'Just stop to think about it,' he explained. 'Money doesn't go on the cost of living. It goes on the cost of conditioning. People don't buy frozen peas because they need them rather than fresh peas. They buy them because they're conditioned to *think* they need them.' Una had long since stopped buying frozen food. Freezers were out as they were expensive to run, unlike fridges which he approved because they were low energy users. Energy-free preservation of food could be easily achieved by drying and bottling, an old skill.

What passed for processed food was a jumble of additives, stabilisers, monosodium glutamate and artificial flavourings, giving a vague impression of what the powder was supposed to be, produced by an intensive industrial process, and wastefully packaged. Fast food from America with its high fat and sugar contents had yet to hit Britain and cause its additional problems with diet and packaging and demands for meat and grain.

Kit wrote a short radio play called 'Sunday Lunch' for a schools' educational series called *Learning About Food* in 1974. His two editions were called 'Feeding Our Future', and asked where food would come from in the year 2000. Would it be pills as science-fiction writers fantasised, or would it be grown under hydroponics in a factory using soil-less systems? Would packaging be non-existent or would it be edible and part of the food itself? Would food have to be grown locally because of high transport costs as oil runs scarce? 'Sunday Lunch' presented a family, a mother and father with a son and daughter named after his youngest children, Justin and Lucy. A television set from the future appears on their kitchen table and shows them a choice of futures for their food supply. It is either all plastic pipes delivering tablets, or a poverty-stricken family eating root vegetables and beans. If they want to avoid both futures, they need to start thinking about where their food comes from.

The western world, Kit believed, was profligate with its food. Something like 100,000 tonnes of grain was used in Britain each year for pet food alone, which could help feed 500,000 people for a year. Meat was becoming more expensive and there was a genuine fear that beef would become a luxury meat within the next ten years, as chicken had been before factory farming was introduced. Since meat is a valuable source of protein, it would have to be replaced with something else such as the soya bean, which was cultivated mainly in Asia and the United States. Soya was used as an additive, a sauce, or part of a meat substitute, but mainly as an animal feed, and a recent bad harvest in the United States made soya more expensive because America was refusing to export it in bulk. Kit explained it like this in 'Sunday Lunch':

> First of all, you used up some of the earth's land to grow the soya beans, then you fed them to the cattle which used up another piece of land to graze on and then you eat the cattle, which contain less protein than the soya bean. Two lots of land and less protein...

'I buy corn from the pet shop, and grind my own flour,' Kit told *Woman's Day*. The grinder was old and basic, like those used by African natives. A loaf of bread cost Kit four pence to make, much cheaper than from the shops. White flour vexed Kit because the industrial process for transforming it from its original state removed practically all that was healthy in wheat in the first place, replaced by artificial substances designed to make the product look good. White, after all, implies cleanliness.

Kit's homemade results were variable as Mark Pedler recalled: 'The sort of house bricks that came out – you needed steam pumps to chew it!' Kit also became irritated by the local baker who insisted on partially wrapping it up with a piece of tissue, which was a legal requirement. To Kit, this was no more than a ritualised theatrical performance of the idea of cleanliness.

There have been several references to the housewife so far, and this was still a period where division of labour within the household fell along traditional lines. When he was interviewed for *Woman's Day*, Lynne Day 'felt' she had to ask Kit if he might not come up against some opposition from the women in question? 'Won't they feel that his criticism of convenience foods and easy-care clothes and all the others bibs and bobs of the ideal consumer society is a chauvinist ploy to get them back into the home?' Kit agreed that they might, but it wouldn't be true:

Heavens, I have a wife and two daughters who are confirmed believers in equality, and I'd never get away with it, even if I wanted to. You know, when the tribe runs into trouble and times are hard somebody gets blamed. We're stuck at a particular spot in the evolution of an equal society and the women are blaming the men. Nobody should be blaming anybody. We should all be working to get out of the mess. The way we live is much more under the control of women than men. Even in homes where the women have their own careers it's the women who still, as a rule, decide what the family will eat and wear and do. Women are more skilled at looking coldly and scientifically, if you like, at their own family's lifestyle.

Una agreed with Kit's views and wanted to do her bit. 'She uses good ol' soap powder,' Kit reported with some satisfaction, 'and with the help of non-chemical water softener (since London's water is very hard) the laundry is perfectly clean and white.' Lucy and Carol were in favour, he reported, but had yet to take the plunge. Kit was also invited to take the message direct to the housewives of Britain who listened to Radio 4's *Woman's Hour* every Wednesday afternoon during January 1974 for a feature called 'Live It Yourself'.

Housing

Kit wanted to design an Advanced Ecologically Sound house (AES) and build in miniature a self-contained room which would be connected to his own home on top of their garage in Clapham. He explained to the *Daily Express* that he wanted to build a house from scratch for under £10,000:

> Dr Pedler believes that given a touch of selective flair and a new appraisal of resources and cost problems the building societies could play a major innovative role in providing new and much more efficient (hence cheaper) housing systems.

For Lucy, it was a seminal moment in her young life:

> The first time I understood the idea of enclosing space was when my father talked about building a second storey on top of the garage, which as a child, I had never thought of. He was describing how he'd knock a hole through the living room into this new room, and it would be his study. It made me realise that you could take air, and build walls around it, and it becomes a room. That was when I first realised, I could do things like that.

Constructed from wood, it would have measured 6.1m by 5.5m. 'Conventional bricks are shockingly inefficient insulators, and iron and aluminium are both heavy users of oil in their manufacture. Aluminium production requires fifteen times more fuel energy than steel. They'll have no place in my house.'

Kit's wooden structure would be very well insulated and designed to be as self-sufficient as possible. Solar panels generating electricity this time would take up thirty square metres primarily to heat water, but Kit believed he could keep a one kilowatt per hour fire and a light bulb burning for each square metre, even when it was cloudy. A windmill would drive a heat pump so if the sun did not generate enough power, warmth could be transferred from the ground into a water reservoir on the south side of the house. Surplus energy would power a 36-volt fluorescent lighting system. The now obsolete filament bulbs, Kit recognised, wasted a lot of heat. Kit's house would contain a biodegradable toilet with minimum water used, and the washing machine would only use recycled water. Propane gas would act as a reserve in his engine.*

His home needed to be decorated selectively. Modern paint depended far too much on chemicals and oil: 'What's wrong with hessian fabrics hung on the wall?' he asked *Strait Times*. 'Many are extremely beautiful, and the only chore is keeping them brushed.'

Kit planned to live inside his prototype for a year, and write a book based on his experiences, and then get someone else to live in it for a further year to prove that you didn't need to be a scientist to do this. 'I shall not actually cut myself off from my family, just eat, sleep, work and perform my natural functions in the house,' he told *Value*.

He presented his ideas to the media over the winter of 1973-74, as he promoted his second book written with Gerry Davis, *Brainrack*.† The house captured the imagination of the media: the *Daily Mirror* were taken with the idea of an engine driven by peanut power, and BBC radio invited him to explain it twice in one week. Kit had built a beautiful balsawood model of a larger prototype which some reports suggested he was now going to build in his large garden.

---

* The Cambridge University Autarkic House project was developing a similar house, but their intention was to use 700 mm of polyurethane for the thermal store insulation; only later was it realised that the CFCs used in the manufacture of polyurethane were a major environmental hazard.
† See Chapter 14.

The government's Central Office of Information visited Kit during early 1974 and made a short film on his ideas. He stressed that his work was still in the experimental prototype stage and that he was actively trying to form a group of like-minded people to help solve the engineering and scientific problems that he was identifying. 'I don't want theorists; I want the people who can deal with the nuts and bolts.' According to *Women's Day*, his call had been answered by at least seventy people who could draw up a list of skills needed for the future. One was a millwright, two were carpenters, and another man was trained in aerodynamics. 'I want people who are genuinely disgruntled and can *do* something.'

Communicating his ideas

By 1974, Kit had grown tired of giving lectures to the public, for it seemed to be achieving very little: 'You can turn people on to pollution for an hour at a lecture,' he told Bob Klass, 'but they immediately go back to the same way of life when it is over. I am forty-seven and I have decided to devote the rest of my life to shaking some sense into an appallingly self-indulgent population.' In their place Kit preferred seminars which were collaborative rather than a one-way thing such as a lecture. He could be confronted with up to two hundred people and at the end of it he believed he would always learn something new. Kit enjoyed a good debate, and Una believed that the way he presented his ideas incited resistance which he needed to spur him on to help develop and clarify his new ideas.

However, Kit's evangelising zeal did not always find an audience. In 1974, he was commissioned to write an article for the *Daily Telegraph* looking at the tenth anniversary of some unspecified event. What they got instead was a highly opinionated article full of 'trendy claptrap'. There was a flurry of internal memos, some of which were 'leaked' to Kit by a sympathetic junior editor. The piece wasn't optimistic enough, they said. After all, smog had gone, and surely the rivers looked a bit cleaner than they had a few years earlier?

Television was the best mass medium to put across the message and be sure of a reaction, even on a late-night programme. In December 1974 he appeared in an edition of BBC2's *Open Door* called 'Design Action' along with Sir Misha Black, and the champion of localised, intermediate technology for the developing world, Ernst Schumacher whose thinking had inspired the work at the Centre for Alternative Technology. An economist and statistician, he had once been an economic advisor to the National Coal

Board and saw oil as a finite resource that would inevitably become more expensive as supplies ran out, located as it was in unstable regions in the world. His influential book *Small is Beautiful* had just been published in 1973. Columnist Astragal, writing in the *Architect's Journal*, was not impressed with the arguments within the edition:

> A man showed a brick and pointed out that the energy needed to bake it would keep an electric fire going for a couple of hours or so. And then the picture changed from brick houses to the Pike-dream autonomous house model [the Cambridge University project], all shining glass which would, in fact, be five times as wasteful in energy in the making. The DIA point was that this house was going to be largely self-sufficient in energy. A pity the point could not have been made some other way because brickwork is the most energy-economical building material we've got except, presumably, straw and timber…

Kit sent a thundering reply, printed in the following issue:

> Astragal makes the astonishing assertion that: 1 'The Pike-dream autonomous house… would be five times as wasteful in energy' as a brick house; 2 'brick work is the most energy-economical building material we've got except straw and timber.' Has Astragal never heard of rammed earth, adobe, and paper houses, and where did he/she get the figures? The complacent assumptions behind Astragal's dogmatic statements are one of the main reasons why both architecture and building technology are so woefully behind the times in this country.

In May 1975, Kit presented *Choices for Tomorrow*. The *New Review* said: 'his worried frown gave emphasis to some pretty strict words about the way we are messing up our environment. He ticked us off for our slavish acceptance of plastic artefacts. More use, it seemed, could be made of natural materials like wood.' The programme was filmed partly at an exhibition centre, a car scrapyard, recycling experiments at the Warren Spring laboratory, and at home. Kit takes the viewer through a tour of modern artefacts, itemises their complicated production processes and asks whether this made the best use for these materials. He explains how so little of what we throw away can be recycled. He appreciated few could make engines, turbines or solar panels, and he demonstrated the benefits of grinding corn to make your own bread. This led R. F. Thornburgh from Maidstone to write to the *Radio Times* asking where he could get hold of the plans to build his own corn grinder. 'Does anyone, for example, produce plans to construct any of these other environmentally sensible pieces of machinery, which, even in their technical simplicity, without plans, are rather beyond me? It seems to me that what we need now is less of the propaganda (preaching to the converted?) and more in the way of positive and practical proposals for the layman.'

Kit replied that he wasn't trying to make a propaganda film, simply to indicate and suggest possibilities in the short time he had available. He said he received one of the largest mails from this programme that he had ever had, asking for more programmes dealing with the 'real nuts and bolts of the changes that are going to be forced upon them by a raw materials and energy famine'. Corn grinders, he added, were already on the market.

Interested people could track down the magazine *Undercurrents* created by Godfrey Boyle which started life in 1971 and involved Peter Harper. This was an invaluable resource for those working on their own AT projects to see what was being done by other researchers and contact them. It was to become Britain's equivalent of the American *New Alchemist Bulletin* or the *Whole Earth Catalogue*, a mixture of new technology, lifestyle, science and radical politics. Kit contributed articles from time to time and was listed in issue 6 as 'Kit – I've sold my Lancia – Pedler', a one-man research team working on cheap methods for autonomous housing.

Interest from industry

Sometimes Kit received interest from companies who were coming to terms with stronger anti-pollution measures that had been introduced by the last Conservative government. Kit knew the approach to take. 'When I speak to engineers about energy losses in industry, I encounter a lot of suspicion,' he told Lorna O'Connell a few years later. 'Money is the metaphor in business, not principles. If I show them how much money can be saved by adopting this or that conservation method, they'll go ahead and do it, thereby reducing the entropy problem too. But it's unrealistic to talk to business people in any but cash terms.'

Usually, Kit turned them down, once claiming he could have become a millionaire had he accepted all the offers he was made, but in 1975 he agreed to advise a firm called Unigate Limited, formed as the result of a merger between United Dairies and Cow and Gate, who made dried baby food. It was not a happy marriage. The company was beset by infighting and factional politics and milk consumption had been declining since the 1960s. It was acceptable for Kit to become associated with them because the company believed in open management and tried to develop an ethos of accountability. It was also a source of much-needed income. Journalist and actor Michael Allaby, who worked for the *Ecologist* magazine, remembered Kit was earning a good living as an 'ecological consultant'.

Kit was interviewed by a local newspaper at the Beaufort Hotel in Bath where the head offices of Unigate were based:

> With Unigate, I've got an opportunity to produce a model for industrial change, a new pattern for our industrial future. North Sea oil is not the panacea. We must look at our own energy use... Sometimes I don't know where to start, but with Unigate I've got a start. Many industries are doing nothing about all these problems partly because the technology for dealing with them is not sufficiently developed, and partly because they're not yet conditioned to do anything. They're still concerned with cash accounting. I want them to realise that energy accounting is more important.

Bath had its own unique and untapped power supply, the hot springs which the Romans utilised for their pleasure. Kit saw the potential to heat thousands of homes from the gallons of hot water that runs to waste into the river. 'It's absolutely staggering. It offends my sense of energy conservation... and people are wrong when they say it costs too much to harness it. They should consider that in the energy crisis it could soon be a saving.'

In 1975, Kit produced a 100-page report called *The Torrington Project – An Industrial Plant for the Eighties*. Much of what he writes about deals with energy efficiency in general terms, to the extent that, within a few years, Kit converted the report to become a potential book on the house of the future. Specific to his brief, he describes in detail how the milk factory plant in Torrington in Devon could improve their energy situation by fifty per cent by redeploying their waste heat. Kit observed that they were spending a lot of money heating the outside of the building.

He examined every work practice to see how it could become an 'environmentally integrated plant,' and even suggesting selling off surplus heat to homes in a nearby village. In July 1976, Kit pointed out how two farms near Torrington, in conjunction with the Ministry of Agriculture and the National Institute for Dairy Research, were already investigating how to redeploy waste heat from refrigeration plants to warm water.

Reports like these have a habit of sitting in what Kit called an 'infinitely pending basket'. To counteract this, Kit later submitted a proposal for the creation of a 'think tank' within Unigate, despite the poor reputation of such groups. Think tanks had been set up by the Rand corporation, the Hudson Institute, and recently by the Heath government. Kit wrote they had been revealed to be 'little more than groups of indulgent romantics who obsequiously reflected the views of their sponsors. Within a large organisation such as Unigate, similar problems appear. However clear-sighted an individual within the organisation is, he or she is bound to be affected by ordinary human pressures of survival and day-to-day operation.'

Kit wrote that large organisations have one universally crippling factor which affects innovation and creative thinking: the notion that stability is only achievable by treading known paths. Creative innovation commonly generated hostility and derision. Kit proposed to circumvent this problem by making certain that hard data is injected into 'management decision pathways at the optimum point... all creative schemes have to be translated into hard economic terms and then presented at board level only'. Although this ran against the principles of open management, it would prevent the two reactions which he described from putting any new idea into the 'infinitely pending basket'. He suggested linking up with research departments in universities who were crying out for good and industrially relevant projects, perhaps even endowing a Unigate fellowship.

He wanted his think tank to investigate current research projects such as reverse osmosis, freeze drying and freeze fractionation which may offer more suitable energy balance for future operations. There should be more product versatility. Unigate made dried baby milk, a process which Kit gently suggested was energy intensive, polluting and complex. Was there a better source of protein available that could replace cow milk? The think tank could examine such processes as leaf fractionation to see whether this is not a more suitable protein production process than milk. 'Leaf protein is fed to cows which make milk which man takes and eats. Protein can be recovered from leaf and eaten by man without the cow.' He adds that lucerne (also known as alfalfa) produces 675 kilograms of protein per acre. Kit's suggestion of cutting out the middleman was a radical idea for a dairy.

Kit was still producing reports as late as June 1977. One report concerned a book on the safety of food additives written by fifteen scientists, most of whom had commercial affiliations and had no issue with the idea. Kit was pleased to see how in one essay the milk industry was trying to minimise the use of additives. He pointed out how in France, the main plank in the Ecology Party's manifesto was to do away with additives for good and they were winning twelve per cent of the vote in municipal elections.

By the time this report was written, Unigate had a new chief executive and chairman, an autocratic man called Jonathan Clements who was determined to end the factional infighting and began to sell off large portions of the company's manufacturing capacity. Kit's ideas such as the Torrington Project would take too long to pay for itself, and such new and untested schemes would have had no place for a conventional man determined to put the company on a sound financial footing.

Finally…

Kit's house on top of his garage in Clapham was never built. The first reason was Lambeth council. In some interviews Kit said that they had been encouraging, and in others he was waiting for their reaction. The *Guardian* sympathised: 'As those who dare to be unconventional will have learned, neither building societies nor local planning authorities take kindly to the experimental and unfamiliar structure.' It was doubtful if any local council would allow someone to construct an additional storey above a garage or in the garden. Anthony Tucker in the *Guardian*: 'And just in case it all sounds a little po-faced Kit is thinking about a rate rebate when his house becomes fully self-sufficient.' Kit loathed the intrusion of bureaucratic bodies, and actively campaigned in the 1975 referendum against remaining within the Common Market on the grounds this was yet another large body spying and intruding upon the individual.

The second reason was that Una wanted to leave London. By now a fully trained child psychiatrist, she was looking for a consultancy, preferably in Kent. He agreed with many others that the coming post-industrial age would require smaller and more closely knit communities within the cities, meaning you would have to get to know your neighbours better. Kit felt that this was a good area to put into practice his AES project, perhaps linking it up with nine other ecologically sound houses to form a micro village. This, too, never happened.

13
Conditioned Brutality in the Lab

> Here then are scientifically valueless experiments involving massive
> and long-term cruelty to animals, performed for no other purpose
> than to give manufacturers some specious legal protection.
> – Kit Pedler in *The Quest for Gaia*, 1979

IN THE AUTUMN OF 1974, Mary Beith took a camera to work at the Dog Toxicity Unit at the Industrial Hygiene Research Laboratories, a division of Imperial Chemical Industries (ICI). Based at Alderley Park in Cheshire, they were testing a new brand of 'safe' cigarettes on beagles. The dogs were restrained in fabric slings which acted like straitjackets, and what resembled medieval stocks around their necks. Muzzles and oxygen masks were clamped around their snouts and they were forced to inhale smoke made from a cellulose-based 'New Smoking Material,' which the Imperial Tobacco Company hoped would replace tobacco and reduce the health risk involved in smoking. Beith was a journalist for the *Sunday People* and the photographs she took made the front page on 26 January 1975. It became a sensation.

ICI was not doing anything illegal; there was veterinary supervision, and they had a Home Office licence for animal experimentation, one of the requirements being that if an animal is suffering from severe pain, it should be painlessly killed forthwith. The newspaper report suggested that the dogs were distressed – the staff's favourite dogs were usually the quieter ones. One animal required two staff members to prepare it, who would chastise it with a blow to the snout from a plastic ruler. Some dogs had been smoking thirty cigarettes a day for three years; they were seen as an investment worth thousands of pounds in a £13 million experiment and had to be kept alive. When the dog's time was finally up, it would be killed and sent for dissection at pathology laboratories.

Beith suggested to an ICI spokesman that 'the dogs were being used for research into human pleasure, rather than pure medical research. He replied that ICI recognised that smoking was a national phenomenon, whether one liked it or not, and they were trying to produce a substance that would reduce the health danger.'

Kit Pedler gave the *People* a quote which was picked up by other papers: 'To subject dogs to these sort of tests is quite unnecessary. If smoke of any sort is repeatedly inhaled, it will cause irritation – but the tests cannot prove anything else.'

The experiment was quite useless. There is no such thing as a safe smoke to inhale, and no matter how many dogs went through this ordeal, nothing could be demonstrated otherwise. The new cigarette was launched in 1977 and proved to be an expensive flop. They were an equally unhealthy alternative.

Supposed protection

Any licence to experiment on animals is issued by the Home Office, governed by the 1876 Cruelty to Animals Act which many felt was no longer adequate. In 1906, a Royal Commission was set up to investigate who applied for a licence and discovered that medical research took up sixty per cent. By 1973, it was less than forty per cent. Animals were being used to test the side effects of cosmetics, poisons and weapons. Of the 5,607,435 experiments performed in 1971, eighty-six per cent of them were without anaesthetic.

If asked, the public (who had no idea what these experiments involved) felt reassured that it was all for their own good. If it could save lives and advance medical knowledge, then fair enough; but how much of this work was genuinely essential, and how much of it was simply trivial? The people carrying out the experiments, or caring for the animals, did not always have any veterinary or medical training themselves. Beith certainly didn't, and she got a job. Home Office inspectors would inspect a laboratory, but they always gave advance notice. As far as scientists were concerned, it was better for the public not to know of their work in case their squeamish sentimentality got the better of them, and there were a lot of sentimentalists about.

Animal welfare societies have been around in Great Britain for over a hundred and fifty years, with antivivisectionist groups among the more recent. The largest organisation was the Royal Society for the Prevention of Cruelty to Animals (RSPCA). It had a huge public profile with branches all over the kingdom, employing full-time staff and inspectors, raising an annual income of £2 million from members who come from all walks of life. Yet some felt that, since the war, it had moved too far from its radical roots and wilfully turned a blind eye towards the treatment of animals both on the farm and inside the laboratory.

Powerful interests were represented within the RSPCA, and they urged the society not to become involved in potentially political campaigning since that would be a breach of its charitable status. This argument had been used to prevent the RSPCA from campaigning against blood sports in case they criticised the patron of the society, the Queen, whose family were very keen hunters.

If you were an antivivisectionist, being a member of the RSPCA was a waste of time. However, in 1970 a group of new members wanted to change that attitude permanently and formed the Reform Group.

Richard Ryder joined the RSPCA in 1970: '[The RSPCA] was entirely about stray dogs and cats, a very old-fashioned organisation. It was an extremely conservative organisation, full of ladies with hats, and was run by retired army officers who were on the staff.' Ryder was a clinical psychologist working at Warneford Hospital in Oxford and had experience of animal experiments himself when he was studying animal behaviour in America. He was critical of their use in research, and became an advocate for animal rights, coining the phrase 'speciesism' in 1970, to demonstrate how human rights and protections were not extended to animals.

He joined the Reform Group whose plan was to get like-minded members elected onto the RSPCA council who could then influence the society. It was a slow process, but by 1972 they had succeeded as Ryder and four others were elected. Despite misgivings by traditionalists, he set up two committees: one would investigate farming and the second would venture into the laboratory. The farming committee was controlled by the RSPCA's then chief veterinarian, who some thought was a 'covert friend' of the industry and delayed action by commissioning a series of reports.

The second group was known as the Animal Experimentation Advisory Committee, and for this Ryder brought in people from outside the RSPCA to sit under the secretaryship of Bill Jordan, a veterinary scientist. Other members included the psychiatrist Dennis Slater, and Member of Parliament for Sowerby, Douglas (later Lord) Houghton. Kit Pedler was invited to become its chairman, on the strength of past comments on vivisection. He also had the advantage of having a media profile which could guarantee publicity.

Kit's experience

Kit had always found animal experiments distasteful, yet accepted them as necessary. His public research papers always emphasised that a test animal was anaesthetised to ensure that it did not suffer and was painlessly destroyed after the experiment was finished. He overruled any feelings of sentimentality due to the importance of his work. He once brought into the Institute a stray female cat to act as breeding stock for more experimental material when supplies ran low. He used the standard argument to his young daughter Carol when she objected to the fate that would befall the animals she came to visit at the Institute: would you prefer a dead cat or a dead relative? That 'them or us' argument comes across in several of his *Doomwatch* episodes, where the only sentimentality towards a laboratory animal was from the one non-scientist in the team, and then she is quickly dismissed.

Kit's mentor, Professor Ashton, was sympathetic. In his younger days as a student at King's College, he made a play for animal rights. After one class, he asked his physiology professor: 'Sir, I can quite see the need for animal demonstrations, but do we all have to pith a frog – would not one example be enough?' He was told to go away and not to be so stupid.

Kit readily admitted that he performed vivisection, but as early as 1967 he was on public record criticising what he considered to be needless and cruel experiments. In an interview for Sheffield's *Evening Telegraph*, the journalist noted how all benevolence faded from Dr Pedler's face when he discussed dolphins being used to attach mines to the hulls of ships:

> This is prostitution of the world we live in. The dolphin is a most elegant, beautiful, and benign creature that never did anybody any harm, with a learning rate higher for some tasks than man. Yet here are these wretched, soulless scientists prostituting one of the most elegant creatures on earth.

He was also appalled to watch on television an experiment where young monkeys were 'curled forlornly in a corner' after being presented with a cloth substitute for their mother. This was 'a piece of monstrous cruelty wrapped up in scientific guise'. No piece of knowledge was worth that much. But no one is perfect, and after his stay in Canada in 1969, Kit brought back a sealskin souvenir for one of his daughters.

Kit was reprimanded for what he had said; but he suspected that, for some of his colleagues, the experiments were designed only to advance their own careers. Kit is quoted by the International Vegetarian Society's website as having said, 'There is conditioned brutality among scientists, especially in the universities of Britain. The time has come to call a halt. The situation has got out of hand.'

Future friend and collaborator Richard Mervyn remembers Kit told him that the need for a result could sometimes bring out a seemingly inhuman reaction in a scientist:

> There was someone he knew of who was so intent on getting the results he wanted in animal experiments that he blinded the animal, so they'd be quieter. He said, 'I don't condemn him, because the problem with science is you're so intent on finding the result that you do things that you wouldn't do in normal life. You're so close to that result, therefore the logical answer is to do what I've just said, but it's morally abhorrent.'

It was this understanding that Kit brought to the committee. Richard Ryder would work and campaign with Kit for the rest of his life:

> Kit's role on that committee was as a scientist, but he was absolutely and emotionally and passionately convinced that animal experimentation was wrong. He was a very passionate man, and I think he was very often depressed. He was a big, strong, red-faced man, bitterly convinced that the world was on its way to ruin, and that there were forces of establishment that were undermining all hope for the future. He really believed in what he wrote about in *Doomwatch* and *Doctor Who*. He added a great deal of passion to the meetings. We were all passionate in our own ways. He didn't do too much of the organising; he was a slightly disorganised person.

Ryder described the Animal Experimentation Advisory Committee as 'radical and effective'.

Angela Walder, who would later become involved in 1976, was a trustee at the RSPCA and remembered Kit's handling of the committee:

> He didn't have any nonsense, he didn't let people waffle on. He kept very much to the point but he was always the one who was most forward in

thinking, so you never sat there as I did in the RSPCA thinking, 'These people are still living in the fifties!' You did sometimes have the problem of thinking 'Oh God, he's in the year 2050 and I'm not there yet!' He was always a forward thinker. He was a very round person, before his time perhaps. You look at *Doomwatch*; that was very much before its time.

Like Kit, Walder had also experimented on animals:

We had the similar backgrounds, so he never felt embarrassed mentioning it. Quite often that would be the case. There were a number of scientists who have come out against animal research after working in it and seen what is going on. I chased up one guy who was a sort of government God on this issue, and I knew when he was working in research, he got a whole team in London going around stealing cats and dogs for research, particularly for St George's Hospital. They admitted it fifty years later, as they always do. Fifty years later no one's interested.

Walder discovered another motive behind Kit's stance. He felt guilty for his role training others to do the same:

I often felt that behind him. He mentioned it more times than he needed to. There's this guy called Colin Blakemore, who worked for the Medical Research Council, and he did the ghastliest experiments on kittens, and Kit had trained him as an ophthalmologist. Kit always had a degree of guilt about this. He was always saying 'I have to make right the wrongs,' and I said, 'There aren't any wrongs! You didn't know what he was going to go forward and do!' But that was the sort of guy he was. He had a sort of conscience, I think.

In later years, Blakemore became chairman of the Research Defence Society, an organisation designed to counter antivivisectionist arguments. Despite speaking out against cosmetic testing and hunting, he became a hate figure amongst militant antivivisectionists, and received death threats.

Although the purpose of the committee was to actively investigate the use of animals in laboratories, it had no official status, and like Home Office inspectors they could not simply walk in and demand to see what was going on. The committee's research officer, David Pennock, would check published papers and was able to make formal visits to research centres on behalf of the RSPCA, but this took time to happen. '[At the beginning] I don't think we would have been welcome in any of them,' Ryder admits. 'We were rather upsetting the scientific establishment and the Research Defence Society was mobilised against us.'

While Kit and the committee were researching, Douglas Houghton launched a Private Member's Bill to toughen up the existing 1876 Cruelty to Animals legislation. He had support from fifty-three MPs, and it was hoped that this, the third attempt at such an amendment, would finally get through. He drew upon a 1965 report from a Home Office committee chaired by Sir Sydney Littlewood. They had investigated alternatives to using animals which laboratories were resisting. They heard from fifty-nine different organisations and claimed that they did not find any evidence that animals suffered. Yet inspection and control were found to be inadequate since there were only fourteen Home Office Inspectors. Littlewood made eighty-three recommendations, some of which included the use of alternatives to animal testing. This was considered impractical by medical researchers on the grounds that anyone could prosecute a laboratory if they believed an alternative testing method could have been used. Parliament did not even debate Littlewood's report until June 1971 following an article in the *New Scientist*.

Houghton wanted to restrict the number of animals being used. For example, in 1971, thirteen thousand monkeys had been imported into Britain. These were captured from the wild, rather than bred for the laboratory. He wanted to have alternative methods employed where they currently existed, such as the tissue culture technique first developed in 1907 by Ross Harrison: 'The search for alternative methods is not a tiresome fad,' Houghton told the House of Commons.

Crucially, Houghton wanted people to see what was going on inside laboratories, which the Littlewood report recommended since the 1876 Act was being used as a shield to prevent the public from witnessing vivisection being performed in their name: 'The doctrine that research must go free, that the number of experiments need have no bounds and the import and use of animals no limit is the doctrine of today. I do not believe that it should be accepted any longer.'

After the bill was passed for its second reading on 11 May 1973, it went into committee stage. This allowed Kit and Richard Ryder the chance to write a letter to *The Times* on behalf of the RSPCA in support of the bill, and to criticise the government for their standard defence of the law as it stood. The letter made public what his committee had been investigating for the past six months:

> We have found abundant evidence that suffering in animals does occur in British laboratories and that the strict necessity for much of the research being done can be questioned... We have found that it includes the testing of weapons, food additives of no nutritive value and weed killers and cosmetics.

This was against the 1876 act which forbids any experiments for purposes other than 'the advancement of new discovery of physiological knowledge or knowledge useful for saving or prolonging life or alleviating suffering'.

Their letter received a response from P. N. Donoghue, honorary secretary of the Institute of Biology, who thought that the tests described by Kit were just the sort needed to 'prolong life and alleviate suffering... It is essential to scrutinise the new products that industry pours forth. The problem is far too complex for the public to be informed of all the possible hazards, so it must be protected.' He thought Houghton's bill was about as practical as asking 'a man of serious intention to guarantee that his affianced is the best and most suitable woman in the whole world. It is his considered opinion and his hope that she is, but he cannot be so omniscient as to be sure... It would ill behove those who march under the proud banner of humanitarianism to forget to apply it to their own species.'

The entrenched view won through, and after successful lobbying by the pro-vivisectionists Houghton's bill was 'talked out' on its third reading in July, a technique often employed by MPs to stop a bill from continuing its passage to law. This caused some angry comment in the papers.

A similar defence of animal experimentation and the Act was argued by Lord Shawcross in *The Times* towards the end of the year, where he stated that current medical knowledge could not have been achieved without animal experiments. This was denounced as a myth by the antivivisection league, and Kit replied in his next letter, published on 15 December:

> Lewisite, a blistering agent once used as a poison gas, was instilled into the eyes of several rabbits, only a proportion of which were anaesthetised. Twenty minutes after administration, the eyelids were lifted off the eye by swelling. In 24 hours, the eye was discharging mucopus.* On the fourth day, the eyelids were stuck together by discharge. On the eighth day, the eyelids were contracting so that the eye could not be opened. On the fourteenth day the centre of the eye started to dissolve and on the twenty-eighth day the

---

* Mucus mixed with pus.

eyeball ruptured leaving only the remains of an eye in a mass of pus (references available).

Does Lord Shawcross consider that this experiment was 'useful for prolonging life' or did it 'alleviate suffering'? And does Lord Shawcross consider that the animals were killed in time to prevent pain?

No one who has watched a sick child dying would dispute the need for animal experiments which could have produced information leading to a cure of that child.

Rightly or wrongly, we as a species make the value judgement that human life is of greater value than that of an animal. Nevertheless, it is now shamefully obvious that large numbers of animals are now subjected to suffering for no reasons relevant to the Cruelty of Animals Act.

Kit sent details of the lewisite tests to the Research Defence Society, but they did not respond.

The fight continues

During the politically tumultuous year of 1974, with its two general elections, three-day weeks, power cuts and strikes, the animal rights issue quietly simmered away, and Kit's committee carried on with its work, largely unnoticed by the public. Meanwhile, within the RSPCA, there was a fierce and public fight to try and stop the direction in which the Reform Group wanted to take the society. There had been attempts by traditionalists on the council to expel Brian Seager, the Reform Group chairman, from the society, but the resulting publicity thwarted this attempt. However, they could not prevent the calls for reform of the administration of the society itself, and at the annual general meeting in June 1973, members voted to set up an independent inquiry to report on their constitution, rules, conduct and management. This created even more lurid publicity, some of it not entirely accurate, as Ryder remembered.

It started when, much to the surprise of the Reform Group, it was discovered that the RSPCA had no written policies. Ryder wrote in his book *Animal Revolution*:

> Such as it was, policy consisted solely of half-recalled council resolutions and the ad hoc pronouncements of senior officers. A huge staff, some five hundred strong, lacked the basic guidelines that a written policy could provide. Often confused and insecure in the midst of the society's then tumultuous affairs, with policy at the whim of one faction or another, staff

understandably played safe. Afraid to take new initiatives which might provoke criticism from council members, they preferred to be cautious.

Some were deliberately obstructive. Angela Walder remembered how it was: 'The trustees are supposed to be in charge. Most of them are doing other jobs, and others were quite often out there doing hands-on animal welfare work. The staff were there with all the facilities 24/7, but they just walked rings around you.'

The eventual Sparrow Report suggested reducing the number on the council by half to twenty-three and electing a new chairman. Council members themselves should have expert knowledge or hold special qualifications. The recommendations were accepted, and the council, headed by the conservative Hobhouse, resigned. The Reform Group had won this battle and disbanded, but the war was not yet over by any means. 'Trying to alter the direction of the RSPCA was like turning around a huge ship. It took time,' Ryder wrote.

With Hobhouse gone, the society voted to oppose all hunting with hounds in February 1976. Angela Walder:

> I think the biggest source of friction within the RSPCA was at the time of the hunting issue. It's extraordinary. Kit used to say he hated hunting as much as I did, and he supported the hunt saboteurs as did I. In fact, I was a hunt saboteur for a while, yet we always had to say when we were talking to one another, 'As bad as this is, the numbers that get killed on the hunting field are minute and the suffering is tiny in relation to the suffering involved in laboratories.'

Animal experimentation needed to be given the same amount of public exposure in the press as hunting, above and beyond letters or a sympathetic article with the usual moral blackmail from the experimenters and their supporters. The RSPCA shied away from engaging with the media, having recently been savaged. The opportunity fell into Richard Ryder's lap quite unexpectedly:

> What happened there was a chap called Laurie Manifold who was the editor of the *Sunday People*. Having seen all the interest in animal experimentation going on in Parliament and elsewhere as a result of our actions, he sent a reporter to visit me called Alan Ridout... 'What can we do to expose this animal experimentation problem that you are campaigning about?' I said,

'Well, why not get some of your reporters into the laboratories, and find out for themselves what is going on, and take photographs.' He said, 'Okay, give me names of the laboratories,' and I gave him a list of about half a dozen organisations that I could think of off the top of my head, that were doing animal research. Then he went away, and I didn't hear anything for months, and then he came back and said that they've got five different reporters in different laboratories, all working undercover and they had all come out with these horror stories and photographs. He didn't show me all the photographs... they were so horrific that they couldn't use them. I asked, 'Why not?' and he said, 'Because the readers would simply throw the paper away. They won't want to look at it.' That was a very interesting judgement. I think the *Sunday People* got it right: they went for the dogs being forced to smoke.

Most papers carried the beagle smoking story the next day and reproduced Kit's words from the original piece. 'We believe the experiments will help towards alleviating human suffering,' an ICI spokesman told the *Daily Express*, neatly quoting from the 1876 act. Kit – or 'Dr Pedlar' as the *Express* called him, repeating the error from the *Sunday People* – 'called for the setting up of a Home Office committee to consider the issue of licences for each individual experiment with animals... He said the RSPCA's powers were severely restricted by a 99-year-old Act which requires a prosecution to be brought within six months of an offence being committed. He said details of most experiments are not published until a year after they are carried out and then it is too late to prosecute.'

Despite the exposé, and the growing public indignation, ICI carried on with their experiment, claiming it was all in the public interest. That thirty thousand people die each year from lung cancer, Sir Jack Challard, chairman of ICI spluttered, was enough reason for the tests to be conducted.

The British Union for the Abolition of Vivisection put adverts in papers addressed to ICI shareholders: 'ARE YOU HAPPY WITH THIS? DID YOU EVEN KNOW?' Dog lovers along with their pets petitioned the Farnham home of ICI's chairman designate, Richard Wright, in protest. 'Stop the Beagle Belsen,' one placard read. Within the House of Lords, Houghton was joined by Lord Platt to denounce the tests. Richard Ryder remembers how 'Lord Platt was very angry with the medical establishment. He'd been president of the Royal College of Physicians and he was angry for all sorts of other reasons I think, but he decided that this was a good one to have a go at them. He was an angry old man. We were all quite angry.'

Lords Houghton and Platt put pressure on the government to intervene in the House of Lords, and the government placed the issue of dogs in smoking tests before the Advisory Committee on the Administration of the Cruelty to Animals Act 1876, a body which consisted of doctors, vets and, in a recent innovation, four lay members to the group.

Acting on the wave of revulsion the experiments generated, another MP tried to amend the 1876 Act in April, which attracted more counterattacks against the 'ignorance and confusion that surrounds animal experiments'. In June, ICI had to refute suggestions that they were preparing to experiment on another ten thousand beagles to test their new product, as they were waiting for approval from the government to put it on the market. But the damage had been done. More extreme animal rights activists launched a raid on the laboratory and rescued beagles which they had heard were going to be dissected by the end of the week. One of the dogs was reported to have been coughing and wheezing like a man who had smoked for thirty years.

Only the RSPCA came out of this whole affair with any credit. At their annual conference in Birmingham, Ryder told them that more evidence had been produced in the campaign against the 'callous and cruel use of animals in experiments, especially those which do not have a strictly medical purpose'. He referred to the rabbits and the blistering agent, but he also disclosed shampoo tests which made rabbits scream, pigs subjected to electric shocks of up to five thousand volts, and the slow, protracted deaths caused by toxicity tests. Helping the argument along was his new book *Victims of Science: The Use of Animals in Research*, which was published in the summer:

> That provoked a lot of debate in Parliament and helped pushed the movement along. The Canadian government attacked it and sent inaccurate reports on my book to the British government, and a junior minister at the Home Office started sending out copies defending animal experimentation and attacking my book. Lord Houghton was very angry about this because it was not the practice of government to name an individual citizen and attack them in this way. He went to Roy Jenkins, the Home Secretary, about that, and Jenkins forced the minister concerned to write a letter of apology to me.

With public opinion firmly in their favour, it was time to get the government to take the issue seriously. The government had indicated at the end of a Lords debate in May that they were prepared to look more closely at the 1876 act. Despite past failures to meet with the Home Office, and resistance from the traditionalists, an official approach to the government was going to be made. This was going to happen nearly two years after Kit began chairing the committee. He was invited to write an article for the *Observer*, published on 8 October 1974, in which he set down his thoughts on the matter, in conjunction with a piece by science correspondent Anthony Tucker.

The page the *Observer* gave to the issue began with a letter conciliatory in tone, stressing they were not calling for the total abolition of the practice: 'It is difficult, if not impossible to support the views of the abolitionists who believe that all animal experiments should be stopped.' No one watching a child die of leukaemia would prevent an experiment designed to prevent a child from dying, and they also accepted 'rightly or wrongly' that animals are of secondary importance to man. Then the letter went to the point and repeated the familiar example of the lewisite experiment, the Research Defence Society's silence on the matter, and the fact that the Home Office's own figures were showing a decreasing proportion of experiments which fell into the medical category, the only one for which the public in a recent survey had approved the use of animals. He then set down the committee's views that the Cruelty to Animals Act 1876 should be rewritten, the Home Office inspectorate strengthened, that the public should be better informed, alternatives should be funded by the government, and there should be 'a ban on the use of animals in procedures which are not strictly medical (such as the testing of cosmetics and toiletries, the testing of weapons and some behavioural research).'

Kit concluded:

> ... the spirit and letter of the Act are now widely broken or ignored and there is no doubt whatever than an increasing number of animals are subjected to horrifying degrees of suffering for reasons which are either scientifically trivial or purely commercial. The law must be changed without delay.

Kit's lengthy article began with the smoking beagles. He pointed out that:

> [the experiments cannot] produce a new discovery since the effect of smoke on the lung is already well known. The knowledge is not physiological since it can never lead to a further understanding of the natural function of body systems. It is also doubtful that the experiments produce information which will prolong life or alleviate suffering since these experiments suffer from the crucial defect of comparing a three-year smoking experience in a dog to a 20-30 year experience in a human.

He wondered if the person at the Home Office who gave ICI the protection of a licence could demonstrate how they were able to endorse experiments which had no substantial value.

He gives other examples of toxicity tests, one of which was also performed by ICI. These involved animals being injected or forced to breathe in a substance, in this case a new fire extinguisher fluid, that was already well known to be damaging. He shows how the authors of the 1948 lewisite experiment had, by their own admission, broken the 1876 act by not using anaesthetic, and by prolonging the test animals' suffering. Scientists in Porton Down laboratories in 1972 had studied the effects of squirting a dye called gentian violet into the eyes of rabbits and make no mention of anaesthetic use during their three-week trial. They had drawn on another study conducted in Germany where the dye was shown to have an irritant effect, and there was no stated purpose for their work.

The Home Office, he writes, only makes available to the public their annual returns, a register of premises which is a card index file, giving the barest of details such as name, address and licence held by the individual. It does not detail what the experiments are for, how many animals are used, or whether the licensees are medically trained. Not even questions by MPs could get further cooperation out of the Home Office. This veil of secrecy was one of the problems highlighted by the Littlewood Report:

> The Home Office takes considerable pains to ensure that details of animal experimentation are not revealed. In fact, the public is forbidden, by law, to witness experiments and the Home Office has recommended that premises for experimental animal usage be out of sight of the general public. Also in many cases, technicians and research workers have been given the impression that their work was carried out under the Official Secrets Act, or that they were in some way sworn to secrecy by their employees.

Kit discovered that he could not examine his own Home Office licence file because there was 'other information in it'.

In the same edition of the *Observer*, his appearance on Radio 4's *Lifelines in Medicine* was reviewed. The programme had debated the issue the previous Wednesday:

On one side there was the ubiquitous* Dr Kit Pedler's easy dismissal of some other scientists' work as trivial; on the other the man who felt that those beagles really liked smoking. But mostly the discussion was sane enough and judging from the complexity of the laws surrounding experiments on animals, it's clear that this a much-debated subject – as one would expect in this animal-loving country.

What happened at the meeting in October at the Home Office, no one remembers. It wouldn't be until 1976 that the issue of reform began to be taken seriously by government despite strong opposition from the Research Defence Council, and RSPCA traditionalists. Bill Jordan, who became deputy treasurer, said in the *Guardian* in 1997 that the RSPCA is made up of pragmatists who believe doing something is better than doing nothing, but who never rock the boat: 'They are an establishment organisation. They never, ever listen to new ideas.'

Kit was still involved in the original committee during 1976, but he too would eventually resign as he felt that the governing body and the RSPCA staff were giving his strong line little support. Richard Ryder became chairman of the RSPCA for two years from 1977, but there was only so much he could achieve within the society.

CRAE

Since 1973, Clive Hollands had been coordinating various animal rights groups and societies in preparation for Animal Welfare Year, beginning 15 August 1976, the centenary of the Cruelty to Animals Act. Angela Walder remembers him: 'He formed various committees: farm welfare committees, the Christian Consultative Council for Animal Welfare, a whole mass of committees all brought together. Amazingly, he brought together people none of us thought would work together because animal people can sometimes be a bit fractious!' For example, he persuaded the League Against Cruel Sports that the hunting issue was too controversial a matter to be included in the year's programme, and yet they still gave their wholehearted support to the campaign.

On 4 August 1976, Hollands joined Kit Pedler, Lords Houghton and Platt, Richard Ryder and Bill Jordan at the Home Office to present the Platt/Houghton memorandum. This paper was signed by peers, MPs from the

---

* Ubiquitous was probably the right word: Kit had appeared on the *Today* programme that morning.

Parliamentary Animal Welfare Group, and members from Kit's committee. It basically reiterated the points Kit made a year earlier in the *Observer*. The memorandum was greeted with a lot of publicity. The Home Secretary, Roy Jenkins, was leaving behind British politics, so the group met with the Minister of State, Dr Shirley Summerskill, a meeting which Hollands later tactfully described in his 1980 book *Compassion is the Bugler: The Struggle for Animal Rights* as 'exploratory'. Ryder remembers that 'she treated us with contempt. Platt and Houghton were so angry that they wrote a letter to the Prime Minister afterwards. After that we dealt almost entirely with the Home Secretary himself.' This was Merlyn Rees who was far more sympathetic.

As a result of the success of this second meeting, Hollands recalled, it was necessary to continue to press for further reforms, and the Houghton group was formalised as the Campaign for the Reform of Animal Experimentation (CRAE). Membership of the group was not open for organisations to be represented by a delegate except in a few special cases.

Angela Walder was a member. She had worked for thirteen years at the Gray Laboratory at Northwood as part of the Cancer Research Campaign. She worked in the animal house, breeding mice used for irradiation experiments. She told the *New Scientist* that she objected to excessive and unnecessary cruelty in their research methods. They were implanting tumours onto the chests of mice which were more likely to ulcerate and drag along the floor of the cage. There had been a decline in hygiene standards since 1970 when a new director was appointed and with whom she fell into conflict. She pressed her views strongly and was sacked in June 1977, accused of removing and painlessly killing animals without permission. The man who sacked her was a retired brigadier called Fowler. Others who spoke out were also sacked or invited to look elsewhere for jobs. 'We tried to use the Home Office Inspectors. But they always rang up the director to say that they were coming, so there was always a massive clean-up. The whole thing was just a mess.' Another casualty was Caroline Dear who remembered that two thirds of her work was 'chasing scientists to get them to tend to animals that were having convulsions or dying'. The Inspectors themselves were not terribly interested in the matter either, and one went so far as to tell a complaining technician to go and work in a sweet shop if she didn't like it.

Walder went to the *Evening Standard* and the *New Scientist*, and there was a war of words between them and Fowler, who described the women as 'dotty'. The remaining technicians went out on strike and some of the staff were given their jobs back. Walder was given compensation, but rather than go back, she began to campaign for reform. A lot of the cruelty, she argued, was simply due to badly designed experiments. Having said that, she felt that 'it would be hard to dream up an experiment the Home Office wouldn't let you do'.

CRAE had regular communication with the department inside the Home Office who were responsible for animal experimentation and could consult with the Home Secretary. No previous animal organisation had been able to achieve this access. 'Clive Hollands and I did most of the organising on that committee,' Ryder recalls. 'I did it in my spare time as I was working in the hospital at Oxford.' It met most of the time in the House of Lords. Kit did not care much for dressing up in what he called his 'establishment-penguin-disguise-kit' but found it necessary when he attended the meetings at Parliament since the policeman on duty would snap his feet and call him 'sir'. If he turned up dressed in his usual preferred outfit of jeans and tops that do not require ironing, 'I get searched for bombs'.

In September 1977, CRAE gave written and oral evidence to the Home Secretary's Advisory Committee which, on CRAE's recommendation, had set up an inquiry into the LD50 (Lethal Dose 50%) test: 'This crude and cruel procedure,' Hollands wrote, 'consists of determining the dosage level at which fifty per cent of the test animals survive and fifty per cent die. Almost by definition one is establishing a level of dosage at which the animals will be made ill, most of them lingering near death before succumbing or surviving.'

Despite the evidence, much of it from scientific bodies, the inquiry chose to make several recommendations but did not outlaw the practice which CRAE felt was unreliable and of little scientific value. However, the report published in 1979 did make some interesting comments on the use of living animals, and the responsibilities of those who carried them out:

> A cruel experiment under the Act is one where the pain caused by it was not justified by any resultant benefit or that it had been improperly conducted – as, for example, by neglect of the 'pain' condition... The human good envisaged must be a serious and necessary good, not a frivolous or dispensable one if the infliction of pain on animals is to be ethically acceptable... No test in which severe suffering could reasonably be foreseen should be started at a time when technicians and other staff could not be continuously available.

The report also recommended that technicians, animal handlers or any staff working in an experimental laboratory should feel free to express unease or misgiving about the welfare of animals under experiment and, if ignored by their superiors, contact the Home Office Inspectorate.

During the late seventies, Kit continued to campaign and broadcast on the issue, sometimes sharing a platform with Ryder. CRAE continued to campaign, but it was a slow process which finally led to the Animals (Scientific Procedures) Act 1986. It was not abolition, and it was not perfect, but it was something. Smoking tests on animals wouldn't be banned until 1997. The RSPCA returned to its more 'pragmatic' views in the 1980s and nineties, even investing with ICI. Arguably, better public relations on the side of the experimenters swung the argument in their favour, especially when compared to some to the headline-grabbing activities of the more extreme animal liberationists.

Angela Walder continued to campaign, and her investigations reinforced an aspect that both she and Kit understood: that much animal experimentation was pointless:

> We've got this problem that people think animal rights activists are bunny huggers, and they don't take on the intellectual argument. During 1980-82, I worked for Advocates for Animals and we were looking up the research that was going on. We did a report which then went back to a committee at the Lords showing how farcical some of this research was. The only one we got stopped was this stupid research a toothpaste manufacturer was performing on greyhounds. They had already paid for four years of adverts saying their product puts a tingle in your taste, and the tingle in your taste was chloroform. Therefore, they had to do experiments to check whether chloroform was dangerous. I can give you a lot worse than that, believe you me.
>
> There was some research going on in Swansea, looking at something in hamster urine, which cost a hundred thousand pounds. When I asked what on earth they were spending all this money for, they said it might lead to pheromones being put into gents' loos to reduce the amount of aggression at football matches. 'Do you know how many animals you killed to do this?' I asked.
>
> There is research that has never been applied, which just shows how crummy it was. It was one of Kit's things – all this fundamental research that never gets applied.
>
> The public should know these things because they moan about money being wasted on other things. There are millions and millions of pounds being spent in research that is never applied; it is totally foolish. Research just for the sake of research and it can't be used.

19
Diabolical Knowledge

'Our nuclear power programme represents a Faustian bargain in which we are jeopardising the safety of future generations and their environment for our own short-term energy benefits and the comforts that go with them. We consider that it is immoral and unwise to pursue a technology which will leave such a dangerous legacy to posterity.' – Letter to the *Guardian* signed by, and including, Kit Pedler and Gerry Davis

AT THE END OF MARCH 1975, nine-year-old Alison Pink delivered a parcel to 10 Downing Street. It was only the size of an Oxo cube, but it represented how much plutonium would be needed to wipe out the entire population of the British Isles. In July the previous year, the Labour government had agreed to allow British Nuclear Fuels Ltd to build a new nuclear fuel thermal oxide reprocessing plant (THORP) at Windscale in Cumbria, doubling its current capacity for extracting reusable uranium and plutonium from spent nuclear fuel.

Alison had with her a petition signed by nine thousand people, according to *New Scientist*, a hundred of whom accompanied her on a march through London organised by the Conservation Society. Some of them carried banners which read 'Radioactive waste can kill', 'Do not open for 25,000 years', and the underlying message of the march: 'Say NO to nuclear power'. It should come as no surprise that one of the marchers was Kit Pedler.

Earlier in the year, Kit was among the signatories to a letter published in the *Guardian* which criticised the government for its pro-nuclear policy, and for not waiting for the Royal Commission on Environmental Pollution to conclude its investigation into the safety of nuclear waste storage. The letter ended on a familiar theme: 'We should make use of all heat produced and not waste it as we currently do from most of our buildings, power stations and municipal incinerators.' Heating water by reproducing processes that went on inside the sun, rather than using the energy that was coming from it, was ludicrous.

The economic arguments for nuclear power are that for such a small amount of uranium, more electricity can be generated than by using fossil fuels. Nuclear power is not affected by price fluctuations in the global markets. It is also seen as cleaner because it emits less carbon dioxide into the atmosphere, only steam. But you can't make a nuclear bomb from coal waste, and oil residue does not take thousands of years to break down; neither can it kill you as quickly as radioactive particles released in the air.

The British government had been investigating whether to buy under licence the cheaper American-designed light water reactors (LWR). They did not have a very good reputation, even in America. The United States Atomic Energy Commission had admitted to 850 'abnormal occurrences' in seventeen operating months of nuclear power stations, and two people had died. Hardly surprisingly, the government turned it down. 'Besides design weaknesses there have been human failures in quality control,' Kit Pedler told the *Daily Express* in February 1974, the month in which the decision was made. 'It could never happen with the British gas-cooled reactor. We've found no way to fault it on safety grounds.'

Kit had pointed out the other argument against nuclear power. It is an incredibly complex system to operate and maintain. Mistakes can be made quite easily because man, as an operator, is fallible. The more complicated the interface, the more catastrophic a simple mistake can be, and in a nuclear situation the accidents could take centuries to recover from. At the Design and Industries Association's conference 'The Truth About Garbage' in Amsterdam in 1974, Kit had been the opening speaker; *The Times* reported:

> On present United States estimates, he said, there would be one 'accident' every 1,000 reactor years. Since there were 100 nuclear reactors in the United States, that meant there would be one 'accident' every 10 years. And, of course, it was impossible to estimate the seriousness of any such 'accident'.

Brainrack *and* The Dynostar Menace

Kit Pedler and Gerry Davis had been researching the issue of the safety record of the American nuclear power plants for their second novel, *Brainrack*. It would centre upon Britain's first privatised nuclear power plant, set in a remote part of Scotland called Grimness (probably inspired by Torness, where Britain's last second-generation nuclear power plant was going to be built). It was the issue of human failure which intrigued the writers. What if simple mistakes were being made by technicians and engineers who were working on huge and complicated machines, where a simple mistake resulted in catastrophe? To err is human, but supposing the errors were exaggerated by the effects of another everyday technological waste product, creating the titular brainrack effect itself?

This product was emitted by a car's exhaust pipe, one of 180 separate chemicals that come out from it: cyclic pentane acetylide. It attacks the brain, reduces the intelligence, and affects a person's behaviour. This 'self-induced idiocy from the motor car!' as one of the characters exclaims, was called the dinosaur effect or brainrack. People begin to make simple mistakes; and this leads to the meltdown of the Grimness power plant, which is described both vividly and colourfully.

The book was published in hardback in February 1974, at the height of the government-enforced power cuts during the three-day week because of the coal-miners' strike. As a result, there were delays in getting this much anticipated book to the shops. With its topical central theme of energy, it received many favourable reviews in the press, and the authors were interviewed together for several radio programmes.

Having irradiated part of the British Isles, and condemned nuclear power and the motor car to oblivion, Kit and Gerry wondered what would come next after nuclear energy if the ingenious technocrats had their way? They began work on their third and final novel, *The Dynostar Menace* (originally *Starshock*), and imagined how, following the cataclysmic events of *Brainrack*, and an explosion at a Russian fast breeder reactor in Odessa, mankind turned away from fission, and towards fusion – the power of the sun, generated by an orbiting fusion reactor. This controversial project was called Dynostar, and by 1986 was within seconds of being 'switched on' by its exhausted crew of technicians – until word reached them that it had to be decommissioned. Someone had got their sums wrong and the vast magnetic fields they would be generating would destroy the Earth's ozone layer. A slight snag lies in the fact that the process to begin the fusion reactor is on an automated countdown.

As the story unfolds, one of the men on board the Dynostar is not prepared to see the work abandoned, and starts to kill off the crew, one at a time. To his twisted mind, all that is needed is a demonstration of the power of the Dynostar for the world to be saved. The survivors try to shut down the station knowing that one of them is a murderer several times over. The authorities back on Earth try to work out who that man is.

Our killer is a very jealous and psychologically deranged scientist who makes their job almost impossible by irradiating the control room, requiring the shutdown procedure to be performed in a different manner. This gives him more time for him to kill off the remainder of the crew. Kit went over to Houston, Texas, in August 1974 to meet genuine astronauts to give the book some trademark authentic flavour.

The book ends optimistically:

> In the year 1989 fusion research was finally abandoned and all further work directed towards the exploitation of natural power sources. Solar energy machines, geothermal probes and wind generators all began to take practical form. By the early nineties, the necessary technology for a post-industrial millennium was assembled and waiting.

It would be Kit and Gerry's final project together, and it was rather fitting that it ended where it had begun nearly ten years before on *Doctor Who*, with a disaster in space. The hardback came out in 1975, and the paperback followed a year later, just when the problems of nuclear waste disposal began to take the headlines.

And they centred upon one remote part of the Cumberland coast.

The Windscale crisis

The proposed new reprocessing plant was going to join a complex that had been hurriedly built when the post-war government decided it needed to have its own nuclear bomb-making programme. Windscale was going to be where the plutonium was to be separated from spent fuel rods. The first civil nuclear power station constructed here was called Calder Hall, opened by the Queen with such hopes in 1957. Now they wanted to build a new plant that would reprocess nuclear fuel not only from Britain's nuclear power stations, but also from countries such as Japan. It would become the only commercial plant in the West handling uranium oxide fuel.

The problem was that Windscale suffered from a long history of accidents and scares, the most serious being the 1957 fire which destroyed the core of one of four nuclear piles. This released radioactive dust into the surrounding area, contaminating grazing fields for cattle. 670,000 gallons of milk were deemed unfit for human consumption. The first peacetime nuclear energy accident made Windscale a household name. Over the lifetime of the site there have been further leaks, discharges, and some deliberate voiding of waste, either into the air or into the Irish sea. The controversy with the Irish government continues to this day.

In October 1973, thirty-five workers were exposed to radioactivity for fifteen minutes in a room which was designed to suck in fresh air in the event of a leak, but did the opposite, expelling the contamination outside. An inquiry found that oversensitive safety devices had been ignored by the workers. Another leak shortly before this one led to forty workers somehow being trapped with radioactive contamination, resulting in workers demanding danger money and adding to the already deteriorating labour relations. A third leak took place in May 1975, where radioactive effluent containing cobalt 60 and caesium 137 escaped into a storm drain and into the river Calder. The leak may have been going on for a month, yet Windscale authorities insisted that the level of radiation was no more than would be found in ordinary drinking water. No doubt Kit had something to say on that when he appeared on Radio 4's news programme *The World at One* on 22 May.

At the end of the year, a locomotive shunting a train loaded with nuclear fuel imported from Japan was derailed at Barrow. There was no damage or leaks, but these events made the public and the politicians very nervous indeed. Windscale wanted to become the nuclear dustbin of the world, with a £400 million contract signed with Japan to process their waste, and there was simply no foolproof method for safely disposing of the waste except storing it underground.

Planning permission for the extension at Windscale rested in the hands of Cumbria County Council, but they were urged to refer the matter to the government. By the middle of 1976, demands were growing for an open public inquiry as objections also came in from the neighbouring Isle of Man. But the local population were very much in favour of the employment prospects. 'Who are these people who come from London in a special train with a poet and a clarinet player?' asked a foreman from a nearby factory in

The Times at the beginning of June. 'What do they know about life in a deprived area like this?'

Just to make things hotter, the Royal Commission finally reported in 1976. The report raised concerns over the safety of fast breeder reactors which British Nuclear Fuels wanted to construct. It was also concerned with safe transportation, and proliferation of plutonium falling into the hands of a rogue nation, or terrorists.

Cumbria County Council duly referred the matter to the Secretary of State for the Environment, Peter Shore; and within a month, news emerged of yet another leakage of low-level radioactive water from a storage silo at Windscale. On 22 December, Shore decided that the most controversial part of British Nuclear Fuels Ltd's (BNFL) bid, namely the thermal oxide reprocessing plant, should be treated separately from the rest of BNFL's proposals, and be submitted to a public inquiry, beginning in June 1977. The tribunal would be led by Justice Parker, aided by two technical assessors. Parker would take the unusual step of requiring all witnesses to take an oath to 'emphasise the gravity of the issues at stake'.

It was against this background that the *Daily Express* asked Kit Pedler to put the case against nuclear power, which would be followed by a rebuttal from the man 'who wants to expand nuclear power in Britain', BNFL's Managing Director, Con Allday. 'This Deal with the Devil', printed in December, attacks the blind acceptance of technological omnipotence in those Kit calls the 'nuclear technocrats'. There is, he says, no technology that can ever be developed which is proof against 'an operator who is late for shaving, has a row with his wife over breakfast, goes into the nuclear control room and presses the wrong button. The combination of insufficiently safe technology and inevitable human error means that as more nuclear power plants are built an accident does not become likely, it becomes an absolute certainty.' He cites leaks that took place at American reprocessing storage centres and where major disasters have been averted. Storage tanks that needed to house waste for 24,000 years had to be taken out of commission after twenty.

Allday begins his counterargument by saying that the nuclear industry is the cheapest, cleanest, and safest of all the power generating industries. He rattles off a list of statistics about deaths from accidents in the coal industry, and looks forward to the inevitable disasters awaiting the oil and gas rigs out in the North Sea. He also uses an argument in the Club of Rome's *Limits to*

Growth to point out how once fossil fuels are consumed they are gone, whereas, in a fast breeder reactor, uranium could be 'spun out almost indefinitely'. He concludes that 'if we are really worried about safety at work, the environment and the economy we should burn more uranium, not less. That would mean that a small amount of nuclear waste would have to be stored, as it has been in complete safety since the nuclear fuel industry began, or disposed of when safe methods are identified.'

It was an astonishingly complacent piece, completely dismissive in tone. He couldn't easily refute the concerns of the anti-nuclear lobby, so opted instead simply to update the old adage 'Where there's muck, there's brass,' and say the future will deal with it. He – or whichever public relations officer really wrote the piece – did not need to put up a huge defence, as further nuclear power stations were seen as inevitable. Hardly surprisingly, the subsequent reaction in the *Express*'s letters pages came down firmly on Kit's side. There was still a long way to go for people to accept that the nuclear argument was the answer to their energy needs.

Allday did not understand the fear nuclear power created. Tony Benn, the Minister for Energy whose diaries for 1977 contain a section called *The Windscale Crisis*, revealed that all was not well at the plant. It got to the point that inept management triggered strike action, and Benn had to consider whether to send in troops to provide necessary CO_2 and nitrogen cylinders. Had it become publicly known, this would have killed off BNFL's expansionist plans. The government took safety very seriously and were not pleased when accidents or leaks were not reported to the Ministry straight away; one case took two months to be reported.

Supporters for nuclear power felt that the nuclear debate was just as irrational and emotionally charged as the vivisection one. When the *Listener* reviewed Kit's appearance on *Man Alive* on 15 May 1975 which looked at waste in general, the reviewer noted that Kit was 'looking – or at least dressing – more than ever like Jesus with the passage of time…' He was accused of:

> … making a whole string of false assertions about the hazards of nuclear wastes, and Dr Ned Franklin, the new chairman and managing director of the National Nuclear Corporation and an honest man if ever there was one, not given a chance to reply. Surely, I ask myself, there is enough genuine information to alarm the layman, if that is what he really wants, without television to concoct it.

The programme was previewed by Joan Bakewell in *Radio Times* who described Kit as:

> ... one of my favourite scientists... and he's not optimistic about being able to safeguard against accidents. At Windscale, where the nuclear waste will remain dangerous for thousands of years, the margin for error stretches beyond the imagination. It represents what the producer David Filkin refers to as 'the madness of leaving this to posterity'.

One viewer from Hull protested at Kit's use of 'scaremongering techniques to discredit the honest attempts at waste control from power stations'. Kit disagreed that he was scaremongering, or disputing the honesty of the work going on at the Sizewell plant in Suffolk, but pointed to another Windscale leak being reported in the newspapers that week.

Building your own nuclear bomb

A few weeks before the inquiry began, the *Daily Express* turned once again to Kit Pedler to highlight just how dangerous the plutonium by-product of nuclear reactors could be. Kit was going to demonstrate how 'easy' it was to build a nuclear bomb in your back garden, or in this case, his new back garden in rural Kent. At first glance, this seemed quite a preposterous idea. He was not going to have access to the plutonium, nor was he going to get his hands on the high explosives needed to trigger the bomb. The idea was a simple one: was there enough information already out there that could, if the will was there (and in the mid 1970s there were enough terrorist groups of all political persuasions to make the authorities twitch), enable them to build a functioning atomic bomb?

The idea had been around for some time. Kit had suggested it as a storyline for *Doomwatch* back in 1970, but what must have been the catalyst for the piece was an event in America a year before. An American student called John Aristotle Phillips made headlines around the world when he claimed to have designed a bomb as part of a research project. It was the size of a beach ball and had one third of the power of the Hiroshima bomb. His design was based on publicly available documents, and some inspired guesswork. He also discovered the name of the explosive used by the US Army to trigger the bomb by simply telephoning the manufacturer. Although it was a design twenty years out of date, if detonated, it still had the potential to inflict severe damage. The interest his project generated was so great that Phillips claimed to have received a phone call from someone purportedly representing the Pakistani government, wishing to buy a copy of the plans.

In the two-page piece published on Wednesday 18 May 1977, Kit Pedler is billed as the consultant to the *Daily Express* project, with an unidentified person designing the bomb itself. But Kit was the man who designed and built the 'safe' bomb from existing and published knowledge, and he had a number of experts to call on for help, including the same people from Imperial College in London who had advised the *Doomwatch* team in 1971 on an episode where students steal a consignment of plutonium and build their bomb.

'We are already in the "plutonium economy",' Kit wrote in his summing up of the experiment called 'The Diabolical Knowledge We Have To Live With'. There was more than 10,000 kilograms of plutonium in circulation in the United States which was not behind the walls of a military complex, but in ordinary private *industrial* premises. There was very clear evidence that this most lethal of materials was going missing, enough to make a bomb which requires ten kilograms. This mainly came from the chips and dust wastage generated from machining, and however carefully that waste was collected there would always be some Material Unaccounted For: the MUF Factor.

How could deadly plutonium just go missing like this? Some believe that it is sold on to the black market, or secretly supplied to friendly countries without arousing world condemnation. On 13 November 1974, an American worker from Kerr-McGee's Cimarron River plutonium plant called Karen Silkwood died in a mysterious car crash. For the past year, she had been concerned by the plant's safety record, especially after several overworked employees had been directly exposed to plutonium, herself included. She also discovered that over forty pounds of plutonium had gone missing from the plant, and this was later confirmed by the company. She was planning to show a reporter her evidence that the plant had been covering up safety violations and falsifying records. The plant was closed in 1975, and the company was successfully sued by Silkwood's relatives although they denied the suggestion that they had killed her. It is a conspiracy theory that rumbles on, but the missing plutonium and the levels of contamination found on Silkwood are facts. President Carter publicly aired his own misgivings over the plutonium production programme. There needed to be safeguards preventing the plutonium from being hijacked in transit.

Kit took his research from university libraries which held material openly published by the United States National Technical Information Service;

books on the construction of the original atomic bombs, and a chance to look at the real thing which was on display at the Atomic Museum in Albuquerque. Assuming the plutonium had been acquired, the article detailed the very complicated process needed to convert plutonium oxide into concentrated plutonium nitrate, using readily available tools such as a sealed-glove box, an electric induction furnace, high temperature crucibles, and a host of various chemicals. The details of the process came from *The Plutonium Handbook* published in 1967, which shows how to refine, purify, cast, machine, and finish the plutonium.

The idea is to create tiny amounts of plutonium 239 and cast them in hollow four-inch-wide hemispheres to avoid accidentally creating a lump large enough to achieve critical mass and explode all by itself. Two steel hemispheres which formed the shell of the implosion assembly comprised the next section to be built, with the explosives arranged around the plutonium in such a manner that, when they explode at the same time, the force drives the hollow pieces of plutonium together at the centre called the initiator, all within a fraction of a second. Neutrons fly out from the initiator and rupture the nuclei of the imploding plutonium in a chain reaction.

In the *Daily Express* piece Kit observed:

> The most severe problem was to achieve simultaneous detonation of all explosive lenses, after the plutonium hemispheres had been driven together. The problem centres about making or buying sufficiently consistent explosive detonators; but with the very high-quality electronic control units I built, this weakness in the design means only that the explosion might be less than the maximum, not that the machine would fail to go off altogether.

In other words, it would not result in the mushroom cloud of lore, but become a dirty bomb, known in the trade as a 'fizzle'.

Kit discovered that only a few parts of the process required a high degree of precision engineering: 'the remainder could actually be rigged in a very crude manner'. The arming device was adapted from a cooker timer and servo motors advertised in the *Exchange and Mart*. Detonation circuits were linked to a telephone, allowing an explosive to be triggered by a phone call. The article goes into much more detail than suggested here, and the paper itself removed a couple of sections, replaced with the melodramatic word DELETED. The photograph of the finished 'bomb' contained a deliberate error, as did the text. In fact, you may spot the deliberate error in the paragraph quoted above. After the bomb was photographed, the prototype and data were destroyed.

The photo used in the paper shows a metal frame with what appears to be a 'football' at one end surrounded symmetrically by circular attachments, linked by wires to the detonator. The finished work was shown to Professor Joseph Rotblat, the recently retired head of the physics department at Bart's Hospital who had worked with the British team at the Los Alamos atomic bomb project during the last war and was the only scientist to quit before the first test explosion. 'Having looked at this, if there was anything wrong with the physics, I would have noticed it. But it looks all right, although I don't know how far it would go.' Hardly a ringing endorsement on the face of it, but had the real thing been built, it wouldn't have mattered. Where plutonium is concerned, a fizz is as good as a bang.

The developer of the Kent bomb concluded:

> Had I known at the outset how easy the task was to be, I would certainly never have taken it on. I am sickened and frightened by what I was able to achieve by recourse to ordinary published information. Perhaps the worst discovery of all was that I was beginning to have ideas about improvements in weapon design. I will never think in this way again.

But Kit understood that, for a scientist, being given a challenge is sometimes hard to resist. Furthermore, thousands of physicist students graduated from universities every year with enough skill to interpret the data from various publications and knowledge of atomic theory.

The Windscale inquiry

Meanwhile, the Windscale inquiry was getting closer, and opponents were mobilising. Mrs Renee-Marie Croose Parry was a German refugee whom Kit knew socially through her role in the creation of the Teilhard* Centre for the Future of Man. It was at one of her dinners that Kit met Club of Rome's Dr John Platt in 1972, shortly after *The Limits to Growth* had been published. Croose-Parry had placed an expensive page-and-a-half advertisement in the

---

* Pierre Teilhard de Chardin had once been a Jesuit, but he was a geologist, a palaeontologist, questioned the doctrine of original sin, and accepted modern science theories on evolution. He also believed that the Earth was enveloped in a layer of thought which he called the noosphere. He died in 1955 but his ideas attracted a following.

Guardian, signed by two thousand people, on behalf of a group calling itself People for a Non-Nuclear World, which raised £10,000 in contributions towards their involvement in presenting their case to the inquiry. It also generated ten thousand letters to the US Embassy in London calling for President Carter to 'denuclearise' the world. The brother of the *Ecologist* editor Teddy Goldsmith, Sir Jimmy Goldsmith, was prepared to underwrite any legal costs of up to £25,000 and had been busy canvassing and lobbying fellow industrialists. The Windscale Appeal would be represented by David Widdicombe QC who waived his fee. Other environmentalist groups were mobilising, such as the Conservation Society, who organised the demonstration mentioned at the top of this chapter. The Isle of Man made available £30,000 to be represented as an objector too.

Windscale Appeal was an umbrella title for various groups which had got together and organised themselves to ensure that the best one was chosen to represent each particular issue. For example, the *New Scientist* observed, the Concern Against Nuclear Technology Organisation was best placed to concentrate on radiological hazards, accidents, and the problems surrounding waste storage, while the Society for Environmental Improvement could argue the case for alternative energy sources. Kit Pedler was called on to put the case of how easy it is to build a nuclear bomb and he prepared a brief, based on his *Express* article. There would also be more traditional opponents from vested interests within the labour movement, such as Arthur Scargill, president of the National Union of Mineworkers, which upset the trade unionists at Windscale.

They had very little time to assemble their case, and it showed. The 'disjointed and careless' submissions made to the inquiry in October 1977 did not impress *New Scientist*'s Ian Breach who covered the full inquiry in exhaustive detail.

Kit Pedler was among the final witnesses called before the inquiry on behalf of Windscale Appeal, alongside Teddy Goldsmith and Dr Charles Wakstein: 'disciples, all three of disaster,' wrote Breach, 'and draughtsmen of its dynamics. If aught goes wrong, locally or globally, it will come as no surprise to these men.' Wakstein showed a film which was apparently rather shoddily put together, showing 'spurious' visuals which did not have much to do with the matter at hand. Goldsmith spoke rapidly on his familiar theme taken from his 1972 argument 'A Blueprint for Survival': 'an almost gleeful litany of apocalypse in waiting'. He was tripped up over a couple of mistakes about industrial workers' health and longevity, which he then claimed strengthened his argument 'to audible astonishment' from the assembled audience.

Kit was sandwiched between these two speakers. His topic, as listed in the finished Windscale report, was: 'Existing security arrangements not sufficient to withstand terrorist attack (not a security expert).' Breach reported that:

> Kit Pedler, as lugubrious as ever, was given short shrift of Guinness-record proportions… Justice Parker thought it better not to republish what, essentially, had already appeared in a Pedler *Daily Express* exercise and ruled that the (eleven page) submission be entered only as a document. The author of *Doomwatch* was in and out of the witness chair in under three minutes.

However, Parker conceded that the long-delayed Royal Commission report thought that Kit's idea was credible.

The decision to proceed with the thermal oxide reprocessing plant was taken following a final Parliamentary debate on 15 May 1978. It opened in 1994 and suffered a serious leak in 2004. Also in 1978, the Dounreay fast breeder reactor, the only one in Britain, was shut down when the government withdrew its financial support for further nuclear development. It will become a brownfield site and open for redevelopment by the year 2030, but only at a total cost of £2.3 billion, whereas the THORP building can only be demolished by the end of this century.

The alternative technology movement

What was happening to the early pioneers of the alternative technology movement to whom Kit was firmly attached? These were still the early days of enthusiastic pioneers, confused thinking and mismatched ideologies. The early objectives of the movement, if it can even be described as such as opposed to an aspiration towards a particular direction, were beginning to become unstuck as enthusiasts discovered for themselves how difficult it was to become truly self-sufficient.

In 1976, *Environment News* reported how one 'social idealist' had bought himself a four-acre farm in the Dandenongs in Australia, planning to make do without fertilisers, pesticides or heavy technology. He hit upon a major snag: time management: 'When we'd spent a year digging our small veggie garden by hand and watching our neighbour hoe acres of ground with a machine much more effectively and in a fraction of the time, we did start using a rotary hoe. To be specific, one gallon of petrol will cultivate half an acre in two hours, a job which might take two hundred hours by hand.' Farming, he discovered, was difficult and exhausting, but it was also rewarding, and he understood why farmers preferred to stay on their land rather than work in the city. Wind power was too expensive as it required the regular replacement of lead and acid within the batteries which were storing the power. 'Is there any point in everyone learning how to make a saucepan, keep bees, drill their teeth or knit a jumper? Trying to become good at too many things means you end up doing none of them well.'

The Biotechnic Research and Development (BRAD) community in Wales had other issues. The families who had moved in with Robin Clarke shared a farmhouse called Eithin-y-Gaer, with forty-four acres of farmland and woods. To begin with, they still needed to use a bulldozer to get the house ready before their first winter and had to keep the local planning officials happy. They were planning to build a completely autonomous house, independent in water and electricity. They installed a solar roof to heat the water, and a heat pump to extract heat from a nearby stream and blow hot air through the house. They were exploring new ways of treating and reusing waste, as well as experiments in agricultural techniques. 'It's very sophisticated and it'll cost a packet,' Clarke told Patrick Rivers in *The Survivalists*.

The well-publicised community found that they could become inundated with visitors which was a big distraction, and some felt it impaired the way the members of the group related to each other. Other personal tensions and dynamics developed within the group. Clarke and his wife left BRAD in 1974 to start a farm on their own in Shropshire, and BRAD was finally abandoned and sold in 1976 to an ashram. 'The essential message from here seems to be that building a solar roof, one's own house even, is child's play compared with close, honest, open communal living therein,' Rivers concluded.

Peter Brachi, a former BRAD member, wrote in *Undercurrents*:

> We each entered the commune with a fantasy; not in the sense of mad delusions, but a well worked out scenario of expectations. For a time, you project, superimposing your fantasy upon reality; until a scene diverges dramatically from one's personal script: your wife walks out; the newborn calf dies; the windmill fails to work; your husband sleeps with the woman downstairs; the barley crop rots. Then you either freak out completely, adjust your fantasy, or draw a deep breath and begin to grow up.

Peter Harper, who coined the phrase alternative technology in the early seventies, had identified the problem as early as 1974. 'Alternative Technology is Dead!', he wrote in *Undercurrents*: 'Most alternative technology folk are middle class… whose only experience is the technology of consumption… they've never experienced the inside of a factory… they forget that the windmills, the generators, the solar panels have to be mined, manufactured, assembled and transported, etc.' Large resources still needed to be available. Advocates needed political and economic reality. It could not all be made at home in isolation or in village units. There were still going to be some ugly sides to AT. There would still be the need for pylons to transmit the power from unsightly and noisy windmills to other parts of the country. What do all these projects mean for the man in Dagenham?

Kit put his own take on what, truly, alternative technology's ultimate purpose was in a short article for *Undercurrents*:

> ALTERNATIVE TECHNOLOGY and the alternative lifestyle are rapidly approaching a crisis where progress could either accelerate rapidly or grind to a halt altogether. Time and time again, thoroughly happy events are organised where windmills are erected, solar panels grow warm, and clichés are exchanged over home-baked bread to an obbligato of folk music. After the regulation discussions of imminent doom, the meetings break up and the participants go back to being parasitic on the very society they hold to be so objectionable that nothing is achieved. Meanwhile the voracious claws of high technology continue to rake the tired earth.
>
> The future of western man is now obviously a neck and neck race between the gentle freedoms of the individual and the completely efficient control processes of ruthlessly organised national bureaucracies. Realistic alternative technologies have one great politically important function; they could restore some aspects of those freedoms to individuals who are fast becoming decerebrated by the media, stripped of skills by the seductions of the commercial world and made to work even harder at dehumanising tasks to earn money to pay grossly inflated prices for the basic necessities of food, warmth and shelter and to buy glittering artefacts of no conceivable function. No changes are in sight and the position grows inexorably worse. If people can really be offered detailed plans of how to achieve their own independence by alternative means, then the centralised purveyors of their basic needs can be isolated and disemployed. But the great problem at the moment is that alternative technology does not work, because it has not been studied and worked out in anything like sufficient detail to make it a viable replacement for the existing status quo.

If a member of an urban commune catches pneumonia he will still need the antibiotics of straight medicine to survive. If a person visits another group, it is almost certain that he will burn petrol, oil or coal in the process. He or she will need to eat a minimum amount of protein, carbohydrates and fat to avoid starvation. Where will it all come from? If alternative and more self-sufficient housing is to emerge in urban areas, repressive rating laws, irrelevant building regulations and autocratic planning authorities of no competence will have to be fought and beaten in the courts. The alternative future is not to do with tools alone, it is to do with the effects of tools and how the overriding influence and power of the commercialised tool makers can be excelled and thus isolated. It is also to do with the courage necessary to spurn the grotesque and dangerous pharmacopoeia offered to the sick by the archaic rigidities of technical medicine. It also concerns the development of alternative food technologies to replace the over-packaged and systematically poisoned imitations of food to be found on the supermarket shelves.

Hard, unremitting detailed study must begin now. The whole fabric of alternative living must be researched, assembled, and disseminated as rapidly as possible before the existing system can be dismantled. There is simply no time to lose; we can no longer afford to wait for someone else to work out the details. There is an enormously powerful and richly humane spirit abroad within the alternative movement. I absolutely believe in its power for change, in its power to give back to a tired and sickened people a self-regard which is being crushed out of them by the all powerful effects of the commercial governmental axis and the faceless bullying of the bureaucrats. To create a detailed manifesto for a viable alternative life we need special skills quickly. Engineers, jurists, healers, scientists, writers, artists. We all fit in, we all have a contribution to make.

At Rotherhithe Street, Surrey Docks, on 29 May until 6 June a festival of alternative living is being held. Will you go, and if so, why?

The festival was called 'The People's Habitat' and was designed to be a counterblast to a global conference going on in Canada called 'Habitat: the United Nations Conference on Human Settlements'. This had been set up to investigate the impact of urbanisation. Dismissed as 'a conference for bureaucrats – the same old questions, the same old answers', the People's Habitat would instead be 'a festival of alternative living', designed to showcase and discuss alternative technology. It was organised by Fiona Cantell of Intermediate Technology Publications, which had been created by Ernst Schumacher, to push forward his views as set down in his book

Small is Beautiful. Both Schumacher and Kit contributed words for an accompanying booklet.

The Surrey Docks were only a mile and a half from Tower Bridge and had been abandoned and mostly demolished since the early 1970s. Locally, the area was known as 'the island' and was now a peaceful place within the metropolis. It started to become colonised and soon London's first urban farm was established. An advert for People's Habitat in *New Scientist* declared:

> Surrey Docks is an example of the destructiveness of our capitalist society. The docks are now unused and half are already filled in, dockers have had to find work elsewhere and the spirit of the place is almost gone. Can it be saved? It can indeed, if the good things of the past and the future can flourish; already old warehouses have been converted to craft workshops and a theatre. People's Habitat will bring an alternative life to Rotherhithe Street during the festival and will try to leave more than pleasant memories behind.

The festival featured practical workshops on the construction of wind generators, solar panels, building skills, urban farming, new uses for waste land, spinning, weaving and many other personal skills. There were discussion workshops debating aspects of changing the human settlement, the politics of alternative technology, devolution, cooperatives, and the use and ownership of land. There would be films, and the inevitable music, ranging from African to chamber. It was a distillation of the past four years, aiming to show how AT could be applied to the urban environment, and not from an inaccessible Welsh farm.

'Is this what Habitat should have been all about?' mused a writer in *New Scientist*. 'Unsung, poorly financed, and meagrely attended…' The centrepiece of the People's Habitat was an unusual windmill for Britain, as it was based on one used by the Cretans. The locals loved it and wanted to keep it to pump water for their allotments which sprang up around the docks, but the conventional Southwark Council wanted it taken down, and for the allotments to go. They had traditional plans to redevelop the site for business.

The day after the People's Habitat finished, Kit could be seen on a Granada Television programme called *Say That Again*, discussing the recent series *A House for the Future*, which showed a family building an energy-efficient house from scratch.

The future for AT was in education. Some of the early activists became lecturers at the Open University, and still lecture to this day on the topic.

The very first course was called Man-Made Futures and attracted seven hundred students. The Centre for Alternative Technology in Wales, which will celebrate its fiftieth anniversary in 2023, neatly solved the problem BRAD had with visitors by encouraging them to explore their work. As well as a practical exhibition for self-sufficiency and AT, it educates the next generation of architects and engineers.

The next generation were going to be given the necessary knowledge and insights. This would never come willingly from government, fixed in the ways of an older generation who wanted to abolish slums and embrace modern time-saving conveniences, without realising that it could create new problems for the future, or those who believed that wealth creation was the only solution to society's problems, and that cheap energy could only come from the inexhaustible power of the atom, or from underneath the ground.

The future in 1976 looked bleak, and Kit was pessimistic, and impatient:

> People are seeing the sort of conditioning to which they have been exposed over the years by big industry… It is going to stop now, anyway, so now we can get back to the lost art of living. People often say, 'You're just an idiot – sort of romantic.' I just say, 'Well, I don't care a damn what you think, it's going to happen whether we like it or not.'

15
The Road to Gaia

> What makes me feel magnificent and superhuman to lie in a field? What makes me feel rotten to lie on a bed of concrete? There is something in my subconscious that tells me one is right and the other is wrong for humans. Therefore, I want to protect it. It's the essence of people. I think the rest is garbage. – Kit Pedler, proposal for a TV documentary series called *Men of Mystery*, October 1976

KIT PEDLER BUILT HIS HOME-MADE nuclear bomb at Great Catts Farm, a few miles south of Canterbury. The move in 1975 had been planned to allow Lucy time to finish her O levels, but it was still a wrench to leave Clapham, especially for Lucy who had been born in that house. Lucy was so put out that, by her own account, she didn't speak to her mother for a couple of months. Eldest son Mark was not impressed when he discovered that Canterbury nightlife was a contradiction in terms, and chose to stay in London and continue his work in the antiques trade: 'He probably said the family left him rather than him leaving home,' says Lucy. Mark's relationship with his father had not been a particularly good one when he was a teenager, although it would improve. Lucy went down to Plymouth in 1978 to study architecture, something her father encouraged.

After thirty years of city living, it must have been a relief for Kit to get away from the dehumanising and polluting environment that had shaped his pre-*Doomwatch* and *Doctor Who* thinking, but he wasn't too far away to visit London when necessary.

Like Kit's childhood home in Suffolk, Great Catts Farm was a very old building, possibly dating back as early as the fourteenth century. It was approached down a very steep bumpy drive which reached the house at the bottom of a dip. In front of the house was a lawn and a couple of habitable outbuildings, including one called 'the hut' in which Carol and her husband Michael Topolski first stayed shortly after the birth of their eldest daughter.

The living room had an inglenook fireplace and the house often smelled of wood smoke. One interviewer in 1979 noted elements Kit had built himself, such as a handmade easy chair in the shape of the British Kite Mark, with broad flat panels on the arm rests that could be used either as supports or working surfaces. There was also the nucleus of a stereo system that Kit was building himself. His paintings and sculptures and collections of antique medical equipment were also on display.

Although the house had a wonderful atmosphere it could be quite cold and draughty. Upstairs there were four bedrooms and Lucy had the top attic room. Attached to the left of the house was a garage with a room above that Kit converted into his office. He also had a big workshop where he continued with his projects.

Kit wanted to see how far he could practically lead a low-impact lifestyle in the direction towards which he had been turning since 1972. One thing that had to go was his fast car. Carol Topolski says:

> I always very much admired him for giving up his fast car. He *always* had a fast car, and he bought himself a Vauxhall Astra or something similar which he calculated to be the most environmentally friendly car in the country at the time. So, from driving a Ferrari or a Veranti everywhere, he went to driving this nasty little box! He put his money where his mouth was in that sense. It was about energy efficiency.

Saving fuel and cutting down on traffic pollution was the intention behind a rather ingenious idea that came not just from Kit, but also from his agent, Harvey Unna. Together, in January 1975, they applied for a patent on 'a battery operated, driver-controlled device for the intermittent low-speed propulsion of a vehicle otherwise propelled by another prime mover such as an internal combustion engine'. Stuck in a traffic jam with the engine running, burning petrol, and emitting exhaust fumes? Switch off the engine, and switch on an electric motor, which moves a roller attached to the tread of the tyre of one wheel. It was also intended to reduce pollution within repair shops and would be a 'low gear equivalent' drive in icy conditions.

Kit wasn't just planning to replace the car's bumper with carved wood, a neglected material in these days of alloys. He designed and built a wooden chassis for his car. Kit told one interviewer from abroad:

> The big advantage of a wooden-bodied car is that all the panels are flat and easily replaceable. Wood is cheaper to manufacture and work than steel and it doesn't rust (if varnished). The industry creates cars in curvy shapes that they claim are aerodynamic and save on fuel. But the effects on economy at normal speeds are negligible and, in my view, styling exercises are just marketing gimmicks to give the motorist a chance to drive something that looks like a spaceship. I'd like to see cars marketed as kits with the buyers making the bodywork themselves out of easily worked marine plywood fixed to angle irons as I have done.

Kit's car was christened the Woodworm Express. By being lighter, the car would be more economical to run. The unknown newspaper that ran this piece ended the article by saying, 'See, I told you. The British are stark raving mad – but delightfully so.'

Great Catts Farm was the scene for another dangerous wind turbine experiment, by Kit's own account in *The Quest for Gaia*: 'One high speed mill I designed and built threw a blade in a gale one hundred feet like an unguided missile and rammed itself nearly a foot into flinty soil.' 'I think he was quite disappointed,' says Lucy. Yet he found that the best design could still be seen working on the plain of Lasithi in Crete, and one was put up at the People's Habitat exhibition. 'It was an extremely galling experience to discover by experiment that all my physics, mechanics and aerodynamics had only led me to discover that the most suitable design of windmill for the post-industrial age was probably two thousand years old.'

Living in the country gave Una a chance to try out all sorts of cottage farm activities. She grew at least twenty different vegetables for drying and bottling; and then there were the goats, one of them being a truculent animal called Heidi 'who gave us delicious milk if she didn't kick over the bucket first as we tried to milk her', remembers Lucy. Una would make homemade goat's cheese in a utility room, which was part of a modern extension to the house. 'The house also came with several geese; unfortunately our dear, enthusiastic family dog Fang scared a couple of them to death, but we did have some lovely goose eggs for supper.'

Lucy remembers Fang well:

At 119 Park Hill, we had this dog called Tansey. The only time I ever saw Dad cry was when he came and told me on my bunk bed that she had died. We weren't thinking of getting another family dog as we were all traumatised by Tansey's death, but one of Carol's friends had a little puppy and there was no home for it. Dad was very against getting another dog as he wanted to mourn Tansey for a little longer.

We all had a family conference and the only way we could persuade him to accept adopting this little mongrel puppy was if he chose the name: Bradley. There was a character in *Doomwatch* called Bradley which must have been the reason. We all hated it so much that Mark called him Fang, hoping that he would become this enormous dog, but he didn't; he was a tiny little dog. We all knew him as Fang – except for my Dad. Since he was home a lot, he would talk to the dog. He said several times how he would give his entire scientific knowledge if he could understand how animals thought. He would have long conversations with the dog and the cats, and he would suppose their answers, so this would be a kind of two-way discussion. He had a particular affinity with animals. He loved Fang very, very much.

Kit was convinced that Bradley/Fang was almost telepathic in the way he could read body language.

Kit continued brewing, which was one of his favourite pastimes. Mark remembers:

Dad was a bit of a drinker and he made his own wine and beer. Boy, was it strong! When he lived at Great Catts, he used to brew it in one of the barns. He'd go for a wander around the garden, which was a big old place, and he would nip into the shed and ten minutes later, come out to see the rest of the garden, really rosy-cheeked. Mum would say, 'Why is Dad being horrid?' I'd say, ''Cos he's pissed.' If he was in a good mood, he'd give me and my pals some.

Although his family were sympathetic to his arguments, they were not terribly keen to embrace the lifestyle wholeheartedly themselves. The young ones, hardly surprisingly, wanted to enjoy the world as it was. 'I don't believe in forcing my ideals on anyone else,' Kit told Lorna O'Connell in 1979. 'My son, for instance, is diametrically opposed to me on the subject of technology. He is very enthusiastic about high tech, and we have very stimulating discussions about it when we totally disagree with other!'

In a unique joint interview with her husband, Una told an unknown magazine:

All our family go their own way and do what they believe in. Nobody forces [their] ideas on anybody else. That's the principle of our family. Kit and I agree absolutely on that. I support a lot of Kit's ideas, but the children are less convinced. Two of them smoke. As far as I know, they all accept packaging, and they all use detergents.

Vegetarianism

In 1976, Kit made the decision to stop eating meat. Kit spoke about it in an unknown lecture given in 1979:

> There is a primary logic of survival built into all of this which I am trying to develop and communicate. It is not a belief system. For example, I do not eat meat or fish, but am not a vegetarian. A vegetarian is a person who has belief, which I respect. But I do not eat meat or fish because there is a profusion of first-class protein elsewhere; and I happen to accept the rights of animals. So, I can combine a logical knowledge of protein need and availability with a feeling about animals and not become an irrational cultist.

Richard Mervyn used to discuss the issue with him when they worked together in 1980:

> He became a vegetarian not because he didn't approve of eating meat, it was because he felt it was uneconomic. He told me: 'If you and I were in the wilderness and you died and we had no food, I'd eat you. If there was a seal around, I'd kill the seal, of course I would. I'm not anti-meat. I want to survive, but I can't approve of that if you've got three fields of food to feed one field of cattle.' This Kit called 'eating towards the sun…' The sun helps plants to grow as part of a natural process. Eating the animal is eating away from the sun. I said, 'I understand that, but I don't like vegetables. This is my way.' Kit said, 'I wouldn't dream of saying you're wrong. I'd point out how expensive it was to eat that steak, and how much land it took to do it.'
>
> He'd give you information like that. If you have a cow that produces milk, what do you do when the cow gets old and no longer produces milk? John Seymour [author of *Self Sufficiency*] talks about this. Honour the cow by using the skin to clothe yourself and use every bit of the animal. Kit understood this in a sense. He was vegetarian by choice and not by creed. If a chicken is not laying eggs, you're not going to feed the chicken, you might as well kill and eat it. There was a practical and pragmatic side to Kit that I rather liked.

Kit believed that since man was not an 'obligative carnivore', who does not need meat exclusively for survival, he did not have the right to kill for pleasure. Killing an animal for no purpose was an offence. When he had to kill one of Una's goats, he then buried it. Unless finely comminuted, dead meat is not a particularly good fertiliser. 'We cannot meet our obligations to sustain life if we condone such inefficiency,' he was reported telling a vegetarian conference by the *New Scientist* in 1978.

Kit aimed one day to become a vegan. He gave up eating fish, and Carol Topolski remembered the circumstances:

> He was invited to go to the Seychelles by some Middle Eastern prince, who said he was interested in things to do with the environment. Dad said he had a spiritual experience with a fish on the beach! We found it rather risible, but after that he gave up fish.

This experience happened in early 1978 at a retreat in the Seychelles which appears to have been organised by a Japanese organisation called the Oomoto Foundation, a benign religious sect. He must have found the guest list enticing. Amongst them was the architect Dr R. Buckminster Fuller; Dr E. C. Sudarshan, a physicist from Texas; Dr Lyall Watson, author of *Supernature*, an interesting book which investigated sentience in plants; the Canadian architect Arthur Erickson; and Trevor Ravenscroft, a man who brought out the idea that the Nazis were interested in occult practices through his book *The Spear of Destiny*. Also in attendance were representatives from religious groups. A curious mix; yet if there was any place suitable for a spiritual experience with a fish, it was here.

Kit and religion

The atheist Kit Pedler sometimes felt that he needed a spiritual dimension in his life. Spirituality does not automatically mean a belief in God, messianic figures, and obedience to priests. Neither does it require a belief in the supernatural. Kit often saw parallels between the priest and the scientist. You accepted what they said without question, had total faith in their power, and you were not encouraged to dissent (as those suspicious of vaccines or sceptical about global warming will attest). What was Kit looking for?

Carol Topolski used to have discussions with her father on belief:

> He was arguing that he felt that some system of belief – call it spirituality – was essential to the human condition. I was arguing rather more pragmatically that I didn't think it was, and he accused me of being an

empiricist. I replied, 'Well, you taught me to be an empiricist so what the hell is that about!'

He certainly had a spiritual side and was interested in spiritual things. He was brought up a Catholic and had cast it all off when he was in his late teens and escaped all that. As a result, we all were brought up as card-carrying atheists, but in my case, infused with the rage he had towards organised religion. But a part of me wondered whether he would have a deathbed conversion because it was something so central to his growing up. In his final years, I always felt that environmentalism and ecology had smacked off the kind of quasi-religiosity that he would have had as a Catholic.

Later, friend and colleague Richard Mervyn also spent time discussing spirituality with Kit:

We never really talked about whether there was a divine being or not. It's the kind of subject you keep off. I always thought he was more agnostic than atheist. He was certainly atheist in terms of organised religion. Certainly, when he started looking into the mind and the complexity of it, he wondered [if it had been designed], but that was what I admired about the man: he was questioning. Bertrand Russell once said, 'The people I'm most frightened of are those who are certain.' Kit didn't preach, but he was always questioning. He once said to me, 'Last Saturday, I was driving back through Kent, to my house, and it was the most beautiful evening. The sun was behind me, coming through the trees, lighting up this fantastic landscape, Bach was on the cassette player, and I suddenly thought, "Did all this happen by accident?"' That was Kit! I thought, 'Oh my god, you're going to come over all religious.' He said it made you think: this glorious music and glorious landscape – did it happen by accident?

Another friend and colleague of Kit's (whom we shall meet in the next chapter) was Jeanette Kupfermann:

There was almost this religious element to him. He was a man of tremendous passion, of enormous curiosity, about everything. He wasn't just a dry scientist; I can't imagine him being confined to a laboratory. Like many lapsed Catholics, I think he was terribly fascinated by religion. He understood the power of it. In his own way, I think he was looking for something that would bring him back into this wonder, the religious awe. He was the transcendental humanist.

Kit felt that a sense of rational spirituality would help the world ease the transition into the post-industrial age. Kit understood why early man worshipped the sun and the elements, things he needed, but had no control over. They instinctively knew they were a part of something wonderful and awesome. For modern man, it meant a respect for the world, and for its natural processes, which were not in the hands of a god creature toying with us. In a 1979 lecture Kit said:

> It would make it easier to communicate the need for adjustment, assuming of course that the belief made sense. And it must make sense, because people have been weaned and brought up on sense – the age of reason. And there is no need to deny reason, but there is a need to extend it. Laurens van der Post wrote, 'We don't seek to avoid reason but the tyranny of reason.'

Kit had other ideas which he explored in a short biography and analysis of the life of scientist Nikola Tesla for Colin Wilson's 1977 anthology *Men of Mystery*. Tesla was an astonishing man, a contemporary and rival of Edison. He could visualise before his eyes, and in three dimensions, any invention he wanted to build. It got to the point where even Tesla found it difficult to distinguish between what was real and what he was imagining. Kit wrote:

> This brings me to my first conclusion. I believe that Tesla was a man who was in touch with a particular and quite mysterious part of reality which is not normally accessible. To write such a statement is for me a profoundly important experience and one which still sends shock waves rushing through my institutionally conditioned mind, but nevertheless I believe it to be true. Tesla seems to have had a reality framework around him which was entirely different in kind from ours... Just as he could see non-existent machines spinning in his own frame of reality, so could he visualise some of the anatomy of the living universe... I believe that the structure of the universe is not just a grey neutral framework of atoms, radiation and galaxies, but is a sentient, living whole which is subject to a continuously evolving design process of which we have no overall concept, but which some individuals can glimpse in brief flashes.

Dr Kit Pedler would not have dared to have published that ten years before without getting labelled a fantasist or a mystical idiot by his colleagues. He too would have dismissed Tesla with the phrases 'maverick', 'populist' or 'showman', words that were applied to Kit during his *Doomwatch* days. 'Having made sure that his unique properties posed no real threat to the probities and dogma of my own speciality, I would have closed the laboratory door behind me with a definite sigh of relief.'

Kit closed his essay by declaring how rewarding it was 'to be able to conclude this chapter by recording that my experience and standpoint has been materially changed in this direction by the act of writing it.' Why? Because he was able to write not just this:

> Contemporary science is now beginning to divide into two separate and largely incompatible systems of thought. On the one hand we have what I call institutional science with its highly developed and essentially mechanical sense of reality and, on the other, a nascent and more fragile belief system which proposes that nature does not break down at all into fully describable systems which when fitted together make a complete and understandable whole. This second category of belief also holds that institutional science is inadequate, narrow and self-limiting and produces biased descriptions of reality which can only fit the method itself and all its limitations. Instead, it questions the myth of objectivity and proposes that there are alternative frameworks of reality and that these essentially depend on the attitude and perceptions of the individual. Although it is an oversimplification, it suggests that the individual is an integral and creative part of the fabric of nature and that his own being and existence would, if fully developed, make this reality just as 'real' as the external, physical and allegedly objective version used by the institutional scientist. This new science, which I hold to be so important to the development of man, is easy to talk out of existence and I know this from personal experience. I worked for many years in various institutional laboratories, and it is only recently that I came to doubt the basic assumptions of orthodox institutional science as both limiting, misleading and inadequate.

... but also this:

> I see individuality as a temporary separation from the fabric of nature. The best picture of this that I can imagine for myself is to see a plane or sheet of infinite extent. The sheet is flexible and individual humans and animals emerge rather as if someone had pushed a finger against the reverse side of the sheet and made a bulge. The bulge becomes a sphere with a thin neck still attached to the plane. Then the neck parts and the individual is free, but just for a lifetime. At the time of death, the sphere goes back down to the plane, reattaches, flattens and flows out into the whole until there is finally no trace of it. But the temporary individuality has not been lost; it has merged with the living entity of nature. We are given a brief leasehold on a separate enclosure. I believe that during the lifetime of some rare humans the neck between the plane of the universe and the sphere of the individual remains actively open during their lifetime and that communication can occur along

it both ways between the entity of the universe and the cognition of the individual.

Kit was inspired to propose a television series called *Men of Mystery*, a kind of drama documentary about 'truly exceptional human beings who actually lived and who really developed their own faculties to a point where they saw images of a richer and more complete universe'. He recorded in *The Quest for Gaia* the two times he had experienced flashes of insight into the world around him: once from looking at a ripening field of barley, once from thinking about photosynthesis as part of the solar drive chain. Both were unsettling experiences. A part of his mind made 'disagreeably rational noises'. He was overtired, delusional, or it was eidetic imagery, but he dismissed these words as useless tautologies:

> The experience was a strikingly different experience of an extended reality, and it showed me that by changing mental set, there is an infinite potential for evolution and change. During these times, my consciousness, my being, is open to the thread of connection... which stretches between the envelope of my individual existence and the living universal mind of Gaia: the neck connecting the sphere to the plane of the continuum.

This was the spirituality Kit needed, similar in idea to that first postulated by the heretical Jesuit Teilhard: the 'noosphere' which enveloped the earth as pure thought.

Kit reviewed Colin Wilson's huge 1979 book *Mysteries* for *New Scientist*, describing it as a 'very important contribution to the subject [which] must be carefully studied by all who entertain the possibility that there may indeed be more things in Heaven and Earth than science at present depicts.'

Kit had liberated himself from the tyranny of reason and broken through his ingrained scientific training. It allowed him to voice in public ideas that were totally at odds with so many in the scientific community. A defrocked scientist no longer, Kit had a new term for himself.

He was a Gaian, a small part of a unified whole of *everything*.

The Gaia hypothesis

It was around about this time that Kit began to take an interest in a recent hypothesis developed by James Lovelock and Dr Sydney Epton, from Shell's Thornton Research Centre. Lovelock was studying how the Earth's atmosphere is sustained by the interaction of organisms and non-organisms which keeps the correct balance of conditions for life to exist within the enclosed system of our planet.

They first put their ideas to the public in an article for the *New Scientist* in March 1975 entitled 'The Quest for Gaia'. The Earth, they argued, can be seen as one complete self-regulating organism in itself, but our current actions could harm its delicate checks and balances of cybernetic feedback, and render it unviable in supporting life.

The name Gaia was suggested to Lovelock by his neighbour, the novelist William Golding. Gaia was the Greek Earth mother goddess. The article argues that we need to rid ourselves of nineteenth-century technocratic thinking, and 'reject the idea that human existence is necessarily a battle against nature. Let us make peace with Gaia on her terms and return to peaceful co-existence with our fellow creatures.' We may need Gaia, but Gaia certainly doesn't need us.

As in all ideas, it was open territory for other thinkers to come in and expand. Lovelock and Epton were more interested in the complex composition of our upper atmosphere and how it was sustained by the biosphere. The Gaian hypothesis was useful for people like Kit to put across their arguments against industrial society, which in itself was only a recent innovation. We are harming ourselves, Kit reasoned, and by Gaian definition, the world itself. The more we oppose and fight against the natural currents of the Earth, the more the Earth will fight back.

Kit told an unknown magazine in 1979:

> Early man was not part of nature for aesthetic reasons, but because his survival depended on this sensitivity. He had to look for clues, like we look for clues in animals. How on earth did he learn to take a wild grass and put it in one place and call it wheat? That took a long time and a great deal of sensitivity from picking it up and eating it. There is a universal behaviour pattern in nature which I call intelligence. All that our industrial society has done is to push that life process backwards, but for a short time only. We thought we could get round it by being ingenious or intelligent, and we've always been self-congratulatory about our ability to destroy. But now the tide is really turning; everything in nature has feedback cycle time: bacteria have developed transferable drug resistance and when they overcome a problem, they become not only stronger, but selectively more numerous.

This new hypothesis excited Kit; he contacted Lovelock by telephone in June 1976, and they arranged to meet in person later that year. In the meantime, Lovelock sent Kit some early research papers which preceded the 1975 *New Scientist* article.

The ancient Greeks believed that we were all part of a common society of Mother Earth or Gaia. Kit agreed that there was a 'oneness' of life on the planet. We the 'beasts, plants and bacteria' were all components of one great 'life machine which it is our destiny to sustain and to which the act of killing is an offence', paraphrased Colin Tudge in *New Scientist* in 1978.

The oneness of life was something Kit had wondered about during his days looking into the electron microscope, studying larger molecules on the wall of a skin cell and seeing where the animal stopped and where the rest of the universe began. At molecular level, it was difficult to tell the difference between an animal or vegetable specimen, but at atomic or subatomic level, it was impossible. Kit had been taking an interest in fundamental physics, which had made some startling advances and discoveries in recent years. There was that sense of wonder shining through, and there were physicists who were struck with that feeling of near spiritual awe with the implications of subatomic physics. Their work questioned the nature of what we perceive to be real. Kit would rap a hard tabletop with his knuckles and declare to his children: 'This is mainly air.'

The Quest for Gaia

By 1978, Kit felt it was time to consolidate his philosophy and put down into a single volume all the ideas that he had been mulling over, debating, developing, and writing about over the past ten or so years, from his earliest thoughts on dehumanised society to his take on Gaia. This would be no academic treatise, nor another doomsday scenario peddled by the author of *Doomwatch*. Drawn from his own experiences, it was going to be a positive book, demonstrating how the post-industrial age was an opportunity for mankind as it breaks free from the stresses and controls of an industrialised world, using knowledge and advantages that no other period of history had enjoyed, to rediscover the lost art of living. This was no harking back to a mythical golden age because Kit knew there was never such a time; but one might exist in the future.

He finished the book in October 1978 and called it *The Quest for Gaia*, possibly borrowing from Lovelock and Epton's article. The original title, scrawled on the folder which still contains the original draft, was *Earth Time*, but that didn't have that personal touch. Lovelock's own groundbreaking book *Gaia: A New Look at Life on Earth* was going to be published a few months later after Kit's.

According to Una, Lovelock was not pleased that Kit had used 'Gaia', but Kit chose it 'to encompass the idea that the entire living pelt of our planet, its thin green rind of life, is actually one single life-form, with senses, intelligence and the power to act'. Lovelock is credited within the text and in a footnote as the originator of the hypothesis in both hardback and paperback editions. Of the ideas of Lovelock and his collaborators, Kit wrote: 'I believe it to be the most important single scientific work of recent time. I am delighted here to pay tribute to their originality and courage.'

The difference between the two books is that although Lovelock agrees some aspects of modern technology are harmful, he chastises the environmental movement for having the wrong 'targets', and rejects the model of society Kit and others aspired to. In later years he was a firm supporter of 'clean' nuclear power and believed fracking was a short-term answer to our energy needs until the population figures declined to a more sustainable level.

The Quest for Gaia is divided into three sections. 'The Anatomy of an Angry Goddess' describes in detail the natural processes of life on Earth, powered by the sun, and contrasts it with the inefficient and wasteful processes devised and continued by 'technologist-toymakers' resulting in pollution which harms the natural cycles of the planet as it cannot be easily broken down or absorbed by the planet. Heat waste had to be reversed otherwise Gaia, which emits only a minimum amount of entropy or disorder, as Kit puts it, is quite capable of taking its revenge.

The second section, *Change and Refutation*, is the most interesting, certainly the most eye-opening to any reader who is unfamiliar with Kit's stance on household technology. It is a total attack on the technological toymakers, the reductionist scientists, and the conditioning processes that industrial society has swamped upon us. It is a demonstration of logic, and how so much of what we now take for granted as essentials are anything but. He breaks down the fundamental needs for the human being to survive into short, snappy chapters on food, warmth, shelter and health.

He examines which modern artefacts would no longer have a place in the Gaian age. With washing machines and top of the range cookers, he analyses the resources and energy consumed in their construction, and the conditioning process employed to make us buy them. He asks, what is the difference between a cooker retailing for £50 and one at £500? Does the more expensive model cook the food any better, or more quickly or healthily? It simply has more gadgets, a more elaborate design, and has had more resources and energy employed in its construction than is necessary. But you are conditioned to think it is *better*. It is a status symbol because you could afford it.

Our food is examined, from white bread to a cup of coffee, to the illogicality of intensive meat production. But he offers, where possible, practical alternatives. Most of what he writes about is very familiar if you had been following Kit's work for the previous decade, but there are a few surprises. His chapters on animal rights, and the modern medicine system, are particularly striking and personal.

He dismisses the plastic toothbrush with bristles that tear the gum, as opposed to the well-applied toothpick, and the variety of harmful detergents and shampoos. He reveals he no longer uses shampoo. What hair remained on Kit he grew longer. As others have found when they stopped using shampoo, after a couple of unpleasant months, suddenly the hair becomes *clean*.

In the final section, *An Age of Gaia*, Kit explores the political machine, the rise of the computer in our lives, and why we should embrace the age of Gaia rather than 'get into our chromium-plated life pods, close the hatch, switch on the multi-dimensional media and wait for the machine to stop'. Kit argues we have already nearly lost an absolutely basic and vital human quality which we once had: 'Colin Wilson calls this Factor X, and I too believe that we could once see much further and with different eyes than we can now; and that this expanded vision has been covered over, muted and almost destroyed by the development of the machine society.' He argues that state education was designed to produce adults with limited skills, fit only for the industrial system but ill-equipped to exist outside it. Kit does not argue for a return to the Stone Age, nor for the abolition of the antibiotic, or for the return of toil in the fields. Kit regarded self-sufficiency as a myth. We all of us are dependent upon the framework of society, and always will be, but there had to be a return to an understanding of the natural processes of life on Earth, especially now with the discoveries through science of how the world works, and our impact upon it.

This section is the most personal to Kit, as he recounts his insights into the universe, and touches upon the discoveries in physics that reveal that what we perceive to be real might not be after all. It is a very brave section and comes as a shock to the reader not expecting such philosophical arguments, which could easily be dismissed as fantasies and used to undermine the essential premise of this beautiful book.

The reviews

There were at least twenty reviews, by Kit's reckoning. Anthony Tucker, who had known Kit back in the days when he was an exciting research scientist, reviewed the book for the *Guardian* in May, and found it 'stark and explicit':

> He is talking to every man, despairing as the magnificent integrity of the earth's independent life structure and life spirit is despoiled, crushed and threatened by the exterminating trivia of technocracy. He does not condemn the scientific method that underlies technology, nor the process of experiment and innovation that drives the technocratic machine. He argues lucidly and simply that these now dominant procedures are vitally flawed because they are incomplete. They exclude all that is most humane, poetic and spiritual in man.

The review Kit was not looking forward to reading was in *New Scientist*, and they chose Sidney Epton. After explaining Kit's initial take on the Gaian hypothesis, he examined the middle section which he found 'idiosyncratic, searching and deadly', and singled out the section on modern medicine: 'But [Kit's] science is often weird, he is inconsistent, he rides hobby horses, he takes extremes as typical. Nevertheless, there is a case to answer.'

Kit's book was not favourably compared to Lovelock's work, and three months later Kenneth Mellanby in the same publication said it was 'just another doom-laden attack on modern technology'. A syndicated feature written by Robert Musel highlighted Kit's warning that the planet Earth 'is not neutral and is the most determined and dangerous opponent ever to face the human race'.

The only real criticism he received came from the left-wing journal *Tribune* which said Kit wasn't socialist enough. Kit thought this was ridiculous because he never pretended to be political, regarding himself as libertarian. The Socialist Party of Great Britain didn't like Kit either because he had campaigned against membership of the Common Market in 1975. In his view politics no longer worked and the real villains were the automatically mendacious large organisations, both public and private. It was no use looking for ideological romances; they were not going to fit our circumstances.

The book did not have the impact or reach of James Lovelock's more conventional take on his Gaia hypothesis. Yet Kit's book threw down the gauntlet directly at the reader, but then suggested that it was for us to pick it up. It would be a liberating experience as he always argued, away from the 'cyber-hierarchy' that was threatening to engulf us, where computers and systems analysis govern our everyday life.

Kit was proud of his book and gave a signed copy to his daughter, the future architect Lucy Pedler:

> Dad said, 'You don't have to read it, but if you don't, I'll never talk to you again!' It slightly explains why I am completely obsessed with waste. I abhor waste. I've always abhorred waste on every single level from a building point of view or from a household point of view, so he obviously got to me through what he talked about when I was a child.

16
Educational Kit

Instead of throwing pupils on to the scrap heap at the age of sixteen or seventeen as they currently do, schools should be teaching children about life and what it offers, not just preparing them for a lifetime of work. Sooner or later the emphasis is going to change for all of us, because the idea of work will collapse. But the answer is not just more leisure or free time, it is the chance to lead a richer, fuller life.
– Kit Pedler, in a speech written in 1979

Despite the attention from the print media, *The Quest for Gaia* did not generate much interest from radio or television, except in Australia. Kit was no longer the first port of call whenever a 'doomwatch' issue seized the headlines. Occasionally he would be asked to talk about his usual sphere of influence, but also to branch into other areas, such as H. G. Wells for *Woman's Hour*, or to review for Radio 4's *Kaleidoscope* a film (*The China Syndrome*), a play (*Toads* at the Nottingham Playhouse) or a TV series (BBC1's supernatural thriller *The Omega Factor*). Other than several educational series for radio, nothing substantial was offered.

Kit was still asked to lecture, although he preferred to conduct seminars or panel discussions, such as those at the International Youth Festival of Hope for Mankind in August 1977, 'The Vegan Spring', a symposium on animal rights arranged by the Vegetarian Society at the Commonwealth Institute Theatre in June 1978, or the open conference 'Eco-politics at the Turning Point' in Rochester in September 1978, where he was reunited with Fiona Cantell, one of the organisers of the People's Habitat in 1976. He made a return appearance to the Sunday Forum at Conway Hall in January 1979, which he had addressed before in 1974; but although eagerly anticipated in the pages of their journal, no record appears to have been made of the planned seminar 'An Age of Gaia: Life in a Post-industrial Society'. Although nice to do, they didn't bring in the money. Kit's earning power was not as great as it had been, and his consultancy work had finished.

The writing side of his life had also effectively dried up when Gerry Davis took his career over to the United States after *The Dynostar Menace* was published, but they remained friends. Kit did not stop writing: he had a love for, and a need to explore, ideas within science fiction, but it was mainly now for his own personal pleasure. Kit's surviving paperwork contains several examples which his agent tried to push forward but to no avail.

Kit was greatly pleased to be asked to write an introduction for a collection of *Dan Dare* comic strips, and did so in April 1979. He attempted, and stopped, a couple of novels. One of these was called *A Mirror for Your Vanity*, of which over a hundred pages still survive. It drew heavily from Kit's own life and experiences as it featured a distinguished researcher into neural biochemistry called Dr Thomas Howard Riker, a lapsed Catholic and survivor of a boarding school. He is disillusioned with the dullness and stifling conformity of academic life, with its lectures and conferences and rife with jealous colleagues. He makes an appearance on television and criticises the use of animals by unethical career scientists, and is forced to apologise to the academic board.

Riker debates endlessly with his inner voice, the foul-mouthed Vox, over his feelings of inadequacy and pointlessness. He takes a trip back to his old school and to his childhood home, before visiting a couple of friends and having a very bad drug-induced trip. He is divorced, and has a couple of meaningless flings, being something of a compulsive womaniser. He has a near-fatal car accident, because of a cheap nut-and-bolt replacement for his brakes, and faces a long recovery. Where this story was going to go is anyone's educated guess, but it is a shame he never finished it.

A couple of unfinished short stories also survive. *The Racing Driver and the House* was a rather pedestrian ghost story finished in February 1975, while *Dr Franken and the Biomim* related how one Doctor Shelley Franken created the biomim, the biological mimic Kit had first written about in his essay for *The Listener* back in 1969. Told from the point of view of a later biomim, we read of how Franken became frightened by the reasoning power of his creation. It wanted to be able to move and see its own reflection. He destroys it and commits suicide. The biomims are recreated by other scientists, and inevitably they take control. We read an account of their experiments on humans in captivity, who have their voice boxes removed and are made to behave like insects. It is a rather neat twist as Kit envisaged that the biomims could behave like insect cultures. Kit had been trying to write a book in 1970 about two machines from fifty years into the future looking back on the recent past, and this may have been a part of it.

In late 1978, he proposed a television play or possibly a film called *The Writing on the Moon*. As the title suggests, it features a discovery by a Russian expedition of an artefact on the Moon, which relates to something buried underneath the Sahara Desert.

An obituary prepared by the Royal Microscopical Society refers to other works which do not seem to have been published, nor survive in his collection. It seems likely that the author based his piece on a resumé (containing numerous biographical errors) sent in by Kit's agents, which they padded out with works in progress, or failed commissions such as another short story called *Old Lady Passing*, or novels like *Casualty* or *Earth Organism*. In 1981, Kit contributed a couple of notes to a compendium called *Science Fiction Writers of the Twentieth Century*, which gives some tantalising details of the type of writing Kit was engaged with:

> My science fiction has always had to do with small logical extensions of current reality. I am currently engaged on *Document from the Year 3*, for example, which deals (post hoc) with the evolution of homo sapiens, and *The Logon* which are the result of mating between a mould and a microchip!

One thing Kit wrote purely for himself to read was a very critical piece of self-analysis, which sounds similar to *A Mirror for Your Vanity*, called *Pedler versus Reldep*. One of these failings, Una suspected, was an element of bluff in Kit's character:

> He did have a very wide knowledge, but he wasn't always correct. He claimed some knowledge that he didn't have. I used to think, at least I have psychiatry, because everything else belonged to him. Well, I heard him say to some visitor, 'I have… a very deep knowledge of schizophrenia.' I knew that all he had done was flick through one of my books. It made me very angry because I wanted to keep something for myself. I wasn't going to have him take away the one thing that was for me.

Attitude to learning

Kit was very interested in education but had a particular problem with a certain type of teacher. As we have seen, his own education had been quite shaky, and he subsequently enjoyed the relative freedom of early polytechnic life to the detriment of his studies. It hadn't been until he had discovered the wonders of anatomy that he experienced a late blossoming. That led one family member to suspect that their father did not rate academic achievement terribly highly, which might explain why he wasn't keen on attending prizegiving ceremonies at Mark's school, despite his son wanting him to be there, and had to be virtually blackmailed by his wife to attend.

It could also be down to what he had experienced with his colleagues in and out of the Institute of Ophthalmology. He thought that science at school 'is often taught abominably'. 'What children want,' he told the *Observer* in 1967, 'is bloody great bangs.' Kit was interested in theories of education, and had a suspicion that teachers had just as restricted a mindset as a certain type of scientist and doctor he deplored. Richard Mervyn remembered a case in point:

> His son was doing A level maths or something. He was doing a test and was having difficulty with a problem. Kit said, why don't you do it this way? It was the sort of problem where if the answer was 0.3 you were right, but you had to show how you got there. He did this, got the mark back, and it was zero. Kit went down to the school and said: 'What are you doing?' It was because he didn't do it in the prescribed way. Did he get it right? Yes: then that is what matters. But he didn't do it in the way that was taught. This was fundamental for Kit with the problems of education.

Kit was always suspicious of how you measured intelligence. In 1976, he made a guest appearance on Tyne Tees' children's show *Look Out* in an edition on robots and machine intelligence. With an audience of children, he used an example from an IQ test which asked: out of four shapes, which is the odd one out? He gave them the 'correct' answer but demonstrated why it would have been more intelligent to have picked a different one. Kit was an excellent communicator, and found he could connect with children as Mervyn observed:

> I had a young cousin staying with us, and Kit visited and stayed talking into the early hours. She said: 'He was extraordinary; it didn't matter how silly

you thought your question was, he took it seriously.' He would answer it in a way that made you feel you asked an intelligent question, and he answered it in a way that made you want to ask another question. [If you said to him] 'I'm sure this is not a very good question,' he would reply, 'Every question is good; if you don't understand something, you ask a question. Just because you don't know something, doesn't mean you're stupid.' He loved talking to children who thought peas came from a packet. He said they've got fertile minds. Children from the ages of five and six have got fantastic imaginations especially if you ask them to draw things. And then imagination gets clamped down by modern education. 'You can't have a floating house.' Kit would say, 'Why can't you? Why can't a house float? Stop crushing children's imagination.' He told me that he used to love every now and then going to primary schools before 'adults had closed off most minds'. He basically thought that people who taught in universities had closed minds because otherwise they wouldn't be teaching at universities! I said to him, 'You taught at university,' but he said, 'Yes, and I got thrown out.'

In the coming Gaian age, schools would have to change and adapt from the original aim of education: to equip the child for the adult industrial or commercial workplace from as early as fifteen and make them useful members of society. In Kit's view, change should be starting now. In a lecture written in 1979, he asks:

> Are children at school being adequately prepared for a rapidly changing future? They are most certainly not. To me the reason for living is personal growth and the sort of education most children are receiving at school gives them no provision for that whatsoever. They are basically educated to get a job in the computerised society, a job which probably won't be there in the near future. They are not taught the personal freedoms or anything important for the full development of human society. I would like to see pupils taught the basic subjects of food, warmth, shelter, health and politics, within which would come the three Rs as a natural consequence. But that, unfortunately, would create a free society, and that is the last thing that a dictatorship of the executive wants.
>
> The work ethic is a very poor conditioning influence. We are on this planet to live and make the most of our lives. It just happens that the society we are living in fails to give any chance of this.

Collaborating with Jeanette Kupfermann

Kit had been a teacher himself, but only for graduates. However, he is supposed to have presented a programme or a course on the retina in the early days for the Open University, and in 1974 prepared a couple of radio lectures on both vision and hearing, and for a series of BBC Schools programmes called *Prospect*. From autumn 1974, school programmes were broadcast on VHF on Radio 4 in the mornings, having first been aired on Radio 3. Kit's first appearance on *Prospect* was as a guest in a 1970 edition called 'Daily Bread' where he talked about *Doomwatch*, and then in 1972 on an edition about governmental responsibility where he was interviewed by James Burke.

In 1974, Kit was commissioned to prepare a five-part *Prospect* investigation into 'The Human Mind'. It looked at whether the brain and the mind were separate identities, or a whole; how the mind is affected by the stresses of modern living; and how we can be manipulated and conditioned by advertising in much the same way that Pavlov conditioned his experimental dogs by associating sounds with food. Finally, Kit looked ahead a thousand years to see whether our minds had become as science-fiction writers would imagine. Significantly, it asked whether we would finally have achieved the ability to communicate by mind alone.

Prospect: The Human Mind was transmitted shortly after entertainer Uri Geller had made his famous appearance on a BBC David Dimbleby programme where he bent his first fork – and became an instant celebrity. No one knew if he was just a superb conjuror or whether he could indeed bend a fork with the power from his mind. Geller's British publisher also published anthropologist Jeanette Kupfermann. Married with two children, Kupfermann had lived for a short time in America, and after a couple of years working in the film industry came back home in England, and took her second degree at University College in London. The theme was religious symbolism in comparative religion. At a party, she met radio producer Stuart Evans who explained about a new ten-part *Prospect* radio series he was doing called *Man and Myth* and asked if she would like to present it with Kit Pedler. She was aware of *Doomwatch* because Robert Powell had been going out with a mutual friend. Kupfermann recalled:

> They commissioned big series in those days. It needed to cover a lot of ground, covering all aspects of man and myth, both psychological and anthropological, all round the world. I went to a provisional meeting at Bush

House to meet Kit, and the minute we met we got on like a house on fire. I realised that he was a proper scientist with a very distinguished background, but he didn't know that much about anthropology. His range of knowledge on other things was enormous: art, literature, mythology; a very well-educated man and very well rounded, but he didn't have the theory. From the very first, he realised, and I realised, that we would be the perfect team because he had the scientific knowledge I didn't have, and I had knowledge he didn't have.

Kupfermann sized Kit up quite quickly:

I realised pretty early on that Kit intimidated me. He was a man of some presence. I imagine that a lot of people felt it was a bit daunting standing up to Kit because apart from his intellectual brilliance, his manner was quite intimidating. He gave the impression of power; he was a powerful man, powerfully built. He was very charismatic, a very good speaker, and when he talked, you listened, he was very persuasive. He was the type of man who didn't suffer fools gladly, quite a brusque man. He was a delayed rebel. It came quite late to him when he broke out of his institutional setting. He always described himself as a defrocked scientist. He said that he would lose his temper very quickly and he would regret it.

They prepared the plan for their unscripted programmes either at the BBC canteen over the road from Bush House or in Regent's Park, but they didn't always talk about work. He revealed how different his existence had been before his operation when he had lived a very fast and loose life:

We used to talk about his marriage and how he felt a bit of a failure in that area. I think with this series, *Man and Myth*, he had to think about people and, in a way, I was his link to human relationships through anthropology. He was much more interested in ideas than the normal human things. He had a burning passion for new ideas.

We more than got on. As far as I was concerned, he was a real gent. He was almost the ideal platonic friend and mentor, the intellectual friend you dream of. We would walk around for hours discussing things, and he had all these ideas. I think one of the reasons we got on so well was that we came from such different backgrounds. Mine is Jewish, which is very emotional, and so different to his own that he was fascinated and drawn to it. My family came from the East End of London before the war, and I had quite a poor upbringing and made it through education. I gathered he came from quite an upper-class background.

At that stage in my life, I was open to all this knowledge, and I was particularly aware of it: he did have an effect on me. He was a natural teacher, a natural populariser. He could simplify ideas and had the gift for clarity. I never went to the theatre or the cinema with him, the normal things that people do. He wasn't interested. He did like art, and his knowledge of it was quite extensive which was his mother's influence. In our *Man and Myth* he could discuss it quite well.

Kit was very good at bringing me along, so to speak. I was quite shy. I had written a book, taken two degrees, but I hadn't quite found my niche yet. He always said to me, 'Jeanette, I suspect somewhere that you have a tiger in your tank and it's got to come out.' He was trying to make me a little bit braver about my opinions. Of course later I became a critic and wrote for the newspapers, and after he died I think he would have been quite pleased to see the influence he had on me.

The first five episodes dealt with ancient myth, with extracts read out from various texts which they discussed and analysed. Robert Graves was particularly mined, with extracts taken from *The Song of Blodeuwedd*, *White Goddess* and *The Greek Myths*. They analysed the Greek plays *Oedipus*, *Agamemnon* and *Clytemnestra*, a 1951 Welsh language play on the legend of Blodeuwedd called *The Lion and the Owl*, and extracts from *The Nature of Greek Myths* by G. S. Kirk and *The Greek Myths* by R. G. Daedalus.

The last five episodes dealt with modern myth, and reflected Kit's wide-ranging interests. *The Man from Laramie*, *Shane*, *Brent River*, *Farewell My Lovely* and Raymond Chandler's essay on crime fiction; *Bad Day at Black Rock* (Kupfermann's own favourite), *From Russia With Love*, and some horror classics, *Dracula*, *Frankenstein* and *Dr Jekyll and Mr Hyde*.

A very modern myth was explored: Erich Von Daniken's controversial 1968 bestseller *Chariots of the Gods*. This was the first of several books which explored the idea that mankind had been visited by alien astronauts throughout prehistory, and this had been recorded in their architecture and sculpture. His work captured the imagination of the public but earned the scorn of the archaeologists. Although he suspected Von Daniken was a bit of a fraud, Kit felt there 'might be something there'. Mark Pedler remembered: 'He was a big fan, although he went off it for a bit. His bookshelves were full of books on ancient Persian mythology and Inca stuff.' Kit thought that Von Daniken offered a modern myth to a technological world. Instead of the faces of ancient gods, it offered aliens in space helmets emerging from spaceships to give knowledge to man.

Kupfermann remembered that the recordings could be a nervous experience for her:

> Producer Stuart Evans was very good and he had been a writer. He was a very volatile Welshman and he used to drink at lunchtime. If you broadcast in the afternoon after he had had a few drinks, it would be fatal. It was like walking on eggshells with these two very brilliant and volatile temperaments, and I was the young girl in between.

The radio critic for *The Listener* was very impressed with the series:

> I warmly recommend *Prospect* to adult listeners. Except for succinct explanations of the meaning of words like gestalt and charisma, it in no way talks down to its audience. In ten programmes, Kit Pedler (scientist) and Jeanette Kupfermann (anthropologist) have explored with great suppleness, elegance and neatness of mind, the subject of men and myths. At the end of the series, a comparison between James Bond and Beowulf becomes a fascinating, and not exclusively literary exercise.

The programme won an award in 1976 much to their delight.

Kupfermann recollects that she next collaborated with Kit on another *Prospect* series called *ESP – An Investigation*, and finally a third called *Our Green and Pleasant Land* transmitted in January 1977, about the effects of pollution and the early ecological movement. Kit did a couple of brief interviews for other *Prospect* programmes and would do one more series of four programmes in 1979 on an introduction to *Quantum Physics*, perhaps tying in with his new interest in the subject, the wonder of which he had briefly touched upon in *The Quest for Gaia*.

The end of the marriage

That last series earned Kit the grand sum of £149. Una was at this point the major breadwinner in the family:

> I think one year he earned just £600, but that didn't matter, I didn't care how much he earned. We had a joint bank account but once he asked me if we could have a separate account. I know now that he thought I would look at the bills and see he was spending money on somebody else. Once he said he didn't think I managed things well and he was going to take over the bank account, but his system for paying bills was not to pay them and instead then they would send him a rude letter, and then he would reply, 'What do you

mean, talking to me like this?' Then they would apologise, and he would pay. Once, the telephone got cut off. Now I was on call, and I couldn't have that.

He wasn't much better with his tax returns, and one year it led to a very unpleasant incident. Carol remembers:

> He hadn't filled in his VAT records, and someone from Customs and Excise came down to the house and said to Dad, 'Well, I have more powers than the police, and I can just walk into your house and look wherever I like.' Dad was beside himself, like Rumpelstiltskin, jumping up and down in a rage in the drive, that this man could do that. He became completely apoplectic.

Kit and Una should have celebrated their thirtieth wedding anniversary in 1979, except that they didn't mark the occasion any more. Great Catt's Farm was proving to be too big to keep, especially since Lucy was now studying architecture at Plymouth University. The reduced family moved closer to the Thames Estuary, to a cottage called Murton's Farm in Graveney, near Faversham. It was to be their last home together as a married couple.

Around this time, a newspaper magazine interviewed the Pedlers at home, giving a rare glimpse into Una's feelings at a time when the marriage was breaking down. Kit enlarged on his view of the family unit which in their case, he said, 'functioned more successfully because of the inherent freedom. Relationships should be free to develop as they really are, or else the structure [becomes] otherwise an imposition. I like my family to be a group of individuals.' Unfortunately, his definition of freedom within a marriage was becoming intolerable for Una.

In the spring of 1980 the marriage finally came to an end. It had been a long and painful break-up, but the crunch came when Kit admitted to his wife that he had met someone else. She was thirty-year-old radio actress Cherry Gilliam[*] from Guernsey, who met Kit while working as a waitress at a vegetarian restaurant in Covent Garden. Mark Pedler remembered:

> She walked up to him in a restaurant and said, 'I'm Cherry, you're Kit Pedler, can you help me?' and that was the beginning of their relationship. I felt Dad

---

[*] Not to be confused with Cherri Gilham, a TV actress and model who was one of the Benny Hill girls and is now a writer and political activist. Cherry Gilliam wrote to Equity to demand that Cherri change her name to avoid confusion, whereafter she was credited as Cheryl Gilham.

was rather flattered that a young woman would go for a man his age. She was probably looking for a bit of security, I think. Dad had been a compulsive womaniser throughout their entire marriage. I can't believe Mum stood it for so long. I remember the day she phoned and told me that she had had enough. She was going to make him a crab bisque, and she was having grouse, I remember.

Una believed that Kit was in love with Cherry: 'I don't think it was just an affair because he decided he was going to stop telling me lies.' Mark adds:

A friend of mine once said to me, 'You know, Mark, your mum is much cleverer than your Dad,' and that's true. In terms of raw intelligence, she was much cleverer than Dad. In terms of debate she was cleverer than Dad. Mum always beat him at Scrabble, and he didn't like that, got quite cross. Cherry was very good with Kit because she was very different, and absolutely adored him, looked after him and let him get on with what he wanted to do.

Cherry came from an artistic background, meaning there would no competitive streak between the two, nor any 'pyscho-analysing over breakfast', as he confided in a friend.

Jeanette Kupfermann met Cherry only once:

It's always surprising when you meet the final love of a great man, so to speak. I remember I was very touched by what he said to me: 'I've finally found the tenderness side of me. I think that's the part of me that all my life has been missing.' He was terribly aware that his life had had something missing. I always got the feeling that with all these scientific investigations, the nature of reality, whatever, was almost a search for this in some way. He was aware of his human failings, that his marriage had failed, and that it was his fault.

Una recalled:

He wanted to live with her; I suggested we should get the house valued, and he would have half the money and I would have the mortgage. We did that and he bought a house in Doddington and went to live with Cherry. During the last few days before he left me, which he found very difficult, he said I was the best wife a man could have, but he didn't want to be married.

It wasn't easy for either Kit or Una to shake off the habit of a thirty-year marriage:

The first time he came back to visit me he asked me for some honey from my bees, so I gave it to him. The second time he asked me for some spinach from my garden, and the third time he asked me for four yards of blue velvet to put on his bedstead and I said I'd look for him. Then a little while afterwards we both saw this was ridiculous because we couldn't get out of the pattern and anything he wanted I would try and get for him. I said to him that I didn't want *not* to see him, but I wasn't going to see him on the premises.

It was extremely traumatic when he left me. I did everything I could not to let our friends criticise him but John [Zorn, his old friend from Clapham, and by now a firm ex-friend of Kit's] said, 'The bastard' and what a relief that was!

17
The Pyramids of Rotherhithe

> We want this centre to dispel the myth that energy conservation and caring for the environment just involves the brown bread and strappy-sandal brigade. – Nigel Tuersley, *South London Press*, 1980

IN MAY 1979, BRITAIN elected a new government. The past few years under James Callaghan had been turbulent. Treasury forecasts had required the need for a loan from the International Monetary Fund, and this meant cuts in domestic spending. Trade unions, who had previously agreed to wage constraints, finally had enough and began a series of strikes. There were no power cuts this time, but the sight of piles of uncollected rubbish and stories of unburied corpses was enough to see the Conservative win.

Revenues from North Sea Oil began to come in and there was little thought given towards appropriate technology. The new government did not want to keep old, inefficient industries afloat with government money, and wanted to curtail the influence of the unions, mindful of how the coal miners had brought down the last Conservative government in 1974. Kit's post-industrial age was just around the corner, but not in the way he had imagined.

If there was to be any hope for the West to embrace renewable energy sources and a softer technology, governments and business needed to be persuaded that it was good for them, the economy and for jobs. Certain politicians agreed, and in 1978 Mrs Renee-Marie Croose Parry formed the Parliamentary Liaison Group on Alternative Energy Strategies.[*]

---

[*] It now meets as the Parliamentary Renewable and Sustainable Energy Group.

Entrepreneurs would have to take the next step, and one of the first was Nigel Tuersley, who had a degree in zoology and a masters in ecology. He initially earned money from buying and renting properties, but this was not a reliable way to earn an income when interest rates were as high as eighteen per cent, with rents set by local tribunals which sometimes did not cover the cost of the local rates.

Tuersley did not need convincing that environmental problems faced the planet, but was put off by the campaigning methods used by certain groups:

> If you look at the environmental movement, it has gone through several stages. The first was conservation orientated, which was a recognition that we were losing species and habitats fast, and the priority was to protect them. The second stage was that the fault lay within our economic systems. The knee-jerk approach was to attack the diseased culprits: corporations, governments et cetera, and that I felt was typified by Greenpeace. The third stage was an awareness that we were all part of the problem.

This last view was promoted by Ronald Higgins in his 1978 book *The Seventh Enemy*, and a documentary for the BBC's *Everyman* programme in 1979. Through inertia and apathy, we all of us were the greatest threat of all, he argued, happily walking towards an open trapdoor. Tuersley believed that the environmental movement needed to speak the language of business, rather than hold a knife to its throat. Public pressure could only help up to a point. 'We need whistleblowers and campaigning groups, still very much so, but we also need those who are working for constructive solutions, not standing on the sidelines and criticising, but rolling up their sleeves and getting stuck in. It's hell of a lot harder to develop solutions than to identify problems.' If business could set the lead in sustainability, there was a chance for a better future.

Tuersley visited the Centre for Alternative Technology and found it to be inspirational. He began thinking about setting up his own foundation, a showcase centre to demonstrate that alternative energy sources can be made to work, and that energy efficiency and sustainability can become a natural part of a commercial and profitable enterprise, and get away from the clichéd image of environmentalists as hippies, middle-class dropouts or angry 'lefties'.

Tuersley took his idea to Paul McClory who ran the Natural Energy Association in Kingston-upon-Thames, a one-stop shop which provided and installed solar panels and cells, wind generators, and books on the subject.

They were regarded by some as a capitalist sell-out and were in tune with Tuersley's thinking. Hugh Sharman had set up the business in its original form back in 1973 and remembers: 'I was trying, somewhat hopelessly, to turn my own home in Kingston into an "eco-house" with a 10kW Elektro wind turbine and a vertical garden on the outside walls. Daft idea, looking back.' McClory edited a publication called *Natural Energy*, and one of his occasional contributors was a 'highly assertive man' called Kit Pedler.

'We got chatting,' says Tuersley, 'and Paul said, "Look, there's someone I think you should meet, Kit Pedler." I met him in Kingston and we hit it off immediately. I explained I wanted to establish a foundation, and how I wanted to mainstream [alternative] philosophies, and he agreed. We pretty well that day decided to work together and make it happen.' With his experience at Unigate to draw upon, it was worth a try.

Kit understood the reason for public reluctance as they lived through turbulent and uncertain times. He told Lorna O'Connell:

> People are really frightened. They want to hold on to their jobs, homes, all the things that mean security, and when people are frightened, they will not want to listen to someone proposing change because change is threatening. I don't blame them. To propose change to an already precarious society is to face either hostility or ridicule... until something happens and blows up in their faces.

The great majority were used to supermarket living and were restricted by financial considerations:

> I certainly recognise these problems as being extremely important. I have considered the possibility that things may go wrong, and I may just be attracting a cult following, but I do feel that I am getting through to all levels of the public, particularly through the media – phone-in programmes for instance. I get an amazing response. It's evident that people are aware of the dangers I'm talking about and phone in with all kinds of suggestions... I'm aware that I'm in a privileged position. I'm educated and affluent. If needs be, I could survive easily on little. I'm also aware that most people are not as fortunate. If the entire fabric of society were to break down completely, as it is threatening to, city dwellers and people in council blocks, for instance, would have no chance of survival at all.

A Foundation, Kit believed, would give the public an opportunity to extend and explore their traditional skills in such a way that they could become more independent.

Earthlife

The Foundation was created as a charity in 1979. It was christened Earthlife by Nigel Tuersley, and both he and Kit would act as trustees. The Foundation would be the head of a group of companies, each set up for a particular project, the first of which would be a centre for alternative technology as the Foundation's showpiece. Money would initially be raised through Nigel's property ventures, and by selling shares in the company.

They needed to find a location to build the centre. 'We initially started looking [for a large estate] outside London. It was Kit who said, "You know, I really don't think this is right. We should do it in a city area." I warmed to the idea and realised that it was absolutely the right way to go.'

Kit brought in architect Tom Hancock, a highly respected town planner who had recently worked on Peterborough New Town, a new regional city which had been designed to accommodate the overspill from London. Hancock believed in social planning and treated the inhabitants as people, not economic units. He had worked for the anti-nuclear movement and for Greenpeace so was in tune with current thinking. He agreed to become a trustee and draw up the initial plans for how such a centre would look. He had very striking ideas and proved to be quite a visionary.

Writing in *Town and Country Planning* in 1982, Hancock remembers he 'immediately took the concept of a major national centre for appropriate technology to Sir Hugh Wilson of the Docklands Joint Committee who suggested that the idea be developed for the Surrey Docks in Rotherhithe'. It was a splendid opportunity. The 120 acres of filled dockland was still empty and derelict. But for the politicians and planners of the time, that was probably what they wanted. Hancock had already looked at the idea of redeveloping Surrey Docks as far back as 1971 and had a 'deep feeling that we should adapt such places to the purposes of our time'.

Hancock recognised Kit as Earthlife's guiding spirit:

> His essential inspiration was to look optimistically at the future, to see that the collapse of our old industry was the sign for a new life-view to take over, that human and natural ecology are the very ground in which a strong, sustainable social economy will be built; and that the miniaturisation of electronics will have its counterpart in energy and resources conservation. He inspired one to think in such terms when creating plan concepts and processes. Earthlife... is the first fruit in urbanism of his contribution.

Kit knew the proposed site well from his visits during the People's Habitat exhibition in 1977. But the fate of the site rested between the joint owners: Southwark Council and the Greater London Council (GLC). They started a competition for any interested parties to submit costed plans. The 120-acre site was a short distance from Tower Bridge, serviced by two railway stations and the river which surrounded the site on three sides. The *Guardian* wrote in 1980: 'It is hard to think of a site with a bigger potential. It should not be thrown away on another shopping centre and batch of office blocks.'

With a site in mind, the search began for more trustees who could advise and lobby on their behalf. Kit could draw upon his contacts and associations and recommendations from the past ten years. 'Needless to say,' Kit wrote to the Labour MP and former Housing Minister Bruce Douglas-Mann when he was approached, 'the workload is minimal and the ideology of the centre entirely neutral.' Mann declined but agreed to be listed as an advisor. Among those who had already accepted, however, was John Silkin, Environment Minister in the previous Labour government; and he was soon joined by Shirley Williams, another former Labour Minister.

The plans that Kit, Tuersley and Hancock had for the Earthlife Centre would require a vast array of expertise, and they attracted a long list of advisors, who are listed in alphabetical order on the Foundation's letterheads. It was a fascinating mixture of teachers from the radical Architectural Association, and from Cambridge University's Autarkic House project. There were experts in wind and water power, more politicians, a former Chief Scientist to the Ministry of Power, radical trade unionists (one of whom tried to turn a weapons manufacturing plant into building socially useful artefacts), biologists, engineers, horticulturists, journalists from *The Ecologist*, the Conservation Society, physicists and artists. Familiar names included the man who helped Kit build his nuclear bomb, Joseph Rotblat, and Professor Derek Bryce-Smith, the man who raised the alarm over lead in petrol and a signatory on Kit's letter to the *Guardian* against nuclear power. There was also successful author Jackie Gillot, the wife of BBC documentary maker John Percival, with whom Kit had collaborated in 1972, and who had been practising self-sufficiency in the country.* Ove Arup and Partners were chosen to be the consultant engineers on the project.

---

* Sadly, she committed suicide in 1980.

Tuersley was the only one who was involved in the Foundation on a day-to-day basis, operating first from Winchester before moving to 17 Warmington Road in Herne Hill, South London:

> Kit's input varied enormously, depending on how much needed to be done. He would come in for key meetings, but I would do the groundwork basically. Kit was acting chairman in a way, but he was much more than that. He was my mentor and an extraordinarily hard taskmaster. He was formidably bright, and so didn't tolerate mistakes. It was a tremendous experience for me. He was a totally proactive man. He was very strongly of the view that we had to get on and do it which is one of the reasons why he found it frustrating dealing with the mainstream all the time who had no insight into the urgency, of which, of course, he was absolutely right.

The Earthlife City

The scope and scale of the £174 million Earthlife City was quite breathtaking. At its heart was to be a huge glass and steel pyramid, as tall as St Paul's Cathedral. This glimmering image would be seen from miles around and would have become a major iconic London landmark:

> It was Tom Hancock's idea for the huge pyramids. It was quite spellbinding. I'll never forget when he unveiled it. I had no idea what was coming. It was a combination of ultra-contemporary pyramids and more traditional developments surrounding it.

The pyramid was to contain the main conference building, an arena and restaurants. On its eastern side, smaller pyramids would contain exhibition centres, displays of 'spaceship Earth' and its life support systems, a display of appropriate technology, a Third World trade centre and an engine museum.

To the south of the conference centre was to be a meditation centre because Hancock was a practising Buddhist. Further south and facing this would be a belt of housing, a park, botanical gardens, and a garden centre. Car parks and roads would be kept underground (no doubt the problem of trapped exhaust fumes would have been ingeniously thought through).

Close to the exhibition centres, small industries would be housed in an area where ideas from research centres could be constructed, marketed and sold, making money for the city, and powered by a combined heat and power plant. Further east near the District Centre for East Rotherhithe Tube station they planned a wilderness park and camping site, which would make a significant contribution to the ecology and life of the Thames. They planned to build a 'fluvarium', a sheet of glass under the water through which visitors could see the whole of the river ecology from surface to riverbed. This would attract not only visitors but students, and school children would be able to see how care of the water could lead to improvements.

Another idea was to plant an 'energy forest' of fast-growing Swedish super-willows in the highly polluted soil from the docks. Felling these would provide raw materials for a plant producing methanol, charcoal and wood gas. The liquid sludge from the methanol would be processed to test techniques for recovering lead and cadmium from contaminated areas.

Further south of the pyramids, and next to the Tube, they proposed using some of the existing waterways to house an organic fish farm, a tree belt, an area for intensive horticulture, and a Science Centre, related to Earthlife. To the west of the main pyramid and the housing belt, Earthlife would have its offices and institutional buildings including a library and resources centre, more workshops, a bakery and a brewery. Residential and hostel accommodation was to be based around here too.

Looking at a modern map of Rotherhithe, all of this would have fitted within the loop of Salter Road, Redriff Road, Lower Road and Brunel Road, along which in some places there was already housing near the Rotherhithe Tube. In the area of available land between the loop and the Thames, Earthlife proposed a riverside development to create a new Rotherhithe village, which would contain craft workshops and shops, studios, small hotels, restaurants, housing and so on, until it reached a river landing point and another dense riverfront village with yet more shops, cafés, galleries and studios. This would take you back to the Earthlife City and its hostels. To save visitors, pedestrians and workers travelling into the Centre by Tube or railway a long walk, the team proposed 'travelators,' moving walkways enclosed inside transparent tubes.

The Earthlife City would regenerate the whole area by bringing in businesses and light industries. It would become the biggest science centre in Europe and make a bold statement for the future of mankind in the post-industrial world. They estimated there would be employment for 1,300 highly professional scientific staff, along with 2,500 skilled and semi-skilled jobs, and 1,500 unskilled jobs, especially window cleaners. The plans allowed for plenty of wide spaces, which Londoners needed.

They believed the scheme would be profitable, according to their three-page proposal:

> Our visitor catchment area will be the whole of London, the UK and Europe and we will certainly get a proportionately larger number. The Science Museum, for example, attracts 4,000,000 visitors per annum, the Planetarium 1,600,000 and Kew Gardens 1,700,000. A similar garden exhibition in Hamburg attracted 9,000,000 in nine months and the Boston Museum of Science outdraws visitors in comparison with all other public places.[*] There are some 1,500 firms in the UK profitably engaged in this area and we expect, from research already carried out, that this number will rise sharply and that each one will be keen to exhibit their products in what will be the prime European showplace for their products.

The Earthlife City needed to demonstrate how it would be energy-efficient and Kit thought hard about how to redeploy its own excess heat. The Festival Hall in London and Battersea Power Station were already investing in surplus heat systems. This he needed to express to the interested parties because the way energy would be deployed at the Centre 'is obviously crucial to the Foundation scheme since it will become an important metaphor of how we think communities are likely to be effectively serviced in a society with fewer energy resources and raw materials'.

In notes retained by Tuersley, Kit wrote:

> Lower-grade waste heat from the foundry and a planned glass recycling plant would be fed into waste-heat boilers, providing steam for the paper mill and for the steam engines in the engine exhibition. Even lower-grade energy from the engines is used to space-heat workshops, and finally used exhaust air is fed to the glasshouses. This will contain a higher proportion of CO_2 which is a growth stimulant for some crops… The glass foundry, for example, may generate too much heat for immediate use at a given time and so the spare heat must be pumped into (thermal) store for use when required. Seasonal differences also affect energy needs and once again, heat storage becomes essential.

Biogas would be created and stored on site from organic garbage, and burnt to create heat for a thermal store. 'Biogas can also fuel the gas engines in the engine exhibition.'

---

[*] Even the Centre for Alternative Technology in Wales earned £25,000 a year by charging 50p per head of its annual 50,000 visitors.

Kit recognised the energy distribution and generation would be subject to 'phase discontinuity':

> Seasonal change, general irregularities of tactical operation within the centre and weather changes all help to create a problem of management which can best be solved by the establishment of an energy control centre... For example, where there is no wind, the wind generators will not work.

The public

A brochure was produced, plans drawn, and an impressive model was built for public display at the Rotherhithe Civic Centre in Albion Street for two weeks in March 1980. They were one among fourteen other submissions on display, and the councils wanted to consider the views of the locals before making their final selection, and so did Kit and Nigel Tuersley. Yet it was Earthlife's astonishing vision which captured the imagination of the public and the press.

The *South London Press* singled out the project on 28 March. Tuersley explained their mission statement:

> Last year £17.1 billion was spent on energy according to the government and thirty per cent of that could have been saved with the use of technology which is cost effective and available now. That shows just how important and vital our centre is in the energy crisis... We are very aware of energy today. And a development like ours is much more relevant when we are facing a future of depleted resources and energy. What we are doing is looking into the future and making the best possible use of the site.

Industries would be attracted to the Earthlife City. He quoted precedents such as Denver, Colorado (where over two thousand energy-related firms had been established since 1973), Silicon Valley in California, and our own Reading-Bracknell area for computer sciences. Earthlife considered that 'a comprehensive industrial training programme' was an essential part of the education function of the Centre. The idea would be to help develop local skills to meet the needs and opportunities of the new industries.

Public reaction to the proposal was overwhelmingly supportive and generated far higher approval figures than its nearest competitor. Even the Department of Industry and Energy and the CBI expressed their support to Earthlife, but it wasn't enough for the traditionalists who wanted heavy industries and jobs, despite the five thousand skilled and unskilled jobs this scheme would have created, working in pleasant and creative conditions. Southwark Council leader John O'Grady told the paper, 'I can't really see this scheme being of any advantage to the people living in the area. It's jobs really that we are after. That's the main issue which will occupy my mind when we consider the plans for Surrey Docks.'

The biggest issue going against the Earthlife Foundation was funding. To get this far had cost them £6,000 which had all come from donations. The Rotherhithe project was under Earthlife Developments which sold a very small shareholding to a city-based construction group. Nigel planned to bring together a consortium of banks, pension funds, insurance companies, and even oil companies, to put up the cash for the project. This was the same financial route taken by a previous bidder to develop on the site, Trammel Crow, an American company which wanted to build an international trade mart on the site. 'But this is exactly where our development differs from other plans for the site – we are not a development company proposing a scheme just to make a profit. We feel our energy city is needed and is completely ideal for Docklands.' Tuersley remembers:

> Kit didn't like dealing with commercial interests, and indeed he was pretty robust in his exchanges at times as I recall. I was the one who would get suited up and go to these meetings. I was less middle of the road in terms of what colour green I was. Kit did have a dire view of our prospects, quite correctly as it turned out. I was the one who had to tread a delicate path between that view of the world and getting something done, communicating with people for whom it was completely new. I remember being extremely irritated myself at the lack of insight from people at that time, even under their own criteria. It would have been a huge commercial success, ahead of its time.

The initial favourable response and the media interest in Hancock's novel glass pyramids caught Earthlife by surprise. When the *South London Press* contacted John Silkin, he replied that although he welcomed the plans, he knew nothing about them:

> When it first hit the news, we didn't realise it would get so much publicity and it rather caught us unawares. We didn't brief John Silkin too fully. We hadn't sent through the stuff in advance because we didn't realise the authorities would publicise it as they did. Instead of phoning us, the paper phoned John Silkin because he had the highest profile. We kept the MPs informed but at times inadequately. We were due to have a trustee meeting

and brief everyone, I'll never forget a letter I'd been asked to write to John Silkin updating him. The word 'illicit' had been misspelt, and Kit went absolutely ape, as though his entire life's work was on the line due to this one typo. He was a hard taskmaster at times, very forthright.

Silkin still threw his support behind the bid, telling the paper:

> The importance of dealing with energy really can't be underestimated. We have coal and oil but as time goes on fewer people are going to want to work in the coal industry and our oil will dry up. I would like to see a scheme like this go ahead, whether or not it's in Docklands. A development like this could never be a waste of a site because it will provide an open space and people involved in the research will be working for the benefit of the community for the next ten or fifteen years.

If given the go-ahead, the first stage would have been completed within three years, and the rest by 1988.

The appointed Docklands Development Organisation (DDO) was to select the shortlist, which was easier to do since some of the bids were uninspiring. 'The other contenders have hardly raised their thinking above the level of hypermarket, office and commercial complex,' wrote the *Guardian* on 22 May. Associated Dairies, better known as ASDA, proposed an £83 million pound theme park with hypermarkets, factories, offices and a static exhibition on the space age. 'Indeed, they are so uninspired ASDA has been told to include elements of other more imaginative schemes, of which Earthlife is one,' said the *Sunday Times* on 11 May, itself dismissive of Earthlife. The DDO's director, Brian Hurst, told *New Scientist* that '[it] would be easy to go for the romantic appeal of schemes like Earthlife's but they would not be realistic without financial backing'.

Earthlife was not among the successful bids, but the DDO liked the scheme's originality and proposed a merger with ASDA, which went through even though they considered their proposals lacking. Before long, the high-technology park plans of Southwark Quays, a consortium of three Westminster architectural practices (which included one of the designers of the Barbican Centre), also sought a merger after they failed to be shortlisted and were the first to team up with Earthlife.

Whenever the media picked up on the Rotherhithe development story, it was the 'imaginative' or 'visionary' Earthlife that attracted the most attention. Would it still be so when merged with other groups who did not share the vision? Kit was very blunt with ASDA at their first meeting. 'That was always a sensitive path to tread because Kit was very concerned not to see the message diluted or compromised in anyway. He made very clear his views on certain things,' Tuersley remembers. 'I had some quite delicate massaging of egos to do afterwards.' Reports of the 'bizarre ménage a trois' appeared in the media over the summer before any formal agreement had been reached with ASDA. Already it was 'being hotly tipped as the favourite as it combines commercial viability with good urban design and visionary ideas', whilst the 'other three shortlisted schemes rely on a dreary shop, office, industry, trade centre formula'.

Tuersley was happy with the merger:

> ASDA wanted a large supermarket, and the rest of their scheme was very conventional, and Southwark Quays was a technology centre orientated concept directed towards the information technology sector. There was a very helpful marriage of ideas. We worked together to produce a composite scheme, not as inspirational, but it was still a very positive scheme and an economic generator.

By the end of October, the *Evening Standard* announced that Earthlife, Southwark Quays and ASDA had formed a consortium to thwart three other bids, which the paper noted were 'foreign backed schemes'. The first of these rival schemes was the Dutch-based MAB Holdings who wanted to build a 'mini-Holland' using the existing waterways. Another Dutch company, Bredero, had combined with Wates the builders, Sainsbury's and British Home Stores to develop 300,000 square feet of shopping.

The third scheme was from Lysander Estates, a partly French consortium which planned to create a traditional style village in the middle of the docks. Businessman Tiny Rowland's Lonrho group also wanted to participate in this plan and build a two-hundred-bed hotel and a massive 200,000 square feet exhibition centre. They would create a village green complete with a village hall, sports centre, and a pub, building 250 houses and flats in pedestrianised streets using traditional building materials. Lysander's scheme would cost £750 million and was designed by Sir Richard Seifert, creator of the monstrous Centre Point tower in central London.

Despite ASDA wanting to build a superstore, and Associated Press requiring a new printing plant for their papers, the Earthlife philosophy still managed to shine through in newspaper reports. The *Observer* enthused:

The design... conjures up an image of a decentralised society. A self-sufficient mixture of developments where cars are unnecessary, communications are cut to walking distances and work is near the home. Life is seen as a single, rich slice of activity; seventy-five per cent of the entire scheme would be operating on experimental energy systems. The four main sections – research structures, shopping, residential and educational – are planned to create a compact, closely knit picture where the parts are connected by a long canal, and the whole is dominated, not unreasonably, by the glassy presence of the Earthlife Centre. And so, while the inspiration of the proposal reflects the possibilities of the future, the architectural shape and scale of the buildings, and of the spaces between them, mirrors the spirit of old towns and cities.

A new model was built for display at the Civic Centre during another two-week consultation period, even though the authorities only required a design.

The selection process rumbled on, with conflicting rumours reported in the press. In January 1981, the 'London Diary' of the *Times* reported that the GLC favoured the Lysander package: 'The rival ASDA consortium has criticised the Seifert vision as being simply a random collection of single-site large developments thrown together and presented as a total urban plan.' The anonymous author was very sympathetic and admiring of Seifert. His son, John, was at pains to tell the diarist that this scheme was a very low-density one, tailored to its surroundings. There would be no Centre Points here. The *New Scientist* reported that Southwark Council favoured the Earthlife bid, as did the Docklands Forum and the Trades Council. There was even talk of combining both bids to beat the impasse. A spokesman for the consortium told the *New Statesman* that it still hoped its scheme would be selected as the outright winner, 'but obviously half a loaf is better than none at all'.

It was to no avail. On the evening of 13 January, Southwark Council came out in favour of the Lysander bid. Tuersley explains:

> He won because he put £6 million on the table, which at least in theory was his bid. Ours was a £9 million bid but with a profit share with the local authorities... which in retrospect they would have done incredibly well from because in the end, Lysander couldn't come up with the six million.

Two years later, and to great publicity, Lysander was finally kicked off the site.

This was not the end for Earthlife, and they were invited to put in a bid for another part of the dockland development area, the Isle of Dogs, and so the Earthlife Foundation formed Thames Islands Estates, and sold shares in the company to raise money.

By this time John Silkin had resigned as a trustee, having fought and failed to win the leadership of the Labour Party. Shirley Williams meanwhile abandoned Labour to form a new centrist group called the Social Democratic Party. Tom Hancock had also resigned but was to be involved in the new scheme, suggesting a framework showing how the docks could be developed anew to a human scale:

> These plans... were as far as I know the first attempt to suggest a positive structuring of the large empty areas of docklands. From them I selected and developed a concept for an intensive mini-Manhattan technology centre to be constructed in the central basin of West India Dock using the two-and-a-half-mile-long wharfs, in all about thirty acres. Surrounded by the mirrored water of the docks, it is called Thames Island.

Despite having some reservations about the new scheme, Tuersley submitted plans and managed to raise two hundred million pounds in a week. It was accepted in principle in July 1981. But this scheme was also doomed to fail, as there were no signs of any decent communications infrastructure being put in place:

> It should have been approached with much more vision and strategic planning and direction than it was. It was considered more a political liability than an asset which was the wrong way of looking at things. It was an extraordinary opportunity, and it should have been approached positively. No one had done any urban science parks, and given the huge depth of expertise in London that was also a no-brainer. Finally, we have a Silicon Valley in miniature being established in the east end of London around Whitechapel in the old street hub thirty years after it was suggested by Southwark Quays, and after Silicon Valleys had been established all over the world with enormous success. It's tragic that we are so slow and myopic in our approach in the UK.

Rotherhithe today

Where the old Surrey Docks once stood, and where the Earthlife City should be now, there is the Stave Hill Ecological Park. This was created in 1984, offered up by the London Dockland Development Council. It was designed to replace the William Curtis Ecological Park, the first of its kind, which had been established a few miles further west on a derelict lorry park near Tower Bridge. It is a tiny fraction of what Earthlife had planned for the area, but it's there.

Had the Earthlife City been built as it was originally conceived, what role would Kit have played? Nigel Tuersley is sure that Kit would not have had his own large office, sitting like a king surveying his creation. It depended on how far it would have fulfilled his ambitions:

> Unless it really worked along the lines he envisaged he would have lost interest and moved on to the next thing. Had his first inspiration, the science centre, happened he would undoubtedly have played a major role in that since that was very much up his street. To an extent once the ideas become mainstreamed a little, Kit would have got bored with it. He didn't like dealing with banks to make it happen, and with the inevitable compromises that it introduces.
>
> He was very much a leading-edge ideas man, and he didn't welcome some of the dilution that happens when you go from the first stage to the second and to the third… The first stage was impossible at that time.
>
> He had extraordinary intelligence. He thought things through very quickly and he used to get irritated by the fallibility of humanity. Kit was impatient. It's as if he knew he didn't have many more years ahead of him.

18
All in the Mind

> I have always distrusted 'experts' and 'specialists' who try to exclude 'laymen'. There was never anything difficult about science, it was only made so by some scientists. – Kit Pedler

PUBS ARE A VERY GOOD place in which to generate ideas, and it was in a pub in Shepperton that Kit Pedler and a Thames film crew (from the lunchtime consumer affairs programme *Money-Go-Round*) began talking 'about UFOs and ghosts and all the rest of it', far from the subject of recycling which Kit had been discussing earlier in the day in a scrapyard with presenter Tony Bastable. Interviewed by Matt Salusbury in 2005 for the *Fortean Times*, Bastable remembered Kit observing that the subject had received very little coverage, and wouldn't it be interesting if someone did a 'proper science programme' on the subject? He proposed connecting the paranormal with the extraordinary discoveries currently being made in physics. Bastable agreed, as did documentary director Richard Mervyn. His executive producer, Diana Potter, took the idea to Programme Controller Brian Cowgill at a Thames features meeting.

According to Mervyn, 'She went in and said, "I've got this idea about physics, the paranormal, and Kit Pedler." Brian said, "Kit Pedler. *Doomwatch*. I like that. Brilliant. Do it." As simple as that. I was asked by Diana, "Do you fancy this?" I met Kit, and we got on like a house on fire.'

No series involving Kit Pedler was going to be straightforward. He did not want to interview people who had experienced the paranormal or had seen something blurry in the sky. A more conventional approach was being put together in 1980 by Yorkshire TV called *Arthur C. Clarke's Mysterious World*. Clarke's sceptical stance shone through at the close of each episode, which led *The Goodies* to have 'Arthur' ponder that the only real mystery was why he was there, since he didn't believe a word of it.

Kit had proposed a similar series in December 1976 called *In Search of Magic* where he argued that today's technological juggernaut had given people a need for the mysterious and the magical. What else could account for the current popularity of Von Daniken, earth energies and ley lines? The series would have kept to a strictly journalistic approach, exploring our own human biases for and against the mysterious. One of the editions was to have been called 'Mind Over Matter'.

Kit had always been interested in the paranormal as he preferred to call it since he was brought up as a Catholic, where prayer to God suggested telepathy. Kit didn't like the term 'parapsychology' as that sounded more like the study of mental illness. Neither did he care for 'psychic' since that implied an act of belief in something untestable. Although he had lived above the premises of the Society for Psychical Research in Tavistock Square, he never joined. But Kit was still fascinated by the notion of ESP, and the untapped power of the mind which had gained currency partly due to the experiments of the botanist Joseph Banks Rhine into the Zener card test.

Like many others before and since, Kit firmly believed that ESP was not just a gift, it was a natural tool that Man had simply forgotten, or 'unlearned'. Mervyn remembered Kit's theory:

> Kit was interested in how the aborigines could follow a track without any mark. He said, 'I think we as human beings are de-educating ourselves with modern technology. Aborigines had a way of communicating with each other over vast distances that is almost accepted as fact; why aren't we experimenting? Because if they can do that, why can't we? But we sort of stop it because we have telephones.' In a way a lot of modern technology shuts off a huge amount of human capabilities that maybe we once had.

Kit believed that the mind could make connections with space and time and the world around us in ways we could not understand. Could the 'new physics' provide a route into understanding certain aspects of the paranormal, if they existed?

Kit wrote in the book that accompanied the series that as a biologist he had imagined physicists to be cool, clear, unemotional men and women who looked down upon nature from a clinical and detached viewpoint: 'People who reduced a sunset to wavelengths and frequencies, and observers who shredded the complex of the universe into rigid and formal elements.' It was only when he started reading the works of Einstein, Bohr, Schrödinger and Dirac that he realised he had misjudged them. 'I found that here were not clinical and detached men, but poetic and religious ones who imagined such unfamiliar immensities as to make… the paranormal almost pedestrian by comparison.'

Kit had already broadcast on quantum physics in 1979 as part of his regular contribution to the *Prospect* series. New physics was rapidly demonstrating that the nature of reality was not as rigid as the laws of old Newtonian physics would have you believe, and our own perceptions were far from straightforward. 'To be is to be perceived' was a now outdated concept. Einstein demonstrated with a simple analogy by throwing a ball from a moving train. What you perceived depended on where you were watching at the time. New physics was not overturning Newton's laws but demonstrating that there were huge gaps and discrepancies within them.

The scientific method

Scientists tended to reject the paranormal because it did not fit into the Newtonian model of God's clockwork universe. 'This is the kind of thing that I would not believe in even if it existed,' wrote a scientist quoted in Kit's book. Another said of the result of a successful series of experiments, 'If the result could have arisen through a trick, the experiment must be considered unsatisfactory proof of ESP (extra sensory perception) whether or not it is finally decided that such a trick was in fact used.' Kit stated:

> I am quite certain that the author of this statement has never applied this extraordinary standard of judgement to his own published research work, and in my own experience as a research scientist, I have never had to apply it to my own published papers. It is, in my view, a stand of some desperation on the part of that particular critic if that is all he can think of as a potential flaw.

He did take heart in a survey conducted for the *New Scientist* by his late friend Dr Christopher Evans. He was 'sternly opposed to the paranormal' and asked whether his mainly scientific readers accepted the paranormal. Only three per cent of the 1,500 replies declared it was impossible. A healthy forty-two per cent thought it was likely, and a quarter regarded ESP as an established phenomenon.

Kit appreciated that paranormal research had more than its fair share of cranks, frauds, and absolute believers, utterly unshakable in their world view. It is also very easy to be fooled, and no scientist wants to be publicly taken in. Practitioners could 'prove' a result by massaging statistics, or simply commit fraud. Kit could never shake off his own training that something should be tested properly, and be possible to be replicated. Scientific inquiry, by its nature, is extremely conservative; any new concept has to withstand rigorous and searching scrutiny before it is accepted.

Kit and Mervyn decided that the series would be quite rigorous in its attitude to experiment:

> Kit approached it from the point of view that he was sceptical from a purely scientific standpoint. 'I'm not going in with a closed mind, I'm going in with an open mind and want to talk to people both within the world of physics and the people working in the paranormal. In the end I will decide and make my pronouncement.'

Kit wanted to demonstrate that the paranormal did not have to be a refutation of scientific work, and that there may be a model for it. He explained his thinking in his review for *New Scientist* of Colin Wilson's book, *Mysteries*:

> My view is that paranormal phenomena will probably yield to investigation of the inter-relationship between system and observer; or sensitive and scientist. By extending Heisenberg's stance it may be possible to measure what the experimenter does to the sensitive and vice versa, but by the same token it may also turn out that this is logically impossible. The scientific method may well have to shift and extend its paradigms to make its own investigation of the paranormal possible. The danger is that if it fails to do so and remains doctrinally insistent on a particular standpoint, it may lose the opportunity to do so altogether and leave the field to unscrupulous entrepreneurs who are in business to create false mythologies of reality – for prestige or profit.

Kit was delighted that Mervyn was not scientifically minded, having failed every science exam he took at school:

He said to me, 'If you can understand this, then an audience can understand it.' A lot of people want to make programmes that get praise from their peers, which I think is the wrong way round. I've made programmes on the English garden and architecture, but I have always wanted to do it in a way that educates with a small 'e', which television used to do.

The structure and content of the series was discussed between Kit, Mervyn and Tony Bastable, who was going to act as a co-presenter on the programme. His job was to be the 'man on the Clapham omnibus', who would talk through points with Kit to make it easier for the audience. Mervyn recalls: 'Tony Bastable backed off to a certain extent and let us get on with it. I loved working with him on *Magpie* [ITV's answer to *Blue Peter*].'

There were to be seven episodes, a mixture of filmed interviews and scenes recorded in a television studio. Kit realised that a great deal of what he needed to film was going to be in America, and so to save money, the seventh programme involved a studio discussion where issues raised in the series would be debated with an invited audience.

The programme was announced on 17 June 1980 at a press conference to launch the Festival of Mind, Body and Spirit at Olympia, but it wasn't until October that Kit, Mervyn and a Thames film crew boarded a plane to America to visit institutions investigating ESP and talk with some eminent physicists.

The laboratories of America

The team visited the Lawrence Berkeley Laboratories in California, where Kit was going to take part in a remote viewing experiment for the programme. Remote viewing is the ability for one mind to be able to communicate with another over a great distance and see what it can see. Experiments had been carried out by two highly accomplished physicists, Doctors Russell Targ and Harold Puthoff, at Stanford Research Institute in California. They had achieved notoriety when they studied Uri Geller, coining the term the Geller Effect. Arch-sceptic and magician James Randi described them as the 'Laurel and Hardy' of Psi research. Randi's background as a stage magician informed his view that those claiming to have genuine paranormal powers such as metal bending, ESP, or faith-healing were acting. Randi had for many years offered a large reward to anyone demonstrating genuine powers within laboratory conditions. By his own account, many had come forward, but few allowed themselves to be tested.

Kit had met Targ and Puthoff a couple of times in the past and was satisfied that they were not frauds or dupes. He was impressed by their stringent precautions to eliminate charges of cheating and collusion which he recognised as similar to the 'double blind experiment' used when a new drug is tested during a clinical trial.*

Targ and Puthoff had performed hundreds of experiments and published their results in two different journals during 1974, claiming that they had achieved a significant number of successful remote viewings. They followed this up with a book called *Mind Reach* where they dealt with the rather hostile and personal criticism they had received.

Acting as a witness to the experiment was Elizabeth Rauscher, a Professor of Nuclear Science and Astrophysics. In Kit's view, she was 'arguably the most articulate and enthusiastic communicator about science I have ever met, and apart from getting a bear hug that regularly cracks a rib whenever I meet her, she is utterly tireless in her pursuit of very high-level scientific conversation. She also laughs a great deal.' She had long held an interest in psychic healing and faith healing, and had co-founded the Berkeley Fundamental Fysiks Group, an informal gathering of minds to discuss quantum mysticism, to find a connection between the consciousness and physics.

On 22 October, the film crew was divided into two groups, half to cover each end of the experiment. A biologist called Dr Beverley Rubik had also joined them to monitor the conditions of the experiment. She had arranged for six properties to be used in the experiment, with one to be chosen at random. The names of the six locations were put into six sealed and unmarked envelopes and then locked inside a steel box.

Kit was going to be viewer, and receiving the images was Hella Hammid, a professional photographer who had been the most receptive viewer discovered by Targ and Puthoff. Watches were synchronised, and the number for the envelope to be selected was predetermined by a random number generator. This gave rise to a strange experience. As he was waiting in his hotel room with the film crew for the experiment, Kit had a premonition. He called for silence, and then wrote down on a piece of paper that during the experiment part of the equipment would inexplicably fail. He underlined 'inexplicably'. The random number machine failed at 3.10pm.

---

* Selected patients are given either the real drug, or a dummy pill made from chalk. Neither the patient nor the doctor who records their reactions is told which is which.

Hella Hammid had no idea where Kit was going to be taken. She was going to remain behind and, for half an hour, sketch what she was seeing, monitored by the other half of the film crew, one of whom would make sure no one tried to interfere. Kit and Rubik went to a place called Indian Rock, which is to be found in the middle of a suburb of Berkeley. For half an hour, they wandered around, taking in the area, and then returned to the hotel room and studied Hammid's results. They were confident that there were significant similarities. Hella was then taken to all six locations to select which one she had 'been' to. 'I was not where you were, I was at Codornices Park,' she confessed.

Kit admitted 'it would have been splendid if we had achieved a hit; it would have complemented the television series. The fact of the matter is that we did not.' But the remote viewing hypothesis has an angle for this: they called it the displacement effect, where the viewer identifies another target on the list. This is suspicious, Kit agrees, but in his opinion, she did remotely view Codornices Park.

The experiment, Kit concluded, was weak and untidy in many respects, but it was clear to him that others can and do achieve successful remote viewing identification. The American government funded remote viewing experiments for twenty years. Kit was hardly likely to have one success on his first try.

For the second episode, Kit took part in another experiment at a psychology laboratory in Cambridge University. The Ganzfeld Experiment also attempts to send images from one person to another, but only next door. To cut down on distractions, the receiver has his eyes covered with half ping pong balls, bathed in red light, and listens to white noise on headphones. An electrode attached to the finger measures how relaxed the subject is, since it has often been found in paranormal research that the mood of the subject can determine the success or failure of the experiment.

The receiver records what he is seeing into a tape machine. On the face of it, this appears to be the most reliable and repeatable experiment in the field, as the sender looks at a picture and after the experiment, the receiver is asked to choose what he saw from a selection. Chance can play a part here, as well as fraud and collusion; but as more experiments are carried out, a pattern soon begins to emerge.

Trevor Hartley was to be the sender for *Mind Over Matter*, and he chose a photograph out of four. Although Kit, as receiver, did perform the experiment, it needed to be re-enacted for the cameras, as it was decided that the bustle of a film crew would be too distracting; but the audio recording of Kit's experience was genuine. 'My thoughts were mixed,' he recollected:

> All I was initially aware of was the red light flooding my field of vision through the ping-pong balls and the soft waterfall sound of the white noise in my ears. For some reason, I became anxious and tense. Looking back on the occasion I think it was due to the different parts of my mind working against each other. Part of me was saying: 'What rubbish you've got yourself into Kit'; another part was saying, 'Go on, you know you can do it if you want to; your rational mind accepts the evidence, so why don't you just settle down and get on with it.' Yet another part was saying, 'My God, what if I succeed. I don't want to be a psychic!'

He could only see vague shapes swirling into view. He wondered if he was trying to imagine shapes, but after a while relaxed himself into describing what he could see. Afterwards, he was asked to look at the four photos, and go through them in detail, comparing them to everything he said in the recording, and finally giving each picture a score from ten (meaning what was said was perfect for the picture) to zero. The actual photo used was one Kit had placed second, a group of women wearing witches' hats. ('Okay, yes, slopes. All triangular slopes pointing upwards with vertical spikes... It's a roof line, viewed from slightly above. Village roof lines and chimneys.') But he was also seeing things from one of the other photos, of palm trees halfway up a mountainside. Unknown to Kit, the sender only chose the photo halfway through the experiment, and the 'fit' of his verbal transcript and the pictures was measurably better during the second half of the session. Kit agreed that it was a complicated result, a good 'hit', but once again displacement had come into play, as they had found with the remote viewing experiment.

Mood did appear to affect the experiments. Dr Lawrence LeShan, an experimental psychologist, was one of several people, mainly sceptics, who tried to create a ghost. They invented Phillip, a man from Cromwellian England who killed himself after a tragic love affair. They spent a whole year without success, until they relaxed, and created a jollier atmosphere. Then things started to happen. Raps on the table began, and the table would move. Precautions had been taken to prevent fraud, and the result suggested they had created 'psychokinesis by committee'.

Spoon bending

The subject of metal bending received its own episode, and it is worth dwelling on since the whole phenomenon only came to attention in Britain in the early seventies when the young Israeli Uri Geller demonstrated his talent on *The Dimbleby Talk-In* on 23 November 1973. Bending a spoon and making it apparently snap by the lightest brushing of a finger made him an instant celebrity, and soon people were trying themselves to bend spoons or forks, using the 'power of their mind'. Some could do it, some couldn't, and others dismissed Geller as a conjuror who had no genuine gift.

If they had been aware of Geller's appearance on Johnny Carson's *Tonight Show* in August that year, they might not have been so convinced. An amateur magician himself, Carson had enlisted the help of James Randi to test Geller on his programme. They made sure that neither Geller nor his team had access to the various metal objects they were going to ask him to bend, nor allow him to use his own spoons. On screen, Geller declined, claiming his powers could not be switched on or off.

Geller attracted the attention of not only Targ and Puthoff in America, but also writer and journalist Arthur Koestler and physicist Professor John Hasted of Birkbeck College in London. They first ran a series of experiments on Geller in 1974, some of which were witnessed by Arthur C. Clarke. The power of the mind influencing the physical world was Kit's first foray into paranormal documentaries, and Jeanette Kupfermann recalls that she did a series with Kit on the paranormal for *Prospect* after *Men and Myths* called *ESP: An Investigation*. It was through Jeanette that Kit met Uri:

> I had just written my first book, and my publisher also published Uri Geller. Uri was in England publicising it, and I was invited to his house and watched Uri demonstrate his spoon bending. He bent something on my hand, and I was quite stunned by the whole thing. Kit was interested in him, and the ESP phenomenon. We got this series commissioned, an investigation, and went into every aspect of the paranormal, such as psychics, automatic writing, and the Filipino faith healers who lay on hands. He was very open to proof. We discussed fraud often.
>
> We met and talked to people like Professor John Taylor and Professor John Hasted. We had access to an electron microscope. We bent a key with a wrench and then examined it under the EM and compared it to one Geller bent in his hand. The molecular structure was different, suggesting great heat had been applied to it. The ESP programme didn't come to any real conclusion although we both had our theories, some of which emerged in his book, but he was never really persuaded one way or the other.

Uri Geller's own website includes two quotes from Kit. The first one is not given any form of attribution or context:

> I have personally witnessed and experienced on two occasions the metal bending abilities of Uri Geller. These experiments were conducted under rigorous laboratory conditions. In these two experiments the thick steel rod I was holding and observing carefully bent, and continued to bend, in my own hand. One rod bent to ninety degrees during a period of approximately six minutes while I was holding it. The other steel rod bent after Uri Geller stroked it and continued bending on a glass table without anyone touching it. The steel rods were provided by myself. I consider the Geller effect to be a phenomenon which should be studied seriously by science.

The second quote comes from Kit's conclusion to *Mind Over Matter* and is made to look as if it is a continuation from, or related to the first. It also lists Kit as still being head of the Electron Microscopy department of the University of London.

Kit was far more circumspect about the Geller phenomenon than the latter's website would imply. He begins by asking, what does he see when he sees film of Geller bending a spoon? Not much, because it is not an experiment; all he can do is talk to the people behind the cameras: 'An experimenter has to declare everything he did very clearly indeed, so that other people have a chance of repeating his work.' For the series, Kit did his own bit of metal bending, except it was a special alloy, nitinol, that has a memory of what shape it used to be and reverts to it when heat is applied.

Richard Mervyn remembered that Kit was quite agnostic about spoon bending; if it was true, why was it some people could influence material and others couldn't:

> Hasted said to us: 'I have no doubt he is bending the spoon. I have no doubt there is a great deal of heat coming off his body and the spoon bends. I put him in a cage and where there is no outside influence. Nobody else is going to accept it but as far as I am concerned it is a reasonable experiment.' But if Kit went in, he couldn't do it. What belief system is going on, what is occurring? If he can do it, why isn't he bending a lamp post? Why just a spoon?[*]

---

[*] Taylor changed his mind about Geller in 1980, taking up the front cover in an American magazine called *Second Look*, which explored the frontiers of science (in other words, the paranormal), and Kit had a copy amongst his papers. Another headline on the cover was 'New Psychic Research Says "Yes" to Paranormal Metal-Bending.'

Hasted had been drawn to metal bending as a result of his fascination with physics:

> Down on the atomic scale, I can't tell you the position of an atom exactly; I don't even know if an atom exists. It only probably exists. It could even be in two places at once. I don't know how many dimensions we're in; I don't know if our space is simple or complex. All of these things are far more bizarre than just a piece of metal deforming.

Hasted conducted his metal-bending experiments inside a shielded room to prevent any contamination. Inside a cubicle is a chair for the subject, in front of which is a small strip of metal which is attached to a small strain gauge, sensitive enough to record any stresses at microscopic level. This in turn is connected to an amplifier and a pen which records any changes to the metal. Any direct touching of the metal is forbidden and can be detected. A dummy recorder sits beside it to detect any outside influence affecting the results.

Mervyn's team interviewed Dr Charles Tart, who was interested in out-of-body experiences, the subject for the fourth episode. He had developed an experiment to measure the brain activity when someone has the experiences. He reasoned that since the mind leaving the body can see, it should be able to read a number left on top of a shelf above the subject. This number is randomly generated for the subject in the film to read during the experience. One such subject, 'Miss Z', managed to read the number on the fourth night, and on two occasions something registered on the equipment.

Faith healing

Programme five dealt with a subject close to Kit's heart: faith healing. Could the power of the mind genuinely cure people, or did it give the patient *permission* to heal, a tactile placebo effect? Placebos had been known to have a positive effect on someone demanding drugs to cure their illness, but it depended upon the patient. Kit had written about his experience of pain in 1966 and how it was really the soothing effect of a compassionate human being that had helped him through it, as well as strong painkillers.

This was to be the one area of investigation he would have most difficulty in accepting 'entirely due to the irrational prejudices and biases implanted in my mind during my training as a doctor. There is still a part of my head that is trying to dismiss the whole thing as a human indulgence. Another part of my head is convinced by a considerable volume of well-designed and conducted experimentation.' Professor Bernard Grad of McGill University in Canada, who was working in the Department of Psychiatry, had been studying the effects of laying on hands on animals, using an experiment designed using exactly the same approach as in a double-blind drug trial.

In a series of notes on the subject in 1973, Kit wrote:

> There is an effect between doctor/patient or healer/sick person which is not based on conventional physiology or treatment. The Chinese call this the 'healing pair'. It is an effect known to healer and patient and both helps the patient and rewards the healer. I think it is based upon very subtle and easily disturbable [sic] communication between the members of the pair. It is not communication by language but perhaps by small subconscious sensory stimuli. It is certainly based upon mutual trust and is, therefore, in one sense dependent on 'faith'. Many medical conditions improve after the meeting of the healing pair. The brain has great command over the body and given this trust in the healer may well alter its behaviour and bring about the healing of the diseased part.
>
> To call these events by the blanket term 'faith healing' may, under some circumstances, prevent the recognition of a serious medical condition and is, therefore, potentially dangerous. Anyone who wants a faith healer should have free access in National Health hospitals, but only provided that the patient has been adequately screened for physically recognisable disease. Conventional medicine could benefit from a greater recognition of these effect. At present it is over-weighted with 'medical technology' and very short on humanity.

There was one thing Kit knew to be fraud. In 1974, he made a documentary for Thames called *Pyschic Surgery – the Invisible Knife*, which he firmly believed was an elaborate conjuring trick, or 'obvious bollocks' as Mark Pedler put it.

Kit encountered sceptics in his own film crew who as he acknowledged in his book gave 'friendly and often ferocious criticism'. Richard Mervyn remembers why:

> It was absolutely fantastic. It was about proof. We were sitting in the hotel bedroom, and one of the team, who shall remain nameless, was very sceptical about all this and he really wasn't coping with it at all, and he wanted proof. 'What do you mean by proof?' said Kit. 'Well, it's possible to prove something.' 'OK,' said Kit, 'I can't prove that tomorrow's Saturday.' 'Don't be

ridiculous!' said the man, 'of course tomorrow is Saturday.' 'How do you know the world's not going to end tonight?' 'Well, it's not.' 'How do you know? Do you know that an asteroid isn't going to hit us? What you can say is I have every expectation that tomorrow is going to be Saturday. Proof is a very difficult thing.'

'Here's a classic one,' said Kit, 'Do you believe in God?' 'Yes,' said the cameraman. 'Prove it,' said Kit. 'Prove there's a God.' 'I can't but I know he's there.' The man was now getting a bit irritated. 'OK, you want proof. Richard, stand up.' I knew what he was going to do. 'I'm going to walk round Richard three times and make him sit down.' So, he walks around three times and I sat down. 'There you are, he sat down.' At this the man went ballistic. 'Ah, but you didn't say within a time frame. You just said you'll walk round Richard three times and he'll sit down.' 'Well, he did.'

This was Kit at his most acerbic. I said, 'Kit, I think we're going to have supper now.' I took him out of the room. He had met a man with a closed mind, who wanted proof, but believed in God, and couldn't prove it. They made up after a few days. Kit said he didn't mind people if they say I can't prove something but found it difficult to accept it if you dismiss it all as rubbish, but at the same time have a belief system that can't be proven. This was Kit at his finest, showing somebody up. The man deserved it. Kit had an ability, a trick up his sleeve to do something like that. He could argue back. He would sometimes get quite spikey, and if he thought someone needed putting down a peg or two, he was good at that.

Physics

Kit would certainly need his wits about him when he met some of the greatest theoretical physicists of his generation. Their contributions would be covered each week, but the sixth episode would focus purely on the new physics. Some of these people were wary about being interviewed for a programme on the paranormal, and Richard Mervyn remembers what happened when they met Geoffrey Chew, Chairman of Physics at the Lawrence Berkeley Laboratories where the remote viewing experiment took place:

> Chew sat in this spartan office and was an incredibly nice man. He and Kit duelled for about fifteen minutes, and I didn't understand a word. They talked about bootstrap theory and string theory, going backwards and forwards, and then eventually, he sat back in his chair, put his hands behind his head, and said, 'OK, what do you want to talk about?' He wanted to find out what Kit knew. Once he was satisfied that he knew what he was talking

about, he relaxed. This man is one of the great particle physicists and he turned to me and said, 'Richard, you don't understand a lot of what we're talking about, do you?' and I said, 'Not a word.' He banged the desk and said: 'Do you know something, Richard, I can't prove that this exists.' I said, 'I beg your pardon?' He said, 'I can't prove this exists.' I said, 'What are you talking about? It's a desk.' 'Well, it is, but if I break it down, there is no difference between the desk and the air really.' 'So, what makes this solid?' 'That's what fascinates me as a theoretical physicist.' And then we were off.

Geoffrey Chew was a very considered man, he thought very carefully about what he said when he agreed to be interviewed. He said, in a sense, theoretical physics had taken over from philosophy. Physics is finding out about things we can't even experiment on. Chew felt it was breaking things down and discovering things in science and life that were phenomenal. He said, 'I don't know a great deal about the paranormal. I don't say it's true or untrue, but what I will say is we're finding things that make the paranormal seem normal.'

Kit was good on the programme because he had no preprogrammed ideas about physics. Kit was on a voyage of discovery, talking to people who, in your normal life, you would never have had a chance to meet. Kit said, 'It is a huge privilege to sit and talk with some of the greatest theoretical physicists who would give us the time of day.'

Arthur Koestler, the man who coined the term synchronicity, gave Kit time because he was a bit like Kit. 'I'm doing an experiment downstairs into whether you could think yourself heavier or lighter,' he said. 'I don't give a toss about science, or scientists. Of course, they'll say this is not correct, or this can't be done. I don't care. Why should I want to influence them? They're never going to believe me, even if it's true.'

We spent time with Fritjof Capra at Berkeley and got to know him. Capra said the same thing: 'People should go off and do these experiments and not worry about what scientists think. Why bother with them?' It is a fascinating subject, and it intrigued Kit especially when he met these top people because he suddenly thought, 'My God.' None of them were interested in the paranormal as such.

Kit compared what the physicist in his lab was saying about the nature of reality to the ancient mystics who, thousands of years ago, could only deduce by using only their reasoning. Dr Lawrence LeShan, in his 1974 book *The Medium, The Mystic and the Physicist*, had compiled short extracts from the writings of about sixty people. He removed words such as 'Brahma' or 'electron' and challenged the reader to decide which was written by a mystic, or by a scientist. Kit's favourite was: 'The universe looks less and less like a great machine and more and more like a great thought.'*

Capra told Kit:

> The question of consciousness of the human mind entered physics when it was realised that the strict division between the observer and the observed, between mind and matter, could be made no longer, and that the observed in physics depends very much on how we observe it, and depends very much on our whole conceptual framework, so that the patterns of matter that we see in physics are, as I like to put it, reflections of patterns of mind. So you have these two realities, patterns of matter and patterns of mind, and the two reflect one another. You cannot say 'mind over matter', or 'matter over mind'; it's not that one causes the other, but they're mutually interrelated and reflect one another, and therefore many physicists, including myself, think now that future progress in physics will be impossible unless we include the nature of consciousness explicitly to our theories. A new type of science will have to enter the picture.

Making sense of it all

Kit would try to merge physics and the paranormal once he was in the studio with Tony Bastable. Kit would explain concepts and feed in ideas, which Bastable would pick up and question, taking a sceptical viewpoint, but allowing the discussion to move on. They were set in front of a black backdrop with few set dressings. To modern eyes, the only distracting thing is the style of the clothes and hair that seals the programme in its time period.

Regardless of appearance, Kit the communicator was in action. His nephew Kerry Glasier remembers:

> The way he talks in *Mind Over Matter* was how he spoke in ordinary life. He could talk about difficult concepts and make it clear as a bell to anybody. He could assemble things in the right order and break them up at the drop of a hat. He had this ability to make the unclear clear. He was an immensely charming man, he did have charisma, and he had a lovely voice.

Bastable felt in talking to Kit that 'you didn't feel you were dealing with a man with 27 million qualifications'.

---

* The quote is from Sir James Jeans's book *The Mysterious Universe*, although in his Tesla essay, Kit attributes it to Arthur Eddington. Both men are seen as founders of modern cosmology.

They needed to find ways in which to illustrate several principles. Mervyn remembers:

> We needed to show the influence of light particles being fired out of photon guns in opposite directions. We did that with two ping pong balls fired from a gun as it were, and a bat. We also did a very simple experiment on Heisenberg's uncertainty principle. Kit said, 'If you take a pressure gauge and put it on a tyre and it reads thirty pounds per square inch, it is actually thirty pounds per square inch minus the amount of air that's gone into the measuring device. You are always going to affect your experiment.'

Mervyn was happy with his finished six episodes: 'I learned a great deal. It opened my mind to a completely different area that I wasn't necessarily ever going to explore. The idea of doing a series about theoretical physics and the paranormal is bizarre, I can't see anybody doing that now.' Bastable felt that it had been a mistake not to make the whole series on film because it could have been more easily sold overseas, making this Thames's answer to the BBC's *Horizon* programme: 'There were more Nobel Laureates interviewed than you could shake a stick at.'

Kit wrote the accompanying book over the winter of 1980 and 1981 and dedicated it to Cherry. It is a clear labour of love; each chapter would ping-pong between the paranormal and physics, with some glimpses into the making of the programme. It was published by Eyre Methuen in 1981, and in paperback by Granada in 1982, who also brought out a paperback edition of *The Quest for Gaia*.

Cometh the critics

The first episode of *Mind Over Matter* was shown to a gathering of journalists and guests at the Royal Institution in Piccadilly. Kit was accompanied by some of his family, including Mark and Lucy, who was studying in Plymouth. Afterwards there was a frank discussion on the programme, and things became unpleasant.

In the episode, Kit spoke about a survey conducted in 1976 by the *New Scientist* into the question of cheating in science. From the transcript of the first episode, Kit said: '… some years ago the *New Scientist* did a survey to find out how many of their readers, scientists again, had actually seen fiddling amongst their own colleagues. And a very high proportion replied yes. But the difference was that in ordinary science, many of the people caught fiddling were promoted, and the people in the paranormal were disbarred from their subject for a long time.'

This statement was challenged by Dr Bernard Dixon, who was editor at that time, and would be repeated in the unfavourable review the magazine gave the programme: 'About two hundred replied,' Georgina Ferry wrote, 'a high number in itself perhaps but not "a very high proportion" of our readership (we were selling about 60,000 copies a week at the time).'

Mark Pedler remembered: 'I actually saw Dad's face when he realised he had messed up the statistics. Lies, damn lies and statistics, and all he could say was, "I think we have to have this out in print." He couldn't actually reply to it because he knew he was wrong.'

This seemingly minor generalisation was disastrous. One tiny error was all that was needed for the sceptics to dismiss his entire thesis, even if the error in question was not strictly relevant to his case. Then again, as Kit once said regarding how he would have reacted to an eccentric mind like Tesla's: 'Having made sure that his wholly unique properties posed no real threat to the probities and dogma of my own speciality, I would have closed the laboratory door behind me with a definite sigh of relief.' He may also have been reminded of something, again which is in the book, which was told to him by the man who trained him as a scientist, probably Norman Ashton: 'Statistics should be used only for illumination and not proof,' and 'Statistics should only be legal between consenting adults.'

Kit wrote a letter to *New Scientist* to clarify the matter, and changes to the dialogue were made to the Thames edition, and for those shown in other areas of the country, but that wasn't enough for other critics. Here is a letter written by Nicholas Walter of *New Humanist*, published in *New Scientist* 28 May 1981:

> It is good of Kit Pedler to correct a mistake he made in the book and the first programme of the... series about the *New Scientist* survey of cheating in science. But it is odd to do so in the *New Scientist* where readers would not have been misled, and not on television, where viewers will have been misled. And it is also odd that the 'quite extraordinary steps to ensure the accuracy' of the series didn't correct such a mistake until it was pointed out at the press reception. One wonders how many other oddities there are, but it may be hard to find out, because my own critical remarks at the press reception were followed by a letter from Pedler threatening legal action against me!

One can only imagine what Walter said to Kit to get such a reaction, but there it is in a nutshell. If he made one mistake, a generalisation, then what else has he generalised? Case dismissed.

Georgina Ferry's review in the *New Scientist* was harsh:

> All the time we are being persuaded, rather than given a range of views and asked to make up our own minds... Tony Bastable's cross-examination hardly discomforts Pedler who is all condescension. Asked what's meant by absolute reality, he raps the table and replies, 'Oh, ordinary everyday reality like this.' This sort of gross oversimplification (which apart from the inaccuracy it entails is rather insulting to the intelligence of the viewer) is fairly typical and is at its most glaring when Pedler enlists 'the new physics' to his support.

Referring to the statistics controversy, she calls the preparation of the series 'sloppy' and criticises meaningless remarks and general phrases such as 'quite a lot of very similar results have been achieved'. The fact that Geoffrey Chew was more than happy to simplify matters by rapping his knuckles on a table was probably something she didn't know.

It was full circle. Kit had decried those who had decried the 'simplifiers' and gleefully launched upon a single error to dismiss something made easier for the layman to follow in 1966 in the *Guardian*. He must have had something of a flashback to more rarefied times as a research scientist, standing on a lonely lectern, waiting for demolition as a flaw is gleefully exposed. Here they were, after him again.

Richard Mervyn says:

> Kit didn't like people that had closed minds. He wanted them to see that there were different views and if they didn't see that he would get quite angry. Kit enjoyed the cut and thrust of debate and wasn't afraid to change his mind or concede a point. He never came in with a hardened view. He also believed that everybody was entitled to a view. 'Oh, I don't know anything about it,' and he would say, 'Nor do scientists. They think they know.'

At the end of the sixth episode, Kit was asked by Tony Bastable for his view, after all that he had seen and explored in the series. Kit addresses the camera, and us, for the last time:

> A scientist would have to be either massively ignorant or a confirmed bigot to deny the evidence that the human mind can make connection with space,

time and matter in ways which have nothing to do with the ordinary sense. Further he cannot deny that these connections are compatible with current thinking in physics and may in the future become accepted as a part of an extended science in which the description 'paranormal' no longer applies and can be replaced by 'normal'.

Despite his bruising encounter with the *New Scientist*, Kit was beginning to experience a new renaissance. In the London area, *Mind Over Matter* was transmitted on consecutive Tuesday nights at 7pm beginning on 12 May, although other regions in the country would show it in the afternoons and on different days. As for the public, the programme appears to have gone down well, and opened the way for more documentary collaborations between Kit and Richard Mervyn. They wondered if a series devoted to physics might be a practical idea, possibly involving Capra. They also proposed a series called *Living Without Oil*, expanding on ideas Kit had explored on the radio. Kit also wanted to do a follow-up to *The Quest for Gaia* with a book of detailed designs which would explore fundamentally different ways of getting the industrial products we now take for granted.

Kit was booked to speak at the Second Eco-Philosophy Conference in Dartington, Devon for a weekend in July and was about to start researching a proposed TV movie based on *The Dynostar Menace*, with the script to be written by Gerry Davis. He had recorded a series of appearances for Radio 4's *Enquire Within*, answering sixteen questions on science, which he had recorded at the end of April and was due to go out starting on 28 May.

He was still campaigning for the Campaign for the Reform of Animal Experimentation, as well as developing ideas for the second attempt at the Earthlife City in the Isle of Dogs. If only he was aware of it, the BBC were planning to bring back the Cybermen in spectacular and unforgettable fashion to meet the new *Doctor Who*. He was finally booked to talk about *The Quest for Gaia* on the BBC's *Paperback* programme on 10 June.[*]

Best of all, he was back on the TV, doing one of the things he loved: communicating ideas, and upsetting the minds of the rigid. He still needed to record the last episode of *Mind Over Matter* which was going to be broadcast on 23 June where he might have addressed the *New Scientist* controversy. He also secretly enjoyed being recognised... 'He had a pretty

---

[*] In the event, Gerry Davis took his place and the programme hosted by comedian and historian Terry Jones became a tribute.

big ego,' remembers Lucy. 'He certainly didn't mind the limelight.' Mark Pedler went further: 'He was vainglorious! When he lived in Kent we went to a fête or something, and he started stooping his head. He said, "I've got a television face, I don't want to be recognised." And of course, nobody did, and he was terribly disappointed.'

The day before the third episode went out, Kit went to visit Carol, who was now living in Brixton, and had recently given birth to her second baby:

> I was just about to go out with a friend. He just happened to have posters or fliers from the television series in his back pocket, and he gave one to me and one to my friend. He was incredibly excited to be back on telly. He told me he'd just been into the vegetarian shop at the end of the street, and how they'd seen it, and how he had been greeted on the streets by passers-by, and bus drivers, He loved all that! And that was the last time I saw him.

*

Kit might have put it a little like this: 'My temporary separation from the fabric of nature ended some time in the morning of Wednesday 27 May 1981.' He had gone into the conservatory which he had built himself at the side of the home he shared with Cherry in Doddington. He was wearing his dressing gown and sat down.

When Cherry found him, she thought he had just gone back to sleep.

19
He Could Be Watching the Sunrise

There he is, sitting in the conservatory he built, his head gently tilted to the left. He's wearing the dressing gown Mum made for him. He could be watching the sunrise, but his eyes are closed. They can't see, of course. I cry for the first time… – Carol Topolski remembering her father's death in The Independent

Lucy Pedler

The last time I saw him was at the Royal Institution in Piccadilly. Dad phoned me on the Saturday before he died. We had a payphone in the student house which only accepted incoming calls. I remember very clearly the conversation. He kept saying, 'How are you?' He rarely called me up and I didn't really know why he kept trying to find out what was going on. It was only in retrospect I understood. We had a really nice conversation. Then Carol called and told me the news.

I went back home that night to Kent. They postponed the funeral so I could take my finals. How I did them I'm not too sure. There were a few more episodes of *Mind Over Matter* shown after he died, and I watched one on my own in Plymouth and remember getting an incredible headache and feeling like he was in the room.

Mark Pedler

After the split with Mum, I went to see him in his new house a couple of times. I didn't fall out with him about it. As I got older and less reckless, we got on very well. Towards the end of his life, he was becoming a bit disenchanted. He didn't like the way the world was going, and it made him very depressed and fed up. His life had been in the doldrums. He was very disaffected in that period of his life. He wasn't spectacularly happy with or without Cherry.

He was autopsied and his arteries were furred up a bit but no more than you would expect in a fifty-year-old man. Curiously, a few months prior to that, he thought he was having a heart attack, so he went to the hospital. They gave him the all clear. It's not actually clear how he died. Everyone assumes it was a heart attack, but we're not totally certain. I presume it happened fast.

Angela Walder

His death came as quite a shock. I had travelled on the train with him the day before, and the next thing that I heard, he had died. There were all sorts of rumours about whether he died or committed suicide or whatever, but I just didn't bother to follow them up on the grounds that it was sad he wasn't here any more. I thought the rumours were a bit odd as he had been happy on the train and chatting away; perhaps there was something deeper going on. The train didn't get into Sittingbourne until gone eleven, and then he had to go on a bit further. I know he'd been out earlier in the day, maybe he had been overdoing it. He was a little bit overweight if I remember rightly, although he shouldn't have been since he was vegetarian, but he was so rushed off his feet, maybe his diet might not have been as good as it might be.

Jeanette Kupfermann

He seemed quite fit. He had been terribly ill before I met him, but he seemed to be OK. At one point he'd driven racing cars and had been a real man's man. I imagine his lifestyle had taken its toll. He was kind of red-faced, what you might call a colic man, and he could lose his temper quite easily. I think you could tell he had been a drinker.

Nigel Tuersley

It was just extraordinary. I was going back to do some work, following some meetings in London. I was just getting off the train at a station in south London, and my secretary met me as she knew I was getting off there and said, 'I have something awful to tell you.'

Lucy

What I remember of the funeral was that the vicar called him Christopher, which Dad hadn't been known by for decades, which signified how little attention he paid to who Dad was. My Dad was an atheist. He would have been laughing in his grave. Carol brought long-stemmed white lilies and she gave us one each which we threw into his grave.

Nigel

It was a very memorable funeral. Kent was extraordinarily beautiful, depressing though the day was. I'll never forget the drive down there.

Richard Ryder

I couldn't get to his funeral or memorial party. I've always regretted that. I can't remember why, probably some hospital work.

Lucy

We had a nice wake in London in a house in Stockwell which belonged to Mum and Dad's old friend Brian Llewellyn, who was managing director of Thompson's Holidays. It was advertised in the *Guardian* or the *Times* or both and said anybody who knew Dad could come along. They played Dad's favourite tune which was a very sad piece by Albinoni. Brian said a few things about Dad, so the wake was as memorable as the actual funeral.

Jeanette

Kit had requested a party to bring all his friends together to celebrate his life; a real proper celebration, not a mournful occasion. For the first time I met all the different threads in his life. I remember Tony Bastable was there. A few people came up to me and said, 'You're Jeanette, heard about you but never met you,' and I'd say, 'You're so and so,' but none of us had ever met, and yet we all had quite intense relationships with him. We only met at this party after his death.

They played his favourite piece of music, which I love myself, and I always think of Kit when I hear it. It is *The Pearl Fishers*, a famous duet by Georges Bizet, a beautiful piece of music which is sung by a tenor and a baritone. It was set at a famous temple in Sri Lanka, and I went there myself a few years ago and thought of Kit. I think he'd been there himself. When I heard that aria, I was quite surprised that it was the piece he loved most in his lifetime. There was a deeply romantic streak in him.

Diana Baur

I remember this packed occasion and thinking what a wonderful idea this was, because it meant that anyone who had known and cared about him would be gathered under one roof to remember him. Everyone was talking about Kit, the one thing they all had in common. Una was on the top floor, and Cherry was down in the kitchen. They both held up remarkably well in the circumstances. There were stacks of people there. It did seem rather bizarre that it was happening.

Nigel

Earthlife lost a visionary, and it took on a different direction. He would have been proud of the next stage, the rainforest conservation. Sustainable resource use in terms of natural capital was not Kit's prime focus at that time. He was much more concerned about the process of social change. He would have been a powerful force in the way the environmental movement went, and today he would have been the voice of reason and integrity. It was very difficult to shift him away from what he believed in.

Richard

Kit was always outside of society because he wanted to question it. It's always the very brave who step outside and say, 'Hang on a minute…' He would describe me as a right-wing anarchist: 'Your anarchism is that you hate the state telling you what to do. Nothing wrong with that; in some respects I understand it. But deep down you are a bit of an anarchist. You want change, but you're not prepared to do anything about it.' I went, 'Maybe I don't want to change it that much.' Kit would say to closet anarchists disapprovingly, 'What are you going to do about it?' That's why we need the people who do want to change things and move things forward.

Kerry Glasier

At the time of his death, Kit was little more than halfway through a life. He had trekked into the base camp of a mountain, fully equipped to go to the summit. He was brimming with ideas and enthusiasm.

Carol Topolski

He always used to say he never quite decided what he wanted to do when he grew up! He was an enormously charismatic man. He was very urbane, and very witty. He had this very fine mind and was terribly interested in, and very good at, debate. Wherever he went he drew people to him. He would have thought of himself as a maverick, someone who thought outside the box.

Lucy

I think he was a very loving, affectionate, interesting, interested, passionate, extremely clever, slightly troubled person; troubled in loving and admiring Mum mentally but not being able to be faithful to her, and troubled by all the issues he was trying to create awareness about.

Una Freeston

To a certain extent, after he died, he came back to us. It was me who did all the arranging for the funeral. We had already bought a double grave at the local church of All Saints at Graveney. That's where he was buried, and that's where I shall end up.

Mark

I never got over his death, and I don't like looking at *Mind Over Matter* or things like that. I've got copies of it, but I just can't watch it. He was a great man.

Mum wanted on his gravestone 'A man of ideas'. That is something that would sum him up.

Appendix I
Medical Papers

Journals and books

1955

1. *Sex of Nuclei in Ocular Tissues.* Christopher Pedler and Norman Ashton, Department of Pathology, Institute of Ophthalmology. *British Journal of Ophthalmology* 39: 362-7. Received 7 March 1955

1956

2. *The Relationship of Hyaluronidase to Aqueous Outflow Resistance.* C. Pedler. *Transactions of the Ophthalmological Society of the United Kingdom* 76 :51-63

1957

3. *A Method for the Direct Observation of Retinal Vessels in the Experimental Animal.* Christopher Pedler, Department of Pathology, Institute of Ophthalmology, University of London. *British Journal of Ophthalmology* 41:174-8. Received 3 December 1956

4. *Studies on Developing Retinal Vessels IV: Effect of Ionising Radiation.* Christopher Pedler, Department of Pathology, Institute of Ophthalmology, University of London. *British Journal of Ophthalmology* 41: 179-81. Received 3 December 1956

5. *Studies on Developing Retinal Vessels V: Mechanism of Vaso-Obliteration* (A preliminary report). Norman Ashton, Clive Graymore and Christopher Pedler. *British Journal of Ophthalmology* 41: 449-60. Received 7 May 1957

1959

6. *Studies on Developing Retinal Vessels VI: Histological Measurement of Fluoride-Induced Swelling in the Retina.* Christopher Pedler, Department of Pathology, Institute of Ophthalmology, University of London. *British Journal of Ophthalmology* 43: 559-65. Received 10 October 1958

7. *Studies on Developing Retinal Vessels VII: Fluoride Induced Vaso-Obliteration and its Relation to Retinal Maturity.* Christopher Pedler, Department of Pathology, Institute of Ophthalmology, University of London. *British Journal of Ophthalmology* 43: 681-5. Received 16 January 1959

1961

8. *The Inner Limiting Membrane of the Retina.* Christopher Pedler, Department of Pathology, Institute of Ophthalmology, University of London. *British Journal of Ophthalmology* 45 (6) 423-38. Received 25 October 1960

9. *Unusual Coloboma of the Optic Nerve Entrance.* Christopher Pedler, Department of Pathology, Institute of Ophthalmology, University of London. *British Journal of Ophthalmology* 45: 803-7. Received 21 March 1961

1962

10. *Studies on Developing Retinal Vessels IX: Reaction of Endothelial Cells to Oxygen.* Norman Ashton and Christopher Pedler, Department of Pathology and Department of Anatomy, Institute of Ophthalmology, University of London. *British Journal of Ophthalmology* 46: 257-76. Received 5 December 1961

11. *The Radial Fibres of the Retina.* C. Pedler. *Documenta Opthalmologica: Advances in Ophthalmology.* February 16: (1) 208-220

12. *The Fine Structure of the Corneal Epithelium.* Christopher Pedler, Department of Anatomy, Institute of Ophthalmology, University of London. *Experimental Eye Research.* March. 1: (3) 286-289. Received 7 February 1962

13. *A Pneumatic Driving Mechanism for Ultra-Microtomes.* C. Pedler and F. Sheen, Department of Anatomy, Institute of Ophthalmology, London. *Journal of the Royal Microscopical Society.* 81: (Pt. 2) 67-71. December. Received 26 June 1962

1963

From 1963 until 1970, Dr C. M. H. Pedler would each year write a summary of work which the Department of Anatomy was undertaking, starting with the Fifteenth Annual Report of the Institute of Ophthalmology.

14. *The Fine Structure of the Cone of a Diurnal Gecko (Phelsuma Inunguis).* Christopher Pedler and Katharine Tansley, Department of Anatomy, Institute of Ophthalmology, University of London. *Experimental Eye Research* 2: (1) 39. January. Received 21 June 1962

15. *The Fine Structure of the Radial Fibres in the Reptile Retina.* Christopher Pedler, Department of Anatomy, Institute of Ophthalmology, University of London. *Experimental Eye Research.* July 2: (3) 296-303. Received 4 June 1963

16. *The Fine Structure of the Tapetum Cellulosum.* Christopher Pedler, Department of Anatomy, Institute of Ophthalmology, University of London. *Experimental Eye Research* 2: (2) 189-95. April. Received 11 January 1963. Listed in Annual Report as 'The Fine Structure of the Cat Tapetum'

17. *The Visual Cells of the Alligator: An Electron Microscopic Study.* M. Kalberer and C. Pedler, Department of Anatomy, Institute of Ophthalmology, University of London. *Vision Research* 3 (7-8) 323-329 July-August 1963. Received 1 August 1963

18. *Some Observations on the Fine Structure of the Visual-Cell Synapse.* Christopher Pedler, Department of Anatomy, Institute of Ophthalmology, University of London. *XIX Concilium Ophthalmologicum.* Acta: Vol. 1 p.645. Edited by Y. K. C. Pandit. New Delhi 1963. Prepared as 'Synapses of the Reptilian Visual Cell'

1964

19. *The Nature of the Gecko Visual Cell: A Light and Electron Microscopic Study.* Christopher Pedler and Rita Tilly, Department of Anatomy, Institute of Ophthalmology, University of London. *Vision Research* 4: 9-10 499-510. November 1964. Received 13 December 1963

20. *An Effect of Dark Adaptation on the Retina of the Lizard.* C. M. H. Pedler and R. J. Tilly. *Electron Microscopy 1964: Proceedings of Third European Regional Conference on Electron Microscopy in Prague.* 2: 321

1965

21. *Rods and Cones – A Fresh Approach.* Christopher Pedler, Department of Anatomy, Institute of Ophthalmology, University of London. Published in *Ciba Foundation Symposium – Colour Vision: Physiology and Experimental Psychology.* Chapter 4. Edited by A. V. S. de Reuck and J. Knight, John Wiley & Sons, Ltd. London. A paper delivered in 1964

22. *Rods and Cones – A Fresh Approach.* Christopher Pedler, Department of Anatomy, Institute of Ophthalmology, University of London. *Biochemistry of the Retina 1st International Symposium.* Edited by Clive N. Graymore. Academic Press, London. A paper delivered September 1964

23. *Anatomical, Electrophysical and Pigmentary Aspects of Vision in the Bush Baby: An Interpretative Study.* H. J. Dartnall, MRC Vision Research Unit UK; G. B. Arden, C. P. Luck, M. E. Rosenberg, Department of Experimental Ophthalmology UK; C. M. Pedler, K. Tansley, Department of Anatomy, Institute of Ophthalmology, University of London. *Vision Research.* 8-9:399-424. Received 23 February 1965

24. *The Compound Eye and First Optic Ganglion of the Fly: A Light and Electron Microscopic Study.* C. Pedler and H. Goodland. *Journal of the Royal Microscopical Society.* 84: (2) 161-179. June

25. *A Simple Exposure Meter for Electron Microscopy.* C. Pedler. *Journal of the Royal Microscopical Society.* 84: (1) 105-106. April

26. *Ultrastructural Variations in the Photoreceptors of the Macaque.* C. Pedler and R. Tilly, Department of Anatomy, Institute of Ophthalmology, University of London. *Experimental Eye Research.* 4: (4) 370-373. December. Received 15 September 1965

1966

27. *The Serial Reconstruction of a Complex Receptor Synapse.* C. M. H. Pedler and R. Tilly. *Proceedings of the VIII International Congress of Anatomy*, Wiesbaden, Eye Structure, 2nd Symposium August 1965. Edited by J. W. Rohen. Schattauer, Stuttgart

28. *A New Method of Serial Reconstruction from Electron Micrographs.* C. Pedler and R. Tilly. *Journal of the Royal Microscopical Society.* 86: (2) 189-197. December. Received 26 October 1966

29. *The Reconstruction of the Outer Plexiform Layer of the Retina.* C. Pedler and R. Tilly. *Electron Microscopy* 1966 Vol.2; *Proceedings of the 6th International Congress for Electron Microscopy*, Kyoto, Japan. Edited by R. Uyeda. Maruzen Co. Ltd., Nihonbashi, Tokyo. p 497

1967

30. *Three Dimensional Reconstruction of Nervous Tissue.* C. M. H. Pedler and R. Tilly. *Proceedings of the Second International Congress for Stereology*, Chicago. April 1967. New York: Springer-Verlag. Not listed in the Institute of Ophthalmology's Annual Report

31. *The Fine Structure of Photoreceptor Discs.* C. M. H. Pedler and R. Tilly. *Vision Research* 7: (11-12) 829-836. November 1967. Received 6 April 1967

Appendix 1: Medical Papers

32. *A Source of Error in the Interpretation of Electron Micrographs.* C. Pedler and R. Tilly, Department of Anatomy, Institute of Ophthalmology, University of London. *Journal of the Royal Microscopical Society.* April. 88 (2) 177-182. Received 3 May 1967

1968

33. *A Computerised System for the Three-Dimensional Reconstruction of Serial Electron Micrographs.* Pedler, C. M. H. *Electron Microscopy: Pre-Congress Abstracts of Papers Presented at the Fourth European Regional Conference.* Edited by D. S. Bocciarelli. Tipographia Poliglotta, Rome. P.573-574

34. *Multiple Oil Droplets in the Photoreceptors of the Pigeon.* C. Pedler and M. Boyle, Department of Anatomy, Institute of Ophthalmology, University of London. *Vision Research.* 9: (4) 525-526. April. Received 25 November 1968. Not listed in Institute of Ophthalmology's Annual Report

1969

35. *A Computer Driven Method of Serial Electron Microscopic Reconstruction.* C. M. H. Pedler. *Advances in Optical and Electron Microscopy.* Edited by V. E. Coslett and R. Barer. Academic Press, London

36. *The Retina of a Fruit Bat (Pteropus Giganteus Brunnich).* C. Pedler and R. Tilley. *Vision Research* 909-922: 909. August. Received 14 January 1969

37. *A Roll Film Camera for the AEI-EM6 Electron Microscope.* C. M. Pedler and G. Mould. *Journal of the Royal Microscopical Society.* 90: (2) 157-160. October

38. *Rods and Cones – A New Approach.* C. Pedler. Edited by W. J. L. Felts and R. J. Harrison. Academic Press, London. *International Review of General and Experimental Zoology.* 4: 219-274. 1969

1970

39. *Retinal Ultrastructure and Pattern Recognition Logic.* C. M. H. Pedler MB, BS, PhD, MCPath, Dept of Anatomy, Institute of Ophthalmology and D. A. Young, Department of Computer Science, University of Manitoba, Canada. *British Medical Bulletin* 26: (2) 119-124. Also delivered by Young and reproduced in 'Proceedings of the Conference on Interdisciplinary Research' in *Computer Science,* University of Manitoba, Winnipeg, June 8-10, 1970

40. *A Logical Simulation of Retinal Function.* C. M. H. Pedler. *Journal of Pattern Recognition.* 1970? Listed in Annual Report 69/70

41. *A Device for Marking Scales on Electron Micrographs. Proceedings of the Royal Microscopical Society.* Further details unknown. Listed as being 'in press' in Institute of Ophthalmology's Annual Report 69/70

1971

42. *Retinal Ultrastructure and Pattern Recognition Logic.* C. M. H. Pedler and D. A. Young. *Ophthalmology: Proceedings of the XXI International Congress, Mexico.* Edited by M. Puig Solanes. *Amsterdam: Excerpta Medica* Chapter IX p564. Listed as 'A Logical Analysis of Retinal Fine Structure' in Institute of Ophthalmology's Annual Report 69/70

General magazines

'Metal Cast of Vessels'. *Medical & Biological Illustration* 5: frontpiece. 1955

New Light on the Retina/A Cybernetic View of the Retina. C. Pedler. *Spectrum.* Central Office of Information. September 1965

There is a reference to 'A New Light on the Retina' in a footnote in *The Television Society Journal* in 1966, which may have been a report of a lecture, and 'A Cybernetic View of the Retina', listed in the Institute of Ophthalmology's Annual Report 1965/66.

The Eye as a Computer. Kit Pedler. *Science Journal.* February. 6: 49-54

Appendix 1: Medical Papers

Ophthalmological book reviews

By Kit Pedler himself:

The Retina Vessels: Comparative Ophthalmoscopic and Histologic Studies on Healthy and Diseased Eyes by R. Seitz MD, translated by Frederick C. Blodi. *British Medical Journal* 15 May 1965

Eye and Brain: The Psychology of Seeing by R. L. Gregory. 'Appearances', *The Guardian* 18 March 1966

Das Auge und seine Hilfsorgane by Johannes W. Rohen. *Journal of Anatomy* January 1966

The Senses Considered as Perceptual Systems by James J. Gibson, and *The Eye: Phenomenology of Function and Disorder* by J. M. Hecton. 'Views of Perception', *The Guardian* 20 September 1968

The Intelligent Eye by R. L. Gregory. 'What's There', *The Guardian* 16 April 1970

Mikrokopisch-histologische Untersuchung unter besonderer Berucksichtigung des Sehorgans. Edited by A. Heydenreich. *Journal of Anatomy* 1970.

With Norman Lockett:

Symposium on Posterior Uveitis & Retinal Diseases: Symposium on Differential Diagnostic Problems of Posterior Uveitis. Edited by Samuel J. Kimura and Wayne M. Cavgill. *British Medical Journal* 20 May 1967

Appendix 2
Known Writing

Television and film

Credited as contributing storyline and ideas:

Doctor Who, 'The War Machines'. 4 episodes, 1966

Doctor Who, 'The Wheel in Space'. 6 episodes, 1967

Doctor Who, 'The Invasion'. 8 episodes, 1968

Uncredited *Doomwatch* storylines and ideas with Gerry Davis (1968-70) with eventual scriptwriter and title:

'The Patrick Experiment' – John Gould as 'Friday's Child'

'Burial at Sea' – Dennis Spooner

'Rattus Sapiens?' – Terence Dudley as 'Tomorrow the Rat'

'Check and Mate' – (1) Hugh Forbes, (2) N. J. Crisp and (3) Gerry Davis as 'Project Sahara'

'Re-Entry Forbidden' – Don Shaw

'The Devil's Sweets' – Don Shaw

'The Flames of Hell' – Kit Pedler and Gerry Davis as 'The Red Sky'

'Pollution Inc.' – Terence Dudley as 'Spectre at the Feast'

'Train and Detrain' – Don Shaw

Appendix 2: Known Writing

'The Synthetic Candidate' – Elwyn Jones as 'The Battery People'

'Hear No Evil' – (1) Harry Green and (2) Gerry Davis

'Lonely The House' – Martin Worth as 'Invasion'

'Massacre of the Innocents' – Roger Parkes as 'No Room for Error'

'The Iron Doctor' – (1) Harry Green and (2) Brian Hayles

'The Will to Die' – John Gould as 'In the Dark'

'The Logicians' – Dennis Spooner

'The Battery People' – Moris Farhi (unused)

'The Pacifiers' – (1) Jan Read and (2) David Fisher

'Inventor's Moon' – Martin Worth (undeveloped)

'Death of a Sagittarian' – Bill Barron (unused)

'Condition of the Mind' – John Wiles (unused)

Full scripts with Gerry Davis:

Doctor Who, 'The Tenth Planet'. 4 episodes, 1966

Doctor Who, 'The Moonbase'. 4 episodes, 1966/7

Doctor Who, 'The Tomb of the Cybermen'. 4 episodes, 1967

Doomwatch, 'The Plastic Eaters'. 1968

Doomwatch, ('Operation Neptune') 'The Red Sky'. 1969

Doomwatch, 'Survival Code'. 1969

Doomwatch (film, final screenplay by Clive Exton). 1971

Mutant 59 The Plastic Eater (unmade)

The Dynostar Menace (unmade)

By himself:

Down To Earth (spoof adverts). 1972

Books

By himself:

The Quest for Gaia. Souvenir Press Ltd 1979 (hardback). Granada 1981 (paperback). Kindle edition released in 2012 by Souvenir Press Ltd

Mind Over Matter. Methuen 1981 (hardback). Granada 1982 (paperback)

With Gerry Davis:

Mutant 59 The Plastic Eater. Souvenir Press Ltd 1971 (hardback). Pan Books 1973 (paperback). Kindle edition released in 2012 by Souvenir Press Ltd

Brainrack. Souvenir Press Ltd 14 February 1974 (hardback). Pan Books 17 October 1975 (paperback)

The Dynostar Menace. Souvenir Press Ltd 18 September 1975 (hardback). Pan Books 1976 (paperback)

Adapted by others:

Doomwatch: The World in Danger. Adaptation of 'The Plastic Eaters', 'The Red Sky' and 'Survival Code' (called here 'A Bomb is Missing'). Edited by Gordon Walsh. Longman Structural Readers Stage 4 1975

Doctor Who: The War Machines by Ian Stuart Black. W. H. Allen/Target 1988/9

Doctor Who and the Tenth Planet by Gerry Davis. W. H. Allen/Target

Doctor Who and the Cybermen by Gerry Davis (based on 'The Moonbase'). W. H. Allen/Target

Doctor Who and the Tomb of the Cybermen by Gerry Davis. W. H. Allen/Target

Doctor Who: The Wheel in Space by Terrance Dicks. W. H. Allen/Target 1988

Doctor Who: The Invasion by Ian Marter. W. H. Allen/Target 1985

Doctor Who: The Scripts: The Tomb of the Cybermen (transcript taken from the soundtrack of the episodes). Edited by John McElroy. Titan Books 1989

Appendix 2: Known Writing

Contributed chapters in books

Short stories edited by Rosemary Timperley:

'Image in Capsule' in *The Sixth Ghost Book*. Barrie & Jenkins Ltd 1970 (hardback). Pan Books Ltd 1972 (paperback)

'The Long Term Residents' in *The Seventh Ghost Book*. Barrie & Jenkins Ltd 1971 (hardback). Pan Books Ltd 1973 (paperback)

'Terence and the Unholy Father' in *The Eighth Ghost Book*. Barrie & Jenkins Ltd 1972 (hardback). Pan Books Ltd 1974 (paperback)

'White Caucasian Male' in *The Ninth Ghost Book*. Barrie & Jenkins Ltd 1973 (hardback). Pan Books Ltd 1975 (paperback)

Essays in books:

'Deus Ex Machina?' in *The Disappearing Future: A Symposium of Speculation*, edited by George Hay. Panther 1970

'Cast Iron Power' in *Radical Technology,* edited by Godfrey Boyle and Peter Harper. Undercurrents 1976

'Nikola Tesla' in *Men of Mystery: A Celebration of the Occult*, edited by Colin Wilson. W. H. Allen 1977

Foreword to *Dan Dare: Pilot of the Future in the Man from Nowhere Volume One*, edited by Mike Higgs. Dragon's Dream 1979

Articles in newspapers and magazines

'Deus Ex Machina?' *The Listener*, July 1969

'Penniless and Without Honour?' Review of *Reason Awake: Science for Man* by Rene Dubos. *New Scientist*, 1970

'Do we Realise What we are Letting Ourselves in for by Taming Insects?' *Daily Mail*, 1 April 1972

'Human Race Against Time at Crisis Point'. Unknown newspaper, 1972

'Europe Debate'. *Sunday Times*, 25 May 1975

'Guardian Extra' (on animal experiments). *The Guardian*, 8 October 1975

'This Deal with the Devil'. *Daily Express*, 12 November 1976

'Building a home-made atom bomb/This diabolical knowledge we have to live with'. *Daily Express*, 18 May 1977

Untitled review of *Mysteries* by Colin Wilson. *New Scientist*, 1978

Untitled review of *In the Centre of Immensities* by Bernard Lovell. *Evening News*. Submitted February 1979

Contributed letters to a variety of journals and newspapers including *Life* in January 1967 attacking an article on the English.

Appendix 3
Known Radio Broadcasts

THE FOLLOWING LIST is compiled from Kit Pedler's radio contracts file at the BBC's written archives at Caversham, and from other sources. Sometimes the two conflict or there are omissions, or the programme has been put out under a different name.

1965

Research Project: The Computer In Your Eye. Broadcast Sunday 15 September 05.30 GMT, BBC World Service. 13' 30". Interviewed at home in Clapham by Paul Vaughan on Saturday 2 July. *BBC London Calling*: '... in *The Computer in your Eye* Dr Christopher Pedler of the Institute of Ophthalmology, London has to use a magnification of 44,000 before he can usefully study the retina of the eye.' Includes illustration.

1968

Fight For Sight. Broadcast Sunday 14 April, 10.10pm, Radio 4. A history of the Institute of Ophthalmology. Recorded Tuesday 12 March.

1969

Postmark Africa. Broadcast Saturday 3 May, BBC World Service African Service.

Of Ombudsmen and Cybermats. Broadcast Thursday 5 June 9.10pm, Radio 3. Recorded Tuesday 14 January 1969. Working title: *My Life in Science*. *Radio Times* featured a picture of Kit Pedler with its listings. Transcript exists at the BBC Written Archive.

Scientists in Session. Broadcast Monday 8 September, Radio 4. Recorded in Exeter on unknown date, and lasting 2' 58".

Speak Easy. Broadcast Saturday 22 November 5pm, Radio 1. Recorded Friday 21 November.

1970

Ten O'Clock News. Broadcast Monday 23 February 10pm, Radio 4. Speaking on 'Test Tube Babies'.

For Schools: Christian Focus. Broadcast Thursday 14 May 10.30am, Radio 4 FM. Recorded Monday 16 March. 'Animals – should we use them?' with Mr A. Silsen and Leslie Smith. *Radio Times*: 'A farmer and a scientist discuss the way we use our world.'

Late Night Extra. Broadcast Tuesday 28 April 10pm, Radio 2. Interviewed about *Doomwatch*.

The World at One. Broadcast Friday 7 August 1pm, Radio 4. On nerve gas dumping.

The World Tonight. Broadcast Tuesday 25 August 10pm, Radio 4. 'Pollution – are we making too much fuss?'

Prospect: Daily Bread. Broadcast Friday 9 October, Radio 3 Schools. Recorded Friday 28 August. About *Doomwatch*.

Today. Broadcast Monday 14 December from 7am, Radio 4. Recorded Sunday 13 December.

The World at One. Broadcast Thursday 17 December 1pm, Radio 4. On contamination of tuna in America.

1971

Today. Broadcast Saturday 23 January from 7am, Radio 4. On President Nixon's State of the Union address where he speaks of environmental reforms.

Doomsday or Doomwatch. Recorded Monday 15 February. 20-minute talk which Pedler writes and reads. Transmission unknown and not written on his contract.

Appendix 3: Known Radio Broadcasts

Late Night Extra. Broadcast Friday 12 March 10pm, Radio 2. Live in Newcastle, on the theme of *Doomwatch*.

Today. Broadcast Monday 7 June from 7am, Radio 4. 'Air versus space.'

Woman's Hour. Broadcast Monday 5 July 2pm, Radio 2. Recorded Monday 21 June on population.

Ideas in Science Fiction. Broadcast Tuesday 26 October 7.30pm, Radio 3. Recorded Wednesday 4 November 1970. In discussion with Dr Christopher Evans on alternative life forms. *The Listener*: 'In this series of conversations, Dr Christopher Evans, a psychologist working on computers at the National Physics Lab, talks about the philosophical ideas underlying science fiction and tries to discover what relation it bears to man's present condition.'

New Worlds. Broadcast Thursday 2 December 9.30pm, Radio 4. Recorded Monday 29 November. Interview and discussion with Dr Warwick Bray.

The Morning Show. Broadcast Wednesday 8 December, BBC World Service African Service. Recorded on Monday 6 December. 4' 30" on biological warfare.

Speak Easy. Broadcast Sunday 12 December 3pm, Radio 1. Recorded on 10 December. 47' 33" discussion programme.

Questions of Belief. Broadcast Sunday 12 December 7.30pm, Radio 4. Recorded Wednesday 8 December at Frensham Heights School. Panel discussion.

1972

Dial a Scientist. Broadcast Tuesday 4 January 11.30 am, Radio 4. Life in 2072 with Kit Pedler, Eric Laithwaite and Cherrie Bramwell.

The World Tonight. Broadcast Thursday 13 January 10pm, Radio 4. Pre-recorded feature on ecology.

Today. Broadcast Monday 17 January from 7am, Radio 4. Recorded on 16 January. About *Doomwatch*.

Late Night Extra. Broadcast Wednesday 19 January 10.02pm, Radio 2. About the *Doomwatch* film.

The World This Weekend. Broadcast Sunday 20 February 1pm, Radio 4. Interview.

Inquiry: The NHS. Broadcast Wednesday 23 February 10.30am, Radio 4 Schools. Interview recorded at home on Tuesday 14 December 1971. Kit's contribution is 3 minutes in duration.

Late Night Extra. Broadcast Wednesday 23 February 10.02pm, Radio 2. Interview about *Mutant 59 The Plastic Eater.*

New Worlds. Broadcast Thursday 24 February 9.30pm, Radio 4. Recorded 22 February, interviewed with Gerry Davis. 2' 18" used.

Speak Easy. Broadcast Sunday 5 March 3pm, Radio 1. Recorded 3 March. 'Whither Science?' 45 minutes.

The Morning Show – East & West. Broadcast Tuesday 7 March, BBC World Service African Service. Recorded 6 March. 2 minutes on the Club of Rome.

New Worlds. Broadcast Thursday 9 March 9.30pm, Radio 4. Recorded 25 February. Discussion lasting 11' 15".

Any Questions. Broadcast Friday 5 May 8.30pm, Radio 4. Live discussion programme transmitted from Horncastle, Lancaster.

Late Night Extra. Broadcast Tuesday 8 June 10.02pm, Radio 2. On motorways, lasting 3' 50". Paid £6.50 in expenses.

Scan. Broadcast Thursday 15 June 8.45pm, Radio 4. Recorded Wednesday 14 June. Discusses feature film and the new TV series. Duration: 8' 25".

1973

The World This Weekend. Broadcast Sunday 15 April 1pm, Radio 4. Unknown subject.

Newsbeat. Broadcast Monday 23 July, Radio 1. On the French hydrogen bomb test. This was a pilot edition for the programme, and the interview was used in the morning and afternoon edition.

Prospect. Broadcast Friday 9 November 11.40am, Radio 3 for Schools. Science and governmental responsibility with James Burke.

Newsbeat. Broadcast Wednesday 5 December, Radio 1. On radiation.

Appendix 3: Known Radio Broadcasts

The World Tonight. Broadcast Monday 24 December 9.30pm, Radio 4. Feature on world resources, recorded on Friday 21 December.

1974

Late Night Extra. Broadcast Tuesday 1 January 10.02pm, Radio 2. Interview on ecologically sound house.

Woman's Hour. Broadcast Wednesdays 2, 9, 16, 23 & 30 January 1.45pm, Radio 4. Six interviews for 'Live It Yourself', recorded Tuesday 4 December 1973.

Newsbeat. Broadcast Thursday 10 January, Radio 1. Interviewed by Paul Heiney for item on peanut power.

The Morning Show. Broadcast Friday 11 January, BBC World Service African Service. Recorded Thursday 10 January. On running an engine on groundnuts.

Late Night Extra. Broadcast 13 February 10.02pm, Radio 2. On *Brainrack*.

Start The Week. Broadcast Monday 18 February 9.05am, Radio 4. Interviewed with Gerry Davis by Esther Rantzen on *Brainrack*.

Open House. Broadcast Wednesday 27 February from 9.02am, Radio 2. Interviewed with Gerry Davis on *Brainrack*.

Today. Broadcast Monday 11 March from 7am, Radio 4. Recorded Sunday 10 March. On smells.

Outlook. Broadcast Thursday 4 April, BBC World Service. Recorded Thursday 28 March. 'Not all garbage is rubbish.'

It's Your Line. Broadcast Tuesday 9 April 7.30pm, Radio 4. Phone-in show. 'Solving the energy crisis.'

Prospect: The Human Mind. Broadcast Fridays 26 April, 3, 10, 17 & 24 May 11.40am, Radio 4 Schools VHF. Edited by Stuart Evans. (1) The instrument and the owner; (2) Mind in stress; (3) Mind under scrutiny; (4) Happiness by order; (5) The expanding mind. Dr Pedler is writer, arranger, and conducts interviews. 'Integral role in the concept and format of each programme'. Only the last episode is credited in the *Radio Times* as *Prospect: The Human Mind*; the others are listed as *Prospect: The Mind*.

History in Focus. Broadcast Monday 29 April, Radio 4 Schools VHF. Recorded Monday 22 April. New York power cuts.

Speak Easy. Broadcast Sunday 19 May 2pm, Radio 1. Recorded Thursday 16 May. One-hour discussion programme.

24 Hours. Broadcast Monday 3 June, BBC World Service. Recorded Sunday 2 June on an unknown subject.

The Jimmy Young Show. Broadcast Monday 3 June from 11.30am, Radio 2. On industrial explosions, regarding the Flixborough disaster that weekend.

Late Night Extra. Broadcast Monday 10 June 10.10pm, Radio 2.

BBC World Report. Broadcast Thursday 8 August, Service ORS. ORS Special project.

The World This Weekend. Broadcast Sunday 25 August 1pm, Radio 4. On genetic engineering.

The World This Weekend. Broadcast Saturday 31 August 1pm, Radio 4. WESOP exhibition to popularise science.

For The Middle Years: Food – Feeding Our Future. Broadcast 25 October and 1 November, Radio 4 VHF for Schools. Producer: Geoffrey Sherlock. Contract: Dr Pedler will interview, write the script and narrate the final recordings. From Teacher's Notes: 'Aim. To provoke thought in children about their food supplies. The listening audience will be about 36 years old in the year 2000. Will there be enough food? If there is enough food will it be in the same form as today or largely synthetic or analogue? With approximately two-thirds of the world's population undernourished today and forecasts, admittedly varied, of possibly double the present population of the world by 2000 it is a problem deserving considerable attention.' Presented as the play 'Sunday Lunch'.

1975

Newsbeat. Broadcast Monday 6 January, Radio 1. On nerve gas.

Newsbeat. Broadcast Monday 3 March, Radio 1. On atom bombs.

Appendix 3: Known Radio Broadcasts

The World at One. Broadcast Friday 28 March from 1pm, Radio 4. On nuclear fuels.

Woman's Hour. Broadcast Monday 14 April from 1.45pm, Radio 4. 'Talk till Two' – a 13-minute discussion.

The World at One. Broadcast Thursday 22 May from 1pm, Radio 4. On the Windscale radiation leak.

Any Questions. Broadcast Friday 6 June 8.30pm, Radio 4. Panel discussion transmitted from Buckwoods, Staffordshire.

PM. Broadcast Thursday 18 September 5pm, Radio 4. Interview on *The Dynostar Menace*.

Lifelines: It's Catching. Broadcast Friday 10 October 6.30pm, Radio 3. Recorded 4 October as 'Lifelines in Science'. Nick Hughes discusses alternative ways to bring variety into life's routines with Kit and medical double act Beetles and Buckman.

The World at One. Broadcast 8 October 1pm, Radio 4. Interview on animal experimentation. Kit's address on the contract is 119 Park Hill.

Prospect: Men and Myths. Fridays 26 September – 5 December 11.40am. BBC Radio 3 for Schools & BBC Radio 4 VHF for Schools. Edited by Stuart Evans. With Jeanette Kupfermann, who is not credited in *Radio Times*. Ten episodes. *Radio Times*: Episodes 1, 2, 4-6 subtitled 'The high life of the gods'. Episode 3 is described as 'a study of ancient myth'. The rest are billed as '*High Noon* and the hero – myth in the modern world'.

Secondary Science: Recorded Vision. Edition recorded Tuesday 5 November 1974 for 1975 broadcast. Script printed in teacher's notes.

Secondary Science: Hearing. Broadcast 3 & 10 October 1975. Producer: Arthur Vialls. Consultant: Dr K. P. Murphy. Radiophonic sound: Richard Yeoman-Clarke. 'The secret codes of hearing'. Recorded Thursday 31 October 1974.

Also recorded in 1975:

Woman's Hour. Radio 4. An insert on humane research recorded on Wednesday 2 July.

1976

Lifelines: Speculations: Man's Effect on His World. Broadcast Thursday 15 January 6.30pm, Radio 3. 'Will mankind eventually pollute himself out of existence?' With Dr Christopher Evans. Repeated Friday 7 January 7pm, Radio 3.

Prospect: An Apology for Science. Fridays 30 January and 6 February 11.40am, Radio 4 for Schools. Edited by Stuart Evans. 11-minute interview with John Taylor recorded Wednesday 19 November 1975.

Kaleidoscope. Broadcast Thursday 6 May, Radio 4. Reviews an exhibition in Brighton called *Phantasmagoria Today*.

The Jimmy Young Show. Broadcast Monday 16 August 11.30am, Radio 2. Interview about experiments with live animals.

Talkabout. Broadcast Tuesday 24 August, BBC World Service. Discussion on survival with James Hugg, Jean Liedoffe and Chris Rainbow.

Unknown. Broadcast Thursday 8 July, BBC World Service. On animal experiments. 2-minute interview. Kit's agent was starting to get fed up with the frequent misspellings of Pedler and Durbridge. He has my sympathy.

Kaleidoscope. Broadcast Monday 2 August 9.30pm, Radio 4. Reviews *Kites* by David Pelham and the *Dream of Flight* exhibition at the ICA.

Secondary Science: Vision. Broadcast 24 September from 9.30am, Radio 4 for Schools. Producer: Arthur Vialls. Writes, presents, and researches. Recorded 8 July 1976.

Woman's Hour. Broadcast Friday 1 October from 1.45pm, Radio 4. Interviewed for 'Thirty Years On'.

Also in 1976:

Interviewed on Radio Medway as part of a series on local sci-fi authors.

Prospect: ESP – An Investigation. Radio 4.

Appendix 3: Known Radio Broadcasts

1977

Prospect: Green and Pleasant Land. Fridays 14, 21, 28 January & 4 February 11.40am, Radio 4 VHF for Schools. Edited by Stuart Evans. Recording dates unknown. Kit to compile, research and present 4 programmes, 20 minutes each. Jeanette Kupfermann is not credited in the *Radio Times*.

Heritage. Episodes 43 'The Entropy Crisis' & 44 'The Post Industrial Revolution'. Broadcast Saturdays 2 & 9 July 1pm, Radio 3. Producer: Brian Cook. 2 15-minute programmes. Kit interviews Jonathan Mimms of the Museum of Engineering. Recorded 21 June. Issued in 1978 by the BBC Transcription Service as a Talks LP.

1978

Today. Broadcast Friday 21 July from 6.30am, Radio 4. Reactions to Russian satellite.

Woman's Hour. Broadcast 21 September 1.45pm, Radio 4. 'The Shape of Things to Come'. On H. G. Wells' birthday, Kit Pedler and Peter Hunot wonder what the man who foresaw the atomic age would be prophesising now if he were still alive.

The Perils of Truth. Broadcast Friday 1 December. 5 minutes used from an interview.

1979

You, the Jury. Broadcast Sunday 28 January 7.15pm, Radio 4 LW. Repeated Wednesday 31 January 11am, Radio 4 FM. 'The majority of experiments on animals are of no value to medicine or science and should be banned.' Opposed by Dr David Smyth. Preparing, arguing, and questioning a witness. Repeated on Wednesday 31. Recorded on Monday 22 January.

Einstein. Broadcast Saturday 10 March. Unknown. Recorded Friday 9 February. Helps, prepares, and interviews.

Bookshelf. Broadcast Saturday 3 February 2pm, Radio 4. Recorded Saturday 6 & Sunday 7 January.

Talkabout. Broadcast Wednesday 13 June, BBC World Service. On living without oil.

Kaleidoscope. Broadcast Tuesday 19 June 9.30pm, Radio 4. Reviews the BBC1 series *The Omega Factor*.

Kaleidoscope. Broadcast Tuesday 26 June 9.30pm, Radio 4. Reviews *Toads* at Nottingham Playhouse. Accidentally gets paid twice. There is also a note written on 24 July querying his expenses, such as train fare, hotel bill paid and a tube fare of £4.55. Accepted in full.

Kaleidoscope. Broadcast Monday 6 August 9.30pm, Radio 4. Reviews the film *The China Syndrome*.

Prospect: Quantum Physics. Broadcast Fridays 21 & 28 September, 5 & 12 October, Radio 4. AKA *Quantum Wonderland*. 'An introduction – which Pedler will research. 20 minutes each.'

File on Four. Broadcast Wednesday 7 November 8.45pm, Radio 4. On experiments on animals.

Also in 1979:

Science Show. Broadcast Saturday 20 October, ABC (Australia). Presenter Robyn Williams. Dr Kit Pedler, research scientist and author of *The Quest for Gaia: A Book of Changes*, talks about his view that the earth is a living organism, and how that view influences the way he lives.

1980

Woman's Hour New Year Day Special. Broadcast Tuesday 1 January 2.02pm, Radio 4. Recorded on Friday 7 December.

Prospect: What Has Science Got to Do With Living? Broadcast Friday 24 October, Radio 4 Schools VHF. Recorded 26 September. Interviewed by Brian Fairman for series, 8' 05".

The Long Term Residents. Broadcast Wednesday 9 March 4.45pm, Radio 4 FM. Read by David March.

1981

Studio B15. Broadcast Sunday 15 February from 3pm, Radio 1. Unknown details. 'Four way' discussion and phone-in about the paranormal.

The John Dunn Show. Broadcast Wednesday 6 May 6pm, Radio 2. Guest.

Appendix 3: Known Radio Broadcasts

The Late Show: Round Midnight. Broadcast Tuesday 12 May from 11pm, Radio 2. On *Mind Over Matter*.

Enquire Within. Broadcast Thursday 28 May 11.50am, Radio 4. To answer 16 questions about science, to be used in various programmes. Recorded Thursday 30 April.

Unknown:

Prospect: Genetic Codes. Radio 4 VHF. 5 programmes.

Appendix Q
Known Television and Film Appearances

Television

1965

Tomorrow's World. Transmitted 9 December 7pm, BBC1. Editor: Peter Hale. Filmed 22 and 26 November at the Institute of Ophthalmology. Paid £30 for filmed appearance and consultation. *Radio Times*: 'In the Making Today. The men, women and discoveries which are changing the way we live. Introduced by Raymond Baxter. Around the world in Medicine – Science – Industry developments are moulding the look of the 1960s in Britain. For better or worse? Good or ill? Film, outside broadcast and studio reports put the face of change in focus for you.'

1967

Late Night Line-Up. Saturday 11 February 11.15pm, BBC2. No contract survives for this.

Late Night Line-Up. Rehearsal and transmission 19 September 11.10pm, BBC2. To take part in discussion on *Tomorrow's World*.

Talkback No. 1. Transmitted Tuesday 26 September 6.25pm, BBC1. Studio 2 at TV Centre. Paid 25 guineas on 29 September. Audio recording exists.

Appendix 4: Known Television and Film Appearances

1968

Tomorrow's World. Transmitted Wednesday 20 November 6.40pm, BBC1. Recorded 13 November at Studio D Lime Grove. Preparatory work and giving interview and demonstration. Earlier contract cancelled due to fee increase.

1969

Horizon: The Miraculous Wonder: The Human Eye. Transmitted Thursday 16 January 8pm, BBC2. Producer: Simon Campbell-Jones. Editor: R. W. Reid. Narrator: Christopher Chataway. Filmed talk and appearance in sequence as arranged. Fee to include prior consultation work. Filming: 5 and 16 July 1968 at Institute of Ophthalmology. Contract cancelled and reissued at higher fee. *Radio Times*: 'Your eyes... are they... Windows of the soul? Receivers of irrelevant information? Respectable substitutes for sex? Something like footballs? Or a piece of the brain looking out at the world? Some of the contributors to tonight's film suggest that they might be. But these are only a few of the ways in which man looks at his eye, and in spite of the detailed medical attention of many centuries, science is still breaking new ground and revealing new information about this remarkable organ. Tonight's programme asks "How important are eyes?" It looks at some current research, at how electron microscopic discoveries are giving new information about the structure of the eye, and at the cause of the most common disease that can affect it.' Exists in the BBC archives.

Doomwatch trailer. Unknown transmission details. Recording: 30 November 1969, Studio 3 Television Centre. Producer: Geoff Ramsey. Trailer 091/4/9/9949. Recorded during a studio day for 'The Plastic Eaters'. 10 guineas for writing and recording short trailer for *Doomwatch*.

1970

Line-Up. Transmitted Friday 27 February 10.30pm, BBC2. Producer: Mike Fentiman. Recorded: 7 February at Studio B, TV Centre. In discussion about book *End of the 20th Century?*

Nationwide. Transmitted Thursday 5 March 6pm, BBC1. Recorded 24 February in Lime Grove. Interview on ethical and social implications of test-tube babies.

New Horizons: People & Computers. Transmitted 23 November. Education programme. Producer: John Cain. Interview filmed at Kit's house on 27 July. Exists in the BBC's archives.

1971

Nationwide. Transmitted 25 March 6pm, BBC1. Interview filmed at home and on location. Exists in the BBC archives.

The Eighties. Transmitted Sunday 4 July 6.15pm, BBC1. Bernard Levin probes some hopes and schemes for the future – medicine. Repeated Monday 5 July 1pm, BBC1.

The Eighties. Transmitted Sunday 11 July 6.15pm, BBC1. Discussing future theatre with Alan Plater, the Ven. Edward Carpenter and Baroness Lee.

Controversy. Transmitted Monday 16 August BBC2, 9.20pm. Professor Sir Ernst Chain on 'Defence and the Responsibility of the Scientist'. Exists in the BBC archives.

Outlook '72. Transmitted Wednesday 29 December 12 midnight, London ITV. Kit Pedler discusses his predictions for 1972 with Alan Hargreaves.

1972

The Urban Spaceship. Canadian Broadcasting Corporation CBC702. A documentary on the design of cities, problems of pollution, crowding, and some suggested solutions with C. M. 'Kit' Pedler, Arthur C. Clarke, and Frank Lloyd Wright.

1973

The Shape of Things to Come...? Transmitted Wednesday 28 November 12.50am, Thames. 10-minute programme presented by Dr Christopher Evans.

1974

That's Life. Transmitted Saturday 30 March 11.20pm, BBC1. Exists in the BBC archives.

Ancient and Modern. Transmitted Tuesdays 26 March, 2 & 9 April 11.25pm, BBC1. A triangular look at the Bible. Kit Pedler in discussion with John Vincent and Brian Morris.

Psychic Surgery: The Invisible Knife. Transmitted Thursday 11 July 11pm (Thames), Saturday 20 July 11.20pm (HTV only).

Open Door: Design Action. Transmitted Sunday 8 December 11.05pm, BBC2. Kit Pedler, Ernst Schumacher and Sir Misha Black are among participants from the Design and Industries Association. Exists in the BBC archives.

1975

Choices for Tomorrow Part 6: Tools for Living. Transmitted Monday 12 May 11.05pm, BBC1. Repeated Sunday 15 June 1.25pm. Other editions in this series were: 'Woodland or Wasteland', 'Water', 'Food', 'There is No Energy Shortage!', 'House Hunt', and 'Cars Without Chaos'. Exists in the BBC archives.

Man Alive: The Waste That Remains and Kills. Transmitted Thursday 15 May 9.25pm, BBC2. The topic is nuclear waste. Exists in the BBC archives.

1976

Look Out: Alternative Technology. ITV Tyne Tees (transmission date unknown). Recorded Tuesday 20 January. Presented by Peter Moth, with Rosie and Colin Swale. Director Michael Snow. Children's programme with a live audience.

Look Out: Robots & Machine Intelligence. ITV Tyne Tees (transmission date unknown). Recorded 17 February. Presented by Peter Moth. Director Michael Snow. Children's programme with a live audience.

The Book Programme. Transmitted Tuesday 30 March 7.50pm, BBC2. With Robert Robinson, T. P. McKenna and Germaine Greer on their choice of new books. Exists in the BBC archives.

Say That Again: House for the Future. Transmitted Sunday 6 July 6.30pm, ITV Granada. Directors: D. Warwick and A. Murgatroyd. Producer: Brian Trueman. Brian Trueman, Don Wilson and Kit Pedler discuss viewers' letters on insulation, solar roofs, windmills, planning permission and their favourite choice of books on ecology. This was the climax to a 14-week series which followed the Grant family as they converted an 1840 coach house near Macclesfield into a house of the future with solar panels and wind power. They stayed there for 27 years, moving in 2003, according to *The Daily Telegraph*. They discovered that insulation is the secret and spent no more than £300 a year on heating at the end. The series was shown at different times throughout the ITV network. Exists in ITN News source archive.

The Book Programme. Transmitted Tuesday 18 May 7.45pm, BBC2. Exists in the BBC archives.

1977

Nationwide. Transmitted Friday 9 September, BBC1. This edition came from Wales. Exists in the BBC archives.

1978

Man Alive: Licensed to Kill. Transmitted Tuesday 7 November 9.45pm, BBC2. Producer: Michael Hogan. Editor: Tim Slessor. *Radio Times*: 'More than five million animals are used in experiments in Britain every year. At the end of the experiments the animals are killed. It's claimed most of them are used to make sure our environment is safe – what we eat, what we breathe, what we take when we are ill. But that assertion is challenged by an increasingly vocal animal-rights lobby – which says most experiments are unnecessary, cruel or trivial. *Man Alive* has filmed in laboratories round the country to find out what we do to animals. And in the studio with reporter Michael Dean will be people who perform experiments and those who say it's time they were made to stop.' Exists in the BBC archives.

1979

Brass Tacks. Transmitted 7 August 8.15pm, BBC2. On energy conservation.

Money Go Round. Thames TV (transmission date unknown). Interviewed in a scrapyard near Shepperton by Tony Bastable to show how the infant science of recycling could work.

Appendix 4: Known Television and Film Appearances

1981

Mind Over Matter. All episodes transmitted Tuesdays at 7pm from Thames. Granada showed Programme 1 on Sunday 10 May 9.30am, Westward TV on Monday 11 at 11.05pm, as did Southern and Channel. Grampian on Tuesday 12.30pm, Ulster and Scottish at 3.45pm. Tyne Tees showed the second episode on a Wednesday morning.

Programme 1. 12 May. From Thames TV press pack: 'In which Kit Pedler defines what the series is all about, emphasising the importance of approaching the subject with an open mind, defining what is a good and what is a bad experiment – and examining remote viewing (where someone in a locked room can see what someone else many miles away can see.)'

Programme 2. 19 May. From Thames TV press pack: 'Here we are introduced to the "New Physics" and how Albert Einstein's discoveries have changed our view of the world so as "not to make the paranormal impossible". Plus a detailed look at how minds can communicate across time and space – and at the Ganzfeld experiment which shows how this may be possible.'

Programme 3. 26 May. Shows how the mind can be exercised over matter and how scientists can affect their experiments by their own state of mind. It deals with metal bending and asks if there are any good metal-bending experiments, or whether we have to rely on the evidence of our own eyes.

Programme 4. 2 June. *The Times*: 'Dr Kit Pedler, who died last week, examines the theory that the mind can really leave the body.' From Thames TV press pack: 'The main theme here is the strange possibility that our mind can affect matter at a distance (called the "Out of Body" experiment), something which has been written about for centuries, and experienced under anaesthetic and at the point of death. It looks at the fascinating work currently being undertaken on the subject – and questions whether poltergeists are real or just the products of our own imaginations.'

Programme 5. 9 June. *The Times*: 'The late Kit Pedler investigates faith healing.' From Thames TV press pack: 'Can the paranormal influence healing? Is there a connection between the healer and the patient's mind? We look at the work of Prof Bernard Grad in Canada who's investigating the connection between the mind and body, and Dr Lawrence LeShan currently teaching healing techniques in America.'

Programme 6. 16 June. From Thames TV press pack: 'Looks at the work of Dr David Bohm which pushes the boundaries of the "New Physics" still further out; at the clues as to why the paranormal is possible and why it appears to flout all the known physical laws. It asks what is the "folded" and "unfolded" universe? It examines the changes physics may have to undergo to take into account the human mind, and the clue this gives us to the future.'

Programme 7. 23 June. *The Times*: 'Tony Bastable reviews some of the important issues that have been raised during the series.' From Thames TV press pack: 'If we accept that the paranormal is here to stay, how do we have to change to take it into account, in the way we live and think? In the studio will be a group of people who have firm opinions on the subject – and we look at their view of how our world is going to alter, and how the paranormal will affect us all.'

Unknown:

Current affairs items on STV, Harlech TV, *Teabreak*, and *How* for Southern TV.

Kit was listed in 1981 as having made, or at least written the following programmes: *The Robot, Energy* (BBC), *The Retina* (Open University).

Film

1956

Oxygen and Retinal Vessels. A film made by Dr Pedler and Dr Ashton for loan or illustration from the Institute of Ophthalmology. 'A demonstration by diagram by experiment on a kitten of the occurrence of retrolental fibroplasia through the obliteration of retinal vessels by high oxygen concentration.' Withdrawn by 1968. Exists at the BFI.

Appendix 4: Known Television and Film Appearances

1975

This Week In Britain and 24 Hours: Science and Survival. 15-minute film by Central Office of Information for overseas. Producer: Tony Hinton. Researcher/writer: Jenny Lucas. Presenter: Michele Brown. Filmed Monday 13 May 1974. Locations: GLC Car Dump, 38 Wood Lane, W12, opposite BBC Studios. 9.30-11am. North Bank of Thames, Battersea Power Station. 11.30-12.00. 119 Park Hill, Clapham, SW4. 2.15pm-5pm. Interview with Dr Pedler at house and garden or walking on Clapham Common; cutaways of environment posters. Includes opening to *Doomwatch*: 'The Plastic Eaters'.

Synopsis: 'From satellites to the electric toothbrush, our everyday lives are dominated by some miracles of science and technology. But there are many people who fear that technology may be getting out of hand and putting man and his planet at risk. Dr Kit Pedler, scientist and writer, who gave "Doomwatch" to the English language, is one of those concerned for the survival of man and his environment. He talks to Michele Brown about the energy crisis and the new responsibility of science to society.'

Paperwork for this edition exists in the National Archive. Exists at the BFI and was shown at the National Film Theatre as part of *Projecting a Modern Britain: The White Heat of Technology* on 29 September 2009.

Bibliography

CD

Tales from the TARDIS volume 3. Extract from *Talkback* September 1967.

DVDs

Doctor Who – Revisitations 3: 'The Tomb of the Cybermen'. 2 Entertain. 2012. Audio commentary with Victor Pemberton.

Doctor Who – Lost in Time: 'The Wheel in Space' Episode 6. 2 Entertain. 2004. Audio commentary between Derrick Sherwin and Tristan de Vere Cole.

Doctor Who – 'The Invasion'. 2 Entertain. 2006. 'Evolution of the Cybermen'. Derrick Sherwin and Terence Dicks interviewed for documentary.

Books

Allaby, Michael. 1971. *The Eco-Activists.* London: Charles Knight.
Banks, David. 1988. *Cybermen.* London: Who Dares
Barker, Russell and Alan Stenning. 1928. *The Record of Old Westminsters 1928* Volume 2. London: Chiswick Press
Bayer, Ronald and Eric A. Feldman. 2004. *Unfiltered: Conflicts Over Tobacco Policy and Public Health.* Harvard: Harvard University Press
Bembridge, B. A., and Rupert Hall. 1986. *Physic and Philanthropy – a History of the Wellcome Trust 1936-86.* Cambridge: Cambridge University Press
Brunt, David and Andrew Pixley. 2000. *The Doctor Who Chronicles Season Four.* London: DWAS

—— 2000. *The Doctor Who Chronicles Season Five*. London: DWAS

Burrows, Roger. 1995. *Cyberspace/Cyberbodies/Cyberpunk: Cultures of Technological Embodiment*. London: Sage Publications

Cambden, Steve. 2001. *The Doctor's Effects*. Great Britain: FX Fanzines

Department of Scientific and Industrial Research. 1960. *Scientific Research in British Universities 1959-60*. London: HMSO

—— 1961. *Scientific Research in British Universities 1960-61*. London: HMSO

—— 1963. *Scientific Research in British Universities 1962-63*. London: HMSO

Dickson, David. 1974. *Alternative Technology and the Politics of Technical Change*. Glasgow. Fontana Collins

Enslin, N. C. de V. 1971. *Should Science and Engineers Call a Halt to Research*. Cape Town: University of Cape Town

Foster George Ross of Bladenburg, Sir John. 1928. *The Coldstream Guards, 1914-1918 Volumes 1 & 2* Oxford: Oxford University Press

Gay, Hannah. 2007. *The History of the Imperial College London, 1907-2007*. London: Imperial College Press

Halliday, Sandy. 2008. *Sustainable Construction*. Oxford: Butterworth-Heinemann

Hollands, Clive. 1980. *Compassion is the Bugler: The Struggle for Animal Rights*. Edinburgh: Macdonald Publishers

Howe, David J., Mark Stammers and Stephen James Walker. 1997. *Doctor Who The Second Doctor Handbook*. London: Virgin Publishing Ltd.

—— 2005 *The Handbook*. Tolworth: Telos

Levy, Marc A. 1995. *Green Globe Yearbook of International Co-operation on Environment and Development 1995: International Co-operation to Combat Acid Rain*. Oxford: Oxford University Press

Matusow, Harvey. 1968. *The Beast of Business*. London: Wolfe Publishing Ltd.

National Association for the Prevention of Tuberculosis. 1937. *Handbook of Tuberculosis Schemes for Great Britain and Ireland*. Great Britain

O'Connor, Alan. 1989. *Raymond Williams on Television: Selected Writings*. London: Routledge

Ravetz, J. R. 1971. *Scientific Knowledge and its Social Problems*. Oxford: Oxford University Press

Rivers, Patrick. 1975. *The Survivalists*. London: Eyre Methuen Ltd.
Ryder, Richard D. 1989. *Animal Revolution: Changing Attitudes Towards Speciesism*. Oxford: Basil Blackwell Ltd.
Scharper, Stephen B. 1997. *Redeeming the Time: A Political Theology of the Environment*. New York: Continuum
Silverman, William A. 1980. *Retrolental Fibroplasia: A Modern Parable*. New York: Grune & Stratton, Inc.
Smith, Curtis C. 1986. *Twentieth Century Science Fiction Writers*. London. St James Press
Sutherland, N. S. 1968. *Pattern Recognition: The Retina and the Machine*. Manitoba
Walker, Stephen James (ed). 2006. *Talkback: The Unofficial and Unauthorised Doctor Who Interview Book: The Sixties*. Tolworth: Telos
—— 2007. *Talkback: The Unofficial and Unauthorised Doctor Who Interview Book: The Eighties*. Tolworth: Telos
Weinberg, Alvin Martin. 1994. *The First Nuclear Era: The Life and Times of a Technological Fixer*. New York: American Institute of Physics
Wellcome Trust. 1961. *Third Report 1959-1960*. London: Wellcome Trust
Wellcome Trust. 1968. *The Wellcome Trust 1966-68 Seventh Report*. London: Wellcome Trust
Wills, Anneke. 2007. *Self Portrait*. Andover: Hirst Books Ltd.

Newspapers

Allday, Con. 1976. Cheap and Safe – Not a *Doomwatch* Nightmare. *Daily Express*, 13 December
Anon. Stanley Aylett. 2003. *Daily Telegraph*, 28 March
Arnold-Foster, Val. 1975. What's Doc Up To. *The Guardian*, 8 October
Associated Press. 1976. Student Designs Nuclear Bomb. *Spokane Daily Chronicle*, 9 October
Baily, Kenneth. 1970. He's Out to Shock You. *The People*, 1 March
Barker, Dennis. 1975. Anti Sally. *The Guardian*, 9 April
Barkham, Patrick. 2010. Oil Spills: Legacy of the Torrey Canyon. *The Guardian*, 24 June
Bedford, Ronald and Hellicar, Michael. 1970. First Assignment Case of the Tattered Tights. *Daily Mirror*, 22 June

—— 1970. Young Doomwatchers to Fight Peril of Science. *Daily Mirror*, 25 July

—— 1970. Menace of the Super-Mice. *Daily Mirror*, 31 July

Bloxham, Peter. 1967. The Cybermen are Waiting. *Sheffield Morning Telegraph*, 11 March

Brien, Alan. 1970. London of Man, Rats and the Absurd. *New York Times*, 6 April

Britain Needs a Doomwatch Says Boffin Writer Pedler. 1970. Unknown paper, 26 February

Chartres, John. 1976. Windscale May Be International Test Case. *The Times*, 1 June

Clare, John. 1972. Who Makes the Decisions That Change Our Environment? *The Times*, 9 March

Clash Over Dogs That Smoke 30 Cigarettes a Day. 1975. *Daily Express*, 27 January

Comnew, Paul. 1972. Drums of Death Fear for 200,000. *Daily Mirror*, 12 January

Critchley, Julian. 1967. Votemeter Finds Many Grumblers. *The Times*

Darroch, Robert. 1972. *Doomwatch* Horror Shock Fact In Britain. 23 January

Doctor Who Creates *Who*. 1967. *The Observer*, 5 February

Doomwatch TV Men Leave. 1972. *The Times*, 7 June

Doomwatch: What is Worrying You? 1970. *Daily Mirror*, 2 July

Dr Pedler's Survival Kit. 1972. *Daily Mirror*, 21 June

Forbes, Donald. 1970. Irrelevant Research. *Corpus Christi Times*, 20 July

Franks, G. 1975. Living Without Any Labour Saving Devices. *Strait Times*, 1 February

Gardener, Raymond. 1973. Prophets of Doom. *The Guardian*, 13 December

Gardiner, Stephen. 1980. Jump into the Future. *The Observer*, 9 November

Gibbon, Alfred. 1970. The Killing Water. *Daily Mirror*, 4 August

Glass, Richard. 2003. Stanley Aylett. *The Guardian*, 28 January

Gonery, Donald. 1967. Are You Just Cardboard characters?/Are We Becoming Cybermen? Syndicated newspaper. Including *Liverpool Echo*, 1 March

Green, Lucia. 1972. Doctor Doom. *Saturday Titbits*

Grosvenor, Peter. 1973. Pedler of Dreams, Making His New Way of Living Come True. *Daily Express*, 28 December

Group Seeks Stronger Animal Test Controls. 1976. *The Times*, 16 August

Hamilton, Alan. 1981. Will Sir Richard win the Surrey Gold Cup? *The Times*, 13 January

Hellicar, Michael. 1970. Don't Ask a Man to Smoke and Drive. *Daily Mirror*, 1 October

—— 1970. Ring of Dark Water. *Daily Mirror*, 28 August

Hencke, David. 1980. Wildlife Reserve Plan for London Docklands. *The Guardian*, 13 May

Holland, Mary. 1972. Ecological Overkilling. *The Observer*, 11 June

How to Move a Government. 1972. *The Times*, 8 March

Insight into Human Eye. 1969. *The Guardian*, 9 September

It Costs Just Peanuts to Run. 1974. *Daily Mirror*, 9 January

Jackson, Martin. 1970. It's the *Dr Who* Team Again. *Daily Express*, 30 January

—— 1972. *Doomwatch* Row Flares at BBC. *Daily Express*, 7 June

—— 1972. BBC gets a New Doom TV Show. *Daily Express*, 1 April

Jeffries, Michael. 1970. A Date with Dr Doom. *Evening Standard*, 6 March

Kennedy, Roderick. 1970. Passing the Pollution Buck to the Next Generation. *Strait Times*, 13 December

Kass, Bob. 1974. Bob Kass Interviews the *Doomwatch* Man. Unknown paper and date

Kilroy, Peter. 1975. Beagle Burglers. *Daily Mirror*, 19 June

Kit Keeps Ahead of the Worst. 1972. *Daily Mirror*, 19 January

Kriwaczek, Paul. 2005. John Percival Obituary. *The Guardian*, 10 February

Life in Test Tube Report by Newspaper Upheld. 1967. *Daily Express*, 5 June

Mackie, Lindsay. 1974. Animal Crackers. *The Guardian*, 23 November

Musel, Robert. 1979. A Living Entity: Earth May Become Man's Fiercest Enemy, 9 September

New Quist for Twist. 1971. *The Guardian*, 28 March

New Warning from *Doomwatch* Team. 1974. *Daily Express*, 14 February

Nicolotti, Aldo. 1970. *Doomwatch* – a New Tonic from the Telly's Sci-fi Doc. Unknown newspaper, February

Northedge, Richard. 1980. All-British Plan for Dockland Super-City. *Evening Standard*, 30 October

Pedler, Kit. 1970. What's There? *The Guardian*, 16 April

—— 1975. Several Urgent Changes are Necessary to Protect Animals. *The Guardian*, 8 October

—— 1976. This Deal with the Devil. *Daily Express*, 11 December

—— 1977. The Diabolical Knowledge We Have to Live With. *Daily Express*, 18 May

Pedler et al. 1975. Nuclear Dustbins for Centuries. *The Guardian*, 7 January

Percival, Daniel. 2005. John Percival: Television Pioneer. *The Independent*, 9 February

Pettigew, John. 1970. This *Dr Who* for Adults is Real Horror. *Sunday Mirror*, 8 February

Plaice, Ellis. 1970. Britain Backs US Plan for Dumping Nerve Gas in Sea. *Daily Mirror*, 15 August

Pollock, Diana. 1972. Design Over Decadence. *The Guardian*, 26 October

Pollution Danger: A Crisis. 1972. *London Courier*, unknown date

Robots With Eyes. 1969. *Daily Mirror*, 1 September

Stuart, Malcolm. 1970. Tuna Declared Contaminated but Fit to Eat. *The Guardian*, 23 December

Stevens, John. 1976. A Son of Nature Bites the Dust. *The Age*, 19 August

Stevenson, John. 1972. Scientist Raps Doctors in Fool's Game. *Daily Mail*, 16 May

Sunrise Zone Plan for Derelict Docks. 1981. *The Guardian*, 15 October

Tendler, Stewart. 1975. Government Considering Whether to Stop Reprocessing Nuclear Fuel from Other Nations. *The Times*, 22 October

Thaw, George. 1975. Books. *Daily Mirror*, 18 September

Theory Warns Earth Can Strike Back. 1979. *Albany Herald*, 9 September

There's a Strong Case for a Real Doomwatch – Says Boffin Writer. 1970. Unknown newspaper

Thomas, Harford. 1980. Pyramids Planned for the Thames. *The Guardian*, 22 May

Tickell, Tom. 1980. That's the Spirit. *The Guardian*, 18 June

Tucker, Anthony. 1965. Cybernetic Insight. *The Guardian*, 3 August

—— 1970. Biologist Gives Up Gene Research. *The Guardian*, 26 February

—— 1973. The West Blows a Fuse. *The Guardian*, 14 December
—— 1974. Dr Pedler Believes the Building Societies Could... *The Guardian*, 14 January
—— 1975. Nuclear Waste Can Kill Us All. *The Guardian*, 24 March
—— 1979. Society in a Fog. *The Guardian*, 10 May
Uncanny Hints of Disaster. 1971. *The Sun*, 4 January
Vision of the Future. 1980. *South London Press*, 28 March
Wade, David. 1969. All Done by Voice. *The Guardian*, 14 June
Welcome To Westminster's Real Life Doomwatchers. *Daily Mirror*, 22 April
What You Can Do with Your Rubbish. 1974. *The Times*, 4 January
Wilkinson, James. 1971. Keep Britain Tidy with Plastic Eating Germs. *Daily Express*, 7 June
Wilson, David. 1969. Article on *Horizon*'s Eye Programme. *The Listener*
Wright, Pearce. 1970. Progress Towards 'Test Tube' Baby. *The Times*, 24 February
—— 1970. Scientists and Social Responsibility. *The Times*, 24 July
—— 1973. Radioactive Blowback at Windscale Contaminated 40 Men. *The Times*, 3 October
—— 1974. Alarms Misled 35 Men Contaminated in Atom Plant Blow Back. *The Times*, 8 June
—— 1975. Another Radiation Leak at Windscale. *The Times*, 22 May
—— 1976. Hazards of Plutonium Reactors Alarm Royal Commission. *The Times*, 20 September
Young, John. 1981. Decision on Surrey Docks Likely This Weekend. *The Times*, 3 January
—— 1981. Lysander Plan for Docks Site is Chosen. *The Times*, 14 June
Young People Take Part in Environment Festival. 1977. *Daily Express*, 23 August
Young Scientist was Terrified of the Future. 1970. *The Times*, 21 July

Periodicals

Advert for Electron Microscope Operator. 1960. *New Scientist*, 4 February: 294
Advert for Lecture at Conway Hall. 1979. *Peace News* 2087-2110
Advert for People's Habitat. 1976. *The Ecologist* 6:1 146

Alternative Technology Comes to Rotherhithe. 1976. *New Scientist*, 10 June: 563

Astragal. 1974. *Architect's Journal*, 18 & 25 December: 1408

Ashton, R. C. 1957. Remarks on Acceptance of the Proctor Medal. *American Journal of Ophthalmology* 44: 5–6

Auger, David. (?) Kit Pedler. *Doctor Who: An Adventure in Space and Time: The Invasion* 46:9

Aylett, S. O. 1966. Three Hundred Cases of Diffuse Ulcerative Colitis Treated by Total Colectomy and Ileo-rectal Anastomosis. *British Medical Journal*, May: 1001-5

Bakewell, Joan. 1975. *Man Alive* preview. *Radio Times*

Mini feature. 1965. *BBC London Calling* 3-4: 413

Bell, Lynne. 1975. Self Sufficient Society: Women Will See Sense First. *Woman's Day*, 6 January

Bentham, Jeremy. 1983. Innes Lloyd. *Doctor Who Magazine* Winter Special 11-13

—— 1983. Peter Bryant. *Doctor Who Magazine* Winter Special 15-17

Bonnell, J. A. 1973. Lead Smelting at Avonmouth. *British Journal of Industrial Medicine* 30: 199-201

Breach, Ian. 1977. Professional Opponents Move In. *New Scientist*, 20 October: 135

Brightwell, Dr Robin. 1971. *Doomwatch:* Does it Really Present Dangers of Today? *Radio Times*, 7 January

Brown, Anthony. 1996. A Renaissance Doctor. *In Vision* 62: 12-14

Burn, Gordon. 1972. Does Quist Give a Damn? *Radio Times*, 1 June: 6-7

Cadogan, Peter. 1974. Science Fiction and World Futures. *Ethical Record*, May: 15-17

Campbell, Dr Patrick. 1970. Interview on *Doomwatch*. *Hospital Times*, 5 June

Chedd, Graham. 1970. *Doomwatch. New Scientist*, unknown date

—— 1971. *Doomwatch* Incarnate. *New Scientist*, 18 March: 622-624

Chemist and Druggist. Unknown year. 111: 490

Clark, Anthony. 1992. Gerry Davis. *Dream Watch Bulletin* 97: 30-1

Clarke, Robin. 1973. Technology for an Alternative Society. *New Scientist*, 11 January: 66-8

Comfort, Alex. 1965. Modified Men. *New Scientist*, 19 August: 456-7

Cowen, Robert C. 1969. Technology's World: The Facts and the Feelings. *Technology Review*, December 6-7

Cowley, Elizabeth. 1970. The Honeymoon of Science Is Over – and Married Life is Not So Rosy. *Radio Times*, 5 February: 2-3

Cox, R. 1974. Sir Stanford Cade, KBE CB. *Annals of the Royal College of Surgeons of England* 54: 94-96

Cunningham, George J. 1965. Untitled. *Annals of the Royal College of Surgeons of England* 35: 3: 168

D'Arcy, Susan. 1972. Doomwatch. *Photoplay*, May: 57-9

Dehumanising World of the Cybermen. 1967. *World Medicine*, 21 March

Dixon, Bernard. 1971. Laboratory Animals: Now is the Time to Act. *New Scientist*, 11 February: 284

Duke-Elder, Stewart. 1966. Biochemistry of the Retina. *British Medical Journal*, 30 April: 1096

Ecological Ombudsman. 1970. *New Scientist*, 18 December: 5

Environmental Crisis and the Artist. 1970. *Bulletin of the Computer Arts Society*, October

Epton, Sidney. 1979. *The Quest for Gaia* Book Review. *New Scientist*, 4 October: 44

Evans, Christopher. 1973. Parapsychology – what the questionnaire revealed. *New Scientist*, 25 January: 209

Events Listing. 1968. *Journal of the Royal Society of Arts* 115: 222

Events Listing. 1968. *Ophthalmic Optician* 8 1-13: 39: 440 & 736

Eye as a Part of the Brain. 1966. *New Scientist*, 10 March: 605

French, Peter. 1970. Presenting the Deadly Dangers of Today. *Radio Times*, 10 December: 60-1

Green, Luciea. 1972. Doctor Doom. *Saturday Titbits* (unknown issue): 28-29

Greenhalgh, Geoffrey. 1978. After Parker: A Review of the Windscale Inquiry and Subsequent Developments. *IAEA Bulletin* 20: 6 1-8

Gray, John. 2013. James Lovelock: A Man for All Seasons. *New Statesman*, 27 March. www.newstatesman.com/culture/culture/2013/03/james-lovelock-man-all-seasons

Gribbin, John. 1974. *Dynostar Menace. New Scientist*, 30 October: 293

Hancock, Tom. 1982. Dereliction: Innovation. *Town and Country Planning* 51: 128-9

Hanlon, Joseph. 1976. Cancer Lab Sacks Animal Technicians in Cruelty Row. *New Scientist*, 18 November: 392

Harper, Peter. 1973. Transfiguration Amongst the Windmills. *Undercurrents* 5: March/April 7-16

Hearn, Marcus. 1992. What the Papers Said. *Doctor Who Magazine* 187: 14-16

Hear Teller. 1971. *New Scientist*, 29 July: 275

Henkind, Paul. 1978. Sir Stewart Duke-Elder Obituary. *Archives of Ophthalmology* 96: 1170-71

In Conference. 1972. *New Scientist*, 28 September: 595

Is There a Tenth Planet? 1965. *New Scientist*, 16 September: 673

Johnson, Timothy. 1966. Exploring the Jungle of the Eye. *Illustrated London News*, 13 October: 12

Jones, Fred. 1968. The Day a Cyberman Went Shopping in St Pancras. *Radio Times*, 21 February

Kenward, Michael. 1972. Book Review *Mutant 59 The Plastic Eater*. *New Scientist*, 20 April:156-7

—— 1973. Alternative Technology – Politics and Yogurt? *New Scientist*, 11 January: 68-70

Law, Frank W. 1962. Science Against Blindness. *New Scientist*, 5 April: 800-802

Leigh, Gary and Tim Collins. 1986. Innes Lloyd. *Doctor Who Bulletin* 36&37: 18-24

Leigh, Gary. 1988. Gerry Davis. *DWB* 59: 10-15

Lewin, Roger. 1971. Who Pays for Plastic Litter. *New Scientist*, 25 February: 440-1

Radio Review. 1975. *The Listener*, 1 December (page unknown)

Listing for Sunday. 1965. *Radio Times*, 18 November (page unknown)

Low, Richard. 1971. In Conference: The Teilhard Centre for the Future of Man. *New Scientist*, 2 December: 41

Marson, Richard. 1984. Whitaker's World of *Doctor Who*. *Doctor Who Magazine* 98:35-8

—— 1987. Gerry Davis Interviewed. *Doctor Who Magazine* 124: 8-12

Mellanby, Kenneth. 1979. Living With the Earth Mother. *New Scientist*, 4 October: 41

Memories. 2012. *The Old Ipswichian Journal* (page unknown)

Mizen, Niel J. 1965. Amplifying Man. *New Scientist*, 14 October: 84-6

Molesworth, Richard. 1997. Ghosts in the Machines. *Doctor Who Magazine* 253:8-9

New Dawn for Surrey Docks. 1980. *Energy Manager*, July/August

Oatley, C. W. 1982. The Early History of the Scanning Electron Microscope. *Advances in Imaging and Electron Physics* 53:2

O'Connell, Lorna. 1979. Last Chance for Survival – an Alternative Viewpoint. *Building Services & Environmental Engineer*, December 20-21

Patterson, Walter C. 1978. The Windscale Report: A Nuclear Apologia. *Bulletin of the Atomic Scientists* 34: 6 44-46

Pedler, C. M. H. 1970. The Eye as a Computer. *Science Journal*, February: 49-54

Pedlerism in Lisbon. 1973. *Design*: 35

Pixley, Andrew. 1992. The Invasion. *Doctor Who Magazine* 189: 23-30

—— 1997. The Wheel in Space. *Doctor Who Magazine* 254: 34-40

—— 1999. The Tomb of the Cybermen. *Doctor Who Magazine* 281:34-41

—— 2003. The Invasion. *DWM Special Edition: The Complete Second Doctor*: 61-2

—— 2002. The Moonbase. *Doctor Who Magazine* 322: 28-34

—— 2004. The Times They Are A-Changing. *DWM Special Edition: The Complete First Doctor*: 59-63

Probing the Paranormal. 1981. *Thames News*

Technology Showpiece for London's Derelict Dockland. 1980. *New Scientist*, 12 June: 231

TV Review. 1971. *Punch*, 21 July: 100

TV Review. 1975. *The New Review* 2: 13-24 61

Review of Quekett Exhibition. 1965. *The Microscope* 15: 247

Richardson, David. 1999. Martin Worth: Doom Merchant. *TV Zone* 55:16-19

Russell, Gary. 1987. Victor Pemberton: Writing *Doctor Who*. *Doctor Who Magazine* 108: 20

Sherwood, Martin. 1971. Controversy. *New Scientist*, 12 August: 386

Sir Alexander Pedler Obituary. 1919. *Journal of the Chemical Society Transactions*. 115: 408-454

Stevens, Ted. 1980. Joint Venture for Surrey Docks Competition. *Architect's Journal*, 20 August

Technology and Conservation Win in Docklands. 1981. *New Scientist*, 15 January: 125

Tinker, Jon. 1972. Britain's Environment – Nanny Knows Best. *New Scientist*, 9 March: 530

Tudge, Colin. 1978. The New Materialism. *New Scientist*, 29 June: 929-30

TV Reviews. 1971. *Punch*, 21 July: 100

Universities and Colleges. 1961. *British Medical Journal*, 9 December: 1581

Unknown. 1981. *American Society for Psychical Research Newsletter* 7:1 6

Uvarov, Dame Olga. 1984. Research with Animals. *Laboratory Animals* 19: 51-75

Vine, R. S. 1976. Cruelty to Animals. *New Scientist*, 16 September: 588

Ward, Colin. 1972. A Doomwatch for Environmental Pollution. *Perspectives In Public Health* 92: 4 173-77

Wayne, Trevor. (?) Talkback – Backlash. *Doctor Who: An Adventure in Space and Time* 37: 8-9

We're Living on A Leasehold Planet... Unknown. c. 1970/1

Windmills: Is Small Safer? 1975. *Undercurrents* 11: 11

Windscale Protest Fund. 1977. *New Scientist*, 19 May: 381

Woffinden, Bob. 1988. *Doomwatch*. *The Listener*, 7 April: 19-20

Wright, W. D. 1966. The Implications for Television of Modern Thinking on the Visual Process. *The Television Society Journal* 11: 6: 128-135

Websites

General sites:

www.cat.org.uk
    The Centre for Alternative Technology's website.

checkpoint.ansible.co.uk
    A collection of science-fiction fanzines including the 1970s, with a few minor references to *Doomwatch* and Kit Pedler.

cyberneticzoo.com
    A valuable resource for the 'Tortoise' and other marvellous robotic creations of the 1950s and 60s, which inspired the Cybermats.

www.dia.org.uk
   The Design and Industries Association website.

www.surreydocksfarm.org.uk
   London's first urban farm in Rotherhithe.

www.nigeltuersley.com
   Nigel Tuersley's own website.

www.michaelallaby.com
   Michael Allaby's website.

mattsalusbury.blogspot.co.uk
   Matt Salusbury's website.

www.urbanecology.org.uk/stavehill.html
   The Stave Hill ecology park on the site of the old Surrey Docks.

www.hometheaterforum.com/topic/188512-benny-hill-show-complete-and-unedited/page-5
   A forum where Cherri Gilham gives an account of why she had to change her name slightly, and also recollections from people who remembered Cherry Gilliam when she was an actress.

Specific pages:

Bellis, Mary. n.d. History of the Microscope: Electron Microscope.
   inventors.about.com/od/mstartinventions/a/microscope_2.htm

Bjork, Tord. 1996. The Emergence of Popular Participation in World Politics. Focusing on the United Nations Conference on the Human Environment in 1972.
   www.folkrorelser.org/inenglish/stockholm72.html

Boden, Margaret. n.d. Grey Walter's Anticipatory Tortoises, from the *Rutherford Journal*.
   www.rutherfordjournal.org/article020101.html#sdfootnote14anc

Burns, Bill. 2012. London Eastercon – SciCon70. Series of pictures and scans from the convention.
   efanzines.com/1970SciCon/index.htm

Buss, Rose. 2007. United Nations Conference on the Human Environment (UNCHE), Stockholm, Sweden, in *The Encyclopedia of Earth*. editors.eol.org/eoearth/wiki/United_Nations_Conference_on_the_Human_Environment_(UNCHE),_Stockholm,_Sweden

Cloosterman, Annemieke. n.d. Useful transcript of the sixth episode of *Mind Over Matter*. www.mindstructures.com/mind-over-matter-video-with-transcription/

Club of Rome – Predicament of Mankind working statement. 1970. PDF reproduction. demosophia.com/wp-content/uploads/Predicament-Club-of-Rome-1970-1.pdf

Cooper, S. N. n.d. XIX International Congress of Ophthalmology. Reproduction of Indian Journal Ophthalmology. 1963. www.ijo.in/article.aspissn=0301-4738;year=1963;volume=11;issue=1;spage=25;epage=29;aulast=Cooper

Espace net. 2013. Kit Pedler's patented 'Improvements in or relating to the contouring or profiling of articles.' GB1153163 complete with illustration. worldwide.espacenet.com/publicationDetails/biblio?CC=GB&NR=1153163

Fleming, James Rodger. The pathological history of weather and climate modification: Three cycles of promise and hype. www.colby.edu/sts/06_fleming_pathological.pdf

Hansen, Robert. n.d. THEN Volume 4 Chapter 1 Aardvarks, Wombats, Gannets and Rats. Chapter of a book on Eastercon in 1970, and NovaCon in 1971. www.ansible.co.uk/Then/then_4-1.html

Hayreh, S. S. 2005. Remembrances of Things Past. Article reproduced from Indian Journal of Ophthalmology 1991 39:140-6. www.ijo.in/text.asp?1991/39/3/140/24447

Jordan, Andrew and John Greenaway. n.d. Paradigm Shift or Muddling Through? British Coastal Water Policy, 1955-1995. PDF copy of the article. cserge.uea.ac.uk/sites/default/files/wm_1997_01.pdf

Kallipoliti, Lydia. n.d. Reproduction of Feedback Man by Lydia Kallipoliti in 2008, concerning early Apollo capsule experiments. www.anacycle.com/Feedback-Man

King's College London. 2012. History of Chelsea Polytechnic 1922-1956. www.kingscollections.org/exhibitions/archives/studentdays/chelsea-college/chelsea-college-through-the-years/chelsea-polytechnic-1922-1956

Langley, Cynthia Medford and Philip Luthert. 2005. Norman Henry Ashton CBE obituary, *Biographical Memoirs of the Fellows of the Royal Society.* rsbm.royalsocietypublishing.org/content/51/1.full.pdf

McDonald, Ian. 2000. Royal College of Physicians: Munk's Roll entry on Sir Norman Henry Ashton, Volume XI, page 33. munksroll.rcplondon.ac.uk/Biography/Details/5316

Mishima, Sai. 2003. Dr David M. Maurice: Fond Memories of my Teacher and Best Friend. PDF reminiscences from an unknown publication on a tribute site for Dr Maurice. www.davidmaurice.com/tribute/tributes.html

Monro, P. A. G. *The Early History of the British Microcirculation Society 1963-1984*, p32. PDF reproduction of a book written for the World Congress on Microcirculation in Oxford, 1984. www.microcirculation.org.uk/who-we-are/

Mouton, Peter R. 2005. History of Modern Stereology, in IBRO History of Neuroscience. ibro.org/wp-content/uploads/2018/07/History-of-Modern-Stereology1.pdf

Patz, A. The Role of Oxygen in Retrolental Fibroplasia. Reproduction of an article first printed in *Transactions of the American Ophthalmological Society* 66: 940-985. 1968. www.ncbi.nlm.nih.gov/pmc/articles/PMC1310320/?page=1

Robertson, James. n.d. Turning Point 2000 featuring details about Renee-Marie Croose Parry. www.jamesrobertson.com/turningpoint.htm

Simmons, Mathew. n.d. Revisiting the Limits to Growth: Could the Club of Rome Have Been Correct, After All? A paper delivered in October 2002. www.mudcitypress.com/PDF/clubofrome.pdf

Mary Beith's obituary in the *Guardian*. www.theguardian.com/media/greenslade/2012/may/20/thepeople-investigative-journalism

Unigate plc history. n.d. Taken from *International Directory of Company Histories*, Vol. 28. St James Press, 1999. www.fundinguniverse.com/company-histories/unigate-plc-history/

Walder, Angela. n.d. Reproduction of *Watchdog* Newsletter Number 63, November 1997 with piece by Angela Walder. RSPCA-animadversion.org.uk/watchdog63.htm

Woolley, John and Gerhard Peters. n.d. Richard Nixon's annual message to the Congress on the State of the Union, 22 January 1970, on The American Presidency Project. www.presidency.ucsb.edu/ws/index.php?pid=2921

Young Scientists: Population and the Environmental Crisis. n.d. A UNESCO report from a roundtable meeting in Paris, 1972. unesdoc.unesco.org/images/0000/000014/001429eb.pdf

Acknowledgements

CYBERMAN: THE QUEST FOR PEDLER was originally published in 2014 by Miwk Publishing Ltd, with a shorter title and a longer word count. The *Doomwatch* script 'Survival Code' has been removed from this edition; it was reproduced with permission from the Pedler and Davis estates, but for space I have had to delete examples of Kit's writings. The text itself has been revised and streamlined with hopefully typos and mistakes removed. My tendency to overwrite has, I hope, been partially remedied, but few facts have been removed. I have added subsequent minor discoveries throughout the text.

Once again, I would like to thank the friends and family of Dr Kit Pedler for their amazing support, encouragement, kindness and trust: the late Dr Una Freeston (who passed away at the age of 93 shortly after I had submitted this new edition), Carol Topolski, the late Mark Pedler, Lucy Pedler, Justin Pedler, Kerry Glasier, Diana Baur, and the late Professor Donald West.

In researching Kit's Suffolk childhood, my thanks go to Sharon Jones, the parish clerk at Mendlesham Parish Council, Pris and Roy Colchester, John Blatchley, archivist of Ipswich School, the *Ipswich Journal*, Rosie Wheat, *East Anglian Daily Times*, and the patrons of Rootschat.com.

For their help with *Doctor Who*, Dave Auger, David Banks, Richard Bignell, David Brunt, James Goss, Toby Hadoke, the late Victor Pemberton, Andrew Pixley, Dr Matthew Sweet, Stephen James Walker, Martin Wiggins and Anneke Wills.

From the world of ophthalmology, many thanks to the late Geoffrey Arden, John Baker, Sohan S. Hayreh, Debbie Heatlie, Helga Kolb, Cynthia Langley, and Jill Wilson from the Royal Microscopical Society. I also thank Lynne Hermiston of the Computer Science Department in Manitoba, and Jon Muzio.

Acknowledgements

For their memories of *Doomwatch* years, many thanks to Judy Bedford, Anthony Brown, Keith Dewhurst, the late Glyn Edwards, Don Shaw, Jean Trend, Adele Winston, and the late Martin Worth. I also thank Scott Burditt and those who contributed to the defunct www.doomwatch.org, without whom none of this would have happened.

For the topic of Alternative Technology, I thank Michael Allaby, Godfrey Boyle, Derek Conway, David Dickson, John Elkin, Dave Elliot, Brian Ford, Philip Glass, Peter Harper, Thornton Kay, Jannet King, Paul McClory, Stuart Rose, Hugh Sharman, Geoff Ward, and especially Nigel Tuersley.

From the RSPCA days, a huge thanks to Richard Ryder and Angela Walder.

From *Mind Over Matter*, my thanks to Jeanette Kupfermann, Kevin Mannion, Richard Mervyn, and Matt Salusbury.

I also wish to thank Cathy Broad, Librarian of the Humanist Library and archives at Conway Hall, London, the BBC Written Archives and the library staff at the University of East Anglia.

Thanks are also due to John Archibold, Nicholas Blake, Andy Davidson, Rob Hammond, Alan Hayes, Chris Patient, Ken Shinn, the original publisher and editor Matthew West, and John Williams.

Finally, to Dexter O'Neill, Phil Reynolds, Connor J. Adkins and all at Fantom Publishing for giving the book a new lease of life.